Contents

Everyone here knows it's all about food.

Acknowledgments

There's a whole planet of people I could thank so I'll start with my dear old Arkansas mom, Grace Ethel Ehmer, my dear old Vietnam/ Korea veteran dad, James Frederick Ehmer, and big brother George Frederick Ehmer. Those are the adoptive family and they rescued my sorry little scruffy butt from a German orphanage at my darkest hour. While we are at it, I will also thank my Mom and my Arkansas uncles along with Daniel Dog Botkin for teaching me how to garden. Someone had to do it.

My sweet daughter Reesa is my constant companion and igniter. She just rocks, big time. I learn something new from her everyday. Reesa, Mommy loves you so much. My husband Jerome provides positive support and unconditional love, plus he cooks the best vegetarian dinners from the garden, how could we be so lucky? Jerome I love you, thank you for being here. Thank you Grandpa Reece, you have always been there for us. I'd like to officially thank all the Lawton people who put up with me all those years. There's a lot of you, and if I forget someone please let me know. I'll put you in the next edition because your name deserves to be here. Thanks go to the Freeman family clan, the Huffmasters, the Millers, Cindy Serna, Fred Crosson, Terry Gresham, Teresa Thomas, the Hobbs, Lon Parks, the Stewarts, and all my cycling buddies, you know who you are. You were there for me when no one else wanted to be my friend and for that I appreciate you so much. Many thanks to Mom's beloved friends and relatives who came out of the woodwork to stand with her as she passed into the Light on January 20, 2010.

There are many people from the Northern California days who I have to mention because they kept me sane. Gail Weissman, Wendy and Amy Clark and family, Tony Tom, Steve Gravy Gravenites, Barry London, Penn and Arne, Gary Fisher and Belle Marko. You were my constant companions on the magical trails, and we learned so much back during those days hanging in your homes together and on our bikes. Going back even further to the Mendocino days, I'll mention beautiful Rainbird Wellwoman, my soul sister who remembered me when my world was at its craziest.

Here in the East, the list just gets longer. My first real friend here, Chrys Ballerano, you are a proven sister. There are no words to express how highly I hold you in my thoughts. The Straw/Manley clan, including Rachel Grey, her handsome man Jim and beloved Albert the dog, you will always be in my thoughts and prayers. Dick and Deb Cavanaugh, the Albany Free School, Leslie Gardner and her wonderful family, the Barr family, the many hardworking folks at the Honest Weight Food Coop (you know who you are), I thank you. John and Amelia Whalen and family, I will always love you. I'd like to shout out to my girl in Hawaii, Lisa Lilja, I'm thinking about you now. Searchangel Illona in Germany, you know you are dear to me. Dear Angelika, hallo my long lost half sister. I am so glad you are here. I see you.

Locally, I must acknowledge the rock solid godmother, Cheryl, her beloved, Sue Cooper, Sue's sister, Judy Waterman and her beloved, Irene, the Frenches, Caleb Carr, Jenny Cruikshank, Sally Maxon, the Ranellucci family, the Griswolds. Always in our hearts are the Hindes family and their beloved Tony. Thank you Laurenne, Vince and Maddie (and pets) for good food, editing, friendship, fermenting, movies and footbag. In MA, I'd like to thank Daniel Dog and family, Amy Anthony, Louise Finn, Mariam Massaro and Paul Rinehart. Mayer, Anastasia and Umba Lena for sharing your homes and lives with us. My ski patrol and snowboard/ski instructor family at Jiminy Peak and Magic Mountain, you keep me on my toes, heelside too. Those of you who first took me high up into the gnarliest mountains here, Sid Perkins and gang, I honor you. My very special ceremony family, including Fidelina Yhari Morales, I welcome you to our private tipi life. Thank you to Starhawk for inspiring so many of us with *The Fifth Sacred Thing* and sharing the reclaiming tradition with the larger world. Most especially, I send great joy and love to and my beloved VWC family in Vermont at Farm and Wilderness. What happens between the worlds affects all the worlds! There's so many good people here on the East Coast that I know and love. If I have forgotten to mention your name, please forgive me, and know that you are in my heart. To my Indian tipi meeting friends and community, Mitakuye Oyasin. I honor you and your ancestors.

Introduction

I might as well tell you right off the bat that this book is officially a fictional autobiography. The fictionalization is primarily to protect the identities of those who participated in my personal drama. *Tripping with Gabrielle* is also completely uncensored. I've often thought about cutting some of the sex, drugs, nastiness and rock and roll, especially the profanity, as a lot of readers might find such language offensive at times. Ultimately, my *fictional* story remains the same as it was written back in 1989, when I first used a Macintosh computer and wrote this book. If you don't like a little extra spice including some fat habaneros with your chili, I'd advise against reading this book.

There are many truths to the story you are about to read, and a couple of fictions. All the names have been changed to protect the innocent from the guilty, and most of the places have been renamed, exaggerated and otherwise embellished to make Gabrielle's story more palatable. The occasional composite character enables privacy for those characters in this book who would remain anonymous. For example, I was never beaten by my biker boyfriend, who also never told me to "Get on the hog, bitch!" I was once good friends with a German dog groomer. She was a biker woman who had a biker boyfriend. He brutally pistol whipped this kind lady for some minor infraction. I'll never forget how he rearranged her face, yet she would not leave him even after paying her own hospital bill. Rather than tell you about this beaten warrior woman who loved dogs, to protect her identity I made her story my own.

To make my book more of a non-fiction, I could have just written about the 50 or so times I got picked up hitchhiking and some guy pulled out his johnson driving 80 miles an hour and hoped he could get off while trying to scare me. That would just get boring so I didn't repeat that story as many times as it happened. On the other hand, at least 95% of the stuff that I write about in this book is indeed true, such as the story about the crazy guy in Chicago who almost got me after a church get together.

Gotta watch out for those church get togethers, you never know what vile words one will find written on a tee shirt, lurking behind a perfectly ordinary suit. *Tripping with Gabrielle* contains stories that I wouldn't recommend to anyone without a strong stomach. Gabrielle, however, manages to laugh it all off and slide along on a wave of youthful sarcasm. There are certainly a lot of references to drugs and alcohol in this book. For the record, I do not condone drug use of any kind, and in fact, do not even drink alcohol. However, my character does. She is a bad, bad girl and she's looking for some naughty action in all the wrong places. She suffers greatly as a result of her hunt for fun. Plain and simple, Gabrielle is just a troublemaker. She's another lost soul just like many of us so it's hard to hate her for too long.

Readers, don't let this book freak you out. If it does freak you out, then try to get a grip and keep reading. Stories like this do happen to ordinary people and to unordinary people too. Life happens. If you take one step at a time into the unknown, pretty soon the Stargate is bound to open up, letting those aliens and star beings and dragons and faeries flow through to your little planet. Dare ye enter?

Parents, if your kid ever gets ahold of this book, remember to tell them that it's not very nice out there in the big bad world, and sleeping in park bathrooms isn't as glorious as they may think. Bathing in a river seems romantic but the truth is, the water's really cold and there's no soap. They may think sticking their thumb out on the side of the road is a free ticket to ride but it's really not free. You pay and pay and pay. There are a very few people who will pick up a hitchhiker these days who they don't know. Out of those few good people, the odds are that one is not so nice with pretty ugly intentions. Be on the safe side. Give the kid a bus ticket, a plane ticket, or a ride to their destination. Don't let them stick out their thumb. I really mean it.

If you readers think you want to trip with Gabrielle you'll have to do it with yoga and a really clean, vegan diet, because that's how she journeys these days. The tripping seemed fine when she was young and stupid, but after a while it just got ugly. The street is a dirty, ugly, lowdown, unforgiving, dangerous place to live. Chances are, you wouldn't like it there.

Next time you see some derelict in the street lying in his or her (Goddess forbid!) own piss, just remember, you may be walking now but you could be lying there yourself, but for the grace of your Creator. Stop and say hello, help that person up, buy them a cup of coffee, a bagel, a bus ticket somewhere. Sit with them in a restaurant, find them a place to sleep, or just give them a kind look if they ignore your initial pleas. Hand them some change. You can do it because they cannot.

I'm not going to tell you what was fiction and what was auto in *Tripping with Gabrielle* but I will tell you this: The wildest stories are true, and the most mundane stuff I put in there so you wouldn't be so freaked out. Gabrielle's story is just ridiculous and there's just no way she should be alive to tell it. It's truly a miracle that she survived all the attempted rapes, the drunk drivers, the crazy men in the middle of the night, the sick individuals who sought to take advantage of her youth and stupidity, the really bad drugs. It's also a miracle that Gabrielle was taken in by so many kind individuals who were able to overlook her ignorance and sarcasm, choosing to help this young woman with food, with shelter, with funds, with job offers, with friendship. Enough of the mushy stuff. It's time for you to sit back, hop onto your couch or net surfing spot, park yourself in your hammock, grab something to eat, something to drink and maybe your favorite stuffed animal. The wildest ride you've had in a long time is about to begin. Need to go to the bathroom? Gabrielle frequently had to pee too and sometimes even more, but finding a place to go in private when you are homeless is a real bitch. Remember that.

How short the life of the butterfly, how beautiful her wings.

The bees are us.

Chapter One

Where the bee sucks, there suck I,
In a cowslip's bell I lie;
There I couch when owls do cry
On the bat's back I do fly
After summer merrily.
Merrily, merrily shall I live now,
Under the blossom that hangs on
the bow.

Prospero: "Why that's my dainty Ariel!"

William Shakespeare

Women refuse to accept the fact of being
castrated and have the hope of someday
obtaining a penis in spite of everything.

Sigmund Freud

Grounding first

I am a refugee from the sixties, a leftist with no Marxist leanings, a bleeding liberal, an animal rights activist, a person who cries endlessly over the stupidest things, an athlete who runs to fat at the wink of an eye, a mystic with very Christian leanings, a woman found in Germany as an infant with no home except an orphanage, and a happy soul at heart. Now that that's over with, how do I begin without sounding smarmy and boring you to tears?

I still remember the second time I went to Germany, this time happily ensconced in the home of my adoptive parents, readily available to whatever mischief might lurk nearby. My first acquaintance with the nasty F word occurred soon enough. I wondered about that mysterious scribbling I found upon the sidewalk on the way to school, right up until I spelled it out for Mama at dinner that night, and she nearly choked on her sliced tomatoes. Oh. It's a bad word? What does it mean, Mom? Add that to my growing vocabulary, and you have the beginnings of delinquency.

I was only seven years old at the time, but the roots took hold and the little weed quickly grew enormous and started its slow decline into seed. The playground should have been a good memory, but I hated the playground at our school in Germany. When Mom and Dad threw me out of the car that cold, cloudy day, demanding I stay at school, I sat on the swings in the fog and drizzle and bemoaned my lonely boredom. I felt no joy at returning to my homeland; Europe was a drag. To me, life on the swing set could certainly do with some improvement. So, I soon teamed up with my neighbors, ruffians every one, and we set out one bright sunny day not to school, but to steal vegetables and fruit from a Deutsch farmer. We stole a rabbit, too.

The scent of cherry blossoms wafting on a light breeze led us into gardens blooming with tomatoes, asparagus, spinach, and cucumbers. Our young senses were accosted with vivid colors of bright orange and red, emerald green and purple that were soon converted into the most magnificent bounty we had acquired yet. The only problem was, what to do with our loot? We hid the unripe peaches and still green veggies in an old cellar, and set forth to obtain our heart's desire, that lovely bunny rabbit who lived nearby.

As my cronies climbed into the top of the rabbit hutch via an overhanging tree to grab an overfed but coveted bunny, I became slightly alarmed at the consequences: who would get the bunny? Could I explain its sudden appearance in our family life to Mother? That question and many others weren't answered, because as we trooped en masse along that winding cobblestone road, here came Herr Farmer, pissed as hell and out for blood.

Driving his crusty old tractor toward one little boy with snot running down his nose, who had tripped on his shoe laces, the farmer cried, "Halt! Das ist mein Kaninchen! Ami-Schwein Kinder, du bist Spitzbube! Mensch..." He looked at me, I looked at him, and then I screamed, "Oh fuck, we're caught!"

Looking around furtively for my fellow thieves, not terribly into self-sacrifice or torture, I knew the only course of action was to disappear from the scene and not get caught. Yes, it's true, the others got caught. "I'm getting the hell outta here, guys, gotta go, see ya!" I'd never make a good soldier, especially a German one.

I escaped behind some trees. I was lucky. The old fart slammed on his brakes while his ancient vehicle practically rattled apart; he leapt out the door and grabbed the boy with the bunny, pulled him onto the seat of his rust bucket tractor, and rolled wobbly off into the pastoral sunset. What a bucolic scene it was, cows grazing peacefully nearby with only a faint haze of dust to show the passage of bunny, boy, and angry farmer. My my, was that ever a close call.

Home beckoned. I really wanted to surprise Mom with an armful of fruit and veggies for our dinner, but something told me it might not be wise. Besides, I was very, very late for a seven-year old girl who lived in a foreign country. Mom was waiting for me in the kitchen, her arms submerged in soap suds. I knew I was screwed when she took her hands out of the dishwater, dried them, then gave me her full and undivided attention.

"Gabby, what were you doing stealing rabbits with that Smith boy?" she rhetorically queried, already ascertaining my guilt by her tone. Mom had only a mere touch of grey in her hair at this time, and her back wasn't yet stooped with the age that only a troublesome child can bring. Her bright, sky-blue eyes shone fiercely as she towered over me, all five feet and ten inches of mad Mom. Doomsday had arrived. "You know better than to go seven miles from the yard, you're not even allowed off base!" Was it really that far? I wondered.

"I'm hungry, Ma," I said, my tummy not wanting to stay for chit chat.

"Don't change the subject," Mom interrupted. "Well, where were you?"

Yup. She knew something. I fidgeted nervously, while Mom continued her tirade of questions. "And what were you doing out of school?" She wiped her red hands on the green and blue plaid apron she always wore when washing dishes, then began to move toward the hall closet.

The Belt lived in the closet.

"I was out of school?" I asked innocently, already knowing the answer to that one. I tried to console myself, fear gripping my heart. No way, she couldn't know about that, too, could she? Mom

4

wasn't making my supper, and Dad hadn't come out of the living room. Something was amiss, and it wasn't anything friendly, either.

"I'm getting the Belt," she hissed, getting madder by the minute at my lies. "Come here right this minute and don't back talk me, young lady, I've had just about enough of you today!" Moving over to the closet to get the Belt, Mom's face was thunderous. She wrapped that black serpentine Nazi Belt around her wrist, and I yelled, "Mama I didn't do it honest!"

She didn't look convinced. Rhetorical questioning got me nowhere fast, but I tried. "Why would I steal a rabbit, you know I wouldn't do that." It wasn't working, so I tried a different tactic. "You taught me better than those Smith boy's, Mom, you know you can trust me, really Mom, don't hit me please... waaah!" Quite lost that particular argument, but what's a mere battle if you can win the war? A few licks here and there are a small price to pay for adventures.

That night was another typical evening at our house. My brother Gerhart was safe from all harm, because he was such a model child that he was even above suspicion. Watching me grow into a mini-tyrant had taught him that the best way to get what you wanted was to be nice to Mom and Dad. He snickered as I ate my dinner, and pinched my ear.

"Cut it out, asshole," I said. "Just because you stay such a goody two shoes all the time doesn't mean shit to me." Gerrie, his short, sandy blond hair and cherubic eyes dazzling every adult he encountered, wasn't even miffed at my poor attitude. After all, I was a delinquent and we knew where delinquents ended up.

"Get over yourself Gabby," he chortled. "And while you are at it, get a life." Gerrie left the kitchen after grabbing my cornbread, and went to his room to work on his third grade math. I would have told on him for taking my food, but Mom wouldn't have believed me, and he knew it.

When questioned again about the day's events, I had survived interrogation successfully, and none of my friends told, either. Sure, I got a whipping, but everyone knew I was guilty, so all in all, I considered this little attempt at fun attractive, and bragged about my rabbit-stealing exploits often to my gang of thuglets.

We planned to steal again, and soon.

5

I used to want to go around without a shirt like all the other heathen German girls. I had this weird scar on my solar plexis, acquired somewhere between birth and adoption, but it didn't disturb my desire for exposing my bare chest. Somehow, the German tradition of nakedness appealed to me, so much in fact that I approached Mom one day to ask permission to run around the yard without my shirt.

I skipped up to my ever busy mother as she hung clothes on the line, as if I wanted a friendly chat, and put the big question to her. Her reaction was not unexpected. Keeping her composure, Mom nevertheless dropped a sheet she was hanging up with clothespins. Her blue eyes were almost shooting daggers that day, for I was like Socrates the gadfly, minus any philosophy.

"No! Absolutely not," she said. "You will wear a shirt at all times or suffer the consequences." And back went good, old-fashioned, definitely not New-Age Mom, up with the sheets, down with nudity. I was an irresponsible self-centered little brat back in those days, and I didn't improve with age, either. After my brief, two-year stint spent suffering in Germany (it rained all the time), Mom and Dad moved us kiddipoos to Oklahoma (it was too hot and boring), where we managed to suffer even more. I always had the burning urge to get out to get out of there but never could figure out how.

It must have been around 1972 when I first discovered drugs, at the tender age of twelve. Not real dope of course, just some rag weed I found while riding my bicycle in a forbidden place we called Bicycle Hills. It tasted pretty bad, but I smoked it anyway and pretended I was stoned. A girlfriend of mine slipped me something in the school bathroom one day that tasted definitely better than that weed I found, smelled pleasantly minty and refreshing, but didn't get me any kind of buzz. Nothing like a clandestine exchange to brighten the day of a juvenile delinquent, though. I was thrilled when my little friend, Jessie Whelan, invited me into the girl's restroom during recess and offered me that very first 'real' joint. My sixth grade class was less than enlightening, and my teacher's blue bouffant was blinding all of us students, so any excuse to embrace escapism was welcome. Jessie pulled the wrinkled doober out of her backpack and shot a furtive look around the bathroom.

"Hey chick, do I ever have some stuff for you!" Jessie whispered. She certainly looked excited. I couldn't believe her Mom let her wear that Black Sabbath tee shirt and those holey jeans. Man, she was one cool chick, I thought.

"Whadda ya got?" I asked. "Something illegal?"

"Are you ready for this?" she asked. "Is anyone in here besides us? I gotta joint, man, a doobie!" Jessie held in her hand a crumpled bit of rolled up paper, filled with who knows what substance. I eagerly grabbed it, then offered to pay cash.

"Wow, Jessie, how much do ya want for it?" I asked, hoping she didn't want too much. "I've got my lunch money, you can have it all." She didn't look very impressed with lunch money. Young dealers never are. "How about fifty cents?" I continued to whine, almost begging. Jessie feigned disinterest, and began to stuff it back into her ragged jeans pocket. I was hooked.

"Can't give it to ya free, ya know," she said. "Dope costs money."

"Can I see it?" I asked anxiously. Shit! I never saw a doober before. Handing her a dollar, I hoped she would wear down. A dollar was a lot of money for a twelve year old back then.

"Well, I guess a dollar is enough," she allowed, pausing to stuff my money into her pocket. Jessie didn't carry a purse, and she lived out of several pockets for days on end. Now the dope was mine, and I was suddenly the proud owner of possible consequences, even a possible juvy record. Visions of drug busts, complete with masked policemen carrying sub-machine guns and handcuffs, danced in my tormented young brain. My parents had unsuccessfully indoctrinated me into the 'See this egg, this is your brain on drugs' theory, but cops terrified me.

"Are we gonna, like, smoke it in here, or what?" I asked in a wavering voice. Uh-oh, what if she wants to do something crazy, like smoke dope in the bathroom? How was I going to get out of it? Jessie stared at me in her non-plussed way, her blond curls and aqua-green eyes making her look like the vision of innocence, all except for the Black Sabbath tee shirt, which totally gave her away. Jessie's lanky, child-body lounged carelessly against a graffiti

7

covered wall while I shook and trembled at the horrors that filled my mind.

"What are you whining about?" Jessie asked. "Ya got no balls."

"I'm not too sure about this, girlfriend," I answered, attempting some bathroom slang. "What if Miss Bitch comes in here and narcs on us?" I was always the paranoid one, while my friends dragged on in bliss.

"Yeah, so what if she does?" Jessie bravely countered. "We'll just kick her lousy fat ass!" I wasn't convinced, not being as tough as Jessie.

"Remember what happened to Mary Alice when they caught her in here with a cig?" I reminded her. Surely that nasty scene would jog her jaded memory. "They like, called her parents, man, and she got her ass beat." Obviously I wavered between wanting to get high and not wanting to get busted. Jessie had the whole affair under control, and offered an alternate suggestion.

"Chick, we're gonna ride the poney, we're gonna touch the sky, and it's all happening at my place tonight, ten o'clock, when the old lady splits for her boyfriend's place." With that, Jessie calmly strolled to the mirror and began to apply lipstick to her pouty lips. I figured she'd at least light a Salem, or something daring like that. I naturally acted as unparanoid as possible, as if I could pull this next one off, knowing it was a school night, knowing Mom would never let me out of the house.

"Cool dude," I slurred nonchalantly. "I'll just tell the parents your Mom said I could hang at your house tonight." Jessie didn't look thrilled, but what the hell. "You don't care, right? I can't exactly go home stoned or stay out after ten ya know." The specter of parental control reared its ugly head. "My Mom is like, strict. Not like yours, Jessie. She can read minds." She still had her Nazi Belt too, and that was my biggest fear of all, except for restriction, which usually accompanied the Belt. I glanced at the stalls, hoping no one overheard us. We exited as a loud bell rang, screeching me out of my revery, jolting me into reality, scaring me half to death. Other girls began pouring in, along with Miss Bitch, the moronic hall monitor who took her duties ultra-seriously and was checking for smokers. What a close call! No one else knew our secret, so our pact with tripping out was safe.

And on and on. Didn't even cop a buzz. Little girls don't know a thing about drugs, but I was soon to discover the joys of sniffing paint by another infamous friend of mine who I began to hang with at the delicate age of thirteen years. Gold metal flake used to get me off royally, but it wasn't a habit I was proud of or planned to cultivate. My actual dope experience would come soon, but not before I got familiar with plastic bags. Every mother's nightmare, they were my new way of life.

It must have been around 1974 when I was fourteen. I was spending the night with one of my forbidden friends, the kind of friend mothers warn their children about, the kind of friend I was constantly seeking pleasure with, my favorite girl of the year, Alishia Waldorf. She fucked, too. Her sister had already had a baby at the age of fifteen, so Alishia knew the ropes. I was still a virgin, and fascinated with her freedom and the fact that since her parent's divorce, she was allowed to do anything she wanted, anytime, anyplace. Someday I would enjoy that same, dubious freedom.

She used to strip to sniff paint with her boyfriend, claiming that the paint got all over her clothes and her mother would catch her during the throes of paint's passionate embrace. I was over my infatuation with shirtless living, and wondered if she had some hidden reason for stripping to her bare pink skin and underwear. One black night in October we were bursting some brain cells together and I was my trembling self, as usual.

"Hey Lishia, this is some kinda spooky old house," I squeaked, surreptitiously glancing around the cold, dark, lonely yard where we were parked. "Are you sure we should be parked out here?" Another sneaky look around—was that a noise in the bushes? Try to act sophisticated. "I heard there was a murder down Lee road and some chick was found face down in the mud, naked and raped." Shit, there it was again, a scraping sound, either a squirrel or a murderer. "Did you hear that noise? What's that noise over there?" Alishia ignored my whining, and busied herself with the intricacies involved in sniffing paint. Tonight, we were doing blue metal flake from Gibson's discount store.

Afraid to look out the window any longer, I hunkered in the back seat, hugging the sticky vinyl and contemplating certain death. Alishia wasn't the least bit worried, and began to strip off

9

her jacket, a prelude to total nakedness. "Man, don't worry," she commanded, "All right?" Heaving a sigh of exasperation, her stringy unwashed hair mussed up and her mascara smeared, she laboriously addressed my deepest fears. "You take all the fun out of life."

Off went her socks, and she pulled out a can of blue metal flake, handing it to me along with a plastic bread bag. It certainly wasn't a very expensive way to fry your brains in olive oil. "Spray some paint in this plastic bag, stick it over your mouth and inhale... that's right." I whisked the whites together with a large, yellow yoke and created the fluffy mass that is necessary for a perfect souffle. But would it fall? I had to do it, she would never take me out to get high again if I didn't. Sucking up the blue fumes, inhaling that sweet, sickly scent, I escaped into a different kind of euphoria than most mothers would want for their children. Maybe that was the reason Alishia was off limits. Whew, what dizziness, what dreamy qualities, what a weird smell. I entered the psychic realm of never-neverland, and flew through Pink Floyd's triangle of time (we were listening to "Dark Side of the Moon").

"Doesn't that feel good?" Alishia asked, as I swayed in time to my own musical beat, my own trip into infinity, my brain cells bursting with each dose of poisonous gas. Perhaps she noticed the fact that I was staring at her increasingly naked body, because she said, "I'm taking off my clothes so I don't get blue flecks all over me after I spaz out," and pulled off her torn Levis. "My Mom is super suspicious ever since she caught Lana in the bathroom, sniffing that black metal flake shit." Alishia removed her bra, the last piece of clothing she had on, and took out the paint can, shaking it up and down. Her washed-out, baby blue eyes glittered unnaturally in the night as she sprayed another hit into her plastic Wonder bread bag. Blue mist filled the stifling car, and I felt very dizzy. The fear of being raped had been replaced by something similar to being pickled, or injected with formaldehyde, or shot with a twelve-gauge.

Now, her boyfriend was this biker type, and he didn't say much. His name was Bubba, or something, and he just drove us around and bought the paint, or booze, or dope, which we immediately consumed while cruising the backroads of Lawless, Oklahoma. His eyes had gotten bigger as Alishia stripped off her cut-up sleeveless jean jacket with the American flag sewn on back and a swastika drawn on front. Bubba began to breathe in eager, hot thrusts, a possible prelude to something I had no intention of watching. I declined another hit of blue metal flake, and Bubba grabbed the can to spray himself some while Alishia began to pick at the back of her left wrist where a scab was growing. Arrested development, I thought to myself, she must have had a weird childhood.

Alishia had a funky tattoo she made herself while serving time in Juvy Jail. She made it by tying some thread around a needle and dipping it into India ink, then poking it through her skin numerous times, right into the flesh. Amazed that her mother would allow her to tattoo herself, I watched her make another tattoo when we were hanging out in her room on a weekend evening, listening to Led Zeppelin and drinking tea laced with vodka (we weren't fooling anyone). This particular one was on the top of her left hand, and the sight of her idea of self-mutilation tore at my stomach as she shook the blue metal flake and Bubba looked on, breathing heavily. Her latest tattoo said, 'DIE.'

I guess I was just bored. Maybe that's why I started running away from home in the fourth grade while living in Newport News, Virginia, supposedly because my Mom threatened to give away my dog. I escaped through the bathroom window on the second floor, gathered my runt of a foundling dog from out front where he was tied to the porch, and proceeded on my merry way to the stables, my favorite hangout that year.

What a day! I cruised along the bridge of railroad tracks, suspended high in the morning air on a level with rustling giant oak trees topped by cirrus clouds fluffing overhead, never stopping to wonder how I would manage to jump one hundred and fifty feet to the rocks below should a train come rumbling round the bend. I never worried in those days.

I found some oats and horse food to munch on at the stables and nibbled around while petting a few thoroughbreds, then snoozed under the stable headquarter's front porch. Later that afternoon I wandered out to the bluegrassy green meadow, wishing I had the nerve to try and catch a horse. After playing on a pile of coal long enough to cover myself in black coal dust, I moseyed on back to the homestead after dark, hungry and tired, my day of excitement over.

Poor Mom was totally freaked when the lady next door 'caught' me and dragged me home. Hey, lay off! I'm going already. The cops threatened to take me away to juvenile jail, but I didn't worry too much—I was used to idle threats. Dad just faded into the background and let Mom lecture me, as he wasn't in the mood for confrontations that night. All in all, everything went back to normal very soon. Oh, by the way, I kept the dog.

Virginia had its moments. I had this really fine fort in the woods which I sometimes shared with my brother, Gerhart. We kept our Salems stashed there but I always forgot they weren't waterproof, and lost many a pack to the elements. Cost me thirty-five cents at the bowling alley cigarette machine in 1969. Where else could a fourth grader buy cigarettes? I didn't have many friends, so I mostly skulked around the woods with my air rifle, picking wild onions and pretending to all the little kids that I was Lone Wolf, the hunter. In the summer I used to run down to the Sand Pool on base and swim all day in the hot sunshine, soaking up the rays and scoping out the guys. All I got at the Sand Pool was grit in my bikini bottoms and exercise, but what can you expect when you're a fourth grader?

Then, the fun ended because I tape-recorded my class at the local public school. All the administrators were white but ninety-five percent of the student body was black. I loved going to school there because most old Superior White Virginia families were too good to speak to my parents (which wasn't conducive to my shrinking circle of friends), but the black kids and their parents were cool and very sociable. Evidently the Eastern social scale demanded that unless a family lived in Newport News for at least five generations, one couldn't converse across the fence over laundry. This left the blacks (who were never accepted into the societal realm), along with the newcomers (who were people like me) to hang out together in ostracism and isolation. Fine with me.

The school was generally chaotic and there was a distinct lack of faculty intervention or control, which was the perfect environment for me to read my books rather than pay attention to the barely audible drone of my teacher explaining her latest attempt at algebraic formulation. Problem was, I was flunking fourth grade and I needed an excuse to tell Mom. In reality, I could have paid attention in class, but I preferred to remain obnoxious. One day I snuck my cassette recorder into class and taped it, capturing the yelling and screaming students and the essence of that public school's integrity. Yeah, it worked all right. Mom pulled me out of the only truly social adventure I could have in that eastern part of the United States, and she did the unbelievable, she placed me in a private Catholic school. "Get ye to the nunnery, young lass!"

In keeping with my delinquent personality, and in order to be true to my own particular code of ethics concerning how adolescents should conduct themselves in school, I immediately got into trouble on my first day of private school. There was this huge, hawk-like nun who hovered at my elbow, blowing her stench my way, practically curling the pages of my book with her foul breath. I was reading a lovely story at the time, and I had gotten to that part where Oliver is being literary and trying to woo Jenny through words of poesy, sweet nothings such as those written by the masters of....

"Young lady, what do you think you are reading?" The hawk-like creature interrupted Oliver's soliloquy, and never knowing the pleasures of physical love, squawked, "This is Algebra class, and we do not allow such filth in our school of Sacred Mary."

"Hey, lay off!" I complained, trying to grab my book back. "You lost my place." Sacred Mary? I'm going to a school named Sacred Mary?

"Give me that book this instant!" Who said nuns were gentle and demure? This extremely agitated nun in particular had beady, little, glittery eyes that glared at me with malice and cunning... she grabbed my book and I never saw it again. We marched in rhythm down the dank, dungeon-like hallway, I to my doom, she to her sacred duty, and the lash was forthcoming to extract penance for my transgression.

Rap! Rap! went the ruler on my fingers, guilty of clutching *Love Story* (luckily, I had already read it once and was rereading to fulfill my voracious desire for good literature and a little smut). The vision in black, Sister Ruth, after snagging me with her gnarled fist on my shoulder and forcibly propelling me to the headmistress's office, did her duty whereby I was reprimanded immediately, and reminded of my lowly status as a 'special student' (they didn't usually accept delinquents at Sacred Mary's, but money talks).

Sheet. What a place. I couldn't cuss or scream or climb a tree or beat up boys or read a half-way interestingly written novel without undergoing intense interrogation about my spiritual motives. My life had hit the pits. Worst of all, the final blow, the horrid truth about private education in Virginia was the clothes we had to wear. I had this green and black pinafore type totally pussy uniform with matching very pussy shoes. And, on top of all the rest, I had the dubious pleasure of finally making straight A's in the fourth and fifth grade, not that I wanted anyone to know I cared about grades, of course.

I still sometimes wonder why I took up hitchhiking in my later years...I must admit that hitchhiking to California had its moments. Strange and unusual people picked me up and offered me various things: food, dope, a place to crash, their bodies. I took a little of whatever I wanted and rejected some of what I didn't want. When you're a hitchhiker, you make up fantasies. I had a great one about Cat Stevens that lasted for three years. Oh, yes, the Great Greek. How that ever began, I'll never figure out. I guess it could have been the drugs, or maybe it was the weird Oklahoma heartland atmosphere that led to my demise as I backslid into California, looking for Cat Stevens, or the ghost of what once was Cat Stevens, which is what I finally found.

Fast forward to college in Waterford, Oklahoma at Southwestern City College amongst the farm girl mentalities. It was 1978 and I guess I just needed an excuse to get out of the 'Area of Operations,' or the AO, as they say in the Army. Tea for the Tillerman by Cat Stevens was the closest album at hand that day with a face that looked remotely like my own. There I was, 18 years old and turning to fat in front of the mirror. I was too young to be all alone in the very large, partially remodeled (partially unusable) chocolate brown, two-story house on a hill above the university by a playground. School was a non-issue because I had essentially stopped going to all my classes.

Lucky to have a roof over my head, I had recently been kicked out of two places. First, I was jostled out of the women's dormitory for loud Fleetwood Mac, dope, and my refusal to join the Dean of Women's alma mater sorority. As a newbie freshman, I indulged my idyll with academia by courting the affections of any adult I thought would listen. Lonesome, I often found myself confessing vices to the Dean's ready ear, all too often allowing auto-yap to override good sense. She knew I smoked dope, she knew I hung out with a woman who was considered mentally deranged (but brilliant), she knew I was ready to have my room searched. But I, stupid me, had no one else to talk to, and interpreted her interest in my life as benevolent, not malevolent.

Wrong. All this and more led up to my dismissal from the dormitory at midnight, the witching hour, in an unceremonious ousting by order of the Dean, who had personally conducted a search of my room and found drugs, yes drugs! An entire joint constituted the stash from which I allegedly dealt drugs to the student populace. She called my dad and told him I was selling on campus, and under suspension (not to mention suspicion). Fine. Fucking fine. Before discovering the chocolate brown house, I found myself camping out in the home of Lura O. Justine, a woman stranger than fiction who wore her scuba knife to class, heard voices and saw little men. There was a reason the Dean thought she was deranged.

My friend, I thought to myself, I'll keep her. At least I had a friend. Soon after settling into Lura's low slung, grime green house, I returned home from my scummy waitress job at the local dive, and found my belongings neatly piled on Lura's lawn, ready for the trash. I banged on the door, I leaned on the doorbell, I screamed my bloody head off.

"Lura, open the door, will you?" I hollered. She had nailed it shut from the inside, it seemed to my delirious mind. There was no answer, but I knew she was home because the tv was blaring out some song about 'Green Acres is the place to be, farrrmm livin' is the life for me...' "What's the idea, anyway," I yelled. No comment. This was getting boring and sweaty. My waitress armpits had huge half moons and my greasy face had zits popping up. This type activity right before supper time did not improve my mood one bit. "I paid you the rent, Lura." I had been rejected, once again, by a person who I thought cared about me. "Why don't you deal with it and let me in to talk, woman?" Shit. No answer yet from behind the green door. I indiscreetly made a scene in the front yard, probably alerting all the neighbors to my impending insanity, my probable nervous breakdown in Waterford, Oklahoma. "You threw my fucking stuff out to get ripped off or rained on or whatever," I yelled at the silence of her puke-green house. It's just not fair, I whined to no one in particular. She doesn't like me anymore.

Tears began rolling down my face as her stolid silence continued. "I thought you were my friend, but you're worse than the Dean!" I whined to the listening Lura, my ex-friend and ex-roomie. Her final insult, the dilemma of two turned against one, and the overall drama of my life left me weak. Slumped on the porch, attired in my lovely, stinky, polyester waitress dress, I sweated elephants, but wouldn't budge from my vigil.

So, out slouches one of her numerous boyfriends to shut me up. Lura had two kids somewhere, but they didn't live with her, that's for sure. Maybe all the rumors about Lura's instability were true. Maybe all the nasty talk about the back-stabbing Dean was true, too. I can't honestly say I wasn't warned. Godzilla the moron curled his lip, revealing white gums, decay, and fangs. Lura's lover set me straight once and for all. "Say lady, whyn'cha get ya stuff and pack it out, huh?" he belched. Do I look like a moving company, I wondered? He spoke again, great wafting tufts of bad breath and gingivitis drifting my way. "Lura don't like you anymore. Her little men told her ya were movin' stuff around the house and they didn't appreciate it."

Little who?

Little men?

"You're joshing me right?" I softly asked, looking around the yard for lurking leprechauns. "Did you really say little dudes?"

"Uh huh."

"I see," I said, but I didn't see any of them, which was in my favor.

He had more to say, and none of it promising. "So whyn'cha jes' git along out a here while ya still can, huh? Split the scene, ya get it?" Bad breath aside, he was still unattractive. Carrying his huge beer belly under one arm, he lumbered back inside.

"Uh huh," I said to the whispering wind and the setting Oklahoma sun. "I'm leaving." Not that anyone bothered to help me with my stuff, and the tv just got louder to drown out my screams, I supposed, but at least I knew where I wasn't wanted. What a scumbag boyfriend. He probably wanted to move in and he entertained Lura's fantasy about little men splendidly, although if he believed it, I never could tell.

Lots of otherwise normal seeming people around Southwestern City College saw little men that year, I was to discover, not just Lura O. Justine. I never saw them myself, being unable to I suppose, but a young nursing student, Mary Ellen, who took me in and rescued me from the lawn of Lura that evening, was a visionary herself. Before I began my transient existence, back in the old days when I was welcome in the dorms, Mary Ellen rushed into my room one night, screaming "They're after me! Let me in the room and lock the door, hurry!" She panted, she heaved big sighs, she collapsed on my bed, barely missing conking her head on the speaker.

I looked up from my book and said, "So like, what's exactly after you, Mary Ellen? Having nightmares about your organic chemistry exams tomorrow?" I was just too smooth and self-controlled, I was buzzing on some great grass and mellow as a tabby cat overdosed on milk. Nothing could faze me out of my dream that night, or so I thought at the time. "Drink a little too much coffee? Popping those uppers again?" I snidely inquired. Hah! I was invincible, I was unafraid, I would protect Mary Ellen from her little fantasy. I droned on like a good doctor, ready to shut the door to subconscious terror, ready to brave the 'elementals.' "You know as well as I do that there are no little men outside my door, I'm going to open it now and show you..."

Sauntering over to the door, I made as if to unlock it to the horrors that awaited us outside, not expecting her reaction, inexperienced in the reality of those little creatures as I was. She freaked! "No, close the door," she whispered. "Don't let them get me, they followed me here from my house," she panted. "Please, don't let them get me!"

17

Out of breath but not out of strength, Mary Ellen bounced off the bed and pleaded with me, pop-eyed with terror. By now, she was sweating and hysterical. I mean, this girl was seriously ill, and had me convinced (almost) that there were really little men outside my door. Then, the mood changed, and things got really weird. Smiling calmly, she wiped the perspiration from her fevered brow, and said, "Gabrielle, you can let me out now," with a calm, cool exterior. "They're calling me, everything's all right now, and all is forgiven."

You be too strange, sister.

"You wanna go out now?" I asked.

"Move Gabrielle."

"But I'm trying to help you, Mary Ellen."

"Move now, Gabrielle." Shit, that girl was dead serious! I still didn't quite get the picture, but I would, soon. Mary Ellen gave me an unearthly glare, and moved toward the door, which I blocked. She became disgusted with our banter and said, "I need out, now. Let me out!" Advancing stomach to stomach, she pushed me out of her way, nearly knocking me to the floor. I became a bit unsettled, losing my cool. Was this the practical nursing student we all knew and loved, member Phi Kappa Phi, lady with the straight and narrow life, highly evolved study habits and Catholic upbringing? I couldn't believe my eyes!

"There's nothing out there," I tried to say, still barring the door to her Great Unknown World. I peeked around the corner down the hall, and didn't see anything, Praise the Lord. "See?"

She said with a slight snarl, "Get away from the door or I'll run right through you to get to my friends." I believed it by that time, and moved aside, looking one more time for little men outside my door. Mary Ellen spoke to someone, and soon vanished into the night. If I hadn't opened the door to let her out, I would have gotten bulldozed, lambasted, mutilated, so off into the night she went, much like Barnabus Collins in Dark Shadows, much like an Alabama tornado in the spring, much like a vampire out for some blood-sucking—that's the impression she left me.

She was outta there, and I was worried.

This lady was one hefty woman with a mind like a steel trap, good grades, and in good graces with the Dean of Women. If she saw weird stuff, surely there was something amiss in Waterford, Oklahoma, and I thought maybe I was in trouble. Well, the fact of the matter is, I was. Don't forget, I was soon homeless and at the mercy of every Tom, Dick, and Harry who might molest me in the night, and I was damn lucky Mary Ellen liked me. She invited me home to her haunted castle, the little house on the prairie behind the big sorority house, 'studio' living at its most efficient, a one room wonder that left little room for intrusion by outer forces (ah, but the inner forces were hard at work as I would soon discover to my chagrin and dismay).

Yes, it's true, Mary Ellen saw little men.

There was a day when we both were off to do laundry or shop or something mundane like that, and I specifically remember leaving the shoes lined up neatly, with a bucket full of warm, soapy water in the center of the floor which we were using to wash the windows. I distinctly remember all this because the house was so teeny tiny that every aspect of living had to be closely monitored to make room to walk in. The one room servant's quarters was abused beyond description when we returned, though. The shoes were scattered and water was everywhere, all over the walls like it had been thrown. Mary Ellen and I had the only keys. All the windows were locked. She looked at me with a glint in her eye, smiled and said, "They're back..."

Things got bad then. Things got really crazy. I lost my mind entirely and well, that's what the rest of this story is about. Are you surprised that an impressionable young woman who's already sort of heading astray would jump ship, leap into the unknown, and pretty much disappear from the world which she had called home?

I decided to withdraw into my own little microcosm of a world, and quit society. Did I say withdraw and quit society? If that means proceeding to flunk out of biology because of non-attendance, giving up on any semblance of reality or friendship with the farm girls and nursing students in City College, the answer is yes, unequivocally yes!

My immediate problem was that of no home, no job, and no transcript to speak of, so I sat on my little haunches in that nice nursing student's house, and called on my Christian God to not forsake me just because I had royally destroyed any academic chance I might have had at CC, and to please find me a house, pronto. He must have heard and taken mercy on my poor misguided soul at that time, because as I was aimlessly wandering around the Administration building, the lady from Financial Aid grabbed me in the hall and breathlessly held onto my shoulder, saying, "Where have you been? We owe you some money!" I cringed under her grip; surely it was a trick. They owed me? For what? Getting kicked out of the dorm? You've got to be kidding. Hey look, I'm a college drop-out, all right? They wrote me out a check for just under four hundred dollars, despite my protests (which quickly dried up), and I rented the chocolate-brown, frame house on a hill I had found that morning while scouting around on my bike for suitable lodgings, without a dime in my torn jeans pocket. Really strange turn of events. The nursing student was awestruck at my good fortune, and her little men had her all to themselves once again. She didn't come knocking on my door anymore, so I gathered they were all happy together.

As I turned in front of the mirror, I noticed the occasional bulimia wasn't working anymore because my ribs didn't show, perhaps since salad wasn't my main meal and granola and oatmeal had replaced vegetable fiber. I had given up my daily run of two to five miles, and taken up the art of pigging out instead. I did not have a job, a school, or any destiny and I was losing my svelte figure brought on by fasting and binging on salads and cottage cheese with the occasional three or four sweet cinnamon rolls. Awesome amounts of fat were to come, as I grew more and more accustomed to consuming unlimited globs of high calorie foods like cream cheese, bread, granola and ice cream, just to mention a few food favorites.

As I listlessly thumbed through a stack of albums bequeathed to me by the last tenant, stoned on some awesome weed acquired from one of my numerous connections, I casually picked up "Tea for the Tillerman," and knew that Cat was my man. Why not? Anything was possible in a town where normal people saw little men and abnormal people like me got answers from God in cold hard cash. I was one strange chickee, and about to embark on a journey that would take me into obesity, big cities, heavy duty drug use, and dangerous liaisons with perverted people.

I gave Waterford one last try before giving up and quitting town but in retrospect I should have just left while I was ahead. Dumb faithful sheep. I visited the Christian youth outreach coffeehouse type place, Serenity House. Two guys in particular stick out in my mind, Tony the skinny blond kid, and Bill, the big, brawny bear with blue eyes and a blond beard. Both were extremely helpful and agreed with me that people who saw little men and who weren't 'saved' were bound for trouble. Yeah, right guys. Tony had a habit of laying around the house, kind of like a male Rottweiler would, with his nether parts clearly outlined through lycra shorts for all the world to view. Sort of a surrender position, if you know what I mean. Several coffeehouse ladies complained about this unnecessary display, and Tony began to drape himself elsewhere. Meanwhile, Bill and I discussed little men. He cleared his throat with a loud "Ahem," and I was certain that a sermon would ensue. It did, of course.

He began intoning, "Now Gabrielle, it's perfectly normal for you to be upset and confused about these demonic influences, but there is nothing to be afraid of." Appropriately reverent hesitation for reflection and affectation. Continue. "Just say, in the name of Jesus Christ, Satan get behind me, and they'll run away." Smugly, Bill glanced at his fingernails, then noticing something on his index, he began to pick at it. I wasn't entirely convinced (or even slightly), so I questioned him further.

"Well, that's good advice, Bill, and you're right about extermination of bad influences, but I still don't get it." Had I missed the point, or just his point? "Why should I ever even see this stuff?" I queried, attempting to play the Baby Christian role and act interested. "I thought the whole idea of being a Christian and 'Satan get behind me' is because Jesus Christ didn't want Satan in front of him, you know, like in His face." I paused for the appropriate dramatic effect. "Neither do I wish to see little men." It was time to extract the truth from him. "Tell me something, Bill, you sound as though you are well acquainted with this problem that plagues Waterford. I don't suppose you have ever seen these little mythical creatures have you? Surely you haven't... tell me you haven't." Jaded as I was, the jist of my question was rhetorical; I had already seen the crazed 'I see little men' look in his eye.

21

Bill finished picking at his nail, and began to scratch his rear end, as if I weren't present. He gave me a superior look, let out a very quiet fart (one of those soft smelly ones), and continued his sermon. "Gabrielle, once you progress beyond being a Baby Christian, as you are now, once you become tried and tested in the fire, you will understand what I'm telling you," Bill gently said. I wasn't convinced.

"Like you, Bill?" I innocently inquired, and didn't say, 'I suppose you have reached thorough spiritual enlightenment, thus enabling you to counsel poor unfortunates like myself who try to understand the nuances of the universe, and fart in private.' I was losing all respect for the man.

Undaunted by my obvious skepticism, he continued. "Right now, you're confused and scared of the unknown, but I assure you, these little men are harmless manifestations of itsy-bitsy pockets of evil." Actually, I'm beginning to be more frightened at the mental state of you Waterfordians than your little men, I silently countered. Bill said, "They're not dangerous, and you too will someday see them." No way, Jose, I'm not going to lose it like you guys, uh-uh, you can forget that noise. With that final answer, Bill hurried back to his Christian duties as Serenity House Deacon. He had countless others in need of evangelism, I'm so sure.

Shit.

Son of a bitch.

I'm getting out of this crazy town.

Saturday came a month later and I split town, unable to pay my bills due to unemployment, cranked out of my head on loud music and pot. It was time to begin my trip into fantasy land, my journey to the seashore, my visit to Mars with a detour to Uranus. I was going after Cat Stevens who would, of course, welcome me with open arms and his millionaire existence into the wonderful world of guitarland, where we would sing together and feed the children forever, amen.

Did I mention that I thought I played guitar? That was my ticket to success, because with Cat, I would bloom into a musical extravaganza, heretofore undiscovered but brought to life with the miracle that guided Cat Stevens into rock and roll fame. I was one mad, crazy wench. I had this exalted vision of myself that went above and beyond mere narcissism, over and away from normalcy, quite out in the stars and pulsating with the black holes of the universe. Yes, it's true, I was self-centered.

I have a friend who is now a clinical psychologist with two Masters degrees, and she tells me that when she got my note about going after Cat Stevens (I always wrote notes to her), she realized I had lost all sense of reality. Letting Renee know about my craziness was my safety valve, because she had lived with me, rescued me from Waterford numerous weekends, slept in a bed with me at sixteen when my parents divorced and her mother died, leaving us alone and untended while our fathers fucked around with loose women, and I could trust the woman with my mind's secrets.

Even though I swore Renee to secrecy, I somehow mysteriously acquired the touching nickname of 'Crazy Gabby' in Lawless, by virtue of the grapevine. She listened to my bullshit then and she listens to it now—nothing has changed, and although I now have returned to planet Earth, and pretend to be reasonably normal, I never lived down the dubious nickname of 'Crazy Gabby,' acquired that year in the late seventies, when I first took flight in my search for the great Cat Stevens. That's right, I finally got a clue and left Oklahoma for a while. But first, a word from our sponsor.

Chapter Two

*In its infancy, slavery was particularly harsh.
Physical abuse, dismemberment, and torture
were common to an institution that was far
from peculiar to its victims. Partly as a result,
in the eighteenth century, slave masters did not
underestimate the will of their slaves to rebel,
even their female slaves. Black women proved
especially adept at poisoning their masters, a
skill undoubtedly imported from Africa.*

Paula Giddings

Casting the circle

I still don't know what happened to all my stuff, but I do vaguely remember hitching my first ride with these totally insane kids who ended up planning to go to California with me, but then we got into a big argument over some trivial bullshit, like why was I looking at her boyfriend that way, so I ended up back in Lawless, Oklahoma, eighty-five miles from Waterford. I was back in the town of Mom and Dad and Bicycle Hills, hangout of paint sniffers.

I trolled away for a while at the college in town, and lasted through exactly one whole semester with a feminist professor who appreciated my dry, thoughtless, meandering wit while I appreciated her choice of poems we explicated in class, not to mention her urbane conversation. Apparently, the rest of the class didn't, because I got an 'A' in Composition II, one of the few students to achieve this great feat under Dr. Schollweise, and my poetry explication has been under fire at every university I have attended since.

Later on in our relationship, we even discussed such mundane matters as veterinary medicine, and what was known back then as Cytomegalovirus, a herpes virus that was common among slum kids in the United States. It was also becoming increasingly common among gay men in New York City, and would soon acquire the acronym GRID, which stood for gay-related immunodeficiency, and finally AIDS, which stands for acquired-immunodeficiency syndrome. I had the idea in my head that Parvovirus was a direct precursor of the powerful Cytovirus, especially after reading some obscure veterinary journals, and wanted to talk about it to someone.

Since I worked one summer in a veterinary clinic as the night time emergency diagnostician, housekeeper, medicinal giver, and needle poker, often tending upwards of one hundred animals, some of whom were on I.V. drips that had to be checked every five minutes, I had quite an interest in zoology and veterinary medicine. In fact, I had often daydreamed about someday becoming a vet myself, doctoring all the sick animals for free, fixing broken bird wings and dead armadillos, rescuing severed snakes from the roads where they lay still twitching in the sun.

I was intensely interested in road kill, but more than death, I was interested in Parvovirus, the latest communicable virus to sweep the nation's animal kingdom, which was even more deadly than automobiles. While majoring in zoology at Southwestern City College, back in my troubled but studious days, I had studied parasitology and genetics, learning all about diseases and mutant viruses. You could say I was interested in morbid things, but really, I just loved animals.

One late evening, while thumbing through the veterinarian's office, trying to stay awake (I worked the ten o'clock to eight o'clock shift), I discovered a treatise on the effects of Parvovirus on dogs, pigs, and monkeys. Since ninety-five percent of the animals I treated that were on I.V.s were Parvo victims, my interest was piqued (no pun intended). Could it be true that Parvo was a form of Cyto, I wondered? This journal said it was a real possibility, but who could I ask? Not one of the solemn vets, that's for sure. They'd kill me if they knew I dug in their offices. I wondered who to spill my beans to until I finally found someone, an academic with an open mind, a true thinker, my Composition II instructor, Dr. Schollweise.

We often conversed over coffee in the teacher's lounge, where students weren't always welcome; it just depended on who was in there at the time. I had just finished pouring a cup when in bopped Dr. Lashlow, who grabbed the pot out of my hand, muttering some inanities about ungrateful pilfering students, evidently imagining all sorts of hideous tortures for students who dared drink coffee in the teacher's lounge. *Sturm und Drang.* After she ambled off, still muttering, I sat down on the couch and expertly balanced a fresh cup on my knee. Ah yes, an undisturbed professor.

Time for intellectual stimulation... I was not disappointed in my captive audience. "Dr. Schollweise, you live in New York City in the summer, right?" I asked her, as she sat quietly beside me on the couch.

"Yes my dear, you know I do," she answered. "I have an apartment in the Village." Her eyes, which changed from lavender to violet depending on how excited she was, twinkled, and she went back to reading her book. Just until I spoke again, of course.

"That's really a radical departure from the rest of the crowd here in Lawless." We exchanged secret smiles. "I was wondering about something I discovered in a veterinary medicine journal during my short career at Southwestern City College, and I want your opinion on it."

"I do remember you had quite an interest in science, Gabby," she said.

"You know lots of gay drama people in New York," I said, not terribly diplomatically for a town like Lawless. "What do they think caused the original Cytomegalovirus?" Dr. Schollweise looked increasingly interested, and lit a More cigarette, ostensibly to wave it in the air. I monologued on. "I have a theory. The Parvovirus that we commonly vaccinate our dogs for has similar qualities to the Cytomegalovirus, and in fact, is suspected by some veterinary scientists to be a mutation of the virus found in monkeys, swine and dogs." What do you think of that? Am I a bright student, or what? I continued. "Pretty *interestante,* huh?"

"You don't think it unusual, do you Gabrielle?" she asked, obviously not unaware of my theoretical argument's validity, yet repressed, as I was, by our local society.

"Well, I don't think it's scientifically unusual, no," I answered. "But people should be aware that the Parvovirus can be vaccinated against, and if Cyto is indeed a strong mutation, a species that 'jumped' from animals to humans like some veterinarians have theorized, couldn't it be vaccinated against in humans?"

She sure the hell sat up and looked real interested after I said that. "Where *do* you get your information, girl?" she asked me.

"All over the place," I answered, then rambled on. "Do you think the medical community in the know is withholding information from the public to get rid of gays and addicts?" It was such a relief to spill my beans to an educated mind.

"We do live in such a homophobic society," Dr. Scholweise observed.

"What do you think of my theory?" I pressed her. Well, maybe not my theory. She considered all my vehemence, took a swig from her coffee, and thoughtfully replied to my soliloquy on veterinary science. Now, this was back in the old days, when AIDS was a new thing with a different name, but Dr. Schollweise was a lady of culture, a feminist who prided herself on being informed, an intelligent being who shone like a beacon in an otherwise meat and potatoes town. She had all the answers. The master spoketh.

"Yes, the gay crowd in New York City has known about transmutated species viruses for a decade, but the medical establishment won't admit to a cover-up, neither will the pork industry." I hung on every word. She was so dramatic, her violet eyes rolling. "We're screwed, Gabrielle."

We looked into each other's eyes with a mutual twinkle of understanding, then went back to our reading. That was the last twinkle of mutual understanding I'd receive for a while, for I was destined to become a homeless street person. Just think, a conspiracy by the medical community and the pork industry to evade the public's outcry, to sell more and more bacon, to strip more and more gay men and addicts of their last resources, ah yes, this was the type of conversation I loved most. Political gossip, so to speak. About the underdog of course.

Alas, soon we parted company, for I was off to hitchhike, or take a bus, or something. Actually, hitchhiking wasn't considered good etiquette in Oklahoma that year, so I took a bus out of there to the Windy City of Chicago, Illinois. Whatever happened to California and Seattle, ocean spray and swaying palm trees?

I should have realized that no self-respecting rock star would hang out in Chicago during one of the coldest, snowiest winters in its history, but did I know or think of that? No, I just wanted out of

Lawless, so I called up a commune of Jesus People and went to live with them for a while. They had a band and a slightly to the left underground newspaper, *Cobblestone*.

They thought a bus was modus operandi for normal people, and despite their long hair, blue jeans, and musical vision, they were good people who followed very strict rules for themselves in order to help street people and drug addicts who frequently came begging on their doorstep, wanting to clean up. JPUSA was as straight as straight could be; no drugs, no sex, no rock and roll (except in church). I got fatter and fatter on the bread of righteousness, and quickly discovered that I simply must find a job and get out on my own—not that they weren't nice people, but I was a bad naughty girl and I wanted some bad naughty action.

I didn't get it in Chicago, that's for sure. With the exception of a Lebanese guy who gave me PCP, I stayed pretty straight. Some friendly Africans took me in and taught me to eat hot stew out of a pot, listening to me babble on about inane events in my silly life as a bookkeeper at Burger Prince on Franklin and Monroe in downtown Chicago, for that's what I had become. Free food for all the white management, and mops and brooms for black serfs. I was a white management. I had this big black guy allotted to me twice daily to carry the deposits (we're talking in the five thousand dollar range) to the bank next door, where we promptly smoked a joint after depositing it. I could score grass in any city, any state, any time.

The blacks wouldn't come visit me over on Hazel Street where I hunkered in my basement apartment, because they said the Mafia controlled that neighborhood and it was too dangerous to visit. I wasn't allowed in their projects either (for my own good, they said, not unkindly). So, I always moseyed home to my barren apartment while waiting for my African friends to come get me for dinner.

We would gather round the kitchen where the chitlins and vegetables bubbled in two separate pots, hot and very hot. I could barely eat hot. I could barely hear, either, because my Africans loved to turn up the tv full blast, turn up the radio to deafening, and yabber in dialects from Nigeria and Uganda above the background noise. No, I didn't understand the theory behind all this, but they were the coolest crowd I had found yet.

The men and boys shared one big bowl of stew with many wooden spoons, the men glancing with pride at their sons and nephews, while the women congregated in the kitchen over hot stoves and bubbling stews. I have a theory about black linguistic development, and why they talk the way they do in their own special slang that we whites like to say sounds 'ignorant,' but that's later, in graduate school, and I must not get ahead of my story. Read a few slave journals and you will find that the eighteenth and nineteenth centuries produced self-educated, black writers whose eloquence rivals that of Charles Dickens and Alexander Pope. Okay, so I'm meandering. Right then, I was just enjoying the scene and the company, even if I didn't know the languages. Black people, in my experience, have big hearts and take a lot of needless shit. Why an all white management at Burger Prince? Why couldn't I sweep once in a while at work? Where was Cat Stevens?

I'd pass this crippled-looking character in a wheelchair every morning while on my way to work, and pass her again on my way to the subway homeward bound. She looked kind of cold because it was snowing outside and freezing. She had a pink flush, a blanket, and a plastic bucket for donations. I had a feeling she was someone other than the woman she appeared to be, and one day we spoke. I spoke first (nickname's Gabby).

"So. Why do you sit on this corner, day after day, week after week, cold and miserable in the sleet?" I asked her. She said nothing yet, so I nagged a bit further, probing deeper into what I presumed was her cult-deactivated consciousness, hoping for a glimmer of enlightenment. "Surely your group doesn't expect you to survive the whole winter on the sidewalk, do they?" This while I'm jumping up and down, slapping my terminally frostbitten fingers together, sucking in car exhaust cooled at minus seven degrees below zero, and having a generally frosty time. Her crippledness spoke.

"I can see you're a Christian lady, I'm a Christian too." She sneezed, poor thing, and shook her head, as if to free it of the cobwebs that bound her to her chair. "I'm doing the work of God, so it doesn't matter how cold it gets out here, I'm willing to suffer for the cause of my church." The woman sniffled, snorted some snot, and coughed. Her black hair hung in soaking strands over a

29

pimpled forehead, and sleet trickled down her plaid blanket into a child's blue plastic bucket. She looked, sadly enough, like she meant every word she said. Yeah, it was cold, but the disapproval of the Church was colder, evidently. Or even the approval, for that matter. At a loss for words, I silently trudged on to Burger Prince, where I would inhale three free fish sandwiches for breakfast.

Soon after that little exchange, she pranced into Burger Prince with her cronies, miraculously recovered from her disability, her chronic injury. I just knew it! Unification Church, she was a Moonie, moonlighting as a cripple and after my money and my soul. What the hell, I might as well hassle them a little, I thought to myself, I'll just smuggle my Bible into a meeting and quote the Scripture at them for fun. So I went with this lady one night to her Moonie headquarters where we sat around a big table and ate this terrible tuna casserole, singing songs of praise to Reverend Moon. That's how they recruit impressionable young things into their cult, by portraying a family image, love and hand-holding, and all that rot. It didn't work on me because I was a renegade who had seen it all before and I didn't think I'd find what I was looking for in Moonie land.

Group-think demanded the immediate separation of all new initiates after dinner to discuss the various and sundry philosophies of Reverend Moon, and the only reason I could see to do this would be to eliminate questions from untoward guests being overheard by other, more easily swayed initiates and less easily swayed hard-core groupies. My opportunity arose to interrupt, which I did. They quickly realized that I was untrainable when I disrupted the group with Scriptural references, and suggested Mr. Moon had a million dollar arsenal which he bragged about on the evening news the week before, so why did they preach peace and goodwill to all?

"But don't you see?" I queried my brainwashed audience right before they threw me out, "Jesus didn't have to use any guns, and he healed the sick, too." Apparently, they heard enough, because two elders grabbed my arms and escorted me to the front door. Reverend Moon didn't need me, I surmised, tromping through cold slush in another silent Chicago evening, all alone with my thoughts. The lady in the wheelchair left me alone after that episode, although we continued to greet each other each morning as I went to work, and she sat in her wheelchair in the snow with sleet overhead. Why give away her secret?

Still no Cat.

I went to live with this Russian couple in Evanston, because the snow was melting, weirdos were hanging out on the street corners and I really was sick of all the dog shit that lay on the grass in Chicago. Evanston was prettier, spring was coming and an apartment was available from a guy who was a missionary in the Congo or somewhere like that. I sublet the place for a while, and when he returned, Nadja and Peter invited me to move upstairs into their spare room. They courted me with Russian cookies an inch thick, teaching me to say 'please pass the chicken' in Russian. I really was one fat chunk of cheese by the time spring finally arrived in Illinois. Even my two fat old Russian benefactors used to point to joggers on our way to the orthodox church we frequented and tell me I should be out there doing that too. Yeah, well try running when you're forty pounds overweight, and see how you like it. I preferred to eat myself silly every night while daydreaming of a better life as a thin person. Fantasy always seems better than fact when you're fat, let me tell you.

Then, one warm evening while we were sitting around the kitchen table and I was practicing my Russian alphabet (p for b and w for v), they invited me to this thing at church. I knew my big moment had arrived—I was finally going to meet Cat! Now what logical reason would I have to think that Cat Stevens would be at a Russian Orthodox-Ukraine church get together, complete with old folks, vodka, and Russian cookies? Good question. Obsession has no limitations, however, and I was obsessed.

As I lurked around the giant food laden tables, gobbling dumplings wrapped around pork and burger, Nadja and Peter came up to me and pointed to the bar, where drinks were served.

"You see that nice man over there?" asked Nadja as she tugged determinedly on my frilly sleeve. Little old Nadja, clad in a pale, canary yellow 1930's type prom dress looked up at me with her trusting, blue eyes, and I loved her. She still gave bad advice. "He is good man, honest, respectable, rich."

31

Everyone's formula for success: link up with honesty, wealth, and respectability. She tried so hard to convince me and got so excited that I was worried for her health. Pink flushed cheeks and glazed eyes stared at me out of that little wrinkled Russian face. I hung on every word, for I had not yet actually seen Vladimir. "You go talk to him, yes? He just your type. Come, I introduce you." Nadja waltzed me over to the bar, and patted Vladimir on the arm that wasn't holding a vodka.

"Vladimir Husak, this is Gabrielle Grople. I leave you two kids alone, yes?" Nadja was about to scurry off to Peter and the dumplings, but I grabbed her arm, not wanting to be left alone with the apparition who stood smirking before me. Him, a kid? He was at least twice as old as me, and three times as ugly! Undaunted by my obvious distaste for her friend, this creepy looking Czechoslovakian, Nadja needed no further signal from me. She was in total control. "Vladimir, give Gabrielle some vodka." With that, she whisked off to Peter, and Vladimir gave me the body ball, the once over, the visual screw. I should have known.

I settled for a drink with Vladimir, who Nadja and Peter had assured me was safe, reliable, and a good Christian kind of guy. Vladimir was certainly no good-looking hunk, not a rock star, and really rather a funky middle-aged, huge, grossly overweight Czechoslovakian with blond, scraggly hair, rotten teeth, bad breath, and purple bell bottoms, hopelessly out of style. Ah, but what the hell, I had some grass and he wanted to help me smoke it.

"Nice to meet you," I said, extending my hand to His Loathsomeness, not at all glad to meet him, but terribly bored with the Russian-Ukraine old folks get together, although I loved them. No Cat Stevens either. He smirked, looked down at my tits, and said, "How do you do?" With a deep bow, Vladimir made as if to touch his lips to my extended palm, but I would not allow it, and wrenched my hand away before it could become polluted with his darting tongue, which lurked nearby.

"You must mean, what's new around Czechoslovakia, yes?" he asked. No, I didn't. I asked the more relevant question, dispensing with small talk. "So, what's new around Russia?" I asked brightly, hoping to stimulate something other than his glands. "Do you smoke grass?" Take the plunge, what the hell, you've been living a cloistered life in the suburbs, get high with the locals for a change.

"Ah yes, I do indeed, why, do you have some?" He encouraged me, batting his eyelashes coquettishly, too much Jane Austen, I'm sure, must have fried his brain. Well, what are we doing in this place then, I asked myself—he's got a car, I've got some weed—you can't exactly smoke dope at Nadja and Peter's, let me tell you, and they noticed every little red eye and roach breath someone might come home with. I needed a place to get stoned in peace, to unwind, to relax and not worry about getting caught by the grown-ups, and punished for getting high. Sure, I got my chance to relax, but did I actually enjoy it, did I actually even get high?

No, I didn't.

After finishing our vodkas (those Russian Orthodox sure know how to throw a church fling), we told Nadja and Peter we were off to see the wizard (off to see a movie or something, I don't remember what lame excuse we gave), to which they nodded their approval and assent. They were absolutely thrilled I had finally found a man. Such a nice guy, that Vladimir—not only does he give his money to the church, he gives his life.

Right.

There we were, in this really scummy decrepit apartment that didn't exactly smack of affluence, and I was beginning to feel major bad vibes from the whole event. Vladimir and I smoked that joint. My inner eye began to warn me that something wasn't right—why would such a nice guy live in such squalor, in this slum? Cockroaches ran amuck, big black hairy things that stole around, right before our very eyes, evidently unafraid of Mr. Rad Roach Spray. They were probably Vladimir's pets.

Suddenly, without any warning, he ripped (yes, ripped) off his suit jacket in a rage and attempted to pounce on me then do who knows what else. I stillettoed around on heels—wouldn't you know it, I dressed up that one night for Nadja and Peter's delicate church sensibilities. Big oaf couldn't catch me anyway. He chased me around, spouting twisted oaths about how he was the Antichrist's follower, and wouldn't you know it, beneath his black suit jacket and tie and shirt, the tee-shirt he wore said FUCK JESUS CHRIST. Now I happen to think Jesus is really a cool dude,

33

because as I said before, He commonly bailed me out of rocks and hard places, not to mention the fact that with all the little men running around in Waterford, I felt I needed more than all the help I could get in the spiritual realm. This didn't thrill me at all. Vladimir then threatened to lick my pussy and smash my face, all in one big slurp and whack. He chased me outside his apartment into the hall, where I hovered by the stairs. Foul Mouth then breathed sweet nothings into my face.

"Come here, bitch, you think you too good for Czechoslovak man, but we are best. I smash your face next, cunt, after I rape you." He was your typical Soviet nightmare, and wanted nothing more than to rape, pillage, and burn. I was the country to be conquered, the war zone to be occupied, the people to be squelched. He was the marauding armies with tanks and howitzers, hum-vees and fire bombs. When all the soldiers were taken prisoner, lined up, singled out, and shot in the head to fall backward into their self-dug graves, Vladimir could then divert his attention from the work at hand, and come to me for a little tete-a-tete. We pranced around the hallway (I hobbled), but he still couldn't catch me.

Vladimir begged and cajoled, temporarily changing his attack tactics in between oaths (I don't think he saw little men—he saw big men!). Looked like a scene from Psycho IV. What should I do? My choices were somewhat limited and unsavory, to say the least. I could A) come back in and let him rape and kill me; B) stay in the hall forever, or at least until daylight, then call for help; C) jump outside into the cold wet damp without any subway money; D) come back in and convince him not to kill me, but to take me home. The things I got myself into would curl poor Mama's toenails. I don't think I will ever tell her about Vladimir and his roaches.

I decided to try my luck at outwitting the guy. I asked him to tell me about this Antichrist character, because I was interested in joining up with the cult team. This got his attention. In the meantime, he still grabbed at me, but I evaded his clumsy thrusts. Poor fat thing was getting worn out. I was fat too, but at least I had some major adrenalin rushes to keep me on the move. The plan was, invite Vladie Baby out for pizza, while acting interested in the maniac...hopefully, my escape was in sight. He said, "You have to be special person to know Antichrist—you have to be invited and say 'Lord's Prayer' backwards three times."

No way, dude, you can forget that noise, I'm no black magic sorcerer, no chance for that!

At this, Vladimir began to shake, and actually seemed terrified. It was as if he remembered a nightmare, or had a flashback. "Antichrist is mean guy—he says Jesus Christ was here to fulfill you spiritually, but he is here to fulfill you sexually. He says he is here with God's permission, and he brings only death." That sounds just like anyone who would wear desecrated tee-shirts to Russian-Ukraine get-togethers, and eat burger and sausage dumplings with little, old ladies and bent-up, old men. I'll bet you just idolize the Antichrist, right Vladimir?

He continued unaware, or uncomprehending, of my thoughts. Good thing he was too zonked out psychically to have telepathy or ESP, because my thoughts weren't exactly like my speech implied. "He has only a short time on the earth, and travels to a different city every month." Fear seemed to turn him on, because the lips slathered as he eye balled my tits. "Let me eat your pussy, bitch. Cunt." Right. A little sex to lighten our moods? A slow screw, perhaps?

I'm, like, supposed to be excited? Glittering, watery, grey eyes, a beet-red complexion, lips curled into a snarl, paunch almost touching me, Vladimir moved closer and closer. Onions and garlic. Ah, yes, the man of my dreams. I promised myself that if I ever got out of this alive and unraped, I'd go home to Lawless, Oklahoma and be a good girl for the rest of my life, never attempting anything dangerous again. I lied. Vladimir was poring over his Antichrist special notebook that only privileged people can look at, which was a notebook binder full of xeroxed misprints representing biblical verses, or so he said. It looked like a royal pile of shit to me. Playing my role correctly required the acquiescence of a wench in waiting, the demure femininity of a damsel in distress, the lassitude of an undereducated waitress at Burger Prince, (my former self) so I acquired the appropriate mask.

"Hey Vladimir, that's totally awesome! You must be a real favorite of the Antichrist to have such valuable manuscripts—oh, do you think what he says about John 3:8 makes sense?" He glares at me with bloodshot eyes. "You do? (I'm not surprised, you creepy oaf!) I've gotta real hunger." To tired to hop, I began to hobble. "Hey, let's go out for pizza I'll buy, whaddaya say, huh?" I had lapsed into the speech of ignorance, in order to fight my way, metaphorically and literally, to freedom from his awful embrace.

He chased me around some more in the apartment, drooling slightly, panting, sweating, stinking. Fucking crazy Czech. Panting heavily, I cajoled in all soft and floozy, cloudy and lofty, perfumed femininity, "Come on, Vladimir, I know you're hungry." You're always hungry for fresh flesh of every persuasion, including my own, and if we stuff you with pizza, maybe you'll temporarily substitute it for random killings which I'm certain, by now, that you commit. You're the local serial killer who's too dumb to get caught, right, Vladimir?

"I've got twenty dollars in my room, all for you, whyn'cha take me home and we can go eat, please?" Whine, whine, wheedle, wheedle—I was making myself sick with all this drivel, but apparently it was working on Vladimir, because his pointed little ears pricked up, his snout poked far up into the dead air of the room (by now I was slightly hallucinating—he had become a giant hog, a pig, a swine dripping with shit from the wallow in which he lay). "We'll take the Antichrist book so I can read it, and you can tell me how to join that fun group you belong to." I hoped, I prayed, I ran back out the front door and into the nasty lobby. He was right behind me. He sneered.

"Bitch, why you think you could ever get in?" Snicker, snicker. Who was I kidding? His secret society would never allow a skirt like me into their hallowed grounds, their circle of blood. I was losing touch with reality, and I knew it. I was almost on the brink of total hallucination, and if not for Vladimir's growling belly, he could have taken me, lost under his spell as I became, hypnotized by his aura of evil which lay dormant beneath the tee shirt. The fat hog glistened with sweat, his stench permeating my nostrils. He probably harbored some mutated form of Parvovirus.

"You have to be special invited person, and it's top secret, anyway." A certain tinny note of fear crept into Vladimir's speech, but he bravely continued. "The Antichrist is a bad fellow and he doesn't let many people into his basement ceremonies." Demons snarled at each other, fighting over the hand of a child, torn from the living soul who was sacrificed to their leader, torn from the lips of the pervert who wanted to eat it. "The place changes for every meeting—I don't even know where the next one is." Aided by drugs such as those derived from datura and hemlock, possessed black magic sorcerers soar in astral travel to meet naked in the sky, on down into the depths of the earth, the hot herb between their legs pushing them onward to sexual release, but they cannot find release, and must drink blood and kill babies to appease that increasing hunger, the hunger between their legs and in each vacant soul.

Dang, yech!

And now the predictable transition from fear to sex. Was I to be the unwitting victim of a snuff film? "Let me lick your pussy lips and stuff my dick up your asshole," Vladimir suggested. I knew that was coming, but he wasn't going to wave that dick at me, oh no, I'd stuff anchovies up it first. My mind was going. Here I was, practically locked into place for a seminal injection, and all I could think about was getting him to eat pizza. I wonder what Freud would have to say about that? Try to look hungry. Think food. Forget about demons and creatures. Get your mind out of the gutter. Stifle that horrendous imagination created by too many Steven King novels and mythical occult histories. Don't let the thought of death by Datura cross your mind. Time to get out of here. Don't panic.

"So, how about some food, huh Vladimir?" Food, Vladimir, not blood. "Ice cream too, okay? My treat, really." I refuse, under any circumstances, to go out with you in public, however, until you cover up that awful blouse you're wearing. "Uh, could you put your shirt back on over that tee-shirt?" Finally, hunger won, or was it the desire to eat something and pretend it was me? Was Vladimir a cannibal in disguise? At least he put on his coat over that disgusting tee shirt, so I assumed we were leaving. Okay, so I got in his car. Yech.

I'm a crazy fool for doing this, but I got my money and got back into the car with Vladimir to go eat pizza (I couldn't let him come back after Nadja and Peter, could I?). We fought over our 'portions' like fat people, and I gave him one of my slices to shut him up. We're talking about a large pizza with extra cheese and pepperoni. Then we went for Rocky Road Butter Brickle ice cream. His dick probably didn't have enough blood flowing to it to keep it hard, because it all went to his stomach for grease digestion. He actually took me home and quit threatening to do unspeakable things to my overdressed body.

I couldn't wait to tell that old trusting pair, Nadja and Peter, that their dream date for me was a vicious, hardcore-sexual-deviant schizophrenic maniac who thought Jesus Christ should be fucked. I wanted sympathy, I wanted commiseration, I wanted understanding, but most of all, I wanted them to believe me (I also wanted to barf). And you know what, gentle reader? They didn't believe a word.

Chapter Three

*Would that you could live on the fragrance of
the earth, and like an air plant be sustained by
the light.*

Kahlil Gibran

Calling the elements

I ran back to Lawless just as fast as a Greyhound can go,
completely disillusioned about Illinois, the Eastern Bloc,
communes, Russian cookies, subways, Moonies, and vodka. I still
loved Africans. Was I determined to keep my promise and be a
good girl? The more relevant question was, how long could I stay
in Lawless and stay out of trouble? Not very long. I immediately
began dropping out of college and acquiring new, greasier,
raunchier boyfriends (I patterned them after Alishia's Bubba),
doing all kinds of weird drugs, fighting with my mother, quitting
jobs, and generally acting like my usual, disruptive self.

By now, my reputation as 'Crazy Gabby' was well established
in Lawless. I didn't know how to reach Renee (could she have
saved me?). I had no one to turn to, nowhere to run. My Mom was
downed out over her divorce from my dad, who had conveniently
taken the fifty-thousand dollars out of their joint savings account,
leaving poor Mom with a job as a cook in the Lawless Public
Schools at the tender age of fifty-seven, when most cooks would
have willingly retired. I loved her, but we had our own, separate
problems, and I couldn't live with her anymore.

Dad had decided to disown me, his second wife dumped for a
third, with whom there was no sharing good, old, money-hungry
Dad. I thought the way Dad managed to get rid of wife number two
was pretty incredible, but I shall go into more detail about his
amorous activities later. It was time for me to boogie.

I think the LSD is what convinced me that I should go West,
young lady, and seek my fortune as a rock star. Suddenly, I was
doing some heavy brain-cell-bursting drugs. After ingesting pink
microdot for the third time that week at the home of some sleazy

G.I.s I knew from nearby Fort Kill, I had this vision and hallucinated myself over to the West Coast, hazed into red, melted into crowds, fell into the ocean of time.

Call it psychic phenomenon, call it smog—whatever, it was me in a crowd, and I was suddenly transported, reminded of my quest for the great Cat Stevens. Anything had to be better than all the classes I was taking and the job I was working half-assed at, so I gave away my belongings (to an Indian lady who let me crash at her pad) in a rash liberal statement of avowed poverty, took my dog, bought a cheap, yellow frame-pack and hitchhiked to I-40. Off I went.

Didn't get very far out of Oklahoma those first few days. This wild looking truck driver picked me up and gave me something to soothe my raging beast. Sugar Boy leaned out his window, ten feet above my head, and drawled, real southwestern like, "Say baby, where ya headed?" Blond, tan, muscled up—well, he looked okay, maybe he'd give me some uppers. He cajoled, sweetly, "My way, huh? Want a ride and some black beauties?"

"Say what?" I asked, sceptical at my first serious ride out of Okieville. He thought I looked as though I took drugs, evidently, so I began to climb up the running board to the passenger side, risking my life and safety once again in the name of adventure.

"Hop in, sweet thing, let's go for a spin down this lonesome highway...." Sung to the accompaniment of Hank Williams' "Your Cheatin' Heart." Yeah, said my thumb to my brain (or was my brain in my thumb?), why not. So I hopped into the truck and we shifted gears. Black beauties, anyone?

He was okay looking in a demented sort of way, but nice, friendly, and under twenty-one. One would imagine after my intrepid, if not entertaining, fiasco with Vladimir I would not climb into foreign vehicles quite so blithesomely, but the lure of drugs was always a quick way for me to forget my senses, and abandon all reason. I forgot to mention that I also noticed how fat I was on the acid while I was hallucinating myself into California, complete with swirling colored strobe lights and a roaring crowd. I had placed myself on a juice fast, the better to trip with (hoping I'd lose weight). The nice blond with the muscles kindly bought me grape juice to continue my weird diet, took me home and told me he was a rough-necker. That night I met his roommates, and a lady with a just-fucked flush on her face who was wearing a bathrobe. I felt so unfucked and superior. I was really into my own selfish thoughts, taking what I could and not giving a shit who thought what.

This type of thinking almost got me into a bedroom scene with wild man the rough-necker, but luckily the phone rang, and I escaped certain penetration. Whew. One of the guys picked it up. "Hello," he said, "Who?" Slamming down the phone, his roommate yelled, "Hey Neal, it's for you man, I think ya gotta go to the rig. Come on, answer the other phone!"

Neal was busy trying to seduce me in the bedroom where I was innocently draped across the water bed, smoking a joint. He didn't look too pleased at the moment, and yelled back, "Tell 'em I'm busy stripping this chick and can't work tonight!" Ominous silence in the living room."Fuck! All right, I'll talk to them." He threw down the pillow he had been fluffing (probably to put under my ass), stalked into the living room, picked up the phone, and said, "Hello? Can I work tonight? Do I have a choice?" Aside to me, he said, "Someone called in sick tonight." To the phone, "Yeah, okay, I'll be right there, that's right, don't panic."

Slamming down the phone, Neal stomped back to the bedroom and began throwing things like hardhats and oil-soaked coveralls this way and that way, most of them towards his black leather bag. He couldn't have been that angry, since he was making thirty dollars an hour for overtime. He gazed at me, lust filming over his eyes. "Well baby, I've gotta go now, so you can sleep in peace tonight." Thank the Lord for small miracles. "But remember, morning comes early and I'll be back to get my piece, honey," he chuckled heinously, "I'll be back for you."

Your what? Your piece? With a parting glance, Neal licked his chapped lips and left the room. I rolled over and thought to myself, "Uh-huh, that's what he thinks, I'm getting out of this place by daylight." I finished my joint, turned out the light, slumbered peacefully on the waterbed, minus the male influence. Ah sweet, deep sleep, how I would come to miss you as the days of my future passed. My puppy dog, Sara Teasdale curled up beside me and we dozed into the night. One of his friends, a sweet country boy who looked like Ma and Pa killed a cow every night for his supper, gave

41

me a belated ride to the highway and my next rendezvous with destiny. I was glad to go—he was cute, but I wanted Cat Stevens. My next ride got me into a hotel room with two guys, one who was a fellow hitchhiker, one who was the money man with the car. Both were after me, neither of them got me. I reduced the fellow hitcher to tears, Sara began to growl menacingly, and the money man left.

This was to be the story of my life for the next couple of years, and I finally realized my plight that night in the hotel room, hundreds of miles away from home (what home?) in Lawless, and cried for the first time (not the last). Next morning, I dumped the hitcher, and got a cool ride with a guy and his wife who I met at the truck stop in Albuquerque, New Mexico. Nice couple, but the wife seemed rather sullen. I would soon find out why. We cruised down the highway to Phoenix, smoked a few doobs, and they invited me to the guy's Mom's house, who had always wanted to meet a hitchhiker. I, the perennial showpiece, the piece.

She lived in a very nice Phoenix suburb, Desert Rock, and genuinely liked me when we met that night. She was a sweet little old lady with blue rinsed bouffant hair and pale pink lipstick, immaculate beyond reproach. She stood quietly, dressed in a filmy, white gauze dress that must have cost a fortune, while Stan introduced me. I squirmed under her inquisitive gaze.

"Mom, I've brought you a hitchhiker," Stan said. "This is Gabrielle," patting my shoulder. "Gabrielle, meet my mother, Lacy." Lacy, neat. That's a fitting name. Do I smell roast beef? Sara was stashed in the garage, so it wasn't necessary to bring her in for introductions, although I did plan to sneak her some food later that night.

I innocuously sniffed the air, then said, "Hello, Lacy, nice to meet you." Feeling some need to redeem myself before I ate them out of house and home, I added, "I'm new at hitchhiking and I don't plan to do it for a living, it's just part time, you know?" I knew I smelled meat, could it be that Lacy made us dinner? Sniffing again, my eyes turned toward the kitchen. Lacy's observant gaze followed my eyes towards the warm smells emanating from her homestyle cooking.

"Well, honey, that's nice," she said. "Why don't you just go into the kitchen and I'll fix you all some roast beef sandwiches." What a girl, what a girl! Overdrive to the kitchen, as fast as the chubby legs would carry me. I was my usual piglet self and broke the juice fast to gobble roast beef, which really pissed off Stan's wife, Candy. Imagine that, what did I do?

The next morning Stan invited me and my dog to cruise around Phoenix while Candy and Lacy shopped. So we wandered over to this dude's house, Tobias, and he showed us his art, his stash, and his gun collection. I spotted a grapefruit tree while out in the backyard, and never having seen such a botanical miracle before, promptly fell to munching on a ripe looking grapefruit.

Tobias, ever the wise ass, warned me after I took a very large bite, "Don't eat that Gabrielle, it'll make you sick!" he giggled. Too late. I gagged, I gasped for air, I nauseously swayed in place, I almost thought I'd died. Never ever eat a grapefruit out of season. The guys laughed so hard they almost puked. Yes, it could have been funny, but not when you're the victim.

When we got back to Lacy's house, and thought all was well, Candy's sullenness revealed itself as jealousy at her husband's infidelity (not with me, but how could she know?), and she screamed, "Where the FUCK have you been all day?" Face red, eyes popping out. "That little hitchhiking tramp is more exciting than your own wife, is that it?" Oh shit, now I get it. She thinks...oh shit! Candy ranted and raved on. "Bitch just lies all the time. How about that great juice fast she was on, what about that, huh?" Candy, a rather hefty woman herself, was at it full speed ahead, and her tantrum turned her cheeks bright red, while her double chin wobbled with the effort of chastising her wayward husband. She looked at me as if for proof. "Yeah, and she comes in here and eats all the roast beef she can get her greedy little lips on, she's probably had them on you too, Stan." Me, with my lips on HIM? No way, he's not my type at all. Infidelity turns me off, totally off.

Evidently, Stan was used to this kind of treatment, because he just smirked while his mother gazed at me with disapproving eyes. But, I continued to ride with them to Venice Beach, California, home of hippydom, street people and strange, strange semi-human mutants. As Candy drove and I snoozed in behind the seats in the camper section, Stan climbed over the seats to snuggle, uninvited by me, shoving Sara out of her deep slumber, and her rightful place beside me. Now I knew why Candy had the ass all the time. She drove on, sullenly glancing through the rear-view mirror, and I begged Stan to please get back in the front seat, as he was married and his wife shouldn't be subjected to this type of abuse. Someday she will shoot you, Stan. They dropped me off at the pier.

Hah! Arrived at Venice Beach, California at dusky dawn, the dawning of time, a brand new beginning. Santa Monica Pier jutted into the sea, waves crashed, I was alive. Bye-bye Stanley and Candy, hope your problems disperse someday. I jumped into the seashore and immediately spotted the Cat, figuring we'd meet any minute (he was on the beach, staring at Sara Teasdale and me as we splashed our way along the shore, she barking and me laughing).

I suddenly decided to rename myself Gabrielle Starfire Laughing Girl, since California was the type of place you could be anyone you wished, legally, even. The specter, the ghost of Cat Stevens followed me everywhere from that point on. The reason he didn't rush across the sand and introduce himself was because he was a shy guy, I told myself. So, I shook the sand off, let Sara off her leash for the first time, and had a seat on the local transient bench in the sunshine by the seashore to watch people roller skate by.

I was having some kind of visual awakening that morning, feeling the salty ocean spray, watching the red hazy dawn, glistening with new life and adrenalin. I wanted to get stoned so I could rehaze myself, melt into the California scene of my acid induced moments. I saw a long-haired, scuzzy type cruising the boardwalk, and he cruised my way. He stopped at the bench I was sitting on, the dawn glinting in his beard (probably other nasties too).

"Say honey, how ya doin'?" he rasped in a beach bum drawl. I was doing fine, thank you, and wondered what he wanted, what kind of payment he would demand, since all males, evidently, wanted some sort of payment from wenches like myself who proffered themselves by merely existing. The momentous question then appeared on my horizon, as he asked, shyly, "Wanna like, do some doobie with me?" Did I hear the magic, spell-inducing words? Suddenly, I was more than interested. He continued to address me, there on the beach. "You look like you party, baby, and I'm your party man."

"Oh yeah?" I asked, still unconvinced after my recent bout with Stan.

"No strings, let's just smoke a joint and enjoy the morning." The stranger pulled out a joint, and handed it to me. Just what I wanted, a little dope to take the edge off, a little smoke to face the day, a tiny bit of bud to reawaken my hallucination. Try to act calm and uninterested.

"Hmmm. Party man he says." Am I cool, or what? Didn't your Mommy warn you about talking to strangers on the beach? "Do you have any killer, or just some of that rag?" It's like, sure I'll smoke your rag, but you must beg me to do it. I'm not an easy girl to pick up, you know. He was unconvinced. My line wasn't the real thing, my tough act was phony, my seams were unraveling; I was obviously a see-through tourist.

"I can tell you're not from around here, honey," he said, looking me over, backpack, tattered jeans and puppy dog. "We don't smoke no shit, baby. Even the leaves have crystals. Dig?" Let's face it, he's blown my cover. Give it up, already.

I gladly accepted the offer, and followed Bill back to his place to smoke, which wasn't too far because he lived on the boardwalk. He kept his motorcycle, a Harley of course, in the middle of the living room, and he made a half-hearted attempt to seduce me on the old rattan couch behind the bike, but he didn't stand a chance against my superior strength (I was a hefty girl) and terrible attitude. Pretty soon his prostitute girlfriend bopped in between tricks, and settled that little problem. She was tall, slender and really built, but what with her heroin addiction and bare minimum apparel, she obviously had a problem. They commenced activity on the couch, while I prowled around outside. Later on, after she had split, Bill said what the hell, I could crash at his place for a while, so I wandered back to the beach to explore and have fun in the sun.

What a life. I was a transient and having an absolute blast. Sara Teasdale, my only belonging that meant anything to me at this point, kicked up her paws, flicked sand from her snout and ran off, saw some dogs, and gave chase. I pursued her, begging her to return to me. Silly dog. Why run away? This really neat guy with long, brown, scraggly hair and geisha pants caught Sara Teasdale for me, and I ran to grab her, dodging skaters and flower vendors as I waded my way through the midday cornucopia of Venice Beach. Oh, the sunshine, ocean spray, warm breeze and wild, crazy people. Pink, blue, purple pastels, flowing robes, torn faded jeans, tie-dyed scarves, and spicy scents, such a visual feast, this Southern California, Venice Beach Boulevard. I was unduly grateful for the return of Sara.

"Thanks for catching my dog, man," I effused. "I couldn't catch her quick little ass." I was panting and out of breath from the chase. "She's seen some dogs she wants to hang with." Sara gave me a dog look, wanting a pat on the head. "I guess she's going bonzo since I never let her loose before." Refusing to pet my wayward dog, I wanted to beat the shit out of her, but that wouldn't agree with the atmosphere of this morning, so I silently swore at her in German (dogs have telepathy), and acted nonchalant.

He tossed his braided hair with the beads on the ends, adjusted his shirt pocket (hmmm, what'cha got for me in there?), and drawled, "Aw, go on and let her run with the other dogs, they'll be back." Next question. "Want some acid?" Dude looked all around as he said this, then at me, square in the eye, fingering his pocket. Figured me out, that's for certain. Wow. Loathe to decline, I pondered my other options. What other options? Like I've been here one day and I'm already getting wasted on the available drug scene.

Turns out Bill was a friend of Fred, a transient beach bum, surfer boy, jack-of-all-trades, part-time smuggler of whatever sold for the highest price that day, not to mention the most well-read individual on the beach. We went back to the pad to visit and turn old Bill on to this awesome purple flying saucer acid (which I would become too well acquainted with in Northern California later that same year). Bill had a long string attached to a bell that stretched from the locked gate of the open air hall to his apartment door. We rang the make-shift doorbell, he let us in and we sat down to look at Fred's stash. My my, did he ever have a stash. Every mushroom and crystal-encrusted sinsemilla bud, not to mention assorted trinkets for tourists and hippies alike fell out of his sheepskin bag.

Cool deal, dude, let's party!

This is how I began to spend my days. My friendly biker benefactor knew everyone on the beach, it seemed. I inquired of the locals whether or not sleeping on the beach was allowed by the infamous LAPD who were renowned for their violence toward beach people. I was told yes, sleeping on the beach was allowed, but not advised, due to the criminal element (no doubt the root of LAPD violence). So, I slept at Bill's and hung out in the daylight hours in the sun with the other tanned crowd. One particularly pleasant Saturday, a day that could have inspired the song "Come Saturday Morning," we were circled around a pit fire, passing the wine and telling stories.

A lovely teenage girl who reigned valley girl supreme got up and told us a horrifying story. Bella, a drama student, certainly had flair when it came to telling a tall tale. "So I'm hanging out, minding my own business and all of a sudden, whammo upside the head I got slugged!" With that spoken, Bella fell to the ground as if struck from behind. Very convincing.

As she lay in the sand, Bella told her story. "I'm laying there in the middle of Venice Beach Boulevard right during rush hour and nobody even noticed what was going on. I was cruising along the beach on my roller skates, checking out the guys, you know, and like, this weird pervert came up behind me on roller skates, no less, and started following me around." She stood up and twirled around the sand as if on skates. She looked over her shoulder, and pantomimed disgust. "I could tell he was after something because every time I stopped, he stopped, you know what I mean? I was pissed and finally turned around and said 'Look, guy, get the fuck out of my face or I'll call the police,' and this fucker slammed me in the head with his cane, or stick, or whatever he was carrying—I dunno, I was out of it." Upon hearing her details, all of us looked aghast, if not surprised, for she was such a colorful being, such a sweet, young thing.

The jazzy teenager covered herself with someone's shawl, pretending to be just waking up. "Finally, after I woke up under some rubbish, I figured out what he wanted. All my jewelry was

47

gone, my bracelets, my headphones and Walkman, everything I owned, even my backpack with all my I.D. in it." She got up, dusted off, pretended to ask for help, and looked around for her pack. "And nobody ever stopped to see why I was knocked out with a bleeding forehead, under some trash, in the middle of the beach in broad daylight. Pretty sad state of affairs, no doubt." It was no pantomime, she was thoroughly disgusted. With a wry glance at everyone, Bella took a slug of wine and a hit of acid, relaxing once more into the background of the campfire set. We sat before the crackling fire as dusk set in, shadows dancing at every corner, the moon faintly glowing south, over the ocean's horizon.

Such a lovely girl, blue and purple creped cotton skirt whirling around her ankles like a dervish, sandaled toenails crimsoned with loving care, enormous doe eyes, shocked with despair—Bella was a vision in 'valley girl,' yet she had been targeted by a madman's lust for what was hers. With a shrug and a sigh, Bella sat back, looking increasingly stoned as someone in the group, I think it was her mother, once again passed her the wine bottle. Poor kid, what a place to be raised in. Venice Beach began to take on ominous tones, and they would become more ominous as my time there stretched into twenty-one days, to be exact.

Hollywood Boulevard during Halloween, 1979, was a strange and psychedelic place to be, especially if you were on Red Dragon acid, guided by a beach bum hippy dude friend. While I gawked at the baby prostitutes, the transvestite multitude, the pimps, the drug salesmen, the leather and skinhead crowd, the flower children garishly made up for this special occasion, we meandered over to this dope dealer's tenement hovel to make a deal. I think I was with Fred that night but I'm not sure, because of the fact that I was out of it.

We got there, I sat on a sagging couch, the guys commenced to argue and before you knew it, I was once again alone in a strange apartment with a strange guy in Hollyweird, California in the middle of the night. Sound familiar? Fred, as deal conscious as ever, had left me without a second thought, and gone off with his 'friend' to look for I dunno what I dunno where. At least it wasn't snowing, and I knew how to walk.

I was not, under any circumstances, going to take any shit from the weirdo who lurked by the couch, staring at me like a scorpion contemplating the violin on the backside of a fiddle-back spider. Stoked up and tripping out, I climbed down some rickety wooden stairs, and got out of there. Out on the street at midnight, with the street lamps glowing orange and red, I watched the jungle of animals roll by, rolling myself. It got scary. Red Dragon acid is potent stuff, and so was the crowd. By this time, the flower children and hippies had gone home, as had the baby prostitutes (with clients, I'm sure). Now, only the skinheads, and leather and chains were out, as were the severely drugged and strung out.

Wasted morsels of humanity.

Miraculously, nobody hassled me. Maybe it was the glazed, crazed look in my eye, maybe it was the speed with which I carried myself, maybe it was the baseball bat in my left hand and the snarling beast on my right (the illustrious Sara Teasdale) who looked as if she had rabies; at any rate, we weren't disturbed, only disturbing. Sara growled and I snarled. I'd had enough of male dominance and I was ready to cause some pain to anyone of these leather guys who took a fancy to me. Together, Sara and I found our way back to Bill's house, after walking for miles, I'm sure, and I tiredly stumbled in at dawn, wanting nothing more than to crash for ten hours. Bill wanted to fuck, naturally. Enough was enough, and I decided to vacate Southern California for the northern headlands and Oregon coast.

Into the sun I went, broke, enlightened (so I thought), and full of spit (rhymes with 'shit'). Some very nice Hare Krishna guys picked me up and took me to their hideaway, but I didn't stay for long, because as I was hoping to discuss symbolic Biblical phrases in the lobby with a female devotee, she tried to get me to go chant downstairs. Now, anything remotely resembling a basement ceremony scares me, and I was interested in eating some melon, which is how they lured me in in the first place, so I initiated the conversation. Or tried to, anyway.

"Yamma yamma ono ono siri siri yamma yamma," the lady said. She swayed in time to her chant, oblivious of my presence. I attempted to make eye contact, and queried, in my politest groupie voice, "Hey, like don't you speak any English?" Shimmering in blue pastel, her holiness answered me, indirectly at best.

"Yes, yamma yamma, but I prefer to, ono ono, chant, siri siri, yamma yamma." Sorry to break your concentration, but where's the melon? Lady looked like she ate one too many qualudes for lunch.

"Well, like is it necessary to always interject chants into your basic sentence patterns?" I facetiously inquired. Why was I such a smart ass? "Can't you take a break?" I eyed the platter of melon meaningfully. "Don't tell me, it's for the cause of the church of Hare Krishna, right?"

She allowed one last chant, then interspersed with, "Siri siri, I do not wish to converse, ono ono, without speaking in, yamma yamma, mantra tongue, ono ono." I was getting dizzy trying to understand her, picking out words, putting them back into sentences. This was worse than German grammar! She said, "Come with me, yamma yamma, downstairs, ono ono, and we will chant, siri siri, together, yamma yamma."

Yummy yummy?

I take it we're not dining out tonight.

I may be broke and I may be a bum, but I refuse to chant for my melon, however starved I might be. I gave up, and bid my farewells to Her Krishna. "Right," I said a bit more politely than the last time. "Well, I think I'll just be going now, you have a good day and enjoy your chanting." She seemed to notice I wasn't going downstairs, and nodded her shaven head as I bid farewell.

"Bye," she breathed, slowly forming the words with her lips before the chanting beast who lived inside her could take over. It almost felt like we had made contact, and I was sad to see her completely possessed spirit as it tried to call out to me one last time. "Sorry," she whispered, probably about the missed dinner.

"It's okay," I answered, hungry as I was. "I understand."

Back up the stone steps, out of their mausoleum, and into the sun. Who needs conversation, anyway? Nothing like spending time with Pentecostal preachers and Hare Krishna chanters—they both speak in tongues, listen to their own inner voice, and aren't exactly with you in a conversation. The only difference between the two was that this particular woman gave me the mega-creeps. I could have sworn I saw leaping lizards and frogs come out of her mouth as she stood there in her blue pastel gown, chanting.

Off to another freeway exit, and what do you think I found? A nice yoga guy gave me a lift back to his place, back in good old Lost Angels, of course, and showed me how he consumed his energy. Dressed entirely in black, he epitomized the New Yogi, and illustrated the steps to enlightenment, or relaxation, if you wish. I liked it.

"Now, all you have to do is twist your ankles around backwards, behind your knees, ugghh, this way, see?" He twisted for my benefit, and I tried to follow suit. No go. I didn't take enough ballet in grammar school for this kind of exercise. "Ommpphh," he said. "Turn your head this way, twist your left arm, arrggg, and put your right hand here, by the solar plexus." Solar plexus? But how? I tried, I groaned, I sweated, I twisted. Still, he drove on, bending even further out of the shape he was born in, the shape God intended all humans to maintain, the natural upright position of chimpanzees, even. Jeez! "See? It feels good. Try it!" Right. Looks ultra simple (for an earthworm, maybe). Okay, I'll try...oww!

"I can't even do the first part, Sasha, how do you expect me to do the rest?" Whine, whine, snivel, snivel. I can't do it and you can and it's just not fair. Relinquishing my enlightened position for a more comfortable one, I gave in and said, "You must be double jointed."

"I'm triple-jointed!" Sasha exclaimed, "How did you know?"

"Just bright, I guess."

Sasha was an anorexically thin, genuinely nice guy. His position looked pretty uncomfortable to me, but at least I was off the streets for the night, and he wasn't chanting. We found a cool natural foods co-op later that evening, where he ordered some carrot juice for both of us, and tried to get me a job, with no luck. I didn't plan to stay in L.A. anyway, but what the hell, Sasha was only trying to help. We went back to his loft apartment. I gazed out at the L.A. night, safe in an upstairs apartment. The stars were barely visible, and the place had a sense of tropical living. I smelled something delicious. It was Sasha, making us some sesame tahini and garbanzo hummus sandwiches along with brown rice, seaweed and tempeh. Nice friend, no sex required or requested. He was evidently happy doing yoga. I left the next morning, still stuck in L.A.

Asphalt was beginning to be a way of life, but I still didn't realize to what extent my transience extended. I was a street person. I was almost a bag lady! I thought to myself that no one would pick me up in a nice car, because I was no longer one of us, I was one of them. Oh well, life was still full of excitement and surely, good things would pursue me in California. I grabbed oranges off trees, picked pecans up off the ground, pan-handled with other young hitchers and felt right at home. I hadn't had to sleep in any park bathrooms, or apply for food stamps, or beg sandwiches from the Salvation Army, or beg bags of food from the Santa Monica relief organization...that would all come later. I was still a fresh pussycat.

There was this guy I met on Malibu Beach who lived in an abandoned car. He had sunbleached afro curls and green, aqua eyes, like the sea. He must have been about twenty years old at the time we met. Mark was a real sweet heart, and we hung out for awhile, meeting again in my life, at a later date. He showed me around the scene, beach boy style. We went to the local taco joint, and tried to scrounge some food from a friend of his. Mark, the beach boy, was well liked, and it seemed that everywhere we went, he knew someone to scrounge food from (or whatever else struck his fancy, because Mark was a true charmer). I suspect he could have been a "house mouse," but he preferred his freedom in an old car that was permanently parked on the beach.

The taco guy got off work, picked us up in a car that did run, and we headed up into the hills above Malibu, presumably to inquire about an old geezer who frequently took financial pity on young transient girls and boys. We got up the hills, behind the rocks and flower gardens and into a yard which was surrounded by botanical extravagance. We had ascended the bourgeoisie into the upper class, we had surmounted the stone hedgeway that surrounded the estate, we had risen up into the higher herbal gardens of marsh andromeda, mugwort, rosemary, thyme, peppermint, spearmint, camomile, sage, oregano. Ah yes, we had arrived. I wish. The old fart was sweet, sure, but his house mouse wasn't, and informed us that the geezer's pocketbook was no longer flowing for the likes of us, so we had to leave, unceremoniously, without any further ado. The house mouse had a lisp, or something, because I could hardly understand him. Maybe it was fake British. Lower lip pouty in distaste, the lean, jeaned, perfumed houseboy let us know his true feelings.

"New, yew cahn't burrew any more monay," he drawled. "Sew jest disahppeyaw, befo ah cahll tha poleese." He glared at us menacingly, his limp wrist hovering suspiciously near the touch-tone phone. Now what country has an accent like that, I ask you? What a creep. California was like that, I would soon decide. Dreams often excluded reality, making it often preceded any real work, the right contacts were always available, and you could make it big just by breathing the air.

Gasping is more like what I was doing. I wanted tomorrow to bring riches, while these dudes were too relaxed to be bothered with tomorrow at all. We drove down the hill and back to the beach. Mark and his buddy said nighty-night, and I settled down to sleep in a very uncomfortable car, cold, lonely, and distressed with my predicament. I never did learn to relax.

Sunshine found me wandering back onto the freeway, trying to get out of L.A. I got a ride with a rather affluent yuppie who took me back to his place (they always took me home, never away), and it turned out that he liked me so much that I could stay forever, as far as he was concerned. I explored the house. Witchy occult stuff, herbal this and that, the usual incense and drug paraphernalia, white wine for lunch with cheese and fruit. Nice shower soap. Mint tea. I could dig this place, even if it was in Redwood City, smack in the middle of the smog-ridden, red-heaving monster, the horribly-steamy, filthy-hulkish brute that is L.A. Anyone who has ever lived there knows what I'm talking about.

Then, the girlfriend swooped in in her black cape, eyes glinting disapproval and mirroring dismay in the heart of my benefactor, her boyfriend. The transformation was amazing. Suddenly, the place was hers, not his, and he became subservient to her every whim. I was not to be part of the menage a' trois he had planned (I was wondering about that). Not bothering to even look at me, she focused on the cowering David, and allowed her wrath to take wings and fly.

53

"What's she doing here, David?" his keeper asked. "Why do you persist in bringing home these, ugh, women off the streets and feeding them MY food from my parties, without ever stopping to wonder what I might think...?" Her stern reproach became a command. I could just picture Ms. Dominitrix with David after dark, when the bats flew out to play.

"Get her out," she demanded. David said nothing, and I was too surprised to speak. "Now." And the final ultimatum, the one he's always dreaded, the one she most frequently tossed out to him, "I'll take away your keys if you don't."

Oooh, you're in trouble David! With that, she swooped her cape and swept down the hall, pausing only to rake me with a horrible glance over my body, head to toe. Fucking house mouse. David, you could have at least warned me about your witch girlfriend. Isis paid the bills and David was her mistress. I was out of the question. Off I went, yellow backpack on my poor aching back, little shepherd mix by my side, off into the bowels of industrialized L.A., off to see a wizard or at least someone to crash at their house, for that's what it boiled down to by then, a place to sleep. Oh, and it was a long, long night that night. My chances were beginning to run out.

This rat-faced, pimple-infested, dark-skinned punk picked me up, ostensibly to give me a ride, but it seemed like he wanted me to give him a ride, especially at three o'clock that morning when he woke me up from a deep sleep on the couch. Evidently, his roommate had come home, so Santo had to make a macho play. His dirty white tee-shirt shone in the moonlight.

"Say, *punta,* wake up and come over here. I said, get your ass over here and suck me off, bitch." Readers, does this line of thinking sound familiar to you? I was in the middle of a very nice dream, and His Machoness kinda pissed me off. He was barely one hundred and forty pounds, at best, and trying to threaten ME? Punk was probably made out of cottage cheese.

Fine.

"What? What's your fucking problem, anyway?" I hissed. He cringed. "I'm not about to do anything for you except probably smash your face if you touch me." Seriously folks, I've said these lines before. "I'm leaving, already. Shit, why didn't you tell me

54

about your raging lust BEFORE you picked me up?" Jerk. "It's kinda a bad time for me to be outside in the streets, *comprende?*" Already, I was gathering my things together and making for the door. He acted all embarrassed and ashamed, but that was bullshit. The begging began soon enough.

"Oh baby, I'm so sorry, I just can't help myself, being around you makes me crazy." He pulled at the crotch of his jeans, demonstrating what wonders he could achieve, watching me leave. "I'm really sorry. You understand, don't you?" Understand what? Pancho looked anxiously toward his roommate's bedroom, hoping to be overheard. "You could stay if you wanted to...in my bed." Why, to catch bed bugs, or some awful disease that will make me crazy if I'm lucky? Go pick your pimples, Panchetto Villa, I'm splitting.

Using my best hissing voice, I brutalized him further. "No thanks, and thanks for nothing." I tried to still my quavering voice, afraid of the night and my next ride. Giving him a hateful glare, I headed out the front door, attempting to seem brave. "I'll see you around, huh? Just ignore me long enough for me to get out of here, all right?"

"But baby," he began.

"I said get lost, already!"

Talk about 'life's a beach...' I'm not exactly enjoying it at the moment. Here I hide, out in the middle of the night, wandering around a dangerous gang and drug infested screaming maniac part of L.A., and I haven't got a clue of where to turn to or who to approach for a place to crash. Finally, after flailing about in asphalt waters for a couple of pointless hours, leaping behind bushes every time I heard a sound or saw a shadow, I walked up to a regular white and blue frame house, knocked on the door, and asked the man who answered if I could please crash on his floor because my ride dumped me. Now if you can believe it, the guy let me in and let me sleep in peace, no questions asked.

He understood my situation completely, I found out the next morning over coffee. As I fumbled around, gripping my caffeine fix with trembling hands, my host and I discussed my prospects for getting a ride out of L.A. I might add that I have come to appreciate that first cup of coffee and those who provide it with the utmost awe and respect. When you don't have enough money for a lousy cup of coffee, things take on a slightly more tangible perspective. As I slurped and we chatted about my rides, Jay and I heartily agreed that escape from L.A. was imperative to my existence as a street person, and a living, breathing, unraped woman.

"Go north, Gabrielle," he advised quite emphatically, convincing me of his knowledge of a gentler folk up in the mountains by the seashore.

"What's 'north?'" I wondered, "Oregon?"

"California, girl, except it's a different world from here," he answered.

"Oh," I said, ready to go right away. Southern California had totally disillusioned me, but I had hopes of a better world somewhere nearby.

"You'll find people more to your liking the further north you go, but it does get radical there, in a different way."

"You mean, there's a different way?"

Jay really seemed to know what he was talking about, so maybe it was the right idea. Anything to get me out of L.A. "Damn, Jay," I said, "That sounds like my cup of tea. How do I get out of here, though?"

"Instead of crazed city maniacs, you'll meet crazed country maniacs," he explained, stirring honey into his coffee. "The country maniacs will warn you before they attack, and if you show you're not afraid, are honest, helpful, and not a cop, they'll treat you real good." Sounded like a bargain to me.

"Truckers?" he suggested.

"My rides always take me home instead of away from here, and I haven't seen any friendly truckers lately."

"Maybe I know someone...no, not right off hand," he said.

"I'll welcome any suggestions," I said, hoping he would direct me to a good freeway exit, or a good truck stop, or a good, safe, friendly ride.

"Go north, Gabrielle, up near Mendo County," he encouraged. Finishing my third cup of righteous coffee, I headed to the door for another day on the road. Sara didn't look too pleased, but she followed me out with a dour expression on her doggie face. Right.

I will do that, Jay, and thanks for being such a lifesaver. If I didn't get out of this town soon, I was certain to become trapped, raped or killed. Surely. Once again, I wearily trudged out to the freeway exit, the words of my friendly host reverberating through my mind. Got to get out of L.A., right away, this minute if possible. Did I succeed? Of course not, not that month.

Chapter Four

I am the son of the plough, of humble peasant
stock, I live in a hut of reed and stalk.
The hair: jet black. The eyes: brown.
My arab headdress scratches intruding hands,
and I prefer a dip of oil and thyme.

Mahmoud Darweesh

Invoking Air, from the East

A couple of Lebanese guys picked me and Sara Teasdale up and decided that since I was just as dark as they were, I could pass Mama's scrutiny and join the family as Azar's concubine. What a great idea. Leave it to the Middle East to bail me out of no man's land into the light of life, a real home, and a real bed to call my own. No, I wasn't going to argue that day. Anything was an improvement over life in the fast lanes of L.A.'s sleazy sidewalks and humorless drivers.

So, I rode home with Azar and Khaled, ready to eat some pita bread which we passed around the table, tearing small pieces off to pick up our veggies and rice. That is, after Mama looked me over REAL good, jabbering in Lebanese at her son about who knows what. Thus, I broke bread with my first foreign contacts in that steamy city, and learned that the term we Americans know as "hi," is the same term Lebanese guys use to say "hi," the difference being that it means "are you high, would you like to be high?" and yes, I would.

We went to a great club after dinner, Azar, Khaled and me, to dance the night away. Sara crashed out in the apartment complex's courtyard, watched over carefully by Azar's little half-American cousin (her mom was white), Lisa Ann. I had the evening to myself with my new friends, the hunky ethnic men. These guys were attractive—Azar was tall and slender, with a friend he said women loved (if you know what I mean), but much to his chagrin I never bothered to find out for myself. Khaled, who was actually an Arab, was short, more muscled up and equally as attractive. Both guys wore gold chains, pounds of them, it seemed, and had very, very long eyelashes, black hair, and big, brown, soulfully deep eyes. They reminded me of lots of hot peppers.

Strobe lights filled the dance floor with pink and red flashing colors, and I watched, transfixed, as Khaled, Azar, and Azar's brother Achmed danced together with their shoulders touching, as they leaned toward each other in a circle with some other Middle Eastern friends, all men. Ofra Haza's Israeli voice cried out soulfully over the loudspeakers, mixing ethnic Middle Eastern folksongs with a disco beat. Was it real? Was this the hallucination I had in Lawless on pink microdot the third time that week?

I was soon to discover that the men not only danced together, but ruled the roost. Everybody thought I was Azar's girl, and I felt that was safest, for I wanted male protection after two months on the wild road. Finally, we went home to sleep, and I called my dog inside to lay beside me on the couch.

Mama was quite sociable, but I never could understand what they all said about me, and counted on Azar's interpretation to guide me. He frequently said such things as "They all want to know why you do not fuck me, because you should be, and women love my friend, it is very big," and so on. Sure, that's what they said, Azar, I believe you, oh great male ruler. In the morning I met Beyzaar, who would soon help me find a job in the credit agency where she worked. Within two days I was employed, living in an apartment with two guys and their mom, learning Lebanese phrases and riding to work every day with Beyzaar, who couldn't understand my lack of deference to the men. I didn't bother to explain it.

Azar told me that guerrillas from the Lebanese 'Christian' Militia' stole into their house one day and tried to kill their Mom. He outsmarted the the intruders to protect his family, and they fled to family in Los Angeles to escape bombings and death. For such gentle people, I would think it impossible for them to hurt anyone. Azar's story subdued me, and I came to respect these kind, gentle people who stayed within the company of their own, and said I was the first American who had ever been nice to them.

One day Azar's brother, Achmed, who was older and should have been wiser, took me to several nude beaches, supposedly to pick up seashells. "Here, Gabrielle," he cajoled. "You can undress here." Achmed pointed to the small crowd of nude sunbathers gathered farther down the beach, then attempted to help me undress. I wasn't in the mood, and felt affronted by his lack of tact.

"You said we were going to pick up seashells, not skinny-dip," I grouched.

"What is 'skinny-dip?'" Achmed asked.

"You know," I said, remembering his lack of proper English slang, "When people take their clothes off to go swimming." Stupid me.

"Yes, yes, you take off your clothes here," he said excitedly, and began to grab at my blouse in eager thrusts.

"No!" I screamed, attracting the attention of the nearby bathers. Achmed looked around uncomfortably, then decided to forget about stripping me down. We hastened back to his Volvo and back to the apartment. Azar's concubine was safe for another day. Things would have continued like this indefinitely, because Azar apparently had some wench he fucked regularly, whom his mom disapproved of, while I held out, gaining steadily in Middle Eastern esteem, due to my virtuous state. Alas, due to a chain of events this was not to be so, for destiny called me to go forth, young lady, and find Cat Stevens. First, disaster struck in the form of male jealousy over some guy named Youssef, who we all know and love affectionately as the Cat, and my refusal to become engaged to Azar.

His friends had to be squelched, his manhood was at stake, his little-big friend was getting impatient. It was on a Tuesday, in the afternoon, if my memory is correct. After a march down Sunset Boulevard which the Lebanese population staged yearly to protest the fact that Turkey never apologized for their misuse of Lebanon many eons ago, so the Lebanese could accept their apologies and forgive them, Azar stumbled into the apartment claiming his gold chains were yanked off his neck by a mugger.

The typical attitude around the apartment, and the general malaise that went with it demanded that we believe Azar's story and sympathize with his chainless predicament. Of course, we all secretly conferred and decided that he sold the chains to buy dope, or whatever. Mama, the exception to the rule, babied her little boy (he was twenty-five).

"Azar, my son, your shirt is torn, your hair is all mussed, let me make you some food, and you'll feel better. How about some coffee?" She appeared to pat him down for possible injuries, although he was merely out of breath.

This is a rough translation, but I could just about figure out what was going on because Mama steered Azar into the kitchen, fussing over him like a pet kitten, and motioned for me to get the coffee (my special job). Those Lebanese loved their coffee, and you already know how I feel about it. The way you make it is to take a little pot with a long handle, pour in the sugar, get the water boiling, then pour in the powdered coffee beans, about a tablespoon. Poof! And up bubbles the chocolate looking mixture, a strong brew for strong stomachs.

I poured our coffee into tiny cups, placed all on a silver tray and went back into the living room, where Azar was lying on the couch with his head in Mama's lap. After we sucked up our coffee, Mama read the grounds and told our fortunes (mine was translated).

Anyway, Azar was 'robbed' at about the same time I got fired from my job, generally for being a lazy typist and mouthing off. I just didn't see the light in those days, and thought I was above everyone else. Yet people continued to take me in, feed me, clothe me, and help me search for Cat Stevens. These days, I look at street people and hitchhikers with compassion, and I have mercy on those less fortunate than myself, but in those days, I actually thought the world owed me a living.

Imagine that.

Suddenly, everybody was pissed off, because I was very visibly around the apartment, eating up the food, and chattering about Youssef Islam, whom I was engaged to. Azar at least recognized the name, although he didn't know who Cat Stevens was, and felt that old masculine jealousy rear its ugly head, along with his little friend.

Mama didn't have any sympathy or mercy on me when I complained about Azar's attempts at mutual penetration because she was appalled that we weren't engaged. So, there's another man in her life, she thought, that little hussy is almost an adulteress. No, dearest Lebanese, I am not your daughter and I'm just another hitchhiker out for what she can get. That was the general consensus

61

of the group, and I did nothing to dissuade them of their opinion; suddenly, I found myself and my tired-of-constantly-moving pup living at Khaled's apartment, fending off his advances, and getting fed up with men in general.

This wouldn't do, I decided, and off to the freeway I went, with pack in hand and little shepherd mix, wiser, older, and slightly fatter for the delay in Lebanon. Transience was my way of life. Highways were my game and good rides were my name.

What a pain in the ass.

Hence, Oxnard and Michael. Not too far from L.A., in fact right next to L.A., is a pleasant amalgam of houses known as Oxnard (sounds like someone sneezed) where musicians and guitar makers dwell, by the sea of dreams. That is where I ended up, due to the fact that this totally gorgeous guy, Michael, picked me up, took me home, commented on what a nice young thing I was, took me back to the highway after lunch, and guiltily deposited me on the streets. I waited for a ride, then went back to Michael's apartment.

"Hi, I'm back," I said when he answered his door that evening. The surprise on his face did not reassure me, but it turned into a bright smile.

"Gabrielle, it's you." Still standing there, he remembered his manners. "C'mon in, you must be tired."

"I couldn't get a ride out of town," I said, which was partly true.

"Don't worry about it, you can stay here for a while, okay?" he asked me, shutting the door behind Sara. "Shall we feed the puppy dog?" That's what I liked, a man who loved animals. Well, it was late, after all. Forget hitchhiking, he was a hunk and maybe, just maybe, he could assuage the heartache I was feeling over the loss of home and the lack of Cat. Yes, yes he did indeed. What a fine night we had, welcome back and stay for a while with me, and I'll play my guitar, we'll smoke a bit of hash and romp together in the sand and see rainbows through the misty ocean spray. I was intoxicated and transfixed; I was infatuated and amazed with Michael.

After our first night together, I made myself at home and began to play mom to his kids, Star and Joy, who were five and seven. I took them to school with Michael, came back, did the dishes, then went with him to paint trim on houses. Michael accepted my presence for the moment, even seemed hungry for the kind of worship I gave him. Yet, the dream of a good life wasn't meant to last.

No surprise to anyone but me.

Michael, Star, and Joy had their share of problems, even though on the surface they seemed like the perfect family. But the biggest problem was, Michael was still in love with the ghost of his wife. I was so happy with them and so unaware of karma that I said to the walls I was glad she was gone so I could have them—Michael, Star, and Joy—for myself. Not good vibes at all; I got cold chills and knew my time was limited. As with the aforementioned words, I unceremoniously was rejected and ejected after about two weeks, and back to the streets I went, only this time there was no returning to Michael's.

"But Michael," I whined, "I was hoping we could live together."

"But we don't know each other, Gabrielle." He hoisted my pack onto his shoulders and out to the car. "I'll take you to a freeway where you can surely get a ride, okay?" I slumped out the door after him.

"Let's go, Sara," I called out. My lazy dog did not want to move, and was curled up next to the fireplace and Michael's calico cat.

"Here's twenty bucks," he said, handing me the money. "If you get into a real bind, call me." Couldn't really bitch about such a good hearted guy, could I? Maybe telling him about Cat Stevens and our impending engagement wasn't such a good idea, but then, I told everyone I met about it, hoping to track down the Cat. Sadly, I knew our life together was quite over, and Michael would go back to his old girlfriend just as soon as I left the apartment. I called Michael up several months later, and he put the kids on the phone to illustrate the fact that they didn't remember me. I still think I got too close to him and he knows it. Or maybe he just got too close to me.

Hmmm. What's gonna happen to me next, I wondered to the stars that night. They twinkled in blue, purple, orange, yellow, and red...they twinkled and shone, speaking to me. "All is well, Gabrielle, all is as it should be, do not tarry too long here, go west, northwest, what's the difference as long as it's movement." I was

63

great at making up conversations with the elements, and I also thought I saw lots of UFOs in Northern California, so maybe my conversations with the stars drew them to me. What's that in the road there, a Corvette? Stopping for me? Yes! Yes! A ride in a Corvette and another Michael? I just don't believe this, it can't be happening.

After many, many hours, Santa Rosa went whizzing past, and suddenly I was heading north to Cloverdale to a glass house in the country (by then I knew how to play the house mouse game), and I had a place to live with a loft bed near the ceiling, Castille soap, granola, shark meat and hiking boots, a Corvette to drive, a carpenter to help, a temper to assuage, oh shit—what had I gotten myself into this time? Yet another Michael, how strange life was in California. It lasted for three months and I ended up better off for the experience. What is the thing about Gabrielle and Michael? Something in Daniel's vision, I think...

The fact was that Michael Coeller wasn't the heart throb that Michael Lockspur was, but what the hell—physical attraction isn't everything (it isn't anything when you're a professional house mouse like me, and bent on pleasing your host). Pleasing Michael had its limits, and sleeping with him was one of them. He used to parade around naked hoping to attract me but I just politely turned my little head, and ignored his little friend (we're talking little), to his dismay and my delight.

The guy certainly had a soft spot for me, but he was just too short, bald, scrawny and funky to turn me on in the least. Luckily, a house mouse was all Michael required, one he could take to work with him on one of his many unfinished projects around Cloverdale, one he could buy things for like good granola and herb bread, one he could visit friends with at cook-outs in the mountains, someone to eat grapes with, you know? We went together into the sunset, sweeping past poverty-stricken transient street people, whishing up the skyline drive into his hideaway by the creek where we once picnicked.

"Gabrielle, what do you want for dinner tonight?" Michael would ask as I lounged in my loft. He might scurry to the kitchen space to look through his food stash, then say, "How about some tortillas with cheese and salsa, a salad, and some Zinfandel?" to which I might reply, "Oh, I dunno," while lazily counting the beams in the ceiling, "I was thinking maybe some sharkmeat or something."

Then Michael might say, "Honey, we're out of sharkmeat, but we could drive into San Francisco tomorrow to get some." Gazing at my petulance, my spoiled pout, my lack of deference, he would cajole, "You can take the Corvette and go alone if you want to." That usually got me into a good mood and shut me up.

"Just don't fry anything," I would remind him while he threw his favorite thing, tortillas, onto a hot iron skillet full of grease. "You know I have to watch my weight." Pointing to my ever-expanding gut, my one hundred and sixty pounds of 'I don't know where I picked it up' fat, my belly roll. He knew I was a pig, but we played the diet game anyway. Michael was skinny as a rail, could eat anything he wanted, and even choked down some of my absolutely disastrous dinners a few times. He was devoted to me.

One day, a day like any other up in the hills of Cloverdale, where I languished in tranquility while the work of the world went on without my assistance, Michael came home and said, "I've got some people I want you to meet." He threw off his work boots, put the kettle on for tea, and looked at the stew I had put together for supper, indicating slight disgust. "Well, you want to go, or what?"

"I dunno, Michael," I replied, not bothering to eat any of the ghastly stew, having bloated myself on fig-raisin granola earlier. "You've got some pretty spaced-out friends."

"Be brave, Gabrielle," he said, picking up a spoon. "I am." Looking meaningfully at the stew, he dug into it with a shade of gusto, but not much.

Sipping the stew, Michael grimaced (I hoped not from the taste), and began to change clothes, heading toward the shower out back. He had asked me to meet people before, and this always prefaced some strange and wondrous discovery in the melting pot of humankind, for Michael had a wide selection of acquaintances, some of whom might land in the vegetable section of animal, vegetable, or mineral. Well, why not? I'm a vegetarian, sort of.

Such was the case of Karen, devotee of Seth, a demonic influence who came into her life via the atypical Californian seminar-type seduction into cultish activities. Karen became Seth

65

every once in a while, and it tripped Michael out to no end. Me too. Poor lady allowed herself to be possessed on a regular basis with succubus, incubus, strange voices, and stranger acquaintances of the spiritual realm. I got awesome bad vibes from Karen, and at the same time pitied her wan face and droopy eyes, devoid of the spirit that was once Karen, young woman turned old, my age yet ancient, no spark or glitter left in her eyes, her limbs curled around chairs as if serpents around a tree. Karen hadn't any soul left to herself—herself was Seth. We talked, sort of, the day I met her.

Michael smirked in the background, evidently enjoying this little exchange. He had a weird streak, which would become much more obvious as time drifted by. Karen was half-awake after a session with Seth, but wanted to talk about her life. I initiated the conversation with a few nosy questions. Naturally. "Karen, what is this Seth creature you keep talking to Michael about?" The more obvious question should have been, 'Do you ever eat?,' for Karen was a stick-person, an anorexic with a balding scalp and what looked like scurvy—pretty strange in a land full of grapes and oranges. I drove on, since she didn't immediately answer.

"Why do you want to be possessed by it, don't you think it might suck your energy out?" I wanted to know, because she was such a devoted believer, she kept tapes of her 'conversations' with Seth. I kind of slid back against the wall and faced her. She vacantly looked up at me, and with a hoarse whisper, answered my question. Karen was certainly polite to strangers.

"Gabrielle, can we talk?" she whispered, drawing me closer to hear her hoarse rasping voice. "It is not everyday that people like ourselves have the opportunity to meet royalty such as Seth." Nice girl, but what a foul stench. "Here, listen to this tape." She plugged in the old cassette recorder, slapped in a worn looking tape with the heading 'Seth Speaks' on it, and a droning monotone filled the air.

"Could it be that Karen was being hoodwinked by some commercial cult?" I wondered out loud to Michael.

"Yes, but not in my case," she whispered. "I know exactly what I'm doing." Noticing her lack of personal hygiene, I wasn't too sure about that. But Michael said she had bucks, so it must have been a voluntary lack. "Well, do you send them money for this stuff?" I asked with a distinct lack of discretion on my part. This question was tactfully avoided. I bombarded her with more questions. "Karen, do you believe in mind control?" Do you realize that your mind is being controlled, poor girl?

"Is it possible that these people are not inclined toward your best interests?" I asked. She shook her head.

"Oh, but they are," she answered. "They care very much for me, Gabrielle." Gazing upward into the heavens of her dusty ceiling, Karen added, "They love me as much as you love Michael." She took a drink of some green stuff that looked like algae, but was supposedly 'Seth's Special Tea,' and said, "He makes me feel sooo good when I channel him, it's just indescribable." Okay, you got me on that one, but your health is shot, Karen, I thought to myself, attempting a different approach.

"Sure, Seth makes you feel good, but what about real life?" He may not make you look very good, but that's the price one pays for possession. "Maybe you could make some, you know, human friends, and forget about ghosts and demons." I sounded like a non-believer preaching to the choir, and it all fell on tone-deaf ears. I tried, I really did. But Karen was adamant in her devotion to the Seth thing, and I'll bet those tapes didn't come cheap, either. Lady probably gave her monthly SSI check to the cult leaders, and lived off whatever they gave back to her.

She dropped into her chair, brushed a greasy strand from her unwashed forehead, rolled her eyes upward, and said, "You have to experience him, know him, love him." Drool began its slow drip from Karen's loose jowls. "Seth is everything. He is all knowing, all powerful, he frequently tells me things about my future, so I'll know how to deal with life."

"But Karen, don't you think..." I began, but she looked up, glancing around behind her back. Trembling slightly, a note of fear creeping into her voice, an expression of terror in her face, Karen said, "I think I hear him calling me, I must go now." With that, she passed out, just passed out on the couch. Oh my gosh, I thought to myself, this is almost like talking to Vladimir!

Michael and I looked at each other, I with the obvious question, he with the knowing smirk. "She does this all the time, Gabrielle. Really a trip, huh?"

"No, I don't particularly think so," I said, disturbed by the flight of Karen's spirit. I didn't want to stick around to meet Seth when he invaded her body. Michael snickered as he stared at the limp Karen where she lay folded in her chair, the subject of a deep trance. I figured she was on death's door, and if she didn't get medical attention soon, would someday never wake up again.

"C'mon," he laughed. "It's funny!"

"Is this your idea of entertainment, Michael?" I asked, askance at his amusement.

"Check her out," he snickered, "That chick's totally gone." What a sicko, I thought.

"I've got the creeps, Mike, can we lock the door behind us and, like, get out of here?"

"Don't you want to say good-bye to her?" he asked, "Tee hee..."

"I don't think she'll notice we're gone. See you, Karen." I headed for the door, planning to wait outside if he didn't want to leave. I felt sorry for the lady, but it was too creepy for words. Besides, what could I do to help her, anyway?

Michael followed me outside, where, thankfully, it was still daylight. All I needed to deal with was darkness. The purple and crimson twilight felt like a huge, silken covering, Grandma's worn cotton quilt, my favorite turquoise Lumber Jack sleeping bag, the waterbed...

Oh. I slipped. The waterbed is in my future, which I shouldn't mention so early in the debauchery of 1980 in Northern California.

Chapter Five

But in his estate shall he honour the god of forces: and a god whom his fathers knew not shall he honour with gold, and silver, and with precious stones, and pleasant things.

Daniel 11:38

Late, late yestreen I saw the new Moon With the old Moon in her arms; And I fear, I fear, my Master dear! We shall have a deadly storm.

Samuel Taylor Coleridge

Invoking Fire, from the South

It was a pretty evening, and not evil night yet, where lurked nearby dark closets and goblins, werewolves and mermaids, sirens and Cyclops. Nightime was the right time for me to get spooked, and if I concentrated on the beautiful weather and scenery, the shades of giant redwood trees, rainbows shimmering on the grass, tiny and large emerald green ferns shimmering in the rainbows, and sinsemilla buds, maybe, just maybe I could tune out the weirdness of my existence as a street person, a homeless person (yes, it's true, I was homeless). Weird people attract other weirdnesses, like for example the folks I sometimes met with Michael.

I would like to say that I didn't encounter many things of this nature, but the truth is, I encountered more weirdness than normality in California, and considering my lifestyle, that was not terribly surprising. Everybody seemed estranged, possessed, Hare Krishna, occultish, demonic, violent, ghost-loving, future-telling, drug-crazed, or something in the categorical subtext of strange. This was why I was welcomed with open arms into the California fringe zone lifestyle. I was obsessed with Cat Stevens (hey, that's pretty cool man, want to smoke some hashish?).

Another of Michael's acquaintances followed us home one night in the form of a pair of red eyes (I kid you not) which visited my loft in the middle of my usually restful sleep. This sounds crazy, but remember, truth is always stranger than fiction, so suspend your disbelief as if you were viewing a Shakespearean play. I'm Ariel ("Where the bee sucks, there suck I, on a bat's back I do fly...").

We visited this guy, right? And he wasn't exactly one of Michael's best friends. Michael was one of those scrawny guys who liked to fuck with people, especially if he had an unwitting henchperson (me) with him to boost his confidence and make him fearless in the face of the enemy. We were driving up in the old Rambler, when Michael noticed Chara's truck wasn't home, so instead of just leaving he got out, motioned to me to stay in the car, and moseyed to the cabin to bang on the door and snoop in general.

Chara was a hard-core cokehead, a dealer, a gun freak, and who knows what else, that much I was aware of from the Cloverdale rumor mill; however, I was ignorant of Mike and Chara's outright animosity toward each other. Michael had simply said, "That Chara is one dangerous dude. Watch what you say around him, okay?"

Yeah. Why are we here in the first place, I wondered. Does Michael owe Chara money, does he want to buy some guns, does he want to get his (and my) butt kicked? Pretty soon, up comes this grey, rusted out pickup, out hops a truly mean looking hippy dude in overalls, and Michael immediately smarts off, bravely aggressive in the face of certain death.

"Say, how ya doin', puss-face?" Was that really called for, Michael? I attempted to smile as Chara pulled out his shotgun, aimed it at Michael's head, and hollered, "What are you doing on my land? Trying to break into the cabin and steal my stash?" Cokeheads are notoriously stingy and paranoid. Chara's ponytail had brambles in it, and his boots were sopping with mud and gunk, so I assumed he had been out in the woods which surrounded his cabin, probably tending the sinsemilla plants. Everyone grew sinsemilla or grapes up in this part of the world. I heard that some people also cultivate mushrooms. Chara looked at Michael with death in his eyes.

"I'll give you exactly two minutes to get the hell out of here, before I shove this gun up your ass." Motioning with the gun, Chara then gestured with it, punctuating his sentences with waves of the gun barrel. I was looking right through two little holes at the end of a long, skinny, black pipe. Two tunnels of pain.

"Who's the young lady?"

I finally get noticed? Chara's coal black eyes wandered over my booted, jeaned, shirted body, while I squirmed and got out of the Rambler, trying to look tough. With my luck, he'd shoot Michael and make me his bondage queen.

"Hi. My name is Gabrielle, and we're not here to rip you off, man. I don't know exactly why we are here, but Mike says we should visit more often." Totally inane and stupid speech, born of fear. Would he believe me?

"Yeah, Chara, and how about that money you owe me for the carpentry job on your barn?" Michael strutted like a skinny little rooster, crowing at his hens. "You haven't finished paying your bill, and I want my bucks." Such a tough guy. Five feet, four inches, one hundred and thirty pounds in his boots, and telling this great hulk of a cokehead what to do? No way. I must be dreaming.

"Tell ya what, Mike, why don't you go back there and check out that building." Chara looked very pissed, all of a sudden, and I figured Mike had finally fucked up with no escape in sight.

We were doomed.

"What building? I always guarantee my work, asshole."

"You didn't happen to notice that the second story loft caved in, did you?" Chara asked, choosing to ignore Michael's fond nickname for him. "It fell on my head, nearly busted my brain, too." Chara's eyes became slits of evil. I could have sworn his irises and pupils were transformed into vertical slits, like a cat's. Could it be that he was really another one of those Parvo creatures?

"I had nothing to do with the stupid loft," Michael said, airily.

"You didn't huh?" asked Chara. "I had a headache for a week. And I owe you money?" Chara absently rubbed his offending head, and still didn't put down the gun. He menacingly looked at me as if I would do nicely for payment for services not acceptably rendered. Their conversation basically got less friendly and degenerated into a shouting match until finally, Michael bellowed

71

idle threats and jumped through the front door of the Rambler, yelling at me to start her up and get out of here. Not before I got a nasty surprise.

Michael told me to watch Chara as he started up his pick-up, and as I backed out of the gravel driveway, I turned around to look behind me at Chara. "Gabrielle, look at his eyes, do you see that?" Michael whispered. I gazed at the sight of Chara eyes turning red, burning an unearthly color of sunsets. I was too shocked to believe it, and I blinked a couple of times, while Chara revved his engine, his eyes glowing brighter as he stepped on the gas.

Shit, I was spooked! No, I told myself, I didn't see that because I didn't look.

At one point I must have yelled out to Michael something like "Step on the gas and let's burn some rubber!"

That night, I was snoozing cheerfully, dreaming of squirrels and hazelnuts when suddenly I dreamed these red eyes in front of me. They swooped down the hill into the window up to my bed and I woke up levitating six inches or so above my loft. Immediately, I uttered, "In the name of Jesus Christ, Satan begone from me!" and the eyes disappeared. I believe in that stuff, even though I'm a naughty girl. Hey, Someone's gotta protect me.

Michael, unlike Nadja and Peter, believed the story I told that night (he's the one who told me to look as Chara's eyes lit up), for I woke him, sobbing in utter fear. He held me in his arms for the first time, and we went back to sleep, platonically, of course.

I had to be the most gullible, ignorant, Northern Californian beach bum, hippy transient that side of San Francisco to not know then what I have finally figured out now. Michael had engineered the whole thing with Chara, from the baiting, to the fly casting, to the reeling in of me. He pissed off Chara to scare the ignoramus out of me. And, naturally, when the red eyes (invoked, perhaps?) boiled out of the sky and down to my humble lost loft, I played my role as debutante and screamed at the appropriate moment. Michael got me in bed (but not for the big 'F' word), and I awoke, more respectful of the evils of the supernatural next morning.

Sorcerers howling at the moon, wolves baying on the moor, werewolves chewing flesh torn from human limbs, vampires cackling, flapping their serpentine wings as the sky mists over with their droppings of blood. Human souls lost forever, screaming in limbo and confusion, fear of the unknown creatures they worshiped clawing at their hearts and minds, yet the sacrifice of babies must continue. Sacrifices to the Seth creature. Evil on the horizon. Shouldn't have spoiled the fellow just because I was scared, should have known better, but did I? No, and I regretted it later on in our relationship while I was on the phone with his mother in Chicago and she was gushing about how happy she was that Michael had found a nice young girl to marry and when was the wedding? Shit. I just knew it. How long could I pretend to be in the middle yet not involved or committed and allowed to live there and drive the Corvette? My poor dog was sick and tired of traveling.

Well, a little longer, because Michael was patient with me and he loved a house mouse, while he played kitty cat. I tried to drive into L.A. one day in the 'vette and got a ticket for speeding at 102 while the cop laughed, clocking me at 89, and took my license as insurance (I never did pay that ticket). Michael realized my boredom was taking me away, so he chauffeured me to L.A. to visit friends (here we go again?) but they were very nice in fact, Mom, Dad, and daughters all. Malibu canyon dwellers.

Several years earlier, back when Michael was a broke, transient carpenter, with only the shirt on his back, they picked him up and took him home with them, where he stayed for a full year, repairing fences and what not. That seemed to be typical California friendliness. We hung out until the family began fighting over who knows what—about three days—then we went back to Cloverdale where the grapes grew on a regular basis by the Russian River.

We wandered around, wondering how to appease my ever increasing restlessness. Did I mention I called Cat Stevens? Through hook and crook, with Michael's help and lots of research, I tracked down Cat's agents, former agents and record producers to the ends of the Californian coast. Come to find out that if an individual really wants to know the whereabouts of another individual who is hiding from the general public (composed of individuals who want to tear his rock star clothes off and eat his underwear), the way to do it is to be casual and act acquainted already with his Eminence, his Majesty but your close friend, the Rock Star of fortune and fame.

Ah, but what the heck. Was the search for the Great Greek really what I was in need of doing, or did it just justify my wanderlust and very existence in Limbo, California? I dunno, it was a good time at any rate. Does one always have to justify one's mistakes, adventures, weirdnesses, wanderlusts? Yes, it's true, I was irresponsible and still stuck in my narcissistic black hole out there somewhere between Venus and Mars, or was it Venus and Apollo, or was I the dreaded boar with my tusk in Beauty's thigh? Alas, Alack! when one lives in Fantasia, one must flow with it.

Yeah, so I called Youssef, and what a bummer it was, no doubt. Got his number in London, something like 'Cat's Fan Club', and he answered the phone in person. What a kitty cat voice he had, smooth as Crown Royale, lusciously accented, deep and resonant like rounded bamboo wind chimes, winter sadness and summer's rain, all rolled into one.

The Cat spoke in a luscious accent from Across the Pond.

"Hello?"

Oh paroxysms of joy! That voice, that tone, that Man! It's him, I can't believe it, I'm so excited I forget to speak.

"Hello?"

I faint, I surrender, I'm yours, oh take me away great Cat. Gotta say something, what do I say? Let's play guitar, when will you jump across the ocean and rescue me from Michael? or let's have crumpets and tea?

"Hello, Youssef? It's me, Gabrielle." Pregnant pause. Did I expect instant recognition from Rock Star Heaven?

"Are you in my fan club?" he drawled very Britishly, and I, charming as ever, replied, "No, and I haven't even been to one of your concerts."

Full of tact.

"How are you, anyway? I heard you gave up music for Islam and the good life in Mecca, don't you miss it?" I called him Youssef, not Steven Giorgio, which was his his real name, or shall I say his given name. That Greek Londoner, he was so exotic! Cat was so excruciatingly polite, and I was bursting at the seams. Visions of us together had haunted me for two years, and I was ready for my life to begin. Now that I had found him, it was only a moment in time before we were married, I just knew it.

"My wife is expecting our first baby," he continued. Tears slowly rolled down my face while my mouth became putty, speechless at this turn of events, shocked out of fantasy (I wish). I mumbled something about how happy I was for him in his new life with Islam and his Islamic wife, and we chatted for a few more minutes (three hundred dollars worth, according to the phone bill). There for that brief, speechless moment, I knew he recognized my pain and was sensitive to it, yet we both carried on like old friends. What a guy! Sigh.

I don't chase married men, so at that point my search should have ended, and it did, sort of, except for the fact that Michael, in his knowing way, plotted his next move. He handled our latest dilemma quite nicely by introducing me to yet another friend of his named Tony, who lived in luscious luxuriance in Carmel by the sea. Or rather, Michael dropped me at Tony's doorstep in the middle of the night because I was getting too restless and hard to deal with due to my recent brush with Cat. Winter was coming soon, and Michael figured Tony'd straighten me out and show me what rock stars (successful ones) were like.

By this time, Michael and I had become very vague with each other, and he knew our time together could come to a close. I wasn't going to be his woman or marry him, cook very well, or do much of anything truly constructive. I was a mainly useless, female human slug, and we all knew it. In short, I wasn't even a decent patron of that old, tried, true, humble, well-trodden path, that of the faithful Californicating house mouse.

Yet, Michael in all his perverted wisdom hung on, even if it meant giving me to some guy for a little fun in the sun. So we arose early the next morning, jumped into the Corvette for an all day drive and he finally unceremoniously dropped me off at some rich guy's house in Santa Barbara. Michael certainly had a sense of humor. I was so excited, although I didn't know why.

Off I went to see the harlequin of acoustic parody, someone exciting who would surely introduce me to the Cat. Off I went from Michael's glass house to hang out in a rich man's castle, a rich man with pussy breath (that's right, he'd been eating trout). Yech.

I politely knocked at around ten p.m., assured by Michael that Tony would invite me in to stay for a visit, and the doorman let me in while I browsed in wait of musical genius. I was digging in the room full of animal furs when Tony came home and politely inquired what the fuck was I doing with his guitar, where was I from, and what did I want?

During this particular period in my life, I thought I was highly cosmic, protected by God, and your basic charismatic movement in the flesh. Naturally, I assumed the world had this same view, so I paraded around without my proverbial clothes while the children laughed at me and wondered why I was theoretically undressed.

You get the picture.

The Gods Must Be Crazy.

It got to be around one or two a.m., hanging out in the castle, and I was sleepy. Tony was short, skinny and probably Italian from Brooklyn for all I knew. I told him about Michael and he kind of sneered, then jeered, in a mild manner, of course, questioning me no further (ah, Tony recognized my shining personality and wants to help me on my quest—what quest? Uh, Cat Stevens?).

He invited me to bed in his bed. Yeah, so I went, but not to fuck I told him. Within approximately seven minutes he had undressed and handed me his dick. I was so naive. Such a naif.

The magic words were breathed into my shrinking ear, and I inhaled a scent very much like tuna fish casserole. Not being particularly fond of pussy breath, I winced and shrank into the pillow, much as Chaucer's anti-hero in "Miller's Tale" must have winced at that fatal whiff of his mistress' 'bearded face,' as he attempted to kiss her, and wound up kissing her cuckold husband's arse instead. Yes, pubic hair was pubic hair centuries ago, and it all smells the same when you don't want it.

"I haven't been with a woman in a long time," his skinny cockiness blew into my tired ear. Sure, you liar, your breath reminds me of dirty underwear, in addition to which you have garlic breath, I thought to myself. These days, I know better than to get into bed, much less a house, even, with some guy and not expect him to try to fuck me. I wasn't a prick tease back then, just a very inexperienced twenty year-old, and not well versed in the swollen, quivering, hot, juicy tendencies of men.

Please, let's digress for a moment.

Surely it is obvious to all that I had to grow up quickly to survive the torrent of semen poised and waiting to be jetted in my direction at the flop of a tit and the jiggle of a cheek. Men live for their dicks. That's why we have wars, they want to shoot sperm at each other...sort of like grown up water guns.

Enough of that, back to my story.

Like I said earlier, Tony was a thin guy. He was about Michael's weight but taller. I was definitely not afraid of him, but still, it was his house and at that point, I really didn't have a clue (my song!) and needed to get some sleep. Although he wished I would surrender, he quickly fell fast asleep in that beautiful house, fully perfumed with cinnamon and sandalwood, myrrh, lavender, patchouli, frankincense, and cloves. Oh man! Olfactory enjoyment aside, that house was one gorgeous hunk of brick. I won't tell you what I did, but it was fast.

In the morning he was gone, and I wandered around his castle, drinking in the rich texture of tiles imported from Morocco, touching the sweeping rubber trees and ferns that spread their fern wings eloquently at each other. I breathed in the vast, cavernous rooms and breathed out jungle growth and oxygen. Raymond, Tony's housemate (house mouse?), emerged from a bathroom and asked me if I'd like to go to bed with him (ho-hum), as he fixed himself Ramen noodles while still in a state of undress. Uh, how do I say no? *Nicht, Speceba. Danke.*

Into the day I went, thumb poised to take me back to good old Cloverville, USA, and who should I run into at a freeway entrance but Mark, the beach boy from Malibu! Was I ever glad to see him, and I took him back to my Cloverdale Hideaway. How silly of me; of course, it's MICHAEL'S little hideaway, and was he ever pissed.

His fur stood up and he waved his tail, growling menacingly as Mark and I entered the glass house that had been my home. Why was he so upset? Oh, maybe he thought I was fucking Mark, but I wasn't, as the story has been told. Michael thought it was okay to dump me on some guy's doorstep that he had once remodeled the bathrooms for, but I couldn't have any of my own friends, oh no. What bullshit, and I was tired of it.

For about two days I didn't miss it, then the rainy season began in Northern California, while Mark and I spent Thanksgiving huddled in a tent, twiddling our thumbs and conversing with these two idiot guys who killed a pond duck for their dinner. I couldn't eat it. I wasn't a complete and total vegetarian until those bozos offered that stringy bird's wing that had recently flapped, and I saw those floppy little duck feet that would paddle no more. I swore off all meat, even salad bar bacon bits after that horrendous day by the duckless pond in the mud. I cared less for the Corvette, the redwood cabin nestled in the trees by the brook, the gifts of hiking boots and a wonderful mahogany and rosewood, chocolate-brown Takamine guitar that sounded like bells (extra-light Ernie Ball bronze), the granola and herb breads, the dried fruits of every persuasion, no, I wouldn't miss it at all.

Mark then had the idea of visiting his Mom and her new husband at their *favela* in L.A., so off we went, thumbs warmed up and stiff in the wind, I conveniently forgetting my last episode with the tar pit that was Lost Angels. We reached Santa Rosa and discovered the well-known hitcher's site was full of young hopefuls like ourselves, bumming a ride to somewhere, nowhere, anywhere. It was a bitch getting a ride. Like, a car would cruise by and PICK a hitchhiker, any hitchhiker, to take out of our group and into an uncertain destiny. What did we care of the dangers of mutilation, murder, rape, sodomy, Gomorrah? We felt invincible, we felt unbeatable, we felt like the world was at our fingertips.

Charlie Manson could have driven by to pick a hitchhiker (car number one, car number two, or car number three—pick your prizes) and no one would have ever thought it was really him. That's how cocksure we all were. At least twenty young car-hoppers, all staked out with claims on various autos, and we didn't know anyone who had been abducted, accosted or otherwise abused, so why worry?

My Mom back in Lawless always said she prayed me out of California, and I'm inclined to believe her, because the headlines were screaming 'Rape, Abduction, Murder on the Highways and Avenues of Palm Beach, Big Sur, San Francisco (and most of all, the favorite city to murder in), Los Angeles.' Paraphrased from the local newspapers, of course. A week whisked by in this manner before we finally got out of there.

No cause for alarm, these kids picked us up by the river where we had been swimming that day, and took us home to feed us ham (okay, I slipped and ate meat). Then we ended up at some guy's house after dark because he let us spend the night. His wife was a witch, and he was a friend of the dead. He told us the story of a ghost named George whom he had met while serving in Vietnam, and said to watch for George that night. I didn't see him, but my sleep wasn't exactly without shivers and creeps. Sometime in the night, I woke up with my hair all fuzzed from electricity, or blue lights, or phosphorus, or George. What did I even know?

I didn't hear any werewolves howling at the moon, nor did darkness spread her dank wings of death over my soul, so whoever George was, maybe he was just a wispy wraith, not an awesome demon. Now that'd be a pleasant change. I knew better, but I tried to be brave. Ghosts aren't really long-lost relatives, or drifting spirits of the deceased, or those violently taken from life at the wrong time. I might as well face the truth, I thought to myself, even if no one else in this place does—ghosts are actually demons in disguise, imitating lost relatives, duping spiritualists into believing their lies; ghosts are voices from the abyss, not Heaven, taunting the living. I knew that. I just wanted to be able to like, flow with it and not freak out about George. I had a theoretical explanation for everything back then.

Ghosts or not, they fed us well in the morning on doughnuts and rolls, coffee, orange juice, and cheese. It was time to resume our journey, so Mark and I bid our hosts farewell, thanking them profusely as they filled our rucksacks with mangos, lemons, oranges, and tea. My, my, what nice people they were.

Hours later, we were still sweating our way slowly and grubbily towards L.A. Rides were not plenteous and the asphalt was dank, oily, and filthy with scum left from the thundering Kenworths and Ferraris that zoomed by, leaving Mark and me in a trail of dusty tears. Took us a while, but we finally made it to Lost Angels.

Mark and I leaned on our communal stash to deaden the pain, and stumbled rather than walked into his mother's tin and stick

79

favela. Dirt floors, a hole in the middle of the front room floor for the cooking fire, black iron kettle on the boil, smoky ash floating, flitting in the dusty air, this shack in L.A.s poorest, gang-infested district was home. Okay maybe I'm exaggerating. I don't remember exactly what all happened, but I think we were drunk, too. She never even noticed.

His Mom, Marie, was great. We had some Mexican tortillas which she made herself, and sprawled out in the living room, relaxed to the core. No questions asked, for after all, this is California where young boys always run astray, hitchhiking around with each other and their friends on the road.

Marie's only comment was, "Oh shit, the old man's gonna want you to go to work in the factory with him, so plan to clear out soon if you don't want to get a job." Then, she thoughtfully went back to sewing up the hole in Mark's blouse. Yikes! A job?

It wasn't a threat or anything, she just warned Mark to avoid a major hassle. These people were real broke (obviously) and didn't quite live up to the poverty line (they lived well below it), so money was an object in their fitness, comfort, and well being. Mark and I slouched into the bedroom and lit another joint, contemplating our plans for the immediate future. We decided that avoidance was the best form of protection, so we split until midnight and roamed the streets while his stepdad came home and ate dinner, then crashed.

We snuck quietly back into the hut, where Marie was waiting with a flimsy nightgown she had for me to wear that night. Even though the wind blew in various cracks throughout the *favela,* even though a lone, soiled horse blanket held off that winter monsoon that dripped moisture from their roof, even wishing I had brought a parka, I politely told her I slept alone and Mark wasn't my warming device to ward off the night.

Next morning stepdad bellowed about the house, and Mark and I took off for real, only to find ourselves stuck in L.A., in the Epicenter of Slum, home of the homeless, founder of smog alerts. Gangs were plentiful, so we watched our step, hiding behind signs, and sneaking along winding boulevards. Couldn't get out of L.A., kept getting bum rides (when we got rides at all) to the next freeway entrance, and so on.

Mark decided to return to Mom and Pop's, while I decided to try my luck minus the male influence. Spanish people picked me up and took me to an old lady's house, L'Tissia's, and I stayed with her for a couple of days. L'Tissia was a very Catholic, very superstitious old woman who fed me constantly and told me all about the glasses of water she kept around the house to allow the inhabitation of good spirits, as opposed to the bad spirits who continually invaded the house. Luckily, she had icons, she said in broken Spanish. I was, by this point, getting worn out on all these spirit creatures that everyone fed, watered, talked to and conferred with. No, I silently screamed at the weird world, once and for all I don't see any fucking little men!

Yes, I agreed that there were indeed bubbles in the water, meaning spirits, and her water must be a welcome sight to all those wandering good spirits. Would this spiritual stuff ever end?

No.

So, off I went, thumb stiff again, feet rather ragged, mind a bit subdued, spirit wishing it had a home (ah, we have reached the crux of the matter, the denouement of my life at that point in time), not with Michael in Cloverdale, but something was keeping me from giving up and going back to Lawless. I stuck with it and decided to hitchhike the four hundred miles back to the land of the Russian River, the valley of grapes, the edge of time. Weird guys began to pick me up, telling me dirty jokes and trying to get a rise out of me. A couple of them tried the old threat technique, like, "If you don't do me now, I'm gonna knife you," etc., but I never fell for it, having dealt with this type of harassment before with Vladimir, and being a rather husky, imposingly hefty woman from all that Spanish cooking.

"Go fuck yourself, let me out of this car, get fucked," etc., I shot back at them. They would continued with, "I'll get my gun and shoot you in the face if you don't fuck me here and now, or at least suck my dick," to which I replied, "Asshole, you either gotta shoot me and deal with God about it, or fight me and suffer severe damage to your dick and balls, because I promise you they'll be the first body part I kick or punch," etc., and on and on. A lady of the gutter, that is what I had transformed myself into (no one else did it for me).

81

I have since come to the conclusion that self-defense begins at home; at home in your body, that is. What man can stand up to a woman who threatens his utmost being, his familial jewelry, his sexual prowess? Not too many, although I have read of instances where women were raped in their homes after being thumped on the head with an iron, a brick, or a club. Obviously, self-defense isn't possible when one is out cold, but this is yet another example of the fallacy of safety when protected in the home.

My experience on the road tells me two things: one, it is necessary to defend one's privacy even when threatened with guns and knives. Two, unless you want to place yourself in the position of being visually and verbally raped (if you can successfully defend yourself against physical rape), do not hitchhike. For all my defensive philosophies, brawn, brashness, cold-hearted castrating attitudes, you could say I was the victim of seminal abuse by proxy. Basically, men who picked me up couldn't scare my pants off, so they jerked off while driving down the highway at eighty-miles plus per hour, and allowed me the dubious pleasure of watching their orgasmic thrashing while they fantasized about raping me. What a thrill. I'm pretty tough and mean, but I worry about petite, demure women and little old ladies, how can they protect themselves in similar circumstances, or in their homes?

I was thinking thoughts like these as I stomped off into the sunset after yet another unsettling ride with an anal-retentive, visual rapist, grateful that he squirted his sperm toward the steering wheel and not toward me, when suddenly a Volkswagon van swerved over onto the shoulder and stopped. The license plate read 'SKY,' so I figured they couldn't be all bad, whoever they were. As I trudged along the highway toward my next ride, I noticed billowy, blond hair drifting out of the driver's window, and although that didn't necessarily connote woman, I surely hoped it did.

"Hey lady, need a ride?" a feminine voice asked.

"How far ya headed?"

"San Francisco," she answered. "Climb aboard." Wow! Some women picked me up! Two gay ladies who lived in San Francisco and would I like to go there and work on their carpentry team? Yes, I would, and off we went, no dicks in sight. Sky was the billowing blond, and Leaflet was her lover. Leaflet also owned the van, displaying her devotion to Sky by the vanity plates. So sweet, romance.

Sleepy and gritty after a long, long drive, we pulled into that rolling city of lights, pastel houses, and co-ops—San Francisco—at dawn. The pink light began to strike orange on the bay while waters lashed at their moorings on the beach, almost as if they might break free and swallow San Francisco. But, of course, they didn't, and we made it safely to the small women's commune Sky and Leaflet shared with two other ladies, Ambrosia and the exquisite Swansong.

I found myself working with Sky's carpentry team, cleaning up after they finished each job. Pay wasn't much but the camaraderie of women was right on target, and I grew leaner with each passing week, mellower, more peaceful. I even became a total vegetarian, eschewing meat forevermore. Two months passed swiftly by, and still I found myself working in San Francisco.

Ah yes, and then I met Swansong. She had been away in Mendocino, hitchhiking around, visiting friends and sinsemilla growers, playing her saxophone in clubs at night, wandering by day. Swansong was a house painter (among her many talents) and worked when she wanted, where she wanted. She had such a delicate touch with trim and an eye for texture and color that her skills as an interior painter were in great demand in the Bay Area, so it was no problem to split for a month or so to roam the wild streets of Mendocino, Albion, Garberville, and Healdsburg.

Grape country.

One day while it was raining outside, as usual, and I was bored with the book I was reading, I grabbed my Takamine guitar and began playing this sad song about Cat Stevens that detailed my love for him and how he wasn't there for me, bluesy stuff held over from my star-struck days in Cloverdale, and I heard this bass thumping in time to my music, a rhythm, a beautiful sound, an accompaniment to my sadly song.

I stopped playing for a moment, then thought to myself, "Oh, what the hell, might as well continue," and played the refrain to 'I Once Had a Love,' my Cat Stevens medley. Swansong continued to jam on her electric bass guitar, seated on the winding staircase where I couldn't see her. Too much! Finally, I had to know who the woman was that was playing my tune, so I threw down the Takamine (gently on the couch) and pounced on the steps where Swansong perched, gracefully strumming her bass guitar.

"Hiya." I opened the conversation shyly, not knowing how the frizzy redhead in the tattered jeans would receive me. "I'm Gabrielle and I noticed you playing my song. That's completely awesome!"

She gazed at me with her sea-green eyes and perky nose, her freckled, open, and friendly face, her smile crinkling the corners of her eyes, and spoke my language even before we talked.

"I'm Swansong. I love your music. You want to jam some more?" She beat a funky Calypso rhythm on her worn, black bass, slipped into a jazzy melody, and reclined back on the staircase, staring at me, frankly questioning me with her look. What could I say? Puppy love at first sight? This lady was the ultimate cool character, she was the way I wanted to be, she was the woman I wanted to become, she was to be my best friend.

Swansong taught me how to wire houses for electricity, and she wired my mind in the process. We sat up nights and read to each other, often reading from one of my favorite books: *The Erotic Works of D. H. Lawrence*, works from *Ovid 1: Heroides and Amores*, numerous translations of *Tristin and Isolde*, not to mention works from Adrienne Rich, Sappho, Shakespeare, and Virginia Woolf. It wasn't just a mental closeness either, for Swansong and I shared companionship with each other, good, deep friendship, such as the kind I once had with Renee in Lawless during my adolescence.

Swansong and I soon shared a room together in the house, and began to make plans for our future, not long-term plans, for that wasn't the California way. She showed me what stores to shop in, made me learn to be unself-conscious about clothes or no clothes, helped me appreciate new scents like Maple, Cedar, Sage, and Jasmine in perfumed oils she bought for us to share, and generally integrated me into her life.

We both liked men, but only from a distance, for she was of the lesbian tendency, while I wanted to avoid men for a while because of my bad experiences on the road. Sky and Leaflet had been together for six years, and didn't like men at all, they said. Ambrosia, a black woman who had a lover in San Jose, thought men were equal with women, and displayed none of the other's militant feminism, but she was a gentle feminist, of course. I liked my crowd of friends, my old house, my life.

The street life in the Bay Area, especially San Francisco and Berkeley left something to be desired, though, and it was just as dangerous to hang out there as it was in L.A., with the additional attitude of relaxation and trust compounding the dangerous atmosphere. The threat of molestation, robbery, or murder was rampant among the flower children of the eighties. Not to mention rape. Yet, at the time, Swansong had a mellow crowd of friends, as did Leaflet. Since they both had been around the block a few times, they remembered what it was like to be a young transient, a teenager with no where to go. Quite a few teenagers went hungry in San Francisco, and some of them came to our house for dinner.

They were children, really, runaways with nowhere else to go. We couldn't legally let them take up residence, nor did we particularly want to, considering their wild lifestyles. Often times, we managed to sneak a few kids out on the back porch so they could sleep off whatever hangover they might have had at the moment, and often we found ourselves phoning around town for a place for the kids to live. They came in beat-up, sometimes they came in raped, and sometimes we were forced to call an ambulance, because they took too many drugs. "There but for the grace of God go I," I thought to myself. Good thing I gave up paint.

Some of these young kids were prostitutes, and addicted to drugs. Pimps bought and sold them, johns bought and sold them, yet it seemed as though no one cared about these homeless runaway children who were too young to get a job, and by the time they were of age, were too steeped in drugs and sex to want one. It was a sad commentary on Americana, but at least, at our house, we tried to help in our own way. Luckily, there were others in the Bay Area who did their unofficial part for the children, too.

I knew this guy named Sinbad who took in strangers at the cheap flophouse on Polk Street in the Tenderloin where he and his lady friend lived, offering them shelter from the storm. He was a personal friend of Leaflet and Swansong's, and he looked like a Hell's Angel biker who had stayed out in the sun too long.

Sinbad was a helper and a hellion (whichever you wished, depending on his mood), a reminder that People's Park was for the drunks and the hippies, not always for concerts. He tore up sidewalks with the crowds of screaming crazies at night to protest Berzerkley's proposed parking lot that was to be built soon. He drank and mixed with rank, horny dudes who often stole merchandise and sold it to the local pawn brokers.

Sinbad wasn't a sailor, although he acted like a pirate. He beat his girlfriend when he mixed reds or qualudes with whiskey and she beat him back. But, he often showed the mercy of Jesus Christ when he fed and clothed various street people who wandered into his path. Sinbad also helped child prostitutes get off the street and into homes of some sort. I couldn't condemn the guy in any way, because he was really a Christian, although he called himself an atheist. Hey, who cares what the fundamentalist bible thumpers might say about him?

Through Sinbad, I became fully aware of those lost souls who wandered the earth because their parents chose to sexually violate them in their earliest years. I became aware of the Night Children.

Oh Mamacita, were those funky kids ever gnarly. I have to wonder now, years later...were they me?

Chapter Six

There was the pain. A breaking and entering when even the senses are torn apart. The act of rape on an eight-year old body is a matter of the needle giving because the camel can't.

Maya Angelu

I used to think my personal power was contingent on my being a good sex object, something good to look at like cherry a la mode.

Ann Simonton

Invoking Water, from the West

Street children, or Children of the Night as they called themselves, sometimes came to Sinbad for advice, because he didn't judge the kids or their lifestyles, and usually gave them cash to dissuade them from turning tricks. I was visiting Sinbad and Judy one evening when three of these young souls came knocking at his door in Berkeley. Visually stunning street prostitutes such as these have the instinctive dress and demeanor that Miami Vice made famous.

I was accosted with Obsession and Poison as Sinbad opened the creaky living room door to welcome Lolita, Jessica, and Xaviera (surely not their given names). I hovered in the light cast by their lavender auras, and yearned to know about their lives. They couldn't have been more than fourteen or fifteen years old, and I wondered if their mothers were worried about them. How could it be that the beautiful children standing before me sold their bodies to strangers, strangers who fulfilled their need for father figures, family members, and lovers?

Introduced to sex at a young age by their incestuous relatives or close family friends, the children lost control of their lives and were inevitably drawn toward physical fulfillment by the age of twelve or thirteen, ready to sell it for money, ready to become

87

victims of predatory pimps, and pederastic customers. Yes, Sinbad helped these children with money, and he managed to place them in homes as a way of ultimately getting them off the streets.

Often, gay, professional men in the city would help find homes for the lost boys. Since the boys were gay themselves, turning tricks with smelly, old men, ugly old closet queens with wives at home, and executive positions in the community, gay men were the only ones the boys would turn to for help. It became apparent to me that not very many gay men were pederasts; that was a myth that straights liked to propagate. Yet, straights didn't want to dirty their hands with something so nasty as gay, drug-addicted, prostitute children, so the gay establishment stepped into the fray when they could.

I was angered when I heard the latest gay-basher put down the homosexual community, for they helped rescue the children, who, like themselves, were living in society's dumping ground. I learned more and more about street people each time I visited Sinbad and Judy, because I usually just listened to the conversation between them and the street kids. Sinbad was like their Father Confessor. So it was that evening in the winter of 1980, as Xaviera settled her little buns on the couch and Lolita went to the kitchen for a bite to eat, that Jessica turned to me with a frown.

"Gabrielle, you just wouldn't believe what that scummy pimp Sam did to Roberto yesterday," she complained, allowing me time to digest this tidbit before continuing with her problem. Her little girl eyelashes batted coquettishly, while she daintily lit a More cigarette. The adolescent had big green eyes with irises lined in black, and I wondered if she had ever believed in Santa Claus.

"What happened?" I asked.

"He beat him up, and Roberto doesn't even work for Sam!" Jessica's curly brunette tresses flew about as she emphatically gestured with her palms turned upward as if to question the brains of pimps. I got her drift.

"That's terrible," I commented, remembering the little boy prostitute Roberto, whose Hispanic father threw him out on the street at twelve years old, for being too 'girlish.' Roberto had had the misfortune of being caught in the closet with his older brother, Juan, who had been forcing him in there for the past two years, or at least, that's what Roberto told us. I was inclined to believe him, and that's why Jessica's story was so disturbing—I believed her too.

"Yeah, it sucks. I'm gonna tell Sinbad."

"You should. Is Roberto okay?"

"If you call a broken nose and a broken arm okay," she answered. Pimps around San Francisco didn't like little boys honing in on their adult action, so they tried to buy them, according to Sinbad, then beat them up if they didn't want to work for pimps. The young boys who frequented the Tenderloin in San Francisco often had male protectors, lovers and friends to live with, so didn't need to work for pimps, nor want to. Little boys often wound up dead as a result of their cry for freedom from conformity, from the rules their parents had once set down for them. Sinbad was the avenging angel of the children.

I knew what was coming next as he sat down next to Jessica and exclaimed, "Who the fuck does Sam think he is, beating up Roberto?" Hot chili alarm, Sinbad's pissed!

"He's a jerk, huh Sinbad?" asked Jessica, snuggling closer to her protector.

"I'll have to teach that sonofabitch a lesson, once and for all." Sinbad looked sinister, and most of all, he looked mad. His red face and red eyes did nothing to hide the alcohol and pot he had digested, but his expression was what made me nervous. He looked like a crazed lunatic, ready for the gladiator's ring, ready to draw his lance and do battle, ready to duel to the death. What a guy. There was no doubt in my mind that Sinbad would beat the shit out of Sam (whom I also knew, but didn't like), and do it soon.

"He's hurt pretty bad," sighed Jessica, almost on the verge of tears. I was too.

"Is Roberto in the hospital?" he asked. Sinbad heaved a sigh of relief when Jessica hastily said no, he had been released yesterday, and got up to go fix Lolita something to eat. Judy was at work, but she held his sentiments, if not his strength, and found herself paying rent for the kids while living in a flophouse, just like Sinbad. They helped by being poor so some street children could sleep alone at night. I hoped someday to make a difference in a child's life, but my life was still so screwed up that it was only a

89

passing fancy, a dream somehow unattainable in my present, rootless state. Those lost kids tugged at my heart, their dearly bought expensive scents reminding me of their homeless plight, and I would not easily forget them.

San Francisco, back at the women's ranch.

It was a day like any other day, except for the fact that Sky came home and discovered Leaflet in the sleeping bag with a seventeen year old. Perhaps I should better acquaint you with Leaflet at this time, enigma that she was. Leaflet was a Ph.D. who practiced some weird mixture of shrinkage for the mentally unhappy in her home (our home). Often we would witness young, distraught women in jeans and sweatshirts, or sarongs and slippers dazedly wandering into the house, looking for Leaflet to solve their problems, or at least listen to them. Was it possible that they too were once victims of adult lust?

The conversation usually went something like this: "Can you please tell me if my appointment with Leaflet is still on?" a young lady would query. "Will you check her book and make sure she knows I'm here?" She would speak not exactly as if to a secretary, but perhaps to one slightly elevated to executive secretary. Whoever happened to be lounging in the living room, which was the 'lobby,' would get the dubious pleasure of rousting Leaflet out of her bed, or her garden out back, or her studio where she painted in watercolor and oils.

"Leaflet, my dear, you have company in the living room, Candie Lang is here for her three o'clock," we would call throughout the rambling, frame house on Christopher Street. As whoever the outpatient was at that particular time fidgeted uncomfortably under our stare, Leaflet would be searched for and sought out, finally approaching her client like a black-widow spider towards her mate. Well, maybe not so predacious, but something to that effect. But she helped them, believe it or not, she helped them overcome various fears and ailments, through self-hypnosis, after the initial polarity massage sessions.

Leaflet would start her patients off with a little dabble into meditation and relaxation, then on to suggestive therapy, finally finishing off with spirit journeying and visualization of goals. I think the most immediate therapy was the mental leaving behind of problems in order to experience the out-of-body experience that Leaflet taught, because her patients were able to block out their personal ailments long enough to get a second wind. Using a few relaxing techniques each day, ladies under Leaflet's tutelage could regain their sense of self, and focus on spiritual self-healing in order to bring about lasting change in their lives. Sort of reprogramming themselves for success. I was impressed with it all, let me tell you. It wasn't just a lot of noise.

Leaflet was popular with the disturbed set, needless to say. Her manic nature put me off, somewhat, so she didn't attract any confessions from me, and I sometimes wondered how she managed to charm her customers out of fifty dollars per hour on a regular basis (which is cheap, I have since learned). Leaflet always had drugs and bucks. She was the only member of our household who possessed a car and a checking account.

Sky apparently was used to Leaflet's sojourns into foreign flesh, but this time was different for some reason. At any rate, by that evening after several long, drawn out private bargaining discussions, Leaflet moved out of Sky's room, taking the bed they had once shared (a beautiful antique, four-poster cherry wood with an intricately carved headboard).

Two days later, seventeen-year-old Nikta moved in, informing us all of her lost virginity, lost to Leaflet in a sleeping bag. Apparently, Nikta had been heterosexual up until her indoctrination by Leaflet into lesbian love. Sky moped and moped, calling in sick instead of working with her carpentry team, eating constantly to assuage her pain, turning her slender body into a slender body with a small pot belly. Poor Sky, her baby blues didn't flash anymore, she had dark pools of emptiness instead. Is this what happens when women fall in and out of love? I wondered. What would Sky do when Leaflet dropped her young lover and wanted her back?

Soon after that, Ambrosia decided to move to Mendocino, and Swan and I went with her. The household just wouldn't be the same with the great twosome broken up into a great threesome, one weeping and two laughing. We pooled our resources and bought an old, funky, beat up 1962 Chevy truck, complete with rusted out bumpers and bald tires. It ran and we didn't have to hitch a ride for a change. My license was gone because of Michael's too fast

91

Corvette, and my too heavy foot, but I took turns driving all the same.

San Francisco faded into vineyards and the redwoods grew bigger, the fog grew foggier, the air grew cleaner as we wound our way up into the hills and through the valleys to Mendocino. What a gorgeous land! I wanted to live and shout with glee at the people who waved, "I have arrived!" I kept my mouth shut, however, and we picked up several women hitchhikers, sharing our car in return for their dope.

One woman gave us tofu she had made, another left us with peyote buds. We ate some mescaline and I sat on the beach at Little River, hearing the ocean call me by name, counting the big, blue jellyfish that washed up on the sand, remembering the pink jellyfish from Marina Del Rey. I saw seagulls winding down toward me, felt the ocean spray mist over my face, time and time again; I didn't wipe it off. I was happy, centered and secure with my women friends in California during rainy season.

Naturally, things were just too good to be true, and life always twisted and turned around. One minute a person could be happy, intent and sedate, another blink in time's eye could bring disaster. Such was the case with Swansong that fateful day, for she was gaily striding toward me, not paying attention to the dangers of modern technology in that pastoral, seaside setting where towering redwood trees crackled their branches in the wind, and huge, emerald and aqua-green ferns swooped and tipped their wings in the ocean breeze.

She waltzed out into the narrow, two-way highway that edged along the cliffs above the beach, and, seemingly out of nowhere, this drunken asshole came swerving around and careened into her with his front wheel grazing her hip (it was an eighteen-wheeler). The force of that glancing blow knocked her over the cliff and into the water—knocked his truck on up the highway and out of sight. Guess he felt like it was none of his business or some shit, I dunno. I was hysterical with pain and shocked out of my revery on the beach. The highway patrol caught him later on that day, because he smashed head-on into a scrub oak—didn't kill him, but I guess poetic justice was served.

Ambrosia and I saw the whole thing in slow-motion, but we reacted by diving into the cold, crashing, dark, blue-green waves to rescue Swansong, who was folded over and floating, head and feet underwater, the small of her back barely showing in the ocean, the small of her back which was forever broken, her wings forever clipped. Swansong would fly no more.

Someone else saw the accident and called an ambulance, while Ambrosia and I silently wept for our friend Swansong, whom we had dragged, sodden and blue with cold, out of the crashing waters which should have been her grave, she said later. Ambrosia worked over her torn body in the sand, pumping water out of her stomach, mucus and seaweed too, while I did CPR and mouth to mouth. She seemed dead. The paramedics came quickly with oxygen tanks, and pronounced Swansong among the living, although barely so. They secured her body tightly to a stretcher, so as not to move her spine any more than they had to, and took her away from us, the ones who loved her, the friends she didn't want anymore.

I called her parents in Wisconsin and told them the terrible news of their bright daughter's misfortune. Tall Swansong. Strong Swansong. Paralyzed and unconscious Swansong, we learned later that day, and her parents moved her to a specialized hospital in Wisconsin before I could say good-bye, for recovery, treatment, and therapy. One week passed in Albion, where we camped out on the ridge. We waited for Swansong to go home. Even though we couldn't see her, we waited for word of her.

Ambrosia and I finally turned around and headed back to San Francisco that sad day, six days after the accident, when her parents left with her in an ambulance helicopter, back home to Wisconsin and her old life, Swansong no more, but Sharon Wilcox of Milwaukee, graduate of the University of Wisconsin, only child of David and Sheila Wilcox. Ambrosia and I were too horror-stricken to stay near Mendocino; we just couldn't live there without Swansong, our womanfriend, our woman lover.

Leaflet fell into hysterics when we told her what happened, while Sky held her, tears streaming down their faces. We all fucking wept. What a waste of good, human, woman possibility. What sadness we all felt when we called her very straight parents and learned that Swan was conscious, but didn't want to contact us

93

or hear from us, and neither did they. Evidently, the Wilcoxes found us responsible for Sharon's gay lifestyle, and disapproved of anyone tainted with the Californian mystique. The news was, Swansong would remain permanently paralyzed from the waist down, and would never walk, swinging her long, red, frizzy hair in the wind as she went. I guess she didn't want to know us in the condition she was now in, and surely felt bitter about the lost life we once led together.

Oh Swansong, I will always love you, I will hope to see you again someday, please don't let go of me forever, you who were my only lifeline in this jungle, California. Sky and Leaflet were back together, of course, since Leaflet and Nikta evidently broke up after Leaflet realized that Ozzy Osbourne and Mozart weren't compatible, and Nikta brought home her boyfriend, whom she had neglected to tell Leaflet about. I don't think anyone was particularly upset or torn by jealousy at the changes. Rob, Nikta's boyfriend, was turned on by women together, and wanted to photograph Leaflet and Nikta together, or involve himself with them (and Sky) in a menage a' quatre.

Out went the teenagers, leaving us back in a foursome, but things just weren't the same anymore without Swansong and with the strain that had permanently crept into Leaflet's and Sky's relationship. Ambrosia and I sadly said our good-byes; she went off to San Jose and I traveled north to Cloverdale once more. Where else could I go?

Michael didn't exactly welcome me with open arms, but he did let me crash there, Marxist that he was, and reluctantly began to act friendly once again. Two transients had moved in with him, I learned, and that night we all four sat in the 'kitchen,' which was simply a vacant space around the stove and sink, and ate our vegetable stew with rice for dinner. Conversation was somewhat stilted, since I was obviously an old-timer at Michael's place, while Tara and her man, Buddy, were anxious to replace me in Michael's esteem. Not a hard task to accomplish, judging from his attitude of disdain toward me. I said to her, in between bites, "So, Tara, where do you plan to have your baby?" She was in an advanced state of pregnancy, which is not a good thing if you are a transient.

Beaming with joy and idealistic, youthful hope, Tara replied, "I'm not worried, Buddy will take care of us, wherever we are." Placid chew, chew, chew. Buddy, who had only one arm and a sneaky look on his face, said nothing. Tara continued to tell me about her love for him, one-armed as he was. "When I used to think of getting married, I never thought I'd end up with a one-armed man who was twice my age, but fate is strange, and we're a perfectly matched couple." She shone beatifically and glanced at her man. He looked to be about forty, while she was my age, a year or two younger, maybe, and I wondered how he had survived as a transient all those years, or if he had always been broke, dressed in tattered shreds of clothing, and homeless.

The two gave me an uneasy feeling, he with one arm, she with her pregnant optimism, for I sensed a certain desperation, and didn't think they could be trusted. Michael shouldn't have trusted them either, he was to find out later, for I kept my mouth shut at the time, leaving him to make his own people forecasts—it would be cloudy, dank and cold, with the local wind chill factor in the teens. A storm was brewing, boiling in the psychic world, ready to wreak havoc on our lives.

A couple of rainy days went by, and I accidently ran into Clover, the lady we had given a ride to in the old Chevy truck, so many eons ago it seemed. She still made her own tofu, and was selling some stained glass pieces at the Cloverdale co-op. They were beautiful—one was of an ebony swan wrapping his wings around a young woman ("Leda and the Swan"), and the other had a purple, amethyst backdrop, with snow-capped peaks and a setting sun in orange, crimson and maroon. Clover and I chatted, I exclaimed in appreciation over her work, she got her money and we walked out into the temporary sunshine, brilliantly flashing in rainbow hues, lighting up the drenched redwood trees, and carrying the scent of the Russian River to us. "What would we do?" I countered, scuffing the foot of my shoe against the gravel parking lot. Clover laughed, and set me at ease.

"Gabrielle," Clover said, a question in her flashing, dancing eyes, "why doncha come out to my place sometime?" I knew from the way she looked me up and down that a liason was possible, but somehow, I just wasn't ready for it. "Nothing you don't want to do," she said calmly. "Maybe make a little tofu, cut a bit of purple glass." She giggled. "Eat a couple of mushrooms..."

"Okay, I'd love to come," I finally said, realizing she was a friend who wanted to be a partner, but unlike some men I have known and won't mention, Clover would never force the issue. We waved good-bye as she set off towards Healdsburg, via her thumb.

Michael seemed secure enough with his new friends. In fact, I think I might have been a bit jealous of the easy way they took over my old resting place, the loft, and left me to sleep wherever I could scrounge a soft, warm space in the round, glass house by the brook. I decided I might as well visit Clover, that heavy-set woman with green eyes like the sea, and perhaps learn how to make stained glass windows in Garberville. Question was, where was Garberville? I knew it was in grassy hills that ran northwest of Cloverdale. The exact address she gave me was vague, something like "Up behind this old cabin, on the left side of the creek." I never, ever, in a thousand years should attempt to navigate foreign lands, looking for an obscure cabin in the woods with stained glass windows. I can't even read regular road maps.

I hitched a couple of rides in the general direction of that small town of Garberville, or so I thought, and finally ended up sleeping in an old car with a young guy who said he knew the way to Clover's house, or someone who sounded like Clover, up in the hills, northwest of where we were camped. I didn't have much choice but to believe the tousled young thing, so I stayed with him in the car and fell asleep in the back seat, while he curled up around the steering wheel. Come morning, I decided he was more lost than previously expected. I headed onward into no man's land toward the by now quite mysterious Garberville. Yes, it's true, I was totally lost. Found this cabin with stained glass windows (a common sight in the hills of Northern California), and figured it was maybe Clover's, since she told me she made stained glass in exchange for rent—although she kept house too. Sounded like a house mouse proposition to me, but I couldn't get an answer to my knock, and sat on the front porch in the drizzle for a long wait.

Darkness fell, and no one came home to the little, innerwoods cabin, so I wandered down the hill some more, flailing away at strange bushes, brambles and branches in the night, and found a miniscule, unoccupied trailer. Hmmm. Into the trailer we went, Sara and me, house mice forever in search of a nest. Seemed like forever, but morning came, bringing a glimpse of sunshine through the clouds, and I scrounged some dried beans and rice, managing to cook them in the iron pot after finding firewood. We went down to the icy creek and pondered our situation. Dirty and scummed out as I felt, I was too frightened to bathe in that unknown creek, although I did later that day. It seemed that no one was home in these here hills, and the silence was overpowering.

Three days went by, during which time I sighted one human being on the other side of yet another, wooded creek, but I talked only to my dog and felt all alone in that forest's green. Exploring around, Sara and I discovered a cabin that had a skull hung on the fence post, denoting KEEP OUT, I'm sure, and we kept out. Wind chimes built from twigs sounded hollowly through the silence, and the trees rustled nearby. Whoever lived in this cabin had a snug, warm place, and I envied these people their togetherness and their home.

My pup and I hiked back to our stolen hovel and prepared the evening fire. Finally some guy in a backpack came and demanded to know why I was in his trailer. I was surprised and frightened of this tall, lanky, blond, bearded woodsman, but he was friendly enough when I explained about Clover (Clover who?), being lost (This isn't Garberville?), and wanting out (Really glad to go). He delivered me to the freeway and explained his lady friend was coming to visit, and shared a joint on the way. The dope was for her, he said. I'm sure he didn't realize I had been smoking his herb for three days, and I felt appropriately guilty of my 'small' theft, but I couldn't repay him or tell him, so I didn't. I have changed so much since those mooching days. When a person has nothing and no one, mooching comes about in a different light. These days, I give to mooches, hoping to repay my debts from long ago. The guilt remains in my heart, never assuaged, never repaid in full. Back to Cloverdale and Michael's glass, geodesic dome.

97

Michael's Corvette was gone and so were his guests. When he returned that evening he was in a foul mood, no doubt because the two sweet things had made away with his carpentry tools which were worth at least two thousand dollars, and were his sole source of an income. He was royally pissed, but at least I got my bunk back in the loft, and went to sleep as he muttered and swore at the vanished thieves, neurotically planning their deaths at the hands of his neighbor, Hank the Hard.

Hank was a very strange individual who Michael allowed to live on his land, providing Hank the Hard watched out for prowlers, poachers and drug smugglers, and kept the weeds under control. Hank's cabin was a two story redwood structure, unfinished (typical of Michael's style), with no stairs leading up to the second floor where Hank actually lived and cooked his meals. The first floor was entirely used up as storage space, with an old tractor, a manual plow, shovels, rakes, and other paraphernalia that never got used, just stayed there and rotted in the mildew only California during the rainy season can produce.

The top loft, or second story, was to be the theater for mine and Michael's final showdown, where I almost bit the dust one night, or ate some air, or took a fall; death brushed my ribcage with its awesome shiverings. Michael was a jealous sort, and when he came in one evening after scrounging for money (he was now broke), he found me at Hank's place, smoking dope, and figured I was fucking the poor bastard. Talk about a temper! As Michael's nearly bald pate surfaced at the top of Hank's handmade ladder, Hank and I felt no cause for alarm, even though we were both wary of Michael's horrible temper, and his recent loss of property surely didn't improve it.

"Have a hit," I said, passing Michael the half gone joint, still quite a cigar, "you'll feel so much better." Somehow, his increasingly scarlet countenance and trembling ears (with little trembling tufts of hair in them) made me a bit nervous—so did his silence and refusal of the proffered weed. Oh shit, what have I done wrong this time, I wondered.

Actually, I never did discover the answer to that question, because Michael screamed "You BITCH!" and lunged at me, grabbing my pants leg and pulling me toward the edge of the second story loft, which had no protective wall to guard me from certain death or mutilation by virtue of the twenty foot fall. Fuck a duck, he's gone berserk! While Hank held Michael's arms, trying to reason with him, I hastily beat a retreat and exited, exalting briefly (very briefly) in the fact that I was stronger than Michael and could have thrown HIM off the side of the loft (but I'm a nonviolent kind of girl).

Well folks, that marked the end of our little 'love affair,' and of my housemousehood in Cloverdale, California. It was mid-December, and right smack in the middle of the oft-mentioned, devastating rainy season, not a pleasant time to be out in the elements. I had no home, very little clothing, no money, and no food. Michael had just tried to kill me, so I couldn't ever go back there to live (although he did later forgive me my 'infidelity').

As I wandered down the road a bit, by the Russian River and towards Mendocino, I pondered the situation. This old couple, Martha and Paul, would surely put me up for the night, and with no hassle, either. Martha was an alcoholic and Paul was no better off, but they had a small ranch with horses, and always asked me to come exercise the dappled poneys, so I thought I might grab a little work and hang around Cloverdale until I came up with some sort of plan.

Chapter Seven

All unhappy families resemble one another; every unhappy family is unhappy in its own fashion.

Leo Tolstoi

Invoking Earth, from the North

I still needed a home. That was what this all came down to in a nutshell. I loved Northern California, so I wasn't ready to leave and go back to Lawless. When I finally did return, kicking and screaming one year later, it was only because my Mom sent a bus ticket and I felt sorry for her (I told myself). Not to mention the fact that I didn't know where my next bed would be, and my dog had been shot for stealing a sheep. Plus, I had a permanent ear infection from exposure to the elements, and couldn't last another winter of five rainy months with no shelter. But, this was all in the future, and if I had known in advance to what state I would be reduced, would I have returned to Lawless after getting kicked out of Michael's?

No way.

One thing you may have figured out by now, my life was pretty dysfunctional. I had no idea how dysfunctional as I was the one living the life, but suffice to say, after multiple diagnoses as an adult with PTSD, ADD, and dyslexia, it is no surprise that I was sort of well, out of whack.

Whacked.

Wacky.

Just crazy. You get the picture.

My mom and I had had problems for a hell of a long time, not her fault and surely my fault, but most of all my father's fault, because he royally fucked up our family, and changed the events of our lives forever. Please, just let the tears rip for a moment. We can play some violins and blame our parents for all our problems, boo hoo. Okay, that's enough, now we can move on and get over it. The crazy stuff all started when Dad came back from Vietnam in 1972

100

with a real bad case of the ass. I was twelve years old by then, with a really big mouth. Up until that particular moment in time, I had been my usual juvenile delinquent self, running around on my minibike which I had rigged with a wire to the governor to make the 3.5 horse power engine go faster, and generally being a pain. I had a horse by this time, a wild, white half-Arabian, half-quarterhorse who rolled in the mud every chance he got and scraped me off under every tree he could find. He became the subject of my dreams, an omen of good fortune during my hitchhiking odyssey. My delinquent friends turned me on to all kinds of smokable items, so I tended to get stoned every time I set out from the house. Basically, I belonged in reform school, but due to my mother's love, I lived with her and my brother, Gerhart.

Gerhart was the opposite of everything I stood for; he was the typical, all-American good kid. He never lied or stole or talked back to Mom for any reason. He played quietly at home and never gave anyone a moment's trouble. We were both adopted from Germany as infants, and we liked being Americans. Gerhart's initiation into being a serious delinquent occurred at my hands, his loving sister, when he was merely thirteen years old, although I introduced him to cigarettes at a much younger age than that. I introduced the next level of deliquency, truancy, one morning when we were already at school.

"Gerhart, let's skip school today!" I exclaimed brightly, hoping to get his attention away from the marble game he was playing with two other boys during recess.

"Get lost, Gab, can't you see I'm busy?" he replied, shooting a cleary out of the marble pit, and winning his opponent's marble. The boys glared at me.

"I know how. It's real easy," I assured him. Gerrie, as we nicknamed him, looked skeptical, and continued to ignore me. I never gave up a good thing, so I said, "All we have to do is forge a note and sneak off at lunch time. Really, I do it all the time!" (This was a bald-faced lie, but I wanted him included in my first skipping scheme). Now, Gerrie had always enjoyed smoking, ever since I taught him to inhale up in an old tree when he was nine, so I figured I could talk him into this today, because we could go off and smoke in peace.

101

Back in the good old days, before we were both wiser, I began my sojourn into wickedness by stealing Mom's horrible L&Ms and smoking one while riding down the block on my bicycle. Now who do you suppose wouldn't enjoy the opportunity to call my Mom and inform her I was smoking while in plain sight of all the neighbors? Of course, everyone wanted to have this golden opportunity to get me because my good old Mom usually defended my rights as a delinquent, and this time, she couldn't.

About five neighboring gossips called Mom that fine spring day, probably jamming the switchboard in their haste to see me thrashed, and that's what happened. I got my ass smoked with a giant bush switch, the kind that feels like it's got little stingers on it. Not that that stopped me. I loved tobacco.

So did Gerrie when I introduced him to the pleasures of a nicotine high that year, 1968, when I was eight and he was nine, and we sat in that old tree top, several houses down the block, and smoked our cigarettes well hidden from nosy neighbors. We both continued to smoke, often stealing away while visiting our great aunt and uncle in Milwaukee, Wisconsin, or our grandmother in Skokie, Illinois. We would tromp far away on cold winter days, just to have a touch of a nicotine buzzeroo. Gerrie preferred Camel non-filters, (brand of the father who never showed any love to his son), while I stuck to and sucked up Salem lights until junior high, when I switched to Kools.

Such a harmless pastime, smoking cigarettes, why not graduate into greater evil by skipping school? I asked Gerrie on the playground that day. He was recalcitrant, at best, because every time I pulled something off, I got caught. He knew it, I knew it, Mom knew it. By this time, in the exalted position of sixth grade, I was accustomed to new and better schemes, and was preparing to make my big break, and run away from home again.

"C'mon Gerrie, let's do it, okay?" I begged.

"I know I'll regret this," he commented sadly, "Ya got any smokes on ya?" Gerrie was finally coaxed into skipping school that day to go smoke, and off we went at lunchtime, after giving both our teachers forged notes, compliments of yours truly. Ah, what joy to escape the confines of schools, the prisons of intellect, the playgrounds of rough sports and broken glass, the grimy green walls of academia.

For exactly one hour we wandered around the alleys and backstreets of our neighborhood (school was one block from the house), smoking cigarettes and talking about the great time we were having. "Gerrie, want another Camel?" I asked, scraping my butt out in the trunk of an elm tree. I sauntered along, swinging my arms nonchalantly.

"No, I feel sick to my stomach," he whined. "Can't we go home now?" Poor baby, he missed his school lunch of lasagna. I decided to play along, just so he wouldn't get vicious.

"Okay, we'll tell the old lady we got out early," I said, placatingly. "She'll never figure out what we did all day." Hmmm. Better threaten him a little, because he might tell her we skipped school. "You won't narc, will you Gerrie?" I asked his pale self. He looked positively putrid. It must have been too much smoke on an empty stomach. One of the biggest power struggles between me and my brother was who would tell Mom what the other had done that day. Bribery was important for secure bargaining, and played no small part in the overall picture of our siblinghood. Here it came. I knew the day would end up like this.

"I won't tell if you give me five dollars," Gerrie replied. Now that was outrageous, that was uncalled for, that represented three weeks allowance or two mowed lawns (my money-maker that year).

"Bull-*shit,* bro, no way will I pay," I screamed at him, ready to fight it out. "You keep it shut or else." Gerrie wasn't exactly quivering and shaking with fear—he could outrun me. There we were, in the alley looking at garbage cans, the stench of rotten something in the air, a scent of dead, rotting skunk or fish, and he was trying to blackmail me. Hah! I would outsmart the little fink, no brother could get away with this shit. I got nasty, but so did he.

"Yes you will, bitch breath, or I'll tell." He managed an evil grin.

"If you tell, motherfucker, you get caught too." I was so tough, such a foul mouth. "What do you think of that, asshole?" Our conversation had disintegrated into this dialogue, which wasn't that unusual, and we were ready to start throwing things. I picked up a rock, intending to smash his little smirky face in. I wished I had some dirty underwear or socks to stuff into his mouth (my favorite punishment), because that wouldn't leave any marks, blood, or bruises on him.

What the hell. We went home, suddenly hostile and too hungry to fight or really care. I had to trust him to keep his trap shut, and he had to trust me not to sabotage his life. Fair trade, I would say. Not that it mattered, because good old Mom had the switch out, and was she ever pissed! Glaring at me, Mom's bright blue eyes were dancing in anger. She had the newly-cut piece of bush in her hand, and was advancing toward my room, where I had quietly snuck in when I thought she wasn't looking.

"Uh-oh. Do you think she knows something?" Gerrie just smirked, and wandered silently into his room, shutting the door to block out my screams of agony. Yes it's true, I got caught very often. In fact, for this transgression, Gerrie got off the hook while I was put on restriction. All he had to do was whine, "But Mama," in his sweetest baby voice, "Gabby made me do it!" Lies, lies, all of it lies.

"I believe it," answered Mama after thrashing me.

"I didn't want to go, honest!" little Gerrie whined, burying his face in her bosom. Naturally, my mother knew his words were as good as gold, as was he, since Gerrie never visibly fibbed, as I previously told you, and I always lied. Gerrie got away with skipping, and I got restriction and a switch. He sat in the kitchen, smugly sipping his chocolate milk, munching his peanut butter cookies, and reading a comic book.

Right about this time, I decided to run away to Jessie Whelan's house, and live in the attic above her garage. Her mom would never notice, because her mom was never home. Jessie was a wild young thing, and I envied her complete and total freedom to roam and make out with boys, and above all, to smoke cigarettes, unhindered by parental guidance. One night before my Mom realized the extent of Jessie's liberation, back in the days when I was allowed over at her house, we sat up all night taking No-Doz, and smoking Salems. She had a bright idea.

"Hey Gabby, let's invite the guys over this morning," Jessie said, hoping I would go off into the sunset while she and her 'man' did their nasty thing.

I wasn't too thrilled with the idea and told her, "It's fucking four a.m. Chick, don't you ever get tired?" Yawn, yawn, yawn. Yeah, well, what the hell.

"So, you a baby still?" she sneered. "I'm calling 'em right now," Jessie said, picking up the phone and dialing. One hour later the boys showed up, bringing beer and more smokes (although by this time I was gagging). How did fourteen year old boys get beer at four-thirty in the morning? Such are the complexities one ponders about life in Lawless, Oklahoma, smack in the middle of the Bible Belt, home of Pentecostal holiness, Assemblies of God, and charismatic mania. Pretty soon Jessie and Rob and me and some guy I never saw before in my life were in the bedroom with the lights turned out and before I knew it Jessie's bra hit me in the face...

I turned on the lights and exclaimed, "What the fuck?" holding her dingy, yellow training bra (she was trained, all right) in my hand.

Rob said, "She likes it, don't you Jessie?" to which Jessie kind of purred, lying under his sweaty armpit as she was in a position of fuckableness. I cruised into the living room and crashed on the couch. The other guy who I never saw before didn't say a word or try a thing. He knew better. Nighty-night boys and girl, I've had enough excitement.

I decided to run away to Jessie's in retaliation for my restriction, and Jessie thought that was cool and fine, but I made the mistake of inviting Meeka, this dumb broad who lived next door to me. We were both in the sixth grade (why did I always want to include other unfortunates in my escapades?), and she had just discovered the art of sneaking out her bedroom window—her mom was always drunk and passed out, and her dad was dead—but she royally screwed any chance I might have had of staying uncaught at Jessie's place.

I didn't realize what a wimp Meeka was until that night when we both were in the attic safely hidden and enjoying our freedom. "Gabby," she whined, her auburn red page boy mussed from attic dust, "I want to go home." A tear silently rolled down Meeka's sweet little face, and she wiped the snot off her nose with a grubby little hand. What a child, I thought.

"I can't believe you want to leave," I exclaimed in disgust. "We just got here."

"I know, but it was a mistake for me to come."

"Well, you're here now," I commented, "And you're not going anywhere." Sitting back to enjoy the evening and my unlimited freedom, I relaxed and almost fell asleep. Meeka sniffled on her sleeping bag in the corner, and I thought all was well, but suddenly out of nowhere blinding lights hit me in the face and my mother's voice called out,

"Gabby, I know you're up there." She sure sounded mad. "Come down right this minute!" I contemplated the idea of letting them come and fucking get me, but nahhh. I climbed sheepishly down, and guess who told my Mom and hers? My sweet friend, the fink, that skinny, pimple-infested, foul-breath, cootie-lover Meeka. She had scrambled down to her mother's arms, and she sat, next to her Mom in the station wagon, ready to go home to her teddy bears. I exploded.

"Why didn't you warn me, wench?" I yelled, "Did you have to call your mom and mention me?" Meeka, true to form, cowered sheepishly in the back seat of her Mom's station wagon and smiled at me.

"I tried to tell you," she said.

I was boiling.

Sheet! "Why did you want to run away in the first place?" Enraged by her weak-willed silence, testosterone took over the left side of my brain.

"I dunno, I thought it would be more fun than this," Meeka said meekly.

"I ought to teach you a lesson, bitch..." By this time, Meeka's mother came to her rescue, following a deep conversation with my Mom, and liberated Meeka from the station wagon and my wrath. They both got out of their car, and came to face me by the garage door, while Jessie and my mom looked on. Tempers were hot.

Mrs. Loften said, "You are no longer welcome in my home, and you can't play with Meeka anymore."

"That's fine with me," I said. "If I catch her butt after school she's had it." Meeka looked a bit uncomfortable, because she knew word would get around the school that she was a narc, and I would probably fulfill my threat, too. Mrs Loften was more concerned about social class than her daughter's safety.

"You aren't from a very good family, obviously," she commented with a snide glance at my fuming Mom.

"Why you..." sputtered Mom, unaccustomed to swearing at people, she didn't have a readily available vocabulary like I did. Mrs. Loften didn't waste much time waiting for Mom to vocalize her true feelings. Sniffing haughtily, she stuck her little snout far into the night air.

"Come Meeka," she said to her silent daughter. Why would anyone name their child Meeka, anyway?

"Yes, Mama," Meeka managed to say. They sauntered back to their protective auto, and drove away. It wasn't quite over with, however, for Mother had some choice words for me.

"I don't want you at this Jessie character's house anymore." Mother had finally realized why I came here so often—lack of authority and parental control called me, like sirens at the edge of cliffs and broken rocks, calling seamen to their deaths.

"But Mom, it's not her fault I ran away!"

"Where's her mother?" Uh-oh. She noticed. I'm doomed.

"Uh, at the store?" I squeaked. "Really, she's around here somewhere." Jessie had long since fled into the house, so I had to handle this occasion all by my self. Mom jerked my arm toward the car, and I knew it was all over.

"Just wait until I get you home and your father gets ahold of you!"

Oh fuck.

I forgot about him.

Home from Vietnam and he liked it better over there, he said. My lip didn't help matters, but when I got home that night, he slapped me clear across the room, which increased my disdain of his military tactics and his awesome power. I would get revenge, I swore, I would get him back. This actually never occurred, because my mom wouldn't put up the front of a typical doting wife and look the other way. She believed in corporal punishment, although

I was a living example of the failure of its intended effect, but my dad wasn't going to slam me around the house with his fist, no way.

"Sam, if you ever do that again you can pack your bags and leave, because there's no call for that kind of punishment," Mom told him. She was totally pissed, and ready to kick him out for child abuse (even though I was more delinquent than child).

"She deserved it, and I'm tired of the little brat," he griped. "I'll hit her again if she doesn't watch it." I stood there by the door, ready to bolt into the night.

"You can belt her, you can smack her," Mom warned, "You can hit her with a switch—but you will never, never punch Gabby in the face again!" That night Dad laid off, because she meant every word of it, but he continued to smack me around for days after that until I finally got him to stop by calling the cops. He used to hit me when she wasn't home, and I didn't usually bug her about it because I didn't want their marriage to break up. Other things happened, however, to change my mind.

Like, for example, the fact that Dad increasingly came home late at night, drunk and disorderly, and threw his weight around the house. "Get in your room!" he would bellow, often for no reason other than the fact that he couldn't stand the sight of my face.

I fought back in my usual way. "Why did you come home from Vietnam and Korea, anyway?" I would ask, "You don't seem to like anyone or anything here in Lawless." I thought some more.

"I'm getting my belt out," he screamed, jerking at his pants to take it off. It was a big belt, too. I was beyond fear, and wasn't bright enough to shut up.

"And, in fact, we liked it better here without you around, bitching at us all the time." With those last, parting words, I dashed out the front door, and didn't come home until late that night, when I was sure he'd be out drinking with his buddies. I was not exactly a model child, but he really had changed since his last tour, and since Mom reluctantly confided in me that he had gotten an Oriental woman pregnant (she had accidently intercepted the letter from Korea), I had no trust or respect for the man who called himself my father. Fucking around on Mom was unthinkable!

But then, things began to even out a bit—Dad found a job at a restaurant, taking over the failing business, working sixty to seventy hours per week that first year, and he seemed happier. I guessed that since the Army had been his whole life for twenty-seven years, he needed a new place to go and feel busy.

He was so busy, he didn't even come home some evenings, but I didn't suspect anything out of the ordinary for the next two years, while I continued to be a renegade, since Alishia had conveniently moved up the street from me (much to our mothers' mutual chagrin), and I had someone to pal around with in Lawless (yes we were). I was too young to worry about my father's activities, and he had finally stopped punching me around so much. It must have been because the local cops gave him a little lecture.

Alishia pulled out her forearm and showed me the track marks. She had been shooting heroin, and wanted to tattoo over the oozing pitted surfaces that were once youthful flesh. Looked like something that guy in 'The Fly' barfed up. She sure had changed from her younger days. Or had she? Now there's a thought, maybe Alishia had just progressed from paint to harder stuff, depending in how poison should be classified. None of those thoughts struck me at the time. I was still impressed with how depraved and depressed my poor friend had become. Me and my buddy, the wild thing Alishia, were having a fine time once again, only these days I was less inclined to believe all her stories, and more inclined to worry about her health. I no longer did something just because she dared me, now that I was fifteen years old, and in high school. One hot, humid June day we were hanging out at the pool on Fort Kill, and I noticed the scars that Alishia couldn't seem to get rid of; they were all over her body, including her legs.

"See, I'm going to make another tattoo here," she said, offering me her oozing arm. "Bubba's gonna help me with the hard parts." She squeezed some pus. "It's gonna be a picture of a motorcycle."

"Alishia, that's totally gross, man, why are you doing that stuff?" I asked, aghast at her terrible health decline since the previous spring, since we had just recently begun to hang together again.

"What stuff?" she asked innocently, while still squeezing her arm. "I quit doing paint three months ago."

"I'm not talking about paint," I said patiently, although I only sniffed a little long ago, and was aghast that she had continued to sniff it for another year. Damn, the wench was declining right before my very teenage eyes. It was scary. "Why more tattoos?" I added.

"Because I like 'em, and so does Bubba. He says they're sexy."

"Okay, so he thinks they're sexy. Fine." I touched her extended forearm lightly. It gave like a squishy sponge. "But drugs are killing you, Lishia."

"Well, I don't do that many heavy drugs, so what's your problem?" she inquired, her dull, gun-metal eyes watching me carefully.

"I want you to listen to me," I yelled, too shocked to be polite. "You got to quit shooting that stuff!"

"I DID quit shooting, Gabrielle, I swear it on my mother's grave." Alishia grimaced as she squeezed pus out of what should have been the hollow of her flabby arm, between the forearm and the biceps. "Have you ever snorted horse?" she asked.

Alishia used to tell me wild stories about her and the Hell's Angels, that they lived in the Wichitas, like grease-soaked mustang poneys, whinnying and fighting over their brood mares. I would sit in my bedroom nights, lighting incense and candles to dispel the gloom, to create my fantasy mythology in which I was the white princess on some old biker's hog, riding into the wind with the moon glowing full, spilling its moonmilk over the atmosphere, droplets of night moisture touching my face. I wanted to fly on the back of a wild beast, far into my fantasy evening, out into the hemisphere where only astrals travel, off to visit the garden of chakras, of Om, of Jesus Christ. In my version, He was a healer rock star, welcoming, friendly, and accepting all who came with open hearts.

Yes it's true, I worshiped Jesus. He was my rock and my fortress, my love and my friend, my father and my mother. He made you my brethren; He made us one together. I knew the Holy Spirit, I knew the wild wind of untamed humanity, of cat's eyes and instinct, of furry paws padding softly in the night—I experienced it all through the spirit of my consciousness, but my subconscious fought back, baying at the moon, feeling like my evil twin, my nefarious alter-ego, Gabrielle the monster.

There I was, daydreaming and praying, having all these spiritual insights about God and His Son and the world and darkness...I suddenly hit on the idea of going rock climbing (I never do manage to concentrate on one thing for very long). From bikers to rock climbing, both settings in the Wichita Wildlife Refuge, where the buffalo still roam and the long-horns still gore unsuspecting tourists.

Rock climbing.

Why not? Hanging out with Alishia was getting to be a drag, and I needed a cleaner crowd. I knew just the bunch to hang with, if they'd have me. Leaping lizards and cactus plants, the Wichitas sucked me in!

My friends in Police Explorers went hiking all the time, and I could go too if I wanted, if I had any balls. I didn't, but finally, one day when I was a sophomore in high school, this guy with a wolf-dog who I knew from around the neighborhood came up to me and said, "Look, I know you're a hippy-radical, all right?" Yeah, he and all his basic training haircut friends knew about me and my lonership.

"Uh huh," I said out of the corner of my mouth, "and you're El Zorro out to save the poor oppressed peoples."

"But we don't always bust hippy radicals," he enjoined.

"If you could catch them you would."

Wayne shook his head. "That's not why I want to talk to you, stupid." I looked at him, and forgave him the slur. After all, I could occasionally be extremely dense, and the Explorer group was a great bunch of folks. I needed a new crowd, but how to tell him? I didn't have to.

"So, what do you want?" I asked, diplomatic as usual.

"Gabby," he smiled, "Come on and go with us rock climbing in the Wichitas this Sunday." He walked off. "We'll be expecting you at nine o'clock sharp," he called over his shoulder. Cool, I thought to myself. They like me!

I was flattered that the short-haired crowd wanted me around at all. Turns out they were members of the Search and Rescue Police Explorers, Blue Ferret Council 33. It was a really hardcore group, and before I knew it I had joined, wore a flight jacket, and carried a nightstick and handcuffs in my ride. What I thought I'd do with that loot I'll never figure out.

We thought we were serious coppers. With my outdoorsy new friends, I began to climb higher and higher peaks, boulder-hopping my way to a new freedom in the natural world, the only world I had ever felt entirely peaceful and happy.

I hung out in the coffee shop with my friends, the future cops, sneaking tokes out in the parking lot while they waited inside for me, knowing my need for drugs. Yet, they accepted me, and let me be myself. We never discussed my drug use, because with them, I was safely an Explorer scout. I rock climbed and hiked, and lost thirty pounds of excess flab before the summer was over. Maybe things would shape up after all, I thought.

No such luck.

At the tender, delicate age of sixteen, I became the child of a Broken Home. It was, as usual, all Dad's fault. Driving around with my baby police friends, I noticed through the grapevine that people were talking about my Dad to everyone but me. Lars and Flanigan had seen good, old-fashioned man-about-town Dad with a married floozy at Hedon's Bar. That did it. Let's tail them guys, and get that license number on her car.

We staked out Hedon's Bar, and sure enough, one week later after many hard and arduous hours at the steering wheel, in the parking lot after midnight, eating takeout sub sandwiches (no wonder cops are fat), we caught them in the act.

Turns out, Celie, Dad's new wench, lived at 23 Harland Avenue on the south side of Lawless, right by Bells High School. We tailed them down Simmons Road that night, on their way to Mr. X's Steak House, and took that wench's license number down to the police headquarters (where we were well-liked), and had them run a make on her plates.

Caught them red-handed.

Mom had suspected for some time that Dad was fooling around, mainly because he used to stay gone (except for the restaurant, where he always showed up for work on time) for days at a time. He would stomp in the front door, disrupting the quiet generated by Mom, Gerrie, and me, while we were seated in a trance around the

112

television set watching that night's Movie of the Week. With my generous help identifying the guilty culprit, Celie, Mom confronted Dad with the news that he should consider moving out.

At any rate, the shit hit the fan. Dad moved out, Mom went through a serious, emotional wringer when Dad took her to court and stole the fifty thousand dollars out of their mutual savings account the day he moved out, and I did as I pleased, unsupervised for the first time in my short life.

Well, that was a big mistake.

Never leave a sixteen-year old unsupervised during her dearth of teenage emotional stability, her downtrodden paths of adolescent hormonal disturbances, her lack of intellectual reasoning. I was not to be trusted.

So anyway, Mom had this pistol she used to keep in her bedroom, and I would tromp in in the evenings, after ingesting large amounts of hallucinogenic or amphetaminic substances, opiates, qualudes...and I would see Gerrie curled up on his bed, watching t.v. in his room with the family dog, but no Mom. I would hunt throughout the house, calling her name, worrying about her. Finally, I would check her bedroom just one more time, and there she would be, with the revolver held to her fevered brow, clicking, clicking, clicking the unloaded gun.

"Gerrie, she's got her gun out again," I said to my brother as he sat, zombied out in front of his tv His bedroom was very dark and musty, and I could barely see him.

"I know, she's had it in there clicking all night." He stared at a commercial.

"Why didn't you take it from her," I asked, miffed and coming down from my trip in a hurry. "She could shoot herself, and then there'd be no more Mom." I began to cry, and Gerrie just sat there, watching t.v. The family trauma was hard on him too, but whereas I externalized everything, and got it out of my system, he internalized it, and suffered the most.

"I took away her bullets," he said. "Now, will you leave me alone?" Tears slid down his face, as we thought about our mother who sat on her bed with a pistol to her head, clicking away and flirting with infinity. "I'm watching this movie, so..."

113

"Okay, I'm leaving," I said, getting up off his bed. "Will you keep an eye on her?"

"Yeah," said Gerrie, "Will you bring me a Budweiser?"

After too many days of suicidal Mom, after being depressed myself for more time than I cared to remember, after leaving Mom one night only to come home and find her passed out and not breathing, then rushing her by ambulance to emergency where they discovered it was too many downers mixed with alcohol, I decided to move away for a while. Mom just wasn't the type to get high, you know? She hardly ever touched a beer, much less massive quantities of tranquilizers.

I'm sure she couldn't help it, because Dad tried to defame her character in court, which must have really hurt her. I went through one helluva nasty divorce myself in later life, not as nasty as hers by any means, but it helped me to understand her better. As a teenager, though, I just couldn't take any more depression, and had to find a way out of there. Somehow or other, I got a grant through Upward Bound, through the skin of my teeth, and began college the summer before my senior year at Lawless High—at last, a trip to the fabled college town of Waterford, Oklahoma. This was all later on, a year after I had tried life with good old Dad and his floozy, Celie.

I moved in with dear Papa when I was barely sixteen. He had this apartment with the floozy, and they let me do whatever I wanted, which was everything. I drank, I smoked pot, I even had people crashing at the apartment at all hours of the night and day, because soon after I moved in, Celie moved out, and went back to her husband with a broken pelvis and a broken jaw. You guessed it, Dad kicked her ass.

It all started innocently enough. I came home one night, drunk and stoned as usual, and went to beddy-bye. Neither of the folks were home, but that was normal since they went out drinking every night. I was sleeping soundly, when suddenly I heard the sound of breaking glass. I got up to look and saw Celie smashing all my perfume bottles and cosmetics that were lined up on the counter in MY bathroom.

"What the fuck are you doing?" I yelled.

114

"Never mind," she slurred, pausing only to look at one of my bottles of perfume for a moment. "It's your father I'm mad at." Then, she smashed it to the ceramic tile floor, scattering scent all over the bathroom. My scent.

"Hey, you're gonna buy me some expensive stuff," I bitched. "How about I just go in the bedroom and smash yours?" I headed to her bedroom, where Dad snoozed in a drunken stupor, but she headed me off at the pass.

"I need to talk to your father," she hissed. "Stay out of it." And she walked into the bedroom, slamming the door in my face. I was totally pissed, but more than that, I was curious—what would happen next? Surveying the mess in the bathroom, I decided that she could just fucking well clean it up herself in the morning, when she sobered up. I headed back to bed, intending to start a fight with the bitch in the morning, but I didn't get the chance, because she started her own fight with Dad.

I heard a large thwack! like the sound of a meat cleaver slicing a roast in half, then I heard a loud *roar!* which was my Dad, who she had punched in the face while he was asleep in an alcoholic daze. Naughty, naughty Celie...

Things began getting louder and more ominous, so I opened their bedroom door to witness what all the screaming and yelling was about. Celie, stark naked, was bleeding from the mouth and nose and had a large welt on her hip, while Dad towered over her at 6'2 (she was a skinny five feet tall), not a mark on him. I couldn't deal with all the blood and they kept on fighting, even though I was looking on at the action. I got out of there.

At four o'clock in the morning, where could I go? It was dark and scary, but I was even more scared in my heart—to see my father beating up a tiny woman, for whatever reason, really shocked me to the core, and I didn't want any more contact with him than necessary. I went to the only friend I could really count on at that time, because you don't go tell Police Explorers about a possible impending murder. I went to Renee.

She was, at the time, living with her dad and his floozy girlfriend, and not very happy about it. Her Mom had recently died, but her dad immediately moved in with this weird creature,

Fey, and began a new romance (or was it an old one, I wondered?). Renee was caught in the middle.

I knocked softly on her window that fateful night, and she let me in the house. Quiet as mice, we crept into her bedroom and went to sleep. Next morning, Fey and Renee's dad, who was actually a very nice, exceptionally gullible guy, didn't even act surprised to see me.

Fey said, "Hello, Gabby," and continued to watch her soap opera, gazing into the depths of American entertainment, tranced out on cheap, mental oblivion, combined of course, with the requisite drinkie poo.

"Hey, Fey," I said.

"Will you be staying long?" she asked, lighting a Bel-Air and taking a swig of her 'tea,' which was actually a whiskey sour, but we pretended it was tea.

"I doubt it," I answered. Fey's blond wig and false eyelashes clashed with the flowered house dress she was wearing, but she didn't usually dress until five o'clock, when most of the clubs opened. Fey was a party animal, and often partied with my Dad and his floozy girlfriend.

"How's your father, anyway? I didn't see him at Hedon's last night." She gave me a crafty look.

"I guess he's okay," I said uncomfortably, wanting to hide in a closet.

"Is he still with that Celie character?" Fey asked innocently. I often wondered if she and my Dad had something going on, she was always so interested in his whereabouts.

"Well actually," I said, "They had a major disagreement last night and she is probably in the hospital this morning," helping myself to some buttered toast. Crunch, crunch.

"Oh," squealed Fey, "How interesting!"

"You should have seen it, it was really bloody." I had her undivided attention for a small moment.

"I'll bet it was," she said. "Who won?"

"Who knows?" I said.

"So," smirked Fey, "That little whore finally pissed Sam off for good, I'll bet."

"Yeah," I agreed with her. "That's why I came over here today." I finished the toast and poured some coffee.

Renee came in the kitchen. She gave me a quick glance, and whispered, "You shouldn't tell her anything, Gabby, she's too weird to handle it." Indeed, Fey had a dreamy, satisfied look on her face as she intently watched a toilet paper commercial. Maybe she would get my Dad, after all. He was stupid enough to let her.

Renee and I decided to split the scene, and went to visit her Mom's house. It was kind of spooky at first, when we walked in and all the windows were shuttered and the shades were drawn, but once we let some breeze in, things looked a little less gloomy. Renee showed me her bedroom, which she had redone in red carpet, including the walls and floor. Her bedspread was red, too. With a little black thrown in for trim, it looked like nothing less than a bordello, and I loved it.

Flash!

I just had a fabulous idea.

First, we must get stoned.

"Want to smoke some weed?" I asked her, pulling my stash out of my jean's pocket, and shaking it under her nose so the olfactory sensation of crystallized herb would hit her full in the face.

Renee crumbled under my considerable pressure, and said, "Oh yeah. Yeah." That was simple enough, and we smoked our first (definitely not our last) joint together in her mother's house, ready to confront the world together.

"It's some killer stuff," I said happily, rolling a joint and letting her have the first drag. "Like it?"

"Gabby, what are you going to do?" Renee asked me a few hours later. She was worried that I might freak out under the pressure of recent events, and wanted to help me stay sane. "Why don't you and I live here?" Renee and I both had the same idea at the same moment. We must have had telepathy.

"Great!" I was so happy and excited I could hardly stand it.

"Yeah, we'll have some fun for sure," exclaimed Renee, clapping her hands. She had been lonely too.

"Let's figure out a way to get my stuff from my Dad's house without having to deal with him, okay?" I asked, lying back on the couch and surveying my new home.

117

"I've got an idea," Renee said conspiratorially, "All we have to do is..." We moseyed on back to the old homestead, where Dad was home, unfortunately, but he didn't give me any shit at all about moving out. He sat on the couch, looking depressed. I didn't want to hear his excuses, for our plan was to get some money for groceries. Renee said she gave her dad guilt trips all the time, and they would surely work on my dad as well.

"How's Celie, anyway?" I asked, hoping she was still alive, not that I liked her or anything, but murder was against the law.

"She's moving out," he replied, studying the evening paper. You didn't really answer my question, Dad.

"Yeah, I figured she would, but how *is* she?"

"Did you know they are opening a new McDonalds in Lawless?" he asked, showing me the front page. "That will be tough on the other fast food joints, especially Hoggies." He ignored my question, but I didn't give up. I still had to know.

"Did you kill her, or what?" Now, you would expect Renee to be squirming by this time, but she stayed cool. I would witness more than my share of her dad's weird wife's behavior, and I think Renee knew it. Okay, so Dad won't talk about Celie. I should have called the cops on him, but I think I was too embarrassed.

"No, I didn't kill her," he mumbled behind his newspaper. He wasn't showing his face to us, and I knew the time was right for me to make my move.

"Dad, I'm moving in with Renee."

He didn't even blink. "As long as you stay here once in a while, I don't care." He fumbled in his wallet and handed me a twenty, which bought a lot more food and gas back then than it does now. Renee and I exchanged glances. Fat chance I'd stay with him again.

"That's for groceries for you two this week," he said. "You need some help carrying your stuff out to the car?" This was easier than I expected. I think his guilt needed to be alone with itself. So, I sort of moved out, returning only to party at the apartment with my friends, drink his booze, and hang out at the apartment complex's swimming pool.

The summer before my senior year at Lawless High, Renee had changed schools to Jackson High, leaving me high and dry with no best friend in the halls, and no place to crash anymore. She had moved in with her boyfriend, although they later moved back to the house on 'I' street, where we had shared so many memories together, and we just naturally drifted away from each other. Renee and I had lots of adventures, like the time the bed broke when Prentiss Tribbly and I got on it, while she and his friend David were already shaking it down, and the time we got busted for ripping off three department stores while they confiscated our grass, and the nights we cruised Second Avenue at dawn, watching the hookers and their johns come out of their hotel rooms. I finally went to Waterford that next summer, and Renee used to come rescue me on weekends, even though I wasn't allowed to leave the campus (I was only seventeen, and it was house rules). Renee saved my life then, and she saved my life when I came back from California—broke, full of drugs, and weirded out entirely on Cat Stevens and the whole transient experience.

I went back to Waterford yet again after graduating from high school, intending to transfer to Big University in Normal the following fall semester, but something made me stay at Southwestern City College, someone talked me into it.

I think it was the Dean of Women.

Chapter Eight

(i do well in old houses, in green grasses,
meadows of ocher dandelions,
yellow and purple thistles, waves of green,
a forest's emerald glade
(i seep into stony walls deep inside the
eighteenth century)
people strolled my meadow's paths
stepp'd lightly o'er my soul,
left memories of themselves,
an imprint upon my mind (echoes fill these
musty halls old veins run through the
marble walls, a bathtub crouches upon its
lion claws, i take a bath)
a meadow full of ocher grass the forest's
green a scent of wildest flowers
my house lives within the forest's bounds,
we breathe the meadow's breath
pine trees sigh, winter falls, summer
springs, still i live within these stony walls,
upon the heath (and memories stain my
heart where people once strolled stepping
lightly o'er my soul)

Invoking Center

Back to the future. While walking down that lonely road in northern California to who knows where, I pondered my options. It was January, raining like a monsoon had come to visit California. The driving, pouring, freezing rain wouldn't let up until at least March or April. I couldn't go back to Michael's, because he would probably kill me this time, and I couldn't go back to Lawless because things were just too weird there, and I couldn't stay on this stupid asphalt road any longer, either. I looked like shit, my hair was uncombed and unwashed, my ears hurt, I coughed up green crap a few times, and my hiking boots and guitar were still at Michael's. Sara Teasdale hadn't eaten all day, and I was worried sick.

My two old ranchers weren't home when I went over there, and even though I spent the night on their porch out back, they never showed up. I waited all the next day for them, but by nightfall I knew they were gone for a few days, and I had to make other plans. I had fed Sara from the shed out back where they kept their horse food and cat food (for the five kitties). She always did prefer cat food to dog food for some reason. However, it was night time again, and I didn't feel like staying on the porch another night, wet and cold, sad and defeated. So, I hit upon a plan for my escape.

I decided to go back to San Francisco, and stay with either Leaflet and Sky or Sinbad and Judy. It wasn't easy getting a ride that night, but some bikers picked me up in their old rattle-trap, and since they had a young girl with them, I didn't feel too concerned. As soon as we got rolling, I noticed the vodka bottle being passed around. I also noticed that the young lady was in tight, tight, short-shorts with a leg-cast all the way to her hip, and I figured out that the guys were not belligerent at me, but just belligerent in general. The driver took a long pull from his vodka bottle and asked me, "Where ya headed?" Swerving to miss a car in the other lane, he took another pull off the bottle and handed it to the girl.

She looked at me (we were both in the back seat) with a worried expression, and said, "Look, you don't have to drive like a maniac!" He was doing at least eighty miles per hour on that swervy road, and speeding up every minute.

"Shut up," he snarled. "Oh, all right," he said in a gentler tone.

"Just because we don't care if we live or die doesn't mean she doesn't," the girl added, looking meaningfully at me.

A canary yellow van passed us, demonstrating that we really weren't the craziest drivers on the road, and the other passenger of our little group, who hadn't spoken until now, yelled, "You gonna let that bastard pass us?" Growing redder in the face and trembling, he screamed to the driver, "Let's kill him!"

Oh shit.

The rattle-trap heaved and gave a shuddering 'ho' as it attempted to speed up. Evidently, the men made the decisions in this family. "How did you hurt yourself?" I asked the fresh-faced teenager sitting beside me, who looked as though she should be in junior high. Her light brown eyes gazed at me appraisingly, and I felt she knew too much to be that young. Peach fuzz adorned her cheeks, and her skin was flushed with excitement. We careened on down the highway at least ninety miles per hour. I tried to remain calm with small talk.

"Motorcycle accident," she matter-of-factly replied. Then she yelled to the driver, "Would you fucking slow down?" I had to get out of that car. I decided to come up with a new tactic, because these guys wouldn't just let me out of the car since I didn't like their driving, that was for certain. Hmmm. Serious situations called for serious action. It was time to think fast or die. I had to come up with a diversion that would work on completely drunk, angry bikers. Should I offer pizza like with Vladimer and would they take the bait? Maybe, maybe not. These guys didn't seem too hungry for food. Think like a biker. Hurry!

"Hey guys," I casually asked, as we plummeted up and down mountain roads. "You want some beer?" I tried to look innocent.

"Beer?" the passenger biker said, "Did she say beer?" I knew they were hooked. The driver slammed on his brakes at the next quick stop store, and let me out of the car. I ran into the store, bought a cheap six-pack with my few remaining pennies, and took it to them, careful to guard Sara from running back into the car.

"Here guys," I said, handing over the beer to the driver. His red eyes glared at me and his scraggly face struck terror in my heart. "I'm going to hang around here for a couple of hours."

"You need to get back in the car," warned the long-haired driver. "You're coming with us." His nasty braided mane hung menacingly down the back seat, and I didn't want to know how long it had been since he washed that thing. It looked like a greasy snake.

"I've got some business to take care of," I lied, trying to look serious. The two dudes were probably too drunk to figure me out, but I eased away from the rattle-trap anyway. "Come, Sara." That dog was just too friendly. She was licking the driver's hand, and about to climb back into the back seat of their ride. Only the girl understood me as she gave me a shy glance. Wish I could have taken her out of that car.

"Thought you were going to San Francisco" the driver muttered. He wasn't convinced. I was becoming worried, since I knew that bikers could become dangerous if they were riled, and when they got drunk, they got mean.

"Man, I'm probably going to go tomorrow, all right?" Try to stay calm. "You can enjoy the beer, unless you want to share a few of 'em with me now." Obviously concerned I might want the beer back, the two greasy bikers stuffed their six-pack down at the floor board by their feet, and peeled out. I was relieved to be out of that old junk heap, one less victim of drunken driving. But now I was stuck at a tiny store in Bakersfield, late at night, with no money and no wheels. Back in those days, I didn't exactly know my way around Callie, or I wouldn't be headed south.

I started walking. Pretty soon this guy pulls up alongside of me, and asks, "Where ya' goin' Mama?" He was a black guy, and he looked just like a Chicago pimp to me, with his diamond studded rings and his numerous gold chains. I didn't think I needed a ride with him, especially after dealing with the bikers. I continued walking. "Oh, Mama, whatcho 'fraid of, me?" He continued to slowly drive by my side, eyeing me on the sly, checking out my bod. How disgusting men are! I decided to speak.

"Look, I don't need a ride, I'm just walking, see?" I didn't notice that I was walking into the worst part of town, and I didn't know the history of sex slayings in Bakersfield; to me, it was just another California town.

"Honey, I know you ain't no hoe, and you prolly know I'm a pimp, but you jus' cain walk out here at this time a night." He looked me square in the eye, and I believed him. Black people have always been cool to me, anyway.

"So, what do you have in mind?" I asked him, still not getting into his pimpmobile.

"Take you home to my sistuh's crib where you cain stay the night." He drove at two miles per hour, keeping up with my stolid steps. I began to slow down, and finally stopped. No bad vibes, no nervous gut instinct telling me not to. I got into his car and we drove away. Sara went to sleep in the back seat. He handed me a joint.

"My name's Bo, and yours?" he asked.

"Gabrielle. Thanks for helping me out tonight." Toke, toke, smoke, smoke. His air freshener dangled from the fur-lined roof of

123

the car, giving off manufactured fumes of jasmine and something else I couldn't identify. It smelled like bathroom but at least he didn't have cockroaches in his car and the vibe remained cool.

"You see, Gabrielle, I can recognize good people when I see them, even though I worship the pimp god." He was serious as a heart attack. Pimp god? Uh oh, psychic check. Did the good vibe just change and go negatory? Nope, still cool. Shew! What a relief.

"What's his name, your pimp god?" I asked, curious at this latest deviation from fundamentalism.

"Belzebubba," he answered.

Now that's funny!

We pulled into the driveway of a tiny frame house on the outskirts of town, and went into the house. It was, by this time, three o'clock in the morning. We finished our joint with his sister, Chaffondra, and I said good-night to the good pimp who helped me out without a doubt. Chaffondra fixed me a quilt on her couch, and before I went to sleep, I asked her, "Is he really a pimp?" She fluffed my pillow, her dreadlocks hanging down onto my face. Chaffondra smelled warm and musky.

"Honey, he been a pimp since I was three years old." She looked at me for a moment, then quietly said, "But he always help his own." And she went into her bedroom, closing the door softly behind her. I was his 'own'? I felt proud all of a sudden to be the friends of these poor people, who could trust at a glance and relied on gut instinct to survive. They took a chance with me, and that's what mattered. Sara curled up on the floor by my feet, chewing the bone Chaffondra had kindly provided her, and we went to sleep, safe and sound for another day. For those of you faithful readers who have made it this far in the book and are wondering which parts of my story are fiction and which parts are autobiographical, here's a hint. Anytime someone does something nice for me, it's true. Anytime someone tries to do something bad to me, it's true.

I didn't know it at the time, but Sara's days were numbered. My friend, my confidante, my protectress. She was doomed from the very beginning. When I first rescued Sara Teasdale from a life of ticks and claustrophobia (she was locked into a duplex I rented, abandoned by her previous owners) in Lawless during my second sojourn back, before I disappeared into California, I knew I had found a devoted dog. She followed me everywhere, and ate whatever I fed her.

I first found my sweet puppy dog in Oklahoma when I was freshly dropped out of college and needed some animal company. After her initial de-ticking, I bathed Sara only every two months. During that first week, she had so many bloodsuckers on her that I had to keep the Paramite dip in one hand and her collar in the other. Needless to say, Sara appreciated my ministrations. But, she was doomed from the beginning. I wished she'd never followed me to Miami, Florida during the year of the pimp god, when I could have gone to San Francisco, as initially planned.

There we stood, in the pouring rain, on a freeway ramp outside of Bakersfield, and I should have known better than to take off out of town with that cute truck driver, but you know me, what the hell. It was a free ride, and I was sick of hanging around, getting little rides to the next little town. Sara was too. Naturally, within a day or two, the kind-hearted, sweet, talkative trucker realized that I wasn't interested in his THANG, so he decided not to bring me back to California as originally planned. We had made a deal: I was to keep him awake for the straight-to-Chicago-strictly-illegal run, and he was to return me to Northern California, in the immediate vicinity of San Francisco. I got a free ride out of the rain, he got a little female company (but that's all he got).

No go. It was either do his thing for him or get out of the truck.

Sara and I found ourselves dumped at a lousy truck stop, right outside of Chicago in the pouring rain. It wasn't exactly what I had planned for that day. So, we were not only wet, we were totally freezing and if something didn't give, we were gonna get pneumonia! And, on top of that, it was dangerous out here in the middle of the midwest for folks like us. No hippies anywhere.

My life was charmed, again, and even in Illinois, I had great luck with guys. Is it my tits? C'mon guys, tell the truth, it's that mammary fixation hard at work on your testosterone levels. Okay, so I shouldn't stereotype men, but I really couldn't help it, even male dogs were tracking Sara down, coming out of nowhere to hump her poor little bones. My poor queenie dog was in heat and it was cold and rainy and I was stuck somewhere outside of Chicago, a place I swore I'd never visit again. Thank the Lord and the

125

Goddess, someone noticed my plight. Sure enough, this gallant came out and talked to me, said hiya, gave me his gloves, putting them on my freezing hands, and lulled me back into the truck stop, where it was warmer, if not friendlier, than the freeway ramp where I had been hanging my thumb in the air. People gave us dirty looks as I took a biscuit to the dripping Sara, who was skulking on the porch, whining to come in and be treated with humanity, not neglect. Ah, if only dogs could talk, but would we even listen? The guy's name was Robert Faulkner, and he didn't even stare at my tits (what a change). I was soaked through and through, but still I sat at this lousy, grimy truckstop full of conservatives who didn't like hippie chicks or rainbow girls.

I was clearly out of my element. Robert the gallant intently gazed into my eyes, and said, "So." Looked me up and down. "How about I rent you a room at this place, huh?" Robert, a youngish forty-something, was the least threatening male I had run into lately, and it was a relief, no doubt, but was he sincere? Sure he was.

"You mean, you want to rent me a room for myself?" I asked, still a tiny bit incredulous, but ready to take the room.

He dug in his pocket, pulled out a twenty, and said, "You rent it." And continued to eat his large chef salad, of which I was also indulging, my own, of course. I liked the guy. He seemed like a philanthropist, my kind of man. But was he sincere? Sure he was.

"So, where do you stay, anyway?" Munch munch, crunch crunch. Sara whined outside, I took her another biscuit. Fuck those conservatives who stared disapprovingly.

"Nowhere in particular right now," I said.

Robert gestured with his left hand, his mouth full of lettuce and cheese, and said, "I got a room with another guy I picked up yesterday. He's from Baahhssttoonn...." Correctly serious East Coast accent required to fully convey the voice of Tom, whom I soon met.

"Oh yeah?" I said, not really interested in anything but my salad. Tom really did talk that way, too. He said things like, "We yoused to play whiffah bahhl out inna paahhking lot...." A real yank. But was Robert on the make, I wondered? Was he planning to get a key to my room and enter in at night while I'm hitting the deepest ZZZ's and dreaming about my fantasy life as a famous rock musician, unprepared for the priapic thrust that he has waiting in his trousers for me? I thought not.

"Look," Robert informed me, "I know you're wondering why I would help you out. I just like to do stuff like that." He was emphatic. Was he for real? He chewed some more of his huge chef's salad with ranch dressing and said, "Would I let you rent the room if I planned to bother you later?" I was wondering the same thing, so I admitted it.

"Well, it's just that I get all these promises from guys all the time, and they always want to fuck me or something." If I was anything, I was blunt, because I hated beating around the proverbial bush, especially my bush, and that was the bush in question at the moment.

Robert was completely understanding, and he slipped me another twenty as I chomped on my vegetarian chef's salad with cheddar cheese and salsa instead of dressing. Trying to lose a few pounds, as usual. He cajoled me. "Now take this twenty, and go buy yourself some gloves in the gift shop. You look cold." More money? I stopped chewing for a moment to accept the twenty. He winked at me, got up to pay the check, and waved from the cash register. "Will you drop by in the morning to visit me? I'm in room 121 with Thomas, from Boston, you know." He lisped, then dropped his hand like a wilting flower. Was he gay?

One thing about me in those days, I never turned down money. Why? Because I was a transient, broke, destitute, miserable, and crazy. I rented a room, took my puppy dog upstairs, and after cleaning up, we collapsed on the bed. For a good night's sleep, take some cold rain and then cover it up with a hot shower, followed by a warm blanket, dry sheets and a clean mattress in a locked room with your guard dog. There you have it. Unless you've been without all of the above for long periods of time, you may not understand just how good it feels to be clean and safe. Next morning, I knocked on room 121's door, and this short, wiry, dark-haired guy in his early twenties or late teens answered the door. He was not even surprised to see me. "Come on in, join the party." He opened the door, and I entered. There sat Robert, calm as can be, relaxing after a hard night, I imagined.

127

"Like to come with us to Florida?" he asked.

"What's in Florida?" I asked, thinking it's got to be better than a cheap truck stop at this forsaken place.

"My parents live there and we can take a plane from O'Hare in Chicago." Noticing my somewhat skeptical look, he added, "First class." Was he kidding? Was I to be kidnapped in the guise of first class, and enslaved to some man's slathering lust? I was tempted, sorely tempted, to say no. I really was. Common sense ruled in this case.

"Florida huh?" Scratched my head a bit in wonder. "Can I take my dog?" He nodded his head, and Thomas sat down next to him and looked up at me.

Thomas was used to this, evidently, because he said, "I'm going too."

"You are?" I asked.

"What else is there to do?" He scratched his head and crossed his eyes, giving me the "duh" look.

"Yeah, I guess you got a point there," I said. "Robert, do you mind taking all of us? It's kind of expensive, isn't it?" I knew it was.

"Money is no object, my dear," he answered. Thomas walked to the window and looked out at the cold, drizzly, grey, damp day, and we both agreed. Florida was better than hitchhiking in that weather. I had one last wish, however, and it should be addressed.

"You know," I said to Robert, "I really want to get back to California soon, could we somehow bring that into the itinerary?" He nodded, like the wise sage he was.

"You'll get back to California, don't worry. I'll help you." And with that, I joined up with the two others in an adventure that took us to the airport in Tampa, Florida, where Robert's mom and pop were waiting for us. Not with open arms, though. Mom looked downright pissed, in fact. Oh great. Another mad Mom.

"I'm sorry, but we don't have room at the house for your... guests (shudder, shudder)." She squirmed under her lavender-rinsed bouffant, and glittering silver dress. She was a vision in retirement home conservatism, and she probably voted for Reagan.

"Then I'm not coming home!" Robert pouted like a bad boy, even though he was in his middle age. I wondered about him, but shrugged it off. Naah. We did get his car, though, a TR-7 that looked like a sort of Fiat Spider, and hauled ass to the nearest Holiday Inn, where we promptly set up house as long as Rob's cash held out. He was our sugar daddy, and we were his baby boy and little girl. Really.

"Rob, will you bring me back a Mountain Dew and some potato chips?" I asked, reclining on the bed, queenly in my repose of one week, fat off the land in Florida, kept for no other reason than because I existed.

Rob, grocery list in his hand, added my latest request to it with no hassle at all, and answered, "Need anything else, Gabby? How about you, Tom?" We looked at each other, looked at Tom who was on the other twin bed watching t.v., and waved goodbye, as he left on yet another excursion to provide sustenance for his kids. Tom lit up a joint, and toked on it, handing it to me.

"I wonder how long old Rob's gonna be able to support us," Tom asked me as we sat there smoking. He shook his curly locks, took a long, deep drag of the fabulous dope Rob had acquired for our little habit, and sighed, "He's going broke, you know."

"I want to know why he's taking care of us," I said, ever the suspicious one, never the trusting fool. "He doesn't even know us, and he's like, buying us dope!" Anyone who bought me dope was all right with me, as long as they didn't want to take it out in trade at a later date, that is.

"You know, he goes to those strip joints at night, then crashes at some lady's house," Tom observed. He looked at me, I passed him the joint, and he continued to explain things to me I didn't understand, but accepted.

"That doesn't surprise me," I said. Tom looked at me thoughtfully.

"Rob says when he finally goes broke he doesn't want you hitchhiking anymore." Well, that's a nice thought, but who can stop a transient from continuing her journey?

"Yeah, well, I got to go back to California and seek my fortune, you know what I mean?" I yawned and stretched my lazy limbs, content as a kitten sucking on a tit, I was. "So, as I was saying, Rob told me that he wants you to have his car," said Tom, ever the practical one. And then he dangled the keys in front of me, the keys to the little jet engine racing machine, the little yellow sportster with the five speed transmission and the temperamental engine (it had already broken down on Rob twice in one week).

"That's pretty fucking nice of the old man, I must say." Previous attempts to watch my weight entirely forgotten, I grabbed a potato chip and sipped my last Mountain Dew. Drank way too much of that stuff in those fatter days. "But I really can't take his car, Tom, you know that." I looked meaningfully at the clock. It was getting late, way past my bedtime, and I was used to getting my finally uninterrupted beauty sleep, the deep, trusting sleep of the wicked.

"Well, the bad news is, we have to be out of here by noon tomorrow." Resignation all over his youthful face, Thomas sighed those big sighs that signify the end of beautiful things. Our idyll was over. It figured.

"Well, are you sure he wants me to have the car?" I couldn't believe it, but maybe if I tried real hard, things would become clearer.

"I swear, he wants you to have it, he loves you," said my temporary partner in transience. Thomas didn't love me like Robert did, but I didn't care who loved whom. As long as nobody touched me, everything was cool. I made a monumental decision, I decided to take the car.

"Let's get some shut eye, and we'll leave in the morning," I said, yawning. "I take it you are coming with me?" Please say no.

"Of course," Thomas answered, as he flicked off the light and turned off the tv.

Of course.

But my puppy dog got killed because we took the stupid car which promptly broke down in Miami in the middle of the night, and I wrote a note to his parents and stuck it on the windshield, then set out with Sara at my heels, as always, but she was pregnant, and I think she committed suicide, because as I watched her linger at the shoulder of that monstrosity highway of five or six or seven lanes, Sara looked me in the eye as I frantically called her, and calmly stepped out into the middle of the oncoming traffic.

In Miami, Florida. Late at night. My poor puppy dog met her death. She yelped as the first truck or car hit her, then yelped in the middle of the road, hit by the first one but not finished, she yelped one last time as the next auto didn't even fucking swerve to miss her, the dog I loved, my best friend in the world, the puppy dog who followed me to this horrible inhumane place in Florida at the stroke of midnight on a Friday night.

My dog was killed. I was without her love forever. I miss my Sara Teasdale puppy dog, even today, many dogs later, I miss my Sara dog. She was my little dog mistress friend.

I began to fear for my own life as cars came close at the speed of light and made my clothes ripple from the force of their passing. It was so dangerous and scary out there that I couldn't even cry yet for Sara, my shepherd mix, my little minx, my animal child. God I hate to remember this part of my story, even for editing which is the darkside of writing that readers never see. It's so freaking sad seeing Sara dog in my mind's eye, dying in front of me on that horrible, lifeless highway.

We finally got off the autobahn death strip, where only machines can survive, and went to the lobby of this hotel to hang out. I was so unhappy, I don't think I had ever been that unhappy. I was the same girl who ran away from home for the first time just because her mom threatened to give away a foundling mutt. Wanting to sob and sob, numb to the reality, but feeling its awful loneliness fill my heart, I still had to get the hell out of that hole, Miami. I put thoughts of my little minx out of mind in order to accomplish my task, in order to return to California. I tried not to think of Sara Teasdale's dog smile, her puppy laugh, the way she always preferred cat food, the way she minced after me on the highways.

I tried not to think about her face as she stepped out into the path of a semi-truck, and her screams filled my mind as I tried not to think of her lying crippled on the highway, waiting for the next truck to finish her off. I tried not to contemplate the fact that it was too dangerous or I would have ran onto the multi-lane freeway and captured her before she was hit again and her screams subsided and she was Sara Teasdale no more. I tried not to think of all her baby puppies lying there on the busy freeway, squashed to infinity, melted into a bloody mess that once was my Sara Teasdale and her babies.

I tried not to think at all.

131

Thomas stuck to me like glue all the way back to California. In retrospect, even though I couldn't stand him, his company was probably better than being alone after the death of my true companion. Sarah had been with me since I left Oklahoma, and with her around I was never alone. This was my first time out on the cold, dead road by myself. Tom could not be shaken. I quickly got tired of his yankee self his disregard for all things beautiful, and his sullen attitude at everything around us, but still he would not go away, or back to Boston, or anywhere but with me.

Fine.

We actually made it to the very steps of my old rancher couple who lived in Cloverdale, on the road to Healdsburg, and I knocked at the door, hoping against all hope that they were home on this long, cold, winter night. I was bone-tired, soul-shaken and driven to their doorstep to be comforted by old people who liked me, and taken into the warm house where I could experience at least for a moment the feeling of family, the feeling of having a home I craved like a junkie craves drugs.

They were home.

I left poor Thomas on the porch and hoped he would go away. After banging on the front door for a while, he finally realized he had been dumped, and went away. Back to Boston, I suppose. I went into the bedroom they gave me, and fell asleep, tears of sadness rolling in lakes and oceans down my face, down my shirt, down onto the bed for one night. I cried for my dog, for my home, for my need to find out who I was, for my lost cause of Cat Stevens, for my lost family life, for my lost, lonesome self. I was a real whiner.

Next morning it was time to go, because Martha headed off to the bar, wanting me to go with her to drink, but I declined, and sadly went my own way. But which way was my way, anyway? I was the last person to know in this case, and I simply pointed my little thumb toward San Francisco. Even though I had passed there with Thomas, I didn't want to take him to Leaflet's place, which was where I was headed. After the long horrendous side trip to Chicago and Florida, I finally made it to the great city by the bay, only to find my previous life with the ladies I loved had disappeared, leaving disillusionment in its stead.

132

I knocked on the door of our old frame house, hoping to find my friends of yesteryear, and a strange man answered, reeking of ganja, and looking like something your dog might drag in, if you had a dog which I no longer did. I asked for Leaflet, or Sky, or Ambrosia, and wondered why they would even allow a male to darken their doorstep, much less answer their faded, feminist door.

"Are any of the ladies home?" I inquired politely, figuring he would know who I meant because Leaflet's van with the vanity plates was parked by the old white picket fence out front. It couldn't be all bad if she was still around. Or could it?

"Yeah, she's in the back room," he drawled. "Who should I say is here?" He looked me over with a leer I had come to recognize- taking in my tattered appearance, my tits and my crotch all in one, raking glance.

This was old, old hat to me, and I glared at him, saying, "Just tell her Gabrielle is here, all right?" You dumb butt, you smell like a bed of freshly manured roses without their bloom. I stomped around on the porch impatiently, until Leaflet came running out and scooped me up in her arms, the Leaflet way.

"Gabrielle!" she exclaimed in her typical blunt way. "You look awful, what happened?" Without much prompting, she figured out what I had been doing for the last five months was bumming around, broke, disheartened and lonely. Sleeping on park benches, pan-handling with the big boys on Fourth Avenue, and taking drugs. Yep, that was me all right, you've got me pegged, Dr. Leaf. I didn't waste time with small talk, and deftly avoided her question.

"Who's the dude, huh?" Grimacing with awful thoughts, I asked her the fatal question.

"Darrell," she said in a low voice. "My boyfriend." Leaflet shyly smiled at me.

I was wondering about that. "Does he, like, live here or what?"

No. Tell me it's not true. You've got to be kidding, aren't you?

"Yeah," she said. "He lives here." She wanted to say more, I could tell. Great sex with Darrell was written all over her face.

"So, you like men now?" I asked, still incredulous.

"Oh, that feminist stuff was all because of Sky, you know."

"Sky?" I asked, too startled to say anything else.

"And I quit my private practice, too," whispered Leaflet into my ear. "We've got very lucrative business now." She smiled at the oaf who stood listening. Yech. He reminded me of Bubba, Alishia's boyfriend. She was a professional who should know better. He was sicker than any case I had ever seen come through her door before.

"You what?" I almost yelled. "How could you? It was so successful!" The oaf ambled off into the house, while we stood on the front porch. I had lost any previous desire to enter my old home on Christopher Street. Not like I ever really had a home anyway.

"We've got a nice private business going." Leaflet winked and drew me close to her, close enough to feel her warm breath on my cheek.

"Leaf, I thought you abhorred men, and he is really a creep. You have a business with that guy?" I was totally incredulous, I was appalled, but the worst was yet to come. Leaflet smiled her bad naughty girl smirk, and I smelled fish, big fish, an ocean of fishiness.

"Don't tell anyone, but we've got a lucrative drug business." Leaflet pointed to the room where he lurked, counting his dollars, I'm sure. "We sell pounds now."

Total shocked silence.

"Leaflet, I just can't believe this," I finally mumbled. "It's ridiculous for someone as intelligent, as feminist, as lesbian as you are to go into business with a man, and to actually sell dope?" I decided to leave very soon, as the dope dealer in question came tromping back onto the porch, a cigarette hanging out of his lower lip, a nonchalant challenge lurking in his eyes... he looked at me, I looked at him, and I knew what was coming before he said anything.

"You're kind a cute, what with all the dykes around." He pinched Leaflet's shoulder, and she looked at him adoringly... this was too sickening for mere words, and I wanted to puke. But then I finally got some good news.

"Gabrielle, you'll never guess who's back in the state!" Leaflet had her typical gleam, and I was, by now, ready for new news. I could believe just about anything after the initial shock waves wore off and my brain began to function again. It was time for some good vibrations.

"What, tell me anything," I said.

"Swansdown's living in Mendocino."

Yes, yes, yes! That's what I wanted to hear, about my old ways and my old, happy life, and the times I had with these crazy women, and the home I used to live in, and the bed I used to sleep soundly in every night, curled up tightly like a kitten, like a safe girl getting some good ZZZs.

"Leaf, that's tremendous, how is she, is she...?" I stopped as she shook her head, and suddenly my bubble burst. Things were not that great after all. Leaflet said,

"Swan doesn't want to see any of us, Gabrielle." She looked slightly uncomfortable. "Especially you."

"Me?" I asked. "Why not me?"

"You remind her of the old life, and she can't be the same person she was with you." Leaf looked downright depressed, and the lunk just stood there beside her, dumbfounded and confused. He drifted back into his room to pick seeds out of his stash, I imagine.

"That's not a good enough reason," I said.

"It's how she feels, evidently," sighed Leaflet.

"But why?" I wondered, why wouldn't Swansong want me back? "Couldn't I talk her into at least seeing me?" Leaf shook her head again, and I decided then and there that she was totally wrong about Swan.

"I'm going to Mendocino, Leaf, could you give me her address?"

Leaf glared at me and stalked into the kitchen to get her address book by the phone, obviously miffed that I wouldn't take her word for it. How could I, she was a dope dealer now, not a shrink. And she was educated, even. She went from a promiscuous, educated psychologist lesbian to a dope dealing, probably just as promiscuous heterosexual, and where in the hell was Sky, for that matter? "You'll only make her mad," Leaflet muttered as she dug in her kitchen drawers for the scrap of paper with Swansong's address on it.

"Where's the lady of your life, Leaf?" I inquired. "I don't see her stuff around anywhere, did she split?" We all know she did, but I was just asking for the record.

135

"Yeah, she moved out about a month ago when Dale moved in with me. Leaflet handed me a scrap of paper with Swan's address and phone scribbled on it. We solemnly shook hands, and I departed the house, never to return, always to remember the good times we once had together. Sigh. Things sure did seem to keep changing a lot, and I kept burning all kinds of bridges behind me. Oh well, enough worrying, I was off to Mendocino.

It was only a few hundred miles away.

Surely I could find it.

I forgot about my city hitching luck, it ran out very often at all the wrong times, and this was one of them. I couldn't for the life of me get out of San Francisco. I called Berkeley to look up Sinbad and Judy, but they had left no forwarding address in the flop house they once inhabited. None of the familiar street kids were turning any tricks that night; it was dark outside, and I was getting scared. I walked very fast along the sidewalks, up and down streets, trying to find my way around downtown.

All the businessmen and women had gone home, it was nasty and muggy, and a man howled at the moon, freaking me out of my revery, making me retrace my steps back to a bush. I hid there for a few seconds, pondering my next move. Was I to be squashed by the great foot of destiny before I made my mark upon the world? Was I to become mincemeat in the grinder of modern crime? Was I to be discovered in the ocean, my torn and bleeding body raped and mutilated beyond recognition by some madman in a parking lot?

I squirmed around San Francisco all night and into the dawn. I watched sailboarders and surfers dig out their wet suits in the morning sun and hit the water, while I sat on the Golden Gate Bridge, on the way to Sausalito, on the way to Mendocino. I had survived another hair-raising evening; with no bed to sleep safely in, I found a park bathroom and took a fitful nap. I had awakened to the day, and went to the bridge where I now sat, gazing below me into the sea where people who had homes to live in sailed their crafts in the mighty surf and spray. I felt like I was nothing, but I didn't jump off the bridge, or even think about it. I was full of juice for life. I had no suicidal thoughts in California, although it seemed as though I acted in a suicidal manner, what with my weird lifestyle, and all. The suicidal thoughts would come, though, just give them a little more time.

These young guys in a worn out, beat up Impala picked me up and said they were going to Carmel. Sure, I'll go. Is that on the way to Mendocino? I really didn't know much about how to take directions, or to get where I started out towards. If I did, I would have gone to Seattle, Washington, not Venice Beach, California, because that was my original plan back in '79.

Seattle, not Venice Beach.

Not California at all.

Chapter Nine

lonely hearts, wish me well,
i am lost in my faerie tale
peep into this looking glass,
roll me on the long green grass
flow'r, bloom me like a rose,
tingle, tickle me to my toes
O flow'r, scent of midnight dew,
do me, do me like you do
petals drop onto the ground,
roses, daisies all around,
chamomile, peppermint, hyacinth too,
O clover, clover, daffodil you,
touch and turn and swoop and sweep,
i'll grab and hold and never keep you
cos all flow'rs shouldn't die,
for who else would sing a lullabye?
little flow'rs, loosen your scent,
i know you are heaven sent
spirits of a botanist' dream,
how very fragile flow'rs seem
baby animals in their wood,
prick their ears to listen good
as you sing your lullabies,
they settle in, and close their eyes
good-night!

Invoking the Goddess

The two guys I linked up with, Joseph and Larry, were into having a good time, and scoping out the area for freebies. "So, where ya headed?" Joseph had asked as I ran toward their car. "We're just kinda out cruisin'."

"As long as you're going north," I said, panting from the short run, "I could use a ride." I got in and we drove away, checking out the scenery and enjoying the day as very young people will. None of us had a care in the world, especially me. I thought I was protected by God, and on a mission to find Cat Stevens, so I seldom concerned myself with such mundane ideas as 'getting kidnapped,' and 'being raped' unless I was in the middle of some life threatening drama. No, it will never happen to me, I surmised, because I'm blessed and probably psychic. Too bad I never read the papers back in early '79 while I was busy avoiding Vladimir, because then I would have been a bit more informed about the wonderland I called home, and the roads I traveled alone. Maybe I would have realized the danger and error of my transient, careless ways. During the time I was traveling around California, between 1979-1980, a young girl of twenty, Colleen Stan, was being held captive by Cameron Hooker and his wife, Janice, in Red Bluff, California.

She could have been me.

Colleen had been hitchhiking from Eugene, Oregon to Westwood, California on May 19, 1977, and was abducted by the two innocuous people on Interstate 5, near Red Bluff. After being blindfolded and gagged, she was taken to Cameron's basement where he stripped her, hung her by her arms, raped her, forced her to wear a 'head box' weighing twenty pounds on her head, and kept her prisoner for the next seven years.

Strangely enough, no one in Red Bluff noticed anything unusual going on at the Hooker house on 1140 Oak Street, for Colleen's screams were stifled with a gag, and Janice Hooker, a young mother of one, enjoyed the escape from Cameron's tortures. Janice watched Colleen suffer indignity and humiliation, only glad she was no longer Cameron's sex slave herself.

Colleen was brainwashed and convinced she was a slave within a year of living in a box in Cameron's basement, and he could train her to do as he wished. This often involved sexual favors, which finally got Janice to testify against him seven years later, for her jealousy knew no limits. Finally, in 1985, Cameron was convicted and sentenced to one hundred and four years in prison. The presiding Judge Clarence B.Knight said, "I consider this defendant the most dangerous psychopath that I have ever dealt with, in that he is the opposite of what he seems. He will be a danger to women as long as he is alive, and I intend to sentence the maximum possible." (*Perfect Victim*, McGuire and Norton)

And to think that I was hitchhiking with anyone and everyone while Cameron Hooker was on the loose and torturing Colleen Stan. No wonder Mom worried.

139

When we got to Carmel, the guys immediately took me to an art gallery where they knew some lady, and scored us some grass, good grass. We wandered on down the boulevard that was Main Street, a beautiful place to visit if you have money, and stopped at a Salvation Army outreach office to get some sandwiches. After munching down on our turkey, lettuce, tomato and mayonnaise on whole wheat (I gave the guys my turkey), we drove on to a park they knew about, and crashed out in the bathrooms for the night.

Not exactly the Carlton, but at least I wasn't all alone, and these two were too young and innocent to attempt to gangbang me. Actually, they had more excitement in more towns than they needed already. I thought they were heterosexual, because they looked like any other young boys, but they happened to be gay, and lovers with each other, hence, the non-threat to me.

Next morning, we drove to Santa Cruz where we promptly filled out some welfare forms for free bags of groceries, and headed for the campus to hang out and eat. Things like this went on and on, as we scavenged through town after town, looking for food, dope and money. I decided to split one morning after breakfast while we were lying on the beach at Monterey, because the boys decided to go big time and rip off a truck parked behind the local Buy-for-More supermarket. I couldn't involve myself in such things as theft, and tried to talk my companions of over two weeks out of their plan.

"Are you sure you want to steal food?" I inquired of Larry, the sandy haired, blue eyed, slim and trim seventeen-year-old who was sitting to my right, stuffing his face as usual. He gave me a withering look. I was fixing a sandwich myself, and planned to stuff my face as well.

"Gabrielle, we have to," he said. "We've run out of scams." He pointed toward the car. "See that car? It doesn't run on pure air, it needs gas." I still didn't get it.

"Surely there's a better way, Larry."

"If we get the goods we can sell them to some people in another town," Larry explained, obviously losing patience. "And therefore we solve all our problems." His partner Joseph, an older man of nineteen, was more on my side, and agreed that theft was unwise, but went along with Larry just the same.

140

"Yeah, Gabby, we gotta get some money because if Larry says we need gas, we need gas." The darkly complected, baby-faced Joseph was subservient, and not very intelligent. Larry would go a long way in crime, because he already had the makings of a shifty-eyed weasel face.

"But Jo, you told me it wasn't a good idea this morning," I griped. "Now you're switching around." I stopped eating the pita sandwich I had made with cream cheese, tomatoes, lettuce, garlic and red peppers. My appetite had quite disappeared.

"I don't want to get caught anymore than you do, but if we have to do this, we have to." He looked expectantly at his lover, hoping for a pat on the head. Larry put his arm around him and licked his earlobe, causing Joseph to positively swoon with happiness. Who needs a dog when you've got a femme?

"Well guys," I said, tossing my leftover sandwich into the trees for the 'coons to eat, "I can't do it, sorry." I looked them over, the two villains to be, dressed alike in purple jeans with button flies, green silk shirts open at the neck to reveal their delicate adams apples, black high top tennis shoes adorning their tootsies. My defection would not be allowed, I was soon to discover, and Larry got irate and irrational.

"You will do as I say as long as you live with us!" he yelled. Larry glared at me and stood up, the better to menace his captive audience of two (trying to impress Joseph).

"Oh yeah?" I snorted, surprised but not frightened. "You got an army to make me?" Standing up, I strolled over to get my backpack. I was heavier and meaner than Larry, and he knew it, although he was the sneakiest.

"No show, no go," he said. That meant, I think, that I had to resume hitchhiking. It was better than going to jail, and besides, I didn't want to mess up my karma by stealing. It was against my religion, and my code of ethics; it still is. I moseyed over to where he stood, the better to menace Larry back. He sat back down, still munching some Twinkies or something, and gave me the evil eye.

"Look, dude, I don't care about hanging with a den of thieves, and I at least tried to talk you out of this idea of yours." I paced along the beach, preparing my speech.

141

"Just fuck off, bitch," Larry snarled, to Joseph's dismay. I didn't really want to fight, so I let the snide remark pass. I kind of liked the two guys, after all.

"We don't have to do this, you know, we could panhandle the money, or something." I was depressed, and didn't want to be alone anymore, so I attempted to reason with him, to dissuade him. He didn't like it one bit.

"Get away from us, you female fool." (Reverse feminism.) "We don't want any women around, anyway, right Joseph?" Expecting an affirmative, Larry jabbed Joseph with his index finger. "Well?"

"But I like Gabrielle," Joseph sheepishly squeaked. "Can't we keep her around?" His brown eyes implored me to go easy with Larry, and not make a scene, but I didn't care to stay and steal, I just wanted to stay and not steal, scavenging as we had been, getting by with my two friends.

"No, she goes, or I do." Larry played his final trump, and I lost that game to a joker. I packed up my very, very few belongings, and headed out to the road, the highway to my future.

"Bye Joseph," I mumbled.

"Bye Gabby," he mumbled back. We touched hands as I walked away. Wasn't I planning to go to Mendocino anyway?

I made it to the freeway and got a ride with some lady truck drivers who worked for the food co-op located in Fayetteville, Arkansas, right smack in the middle of the Ozark Mountains. I would have gone back there with them if they'd invited me, but they took me somewhere far better, it turned out.

The driver, a gorgeous woman who wore a scarlet and black-checked work shirt, with faded black Levis jeans and Vasque hiking boots asked me, "Where you headed, Lady?" Looking me in the eye, she smiled.

"Uh, where ya'll headed?" I asked, sheepishly. "North?"

"Welcome to the world," she answered, opening her door for me. "Honey, you look all plumb-tuckered out." She turned to her partner, and they exchanged looks that seemed to say, 'What should we do with this one?' I hunkered in on the right side of the front seat, while Keisha, the passenger, climbed into the comfy camper covered in Persian tapestries. She was dressed in overalls and a tank top, and looked like her pectorals and biceps did some heavy lifting. I thought they were both very attractive, but I was just a street bum, wearing tattered rags. How embarrassing to be unclothed and unwashed in the presence of these two lesbian women, who wore their bodies for clothing, at home in themselves like wild, young animals in their lair.

"I'm, uh, going to Mendocino to look up a friend of mine," I said meekly. "I've kind of been bumming around the countryside, checking out the ocean." Come up with a reason, you idiot! I cursed myself for looking so stupid in front of the athletic couple, but couldn't for the life of me give them a good enough sounding excuse for the life I led, the bummery I did. Keisha and Violet didn't let it bother them, or hid it from me so as not to hurt my transient feelings, and the class consciousness issue was never raised. Even though our lives were totally different, I think they didn't care what I did, for they looked deep into the spirit inside, and realized I wasn't in my right mind.

"You need a ride to Mendocino, right?"

"Yeah, that would be fantastic," I said. Violet drove on, picking up speed as she rolled on up to the next U-turn on the road, and turned around, heading north up Highway One, north to the redwoods and the black ebony headlands, north towards the Oregon coast, the Pacific Northwest, the ocean of my dreams. The Land of Oz. The home of Swansong and River, Tarah and Betsy Albionacious, Alternative High Schools for Pat Benatar lookalikes and salmon and abalone fisherfolk. The fork of the Russian River.

"But you weren't going that way," I implored, "Don't go out of your way for me!"

"No problem, Sweetie." Violet turned to Keisha, who looked back at her partner, her loving friend, the woman she worked and lived with, the nighttime confidante she wrote poetry to and took for long walks on the beach. I wistfully dreamt of their life together, gathering the tattered morsels of my own.

"As far as I'm concerned," Keisha said, "We were heading that way anyway." She shrugged. "Besides, I haven't been to Mendo for at least a year." Squeezing her lady's thigh, Keisha contentedly sighed. "We need a vacation, after hauling that last load of oats, rice and wheat berries."

143

"I never knew people could eat so many wheatberries," Violet mused, swerving to miss another semi that strayed too far into our narrow lane. Highway One is a twisty, two-lane road, but the coastal scenery is awesome.

"You'd think they'd sprout corn," Keisha commented. The conversation was really tripping me out, and I had to know what wheatberries were, and why they should sprout corn.

"What sprouts corn?" I asked. "Wheatberries?" They both cracked up, and naturally, I did too. Violet was the first to contain herself, and stopped laughing long enough to speak and avoid swerving into that huge redwood tree over there.

"People eat a lot of wheatberries in the north, and they sprout them for wheatgrass, which they juice." She breathed warm laughter over me one last time, her eyes twinkling. "Still confused?"

"Oh, you mean they drink it?" I asked, beginning to get the drift. "They drink wheatgrass juice?" Keisha gave me a quick hug, which I had been needing for days.

"You got it," she laughed.

So, I got a ride with two very cool women, and felt very happy to be back in the women's community, where tits and ass weren't necessarily a bargaining commodity in the search for one's next ride. Women usually don't sexually intimidate or rape other women as a rule, and I slept peacefully that night, in the back of the semi where they had stowed their sleeping bags and other gear, like hammocks.

As I lay dreaming in Violet's sleeping bag (she climbed in with Keisha), my subconscious mind began to play tricks on me. White poneys began to dance at my eyelids, dreaming up ways to seduce me with their power, their power to predict the future. I woke up with a start, and missed that white poney who had lov'd me so, he lov'd me so, and protected me, he did, O yes, my white poney, just for me. Shaking my head again, I felt in a Chaucerian trance, as Middle English kept creeping into my speech patterns and making me dream in verse.

I couldn't quite figure out how my white horse had captivated me, but it felt so good and so safe I accepted it as an omen of good future times, and fell back to sleep, dreaming of green pastures and mountain tops, crested with snow. I dreamed I was in a castle by the sea, surrounded by black rocks ebony faire, and the sea's aqua and emerald waves crashed at the bottom of my cliff, but I was only touched with the ocean's spray. Fog surrounded me and the surf leapt higher and higher and suddenly, I was in the water, dropping down, lower and lower to the depths of the sea, where tentacles of weed things wrapped their dark, slimy tendrils and folds around my toes and fingers... I drifted lower and lower to the bottom of the ocean, to the depths of the sea and fell asleep. I was asleep.

Sun woke me, splashing its yellow bright light rays as Violet rolled open the door from the inside and let the streaming dawn, the crescent sunrise open up the day to us, wake up the senses we possessed with the promise of a new, better day. I stretched and yawned and flexed my arms and my thighs, curling my toes and cracking my finger knuckles, bending my knees and tightening my abdomen.

Keisha rubbed her eyes, emanating a scent of sleeping woman, and said in a sweet, soft voice, "What time is it?" She grinned a playful grin at Violet and added, in a more masculine tone, "Where's my coffee, wench?" They both cracked up, and looked at me, causing me to crack up too. They were so silly together, it was ridiculous, but not in real life, just in the escapades and charades they put on for me and other people they encountered. Violet and Keisha had the kind of relationship that can only happen when two people truly find friendship in each other's arms, and constantly played games that only two equals can play without killing each other.

They wrestled around on the sleeping bags, each pretending to be on top. Violet tried to get Keisha in a neck-lock, but Keisha prevailed, and threw her to the side of the floor with a hard but gentle thud, and won the match. (By that time, I was jealous—how come I didn't have a girlfriend?). "I said, get my coffee, woman," Keisha ordered, snickering with an evil grin.

Violet got up to go get Keisha's caffeine fix. "You want to come?" she asked me. We walked over to the store across the street, arm in arm, and bought some coffee beans, grinding them back at the truck for the paper funnel through which we would

145

drain their life-giving juices for our morning ablutions. California was just a great state, as far as I was concerned.

Driving along Highway One, we passed increasingly bigger and bigger redwoods, winding up sharper and sharper turns on the two-lane road, gazing out at the panorama that greeted us from the west. The great Pacific. Whales snorted splurts of steam and sputsom into the atmospheric haze surrounding the ocean's horizon, and we could barely see them, but they were there, singing their whalesong.

I was entranced in my company and the day, salty breeze tickling my nose with olfactory memories of deja vu, and I felt like I knew the place from some ancient past. I felt like I remembered something that lay in my very DNA, the oversoul of humanity before me, the group mind of all who had walked my path to this great seashore in the far North Pacific coast. I was one with the universe. I was going to Mendocino.

Off we went, to the New England style town on the coast, high up on a cliff, above the ocean spray and white beaches, above the hidden caves where seagulls kept their young. We emerged at the tip of a small, one-horse operation called Albion, and they let me out. "Mendocino is just ten miles up the road," Violet gestured with her hand. "See that bridge? That's Little River, home of the 'Little River Band.'" She gunned her engine, and Keisha spoke from the other side, as I alighted, clutching my tattered yellow pack which contained my old clothes.

"Have fun in Albion and Mendo, Gabrielle." She blew me a kiss. "Sure did enjoy having you along for the ride." I wondered what the deal was.

"Aren't you two going to Mendocino for your vacation?" I asked.

"Nah, we haven't taken a vacation in three years," Violet said. "Be careful, now, and let us know how you are doing, all right?"

"All right, and thanks for all you've done for me," I answered, and waved good-bye, clad in Violet's grey overalls and Keisha's purple blouse with the puffy sleeves. I wore a pair of woolen socks they had donated to my cause, which made my worn-out hiking boots much more comfortable. I turned, and faced the only store in town, at the end of the only asphalt road in town, and walked toward it. Albion turned out to be the place where I would live my last days as a Californian transient, and the place where I truly felt at home in California. Maybe it had something to do with the fact that soon after I arrived, I had a place to call my own, a tree house, sort of. In the woods. Hanging around out in front of the store/post office, I observed the passers bye. Hippies, hippies, and more hippies. Not a well-dressed conservative in sight.

Pretty soon, a short, waddly guy wearing a saffron robe came up to me and said, "You need a place to crash?" What psychic phenomena, what ESP, what observant behavior he had! I didn't say anything as River looked me over, not in an unfriendly or sexually aggressive way, and said, "I don't mind if you want to crash at my place."

"How do you know I need a place to crash?" I asked suspiciously, wondering if it showed that much, which it did, of course. "I came up here to see a friend of mine."

"Who?" He questioned, probably wondering male or female, lover or friend, relative or non-relative. Nosy, wasn't he? Bold, too.

"Why should I tell you?" I eyed him in my smart-assed way, and looked him over, head to toe. I can do it too, you know.

"Because I'm your ticket to a place to sleep, that's why." River was getting bored with this exchange, but persistence wins the goose, I always say.

"Okay, her name is Swansong."

"Swansong's out of town."

"She is?" Typical Swan to be gallivanting about. I decided he was for real, and followed him back to his van, weary at the day's end, hoping for a good night's sleep, and a hot meal. Maybe even some smoke.

"I teach second grade at the Whale School," River said as we tumbled over and around and up and down a winding country path that climbed up into the ferns and redwoods that dotted the landscape. "What do you do?"

"I don't do much of anything," I answered, abashed at not having a visible means of support.

"That's okay, a lot of people around here don't do much of anything," he explained. "The place is economically depressed." We came to a halt at the edge of the thickest bracken and forest I

147

had encountered yet in Northern California, and climbed out to hike through treacherous bramble and thorn along an invisible path (I didn't see it). I carried some of River's gear because he had to haul everything in and out by hand, including water from the well, which we stopped to get.

"This place is wild," I panted, breathless from the exertion, but enjoying the trek through the wilderness just the same. Mist hung in the air as huge ferns waved their tendrils mysteriously in the non-breeze... look, over there, was that a rainbow?

"Is that a rainbow over there?" I asked, pointing to a particularly foggy patch over by a group of red and purple wild flowers.

"Yep, sure is," he smiled. "There's lots of 'em out here." He took a deep breath, shifting the two buckets of water he carried. "Feel that fresh air, isn't it great?" Imagine, breathing in rainbows.

"I've never seen a place this beautiful," I whispered.

We came to a log cabin with sun roof windows that dotted the top and side, and dropped our loads, splashing some of River's water.

"Here we are," said River, setting down his bucket of water.

"Whew, that was hard," I panted. "Do you always have to carry this much stuff in and out of the hill?" I collapsed on the ground, feigning exhaustion. "How far is it up here?"

River scratched his bald pate, and said, "About a mile." And he wasn't even breathing hard! Fat and all, River was one strong guy, with legs like a hobbit and furry toes, too.

We made tea, and went upstairs to his loft to drop some shroomies and smoke some herb. I ate a peyote button he offered me, almost gagging on the raunchy flavor of rotten wood, then munched on two huge mushrooms, which tasted barely any better. Yech. But did I ever trip, lost in the forest and the faerie wonderland of rainbows and unicorns shimmering on the grass. I fell into a deep trance, while River lit candles and started playing his lute. Eighteenth century lute music fit right into the mood we were in, and I drifted off to escape from my mind and myself, to fly away in the clouds and swim in the ocean and suck up the sea air. It was night. We surrendered ourselves to the darkness, and listened to the sounds of deep forest creatures, chirping and singing and rustling the leaves. The sky hung low, clouds covered us as their mist curled and wrapped each plant with cotton, each green, living, budding life that reached up to touch the sun, sparkles of light hitting crystalline drops that clung, precariously, to little leaves. I was tripping out.

Safe in the haven of woods and streams, furry creatures padded about on cat feet, tiny claws climbed huge, towering hulks, redwood trees housed life in furry forms with young hidden in furry nests. Pouches formed along the mushroom landscape, dripping with sweat and steam and mist and spray, carrying spores of psychedelic psilocybin mushroom friends, little friends of the forest, inhabitants of our spirit's emerald glade. Deep in the forest's nest, we rested our weary spirits, and flew with the merest whisper of ocean breeze into the starry evening, into the starry night.

Winter comes, softly at first, a slight falling away from summer hues...sky colors flashing in sunsets, o'er mountains of yellow, haze and bronze... winter wind chimes, homemade out of leaves, acorns, pecans and dry branches, handmade by nature herself... silence walks, mildly and then, a weakening of life lifts leaves high, sky flashes into grey fog, o'er fields with wheat, corn and cotton...evening song is made of owls, hooting, squirrels scurry after nuts, it won't be long now, they fear...sleet arrives, hardly gentle, it creeps into little animal ears...sky frightens summer away, o'er cloudy banks of mountain homes...night time blackens in the frost, screams of wind thru corridors that once housed little bobcats...blackest night, starry sky, winter won again with fiery cold, sky fills and languishes in moon shine o'er forest oaks, pine trees, and moss...chirping sparrows say spring comes soon, it's not far away....

I awakened from my slumber, the white poney dancing in my subconscious, the hallucinogenics dancing on my brain. River was making coffee for the two of us, grinding sweet mocha beans with an archaic hand grinder.

"Have a good trip?" he asked, obviously in a good mood from his own experiences on the peyote and mushrooms.

I drifted slowly into some semblance of reality, and shook the ferny cobwebs from my brain, the last vestiges of Mother Sea. I slaked my thirst for fantasy sucking in one, last draught of fresh dream, and said, "It was all so beautiful, it was all so foggy and misty and the animals...."

"I know, I know." River grinned at me and finished grinding, then shook out the small particles that smelled so wonderful and filled our nostrils with such longing. "Want a cup of coffee?"

Chapter 10

butterflies, all of us we land on separate
flow'rs, dancing lightly on yellow,
gold and purple petals whisked off
our butterfly feet
with each wind we drift apart,
scatterbrained as the breeze,
our thoughts never staying with us long
enuf to remember games, O how we love
games. "your petal or mine?"
she winks at her friend and
disappears into the dusk,
the invitation long forgotten
O how short the life of the butterfly,
how beautiful her wings, yellow,
gold and purple, bright in the sunshine
dewdrops sticky on butterfly feet as she
melts into her flow'r and whispers
good-bye to her life of one day.

Invoking Weather

River walked me out into the woods, at least a quarter mile further than his cabin, and delivered me to a hollowed-out redwood tree trunk with a pot belly stove inside, and colored glass windows located in the notches where branches used to be. The place was about thirty feet in diameter, and pretty rustic, to say the least. It was also located so far back into the forest that I doubted I would ever find my way out, especially at night.

"This place used to belong to two lesbians," River explained. "It's always been a habitat of women." He waited for my response, probably expecting me to whine and carry on.

"I love this place!" I exclaimed, all misgivings saved until later.

"Good," he said, a bit surprised. He wasn't aware of my recent midnight catnaps in dreary, smelly, dangerous park bathrooms, and I didn't tell him.

"You mean I can live here?" I asked, strolling around, stepping on moss and cracking dry twigs underfoot.

"Sure, why not?" he asked.

"What about the owners?" I couldn't believe they wouldn't want their house back.

"I own it now." River said proudly. "You want it, or not?" He climbed into the tree trunk house, the art deco natural extravaganza, and extracted the lid to the pot belly stove.

"Yahoo!" I yelped, leaping up into the air and acting like some housewife who just won a dishwasher on 'Wheel of Fortune.' "I'll take it."

"Don't ever light the stove without this lid," he cautioned with a stern look, "And don't ever leave the place with an unattended fire." Even though the forest was damp, I could see what he meant about the danger of fire. The old stove's chimney was cracked in places and barely attached to the stove, which was barely standing on four very wobbly legs.

"Yeah, okay," I said quickly, ready to agree to anything. I wanted this beautiful, falling apart, fire-trap of a tree house.

"I'm going into town later, want to come with me?" River asked, as he began hiking back down the hill and into the forest's green, following some path that I couldn't see. Where did he go? I wondered, leaping to action and running after him.

"River, wait for me!" I called out to his vanishing form. How in the heck I would ever find my way out was a question I wondered about often, and always ended up staying home at night for fear of getting hopelessly lost. Good, I had him in sight. All this running and climbing would make me model thin, I thought to myself. Fat chance.

"Sure, I'd love to go," I said, finally catching him. I ran down the hill and gave him a huge hug. "Thank you so much, River." I was almost close to tears, my transient-hardened sensibilities moved by the good people I kept meeting, people who saw my need and didn't question it. River blushed, unaccustomed to such displays of affection, living all alone in his cabin in the woods.

"Aww, shucks, it isn't much of a house," he drawled. "But at least it will be yours, Gabrielle." He looked up at the sky through the tree tops.

"It's really nice of you," I said. "Are we going into town now?"

"We'll go when the sun gets over that way, west," he pointed. "Watch for it, okay?" Sure, I could tell solar time. We gave a short wave, and I entered my jungle-infested, overgrown with ferns and weeds and a civic cat tree trunk house, my home at last, far away from Lawless, Oklahoma, deep into the heart of Northern California. I could smell the ocean breeze, and almost hear the surf which crashed nearby. I set about cleaning and rearranging the place, and decided to hike back out for water.

Wandering around aimlessly, I soon discovered that I was lost, and couldn't find my way out of the forest. There, over a copse of trees, was some type of weird cabin, and a guy was chopping wood out front. I took a chance and said, "Hiya!" to the blonde in the green overalls with the muscles. "Can you direct me back to River's place?

"Yeah, see that path over there?" He gestured with the axe (he was kind of cute, in a long-haired way), but I still didn't see the path.

"No," I answered, looking around blindly for the path. What path were they talking about? "That's why I'm lost."

"You must be new around here," he said, not unkindly. "See it over there by those wildflowers?" He pointed to a small copse of redwoods with purple and yellow flowers strewn under them, along with a group of huge, emerald green ferns. What path?

I was feeling really stupid. "Could you show me?" He walked over to the miniscule trail which was about an inch wide. He stood there until I walked over and actually saw it. Looked like a barely used deer path to me.

"This is it," he said, grinning ever so slightly. "Been in the woods long?" Extending his grimy, sweaty palm, he shook hands with me, formally. "I'm Max."

"I'm Gabrielle," I said politely. "And I just moved into the cabin up the way." I didn't want to tell all, but he figured it out.

"Oh, you got Cedar and Star's place." Obviously. "You need some help renovating it, just give me a holler," Max offered, as he went back to chopping wood with a vengeance I would soon learn to emulate, as winter neared our neck of the woods.

"Okay, see you later, Max." I started along the path, barely discerning it among the brambles and thorns, bumping into trees and scraping under branches. "Where's the well?" I almost forgot my mission.

"You've bypassed it by a quarter mile," he smiled. "Here, I'll let you have a can of my water, okay?" As he started into the house, I ran after him. Enough was enough.

"Look," I said, stopping him in his tracks. "I need to learn to deal with this place, but thanks anyway, Max." I just couldn't bum the poor guy's water which he had laboriously lugged up the mountainside, but I did accept his spare can (I didn't have one.)

Such was my life in the forest, and such were my days passed, doing menial tasks like hauling water, helping River, exploring the countryside and getting lost all the time. One time I was snoozing in my sleeping bag, which River had kindly provided for me, and I got up to go take a pee. Well, taking a pee in the woods in the middle of the night is an experience, and somehow or other, I actually strayed too far from my home, and got lost, naked and wrapped in a sleeping bag.

The next morning, after spending a fitful and wet evening in the woods, dreaming of Bigfoot and worrying about my plight, I confronted a farmer in his field, and asked him the way back to River's. He took one look at my sleeping bag-clad body, and didn't even bat an eyelash. "That a way," he said, pointing west, "Up yonder in those trees."

Occasionally I would hang out with Max, who read palms and Tarot cards. I was a bad girl, and, consumed with curiosity, allowed him to read my cards, my palms, and tell my future. It is not allowed, Biblically speaking, but I did a lot of things back then that I shouldn't have. I didn't suffer any negative spiritual effects, although I did get weirded out one day on mescaline, and saw strange, dark, tendrils of something or other hanging all over Max's shoulders and hands. He said it was just some spirits that came once in a while to disturb him. I stayed off the cards after that experience.

I hitched to Mendo on a regular basis and got a job as a maid in a Bed and Breakfast inn, which paid me enough to get by on, and not much else. I did some electrical wiring with this guy for two weeks, and collected and sold wood with Max a couple of times. My Mom sent me some money every month, and called the Albion

General Store, asking for me. I still didn't want to go home to Lawless, even though the tree house life was a lonely time.

I met some sweet reclaiming witches and hung out with them at their women's community in Little River, often bringing them little gifts of wheatberries, which I bought at the co-op for a very cheap price of five dollars for twenty-five pound bags. They sprouted wheatgrass, and we drank the juice. One night we were gathered around the campfire, and they asked me if I wanted to take part in the winter solstice ceremony. We lit candles and placed small tokens upon the altar, then smudged ourselves with cedar and sage. Sprucewood, our ritual leader for the evening, began leading us in the invocation. "Oh Mother Earth, we stand firmly upon you, grounding our energies," she intoned, swaying gently, her robe slightly rippling in the night breeze. We all began to feel grounded as we stood together in circle together round the fire.

"Dirt beneath our feet, stars above, lava and inner Earth dwellers below us," murmured Sandalwood, Sprucewood's lover.

"Earth power courses up through our chakras," added Truefern, dressed in black geisha pants and a crimson shawl. It was time to invoke the four directions, after which we would call upon the sky spirits, and the Great Spirit within our hearts.

"We are now calling upon the spirit of the North, who rules the Earth," Sprucewood continued. And on and on like that.

"As we continue to send out prayers protect our Mother Earth," I added, tossing some sage into the fire. They sprinkled incense on a flat, black rock within the fire, which caused the incense to whoosh up in smoke, crackling with forest scents. This was fun, I thought, lost in a revery with the others as the moon shone full overhead, and bright stars twinkled upon our innocent Earth blessings.

"Look Gabrielle," someone said suddenly, "There's three blue stars right above your head!" Everyone oooh'd and aaah'd, making me feel like the token stranger, which I was, since I was the only self-professed Christian present in this group of pagan women who worshiped the Goddess and protected the Earth. They were what I would call "Christ friendly," as are many pagans. Since He hung out with all kinds, and didn't judge others for their particular faiths, I felt like it was okay for me to spend spiritual time with these

155

good women, way better than church. They liked and accepted me for who I was, without expectations. Besides, I thought to myself, if this is being a pagan, then I'm mostly pagan too. But blue stars? Above my head? Where? Albion and the headlands of Mendocino were kind of like Mount Shasta in that extraterrestrial sightings, blue, pink and yellow flashing lights, satellites and strange constellations were commonplace. I was not used to seeing strange occurrences in the sky, but I got so used to it that when I returned to Lawless, I looked for signs in the sky for a full year before giving up, and looking down.

Tonight was no exception. The blue stars, my witch friends said, had followed me to their place in the night. This brought me new respect and admiration for my psychic powers, which of course I didn't possess, but I enjoyed the extra attention, no doubt. I was Gabrielle Starfire Laughing Girl, and this was my home.

One night, I was driving around in Leda's car, buying groceries for the group, and I saw one of the local dudes get thrown out of a car onto the street. He didn't get up. I drove over to him, and parked my car in the road with the flashers beaming to protect us from oncoming traffic. He was drunk as a skunk, with what looked like a broken arm from the fall.

"Jack, what happened?" I asked, reeling from his alcoholic stench, but helping him into the car just the same.

"Gabrielle?" he asked drunkenly. "Is it you?" He slouched over the dashboard, and we drove off. I stopped shortly after to seatbelt him, because he was rolling around in the front seat, out of his mind on alcohol.

"How come you got thrown out of that car?" I inquired, not that it really mattered. This type of stuff happened all the time up in my neck of the woods.

"I don't know," he said, slathering his words all over me. "Tom got pissed, I guess." Head lolling to one side, Jack looked at me with watery, blood-shot, grey eyes. I took him home to his wife, who wasn't surprised at his condition. This earned me a reputation in the town of Albion that saved me from things like rape (by drunks like Jack), and hate (by their women). Someone got raped soon after this incident, but Mary, Jack's wife, told me that if any guy ever hurt me, the ladies in Albion would kill him.

I believed her.

This was because of the fact that I didn't steal dudes from their women, and I didn't leave them in the road to die. Since Albion was composed of mostly dope-growers, fisherfolk, and ex-cons, my protected status was completely necessary to my survival. The cops wouldn't even come into the town, only feds when they were sniffing out sinsemilla plants, and there were tons of those growing in these woods.

I made friends with a young girl, a prepubescent beauty named Tarah, whose Mom was rather a slut. The night I met Tarah, the fisherfolk were having a free abalone cook-out over at Redfern's place, and Lydia, Tarah's Mom, took off all her clothes and started doing the pelvic thrust in several guys' faces. They followed her into the woods soon after that, to do some dirty, I'm sure.

I said to the closest ear, "Man, that lady is sure wired!" Watching my words was important in this town, but I was kind of shocked at the scene Lydia put on.

The closest ear turned to me and said, "That's my mother." A pair of young, green eyes and innocent pink cheeks looked up at me, pure virginal child.

"Oh, I'm sorry," I said, embarrassed at my faux pas.

"She does that all the time," explained Tarah matter-of-factly. "It really makes me sick, but what can I do?" I looked at the poor little girl, and said,

"Do the guys ever hit on you, too?"

"Yeah, but I kick 'em in the balls," she deadpanned. Whew! At what cost virginity is held dear, I thought.

"I'm Gabrielle," I told her, wanting to help in some way.

"I know," Tarah answered, "You've got a rep."

"I do?" I asked her. "Says who?"

"Oh, everybody. They say you have three blue stars that follow you around." Yeah, I knew that.

I looked up, and sure enough, there they were, blinking furiously in phosphorescent beauty, set like aqua-marine jewels in the clear, night sky. "They say nobody will ever fuck with you, either," Tarah added.

"Really?" I asked. "Why?"

"Because you help people out." She was all of thirteen with gangly legs. "You want to hang with me for awhile?" Tarah asked me shyly.

"Sure," I said, lonely myself. "You got a problem with any of these dudes?" I was ready to protect this little girl from all the dripping dicks that were hung in the night's gathering, and my maternal instincts arose very powerfully to the occasion.

"I'm just afraid to walk home alone," Tarah said sadly, sniffling a little. "I think my Mom's gone for the evening." So, I walked her home to her shack on "E' Street, which was a string of shacks owned by a wicked-looking woman who ran the street like she was mayor, or something. Sally, the owner-landlady, was really quite nice, I found out later. She just had to look tough and mean to keep a handle on the wild crowd who inhabited 'E' street. We crashed in Tarah's cabin, and the next morning still didn't bring her mother home, so she decided to stick by my side. Fine with me. We strolled on 'down the ridge' (I lived up the ridge) into town to the general store and hung around on the steps, smoking some grass and greeting the passersby.

"Oh, there's Juniper," Tarah exclaimed. "Hey Juniper!" The little dickens waved and ran over to him, dragging him by the arm to where I sat, roaching the joint.

"Hi," said the jolly man with the goatee. "I hear you are Tarah's avenging angel."

"Could be," I answered slowly, not knowing this individual who reminded me of River, only he was taller and didn't have hairy toes. His blue eyes twinkled with merriment.

"You ladies care to dine at my place for lunch?"

"Sure," said Tarah, before I had a chance to decline.

"Come with me, ladies," he said, opening his van door for us. I kinda liked him by now—who wouldn't like Juniper? He was a gourmet chef at the Mendo haute cuisine hideaway, and he always came home with leftovers, like divine cucumber soup, and french bread sticks, and raspberry mousse. Juniper had an open hand and an open heart for anyone who came his way.

"He's gay," Tarah whispered, as we waited in Juniper's van for him to come out of the post office.

"Well, at least he doesn't bother you," I replied.

"I know," she sighed resignedly, "that's why I like gay men so much." What a life. We had a wonderful lunch with Juniper and his lover, Redwood, and many lunches in the future. He was a real sweetheart who often took Tarah to his house to sleep, so she wouldn't have to deal with her mother's many, many suitors (like dogs after a bitch in heat).

"Hey Gabrielle, River tells me you're a friend of Swansong," Juniper said between bites of watercress sandwiches with the crust trimmed off.

"Uh huh," I grunted, chewing and swallowing my cheesed potatoes.

"She's back in town today, I saw her pull up."

"Really?" Surprised, I put my fork down. This was important news, because I had almost forgotten about Swansong during the three months I had lived in Albion. "I'm almost afraid to go see her," I said.

"She's madly in love with some flute player in Mendocino," Juniper said, swallowing a gulp of chamomile tea, "But I'm sure she'd be glad to see you." So. Swansong had a girlfriend, I mused. That's a good sign of her recovery.

"Can she walk?" I asked, still hoping for some miracle from God, because I had been praying for her for the year it had been since I'd seen her last.

"No, but she gets around quite well," Juniper answered. "She never talks about her past in San Francisco, but I know you two were together when the accident happened."

"We were together in more ways than one," I said, suddenly missing Swansong so much I began to cry, tears rolling down my face. "I loved her so much, and to see her crippled almost did me in," I sobbed.

"There, there," Juniper and Tarah comforted me. "She's all right now, and what's done is done. Go see her, Gabrielle."

They both looked at me, and I decided to do it. Tarah and I finished lunch, and walked back to the store to hang out. There was a huge box sitting near the front entrance, and a sign that said, 'free puppies.' I just had to look, and there, inside, were cuddly bundles of fur that turned out to be half St. Bernard, half something or other. I reveled in the feel of furry flesh on my hands, and an older lady with wavy, auburn hair said, "Take one, they're free."

"They're yours?" I asked, picking up the biggest pup. He was soft and tan and white and furry. He licked me with his pink tongue, and his light brown puppy eyes stared into mine. His huge paws scratched my arm, and a trickle of urine ran down my blouse.

I fell in love.

Mousaka.

So I took him, and Tarah absolutely squealed with delight. "A puppy, a puppy, oh, let me hold him...." I didn't want to hand him over, suddenly flooded with dog love and protectiveness, but I handed the puppy to the little girl, remembering what I was like at her age, and how much I loved dogs then, and how connected they were to my very existence as a child.

"Let's take him home to my place, all right?" I asked her.

"Yeah, let's take the little baby boy home," she sighed contentedly, and we traipsed the three miles back to my cabin in the woods. We named the little jewel 'Mousaka' because I liked the sound of the Greek word for lamb stew, and cosseted him in our female nest.

I did go see Swansong soon after that, but I let Tarah babysit Mousaka (who later became her devoted protector, a huge monster that made dicks wilt as he stuck his snout into offending crotches, sniffing out potential pedophiles).

I was afraid of my initial encounter with my old friend, my old companion, my sweetest lady. I didn't know how she would react to me, and Leaflet's words reverberated through my consciousness, 'She doesn't want to see you, Gabrielle.'

Aw, the hell with it, I wanted to see her, so I moseyed on over to her homestead one bright, sunny day in October, right before the rainy season began, and looked around her wood-strewn lawn, afraid to journey the ten yards farther that led to her doorstep, and bang the little knocker. Ducks quacked at the unseen pond around the corner, as I let fall the knocker thrice, and impatiently (shyly) stamped my feet, hoping against hope that she would still miss me, and want to be my friend. Just as I decided she was gone (good!) I heard a rustling and another quack, this time closer, and Swansong came wheeling around, a duck following closely behind her.

Another duck came into the picture, and I found myself staring at her and her two duck friends. "Swan," I said uncertainly, "How are you?" I greeted her, trying not to weird out at the sight of her chair, and looking instead at her flashing, forest-green eyes, and her frizzy golden hair that looked red in shadows, but was bleached blond by Albion's northern lights, hot sun, and white beaches. Swan checked me out, noting the old, worn-out hiking boots that I had salvaged from the back of Violet's semi-trailer, her eyes traveling slowly up my body, slowly taking in my slimmer hips, frazzled, faded-out Levi's, black 'Led Zeppelin Lives!' tee-shirt, and finally resting, gazing deeply into my eyes with locking eye-beams. Same old Swansong, I thought. Hasn't changed a bit.

"So, you've moved into Star and Cedar's place," she said cooly, still locked into my eye beams, telling me tales of Wisconsin winters and hospital summers spent recuperating from her accident. We exchanged wordless thoughts as I gazed into her eyes and learned where she had been, and how she had survived.

"Yeah, I've done a lot of work on the place." Proud to say I've worked, I expected her to be impressed. She wasn't. "I really like your ducks," I added, continuing with inanities, continuing to wonder about Swan's life, as she and I spoke with our eyes, not our mouths.

"So has everyone else," she said, "Worked on the house, I mean. It gets infested with jungle every spring and summer, you know." No I didn't, because I had only been there in early autumn. Briefly I wondered how she could ever manage that jungle I called home confined in her wheelchair, but another close look at her bulging, oiled biceps convinced me that with her high-tech chair with racing rims with sealed, Phil Wood hubs and Continental light-weight, 700cc tires, that girl could go anywhere, and I mean the boon-docks! Wow! What a fine piece of machinery... I fingered the delicate, bladed spokes on her right wheel, and Swan noticed, obviously.

"A college friend of mine from Milwaukee built me this bike," she said quietly. "He has a bike shop on campus corner."

"Great bike," I commented, touching the taut tires which held 135 psi each. She looked sad for a moment, then her steely resolve took over.

161

"We used to belong to the Fire Dragons, a Cat II racing club," Swan said brightly. "Back in the old days when I lived in Wisconsin with Mom and Dad." Damn. Now I like bikes, and I have a few myself, but this little system Swan was riding must have weighed a grand total of ten pounds max, and that was mostly wheels, because the frame looked like it was built out of titanium.

"What's it made of," I asked. "Titanium?" The frame's unpainted surface was smooth, blue-grey, with a thin, clear finish.

"Only the best," Swan said. "He was terribly in love with me once."

"Yeah, and what happened?" I asked, warming up to the conversation. Swansong grinned, and I grinned back, knowing the answer before she said it. "You fell in love..." I began, and we finished the sentence in unison.

"With a woman!" We both cackled, and it seemed as though we had never been apart. "Well, at least he forgave me later," she said with a devious twinkle in her eye. "He knew I was lez from way back." We exchanged smiles.

"Some guys never learn, do they?" I asked.

"Never," she said.

"Lady," I began, "I've missed your face." Tears sprang to my eyes as I gazed at the lovely Swan, the fallen but not beaten Swan, the woman who renamed herself after an old Navajo Indian healer, 'Swansong Well Woman.' I wanted to give her a big hug, but we hadn't reached that point by any means. She was enveloped in her shell of reserve, and I was still on the outside, looking in. I wondered how long I would be held at arms length.

"So," she said, gently easing back into friendship. "Would you like to ride into town with me?" Missed that last remark, I guess. Oh well. Enough smarm.

"You gonna get groceries, or just hang around?" I asked.

"I'm following this flute player around, see, because I've got a crush on her," Swan said, adding, "She doesn't even know I exist." Didn't seem to bother her any, I observed. Crushes are always safer than the real thing, I thought to myself.

"Uh, yeah, I'm not doing anything."

She drove, I rode. We began to laugh again.

Thus began the tentative relationship between me and my lost Swan. We hung around together and she fed me natural foods, carefully whipped up in her kitchen. She let me stack wood for her fireplace and sleep on her couch or in the moon room. I used to always venture into her bedroom, wanting to talk, but the bedroom was off limits to me, and although I saw several men from town go to and fro in the morning from her bed, I never saw the female flute player.

Maybe Swan used the guys because they were non-threatening emotionally, since she truly dug the female sex. Whatever reasons Swansong had for laying off the ladies, it bolstered her charismatic hold over everyone in Albion, for you see, I was only one of many worshipers. Everyone loved Swansong.

Days, weeks, months passed, and I took more and more peyote and mushrooms, hallucinating myself into flying saucers and colored strobe lights. This was indeed the vision I had on acid in Lawless, this was the California of my dreams. Only trouble was, reality kept getting in my way. Like the time I was sitting with Betsy Albionacious's old man, and she was wandering around Mendocino with four of her seven children, going to the movies or something-anyway, there we sat, Sandburr and I, putting on the acid, putzing on the Ritz. Tarah had Mousaka, as she often did, so I was free to roam the streets.

"Sandy, that last hit didn't faze me one bit," I told him, grinding my teeth, twitching my eyelids, the tick in my forehead barely apparent, "Can I have another one?" Sandburr, Sandy to his friends, a slim and lanky six-foot-four inch long-haired carpenter, could hold two hits of Purple Flying Saucer acid, but could I? He didn't think so, and said,

"Gabby, why don't you wait a couple of minutes longer, until the first hit takes effect." He wasn't even twitching.

"Why?" I asked, "You didn't. I can handle it, I take drugs all the time."

"You really should just wait a few minutes," he reasoned, but to no avail. I twitched and ticked.

"With a built in resistance, it takes more to get me off," I groaned, lost in the throes of an overdose already. Convinced I needed more, I kept trying to convince him.

"Look, Babe," Sandy said, "This is potent acid, and I'm a lot bigger than you." He didn't twitch, grind his teeth or tick, and I should have listened to the man, but no, of course not, I knew everything there was to know about hallucinating (I thought!).

"I want another hit, please Sandy?" I whined.

I begged. He gave me another hit, and I sucked it down fast.

Suddenly a freight train picked me up and a flying saucer landed. I was in an elevator going up but falling down, and little voices in the sky beckoned me to join them in their space ship, but I could not get out of my body, and remained grounded.

"Sandy, I shouldn't have taken that second hit," I cried, feeling like the top of my head had been sliced off by a Samurai warrior, and wanting desperately to escape from the prison of my poisoned body.

"Gabrielle, now don't freak out, all right?"

"Sandy, I gotta go, I gotta get out of here!"

"You need to keep cool. Look, we'll go to the beach."

"My head is burning, I'm gonna die!"

"You are not going to die, just stay cool."

"I have to go now, I'm leaving, I have to go."

"Hey, wait for me!"

I ran the three miles to the beach below Albion, and collapsed, briefly, on the sand. The moon shone blue light over the ocean, and orange and green-yellow stars blinked on and off, furiously. I just knew that the space people had come for me, and they were hovering overhead. I got up and ran down the beach, the strychnine in my body hurting, my brain cells bursting at the rate of a thousand per second, my synapses missing their mark, my neurons gone berserk. I needed some vitamin C; suddenly it became an obsession.

"Sandy, I'm gonna die if I don't get an orange and come down!" (everything was '!!!') I whined, crawling around with my face in the sand. He was a good friend, and kept me from totally losing it and never coming back.

"It's six o'clock in the morning, and you won't find anything open right now, Baby," he soothed. "But I've got some Vitamin C tabs at the house, if you want to go back. He wiped the sand off my nose, while I clutched my head in mock terror.

164

"Nooo," I cried, "I need it now, I can't make it, my head is burning!"

"Okay, we'll wander into Mendo and see if we can scrounge some fruit for you, Gab," he decided, helping me to hang onto a thread of reality, helping me to not lose my mind. We walked into Mendo from the beach, another five miles (but we were tripping), and walked to the window at the kitchen of the Seagull Restaurant, where we frequently hung out and drank coffee, and shot the breeze. There was a guy chopping onions for the morning omelets, and we had no shame in approaching him for a free hand-out.

"Hey," I cried, "Can I have an orange?" He looked at me, his ponytail well out of the onions, his long hair telling us he was cool.

"Sure, hold on a minute," he said, turning to walk into another room we could not see, and returning with three oranges. Looked at me quizzically. "Here, eat."

"Oh, thank-you, thank-you, thank-you," I effused, happy to get the 'C' fix that I needed to replenish my stores the acid had eaten away. Or so I thought—it's amazing what obsessions will make you do. We finally made it back to Sandburr and Betsy's house, and the children were home with their mother, the dogs barking, the horses neighing, the chickens cackling, the roosters crowing....

Betsy laughed when I told her I had OD'd, and gave me some orange juice. It took me two full days to come down, two days spent at their small farm in the mountains, watching the animals, having visions about the German Shepherd in particular, who I felt certain was an angel in disguise after my acid-induced revelations. I swore off hallucinogenics forever, and actually stayed clean for a short period of time, long enough to realize that Cat Stevens had been following me around Albion.

It was all Tarah's fault, she's the one who started me back on that particular trip, right around Christmas time. It was raining cats and dogs, chipmunks and squirrels, piglets and poodles. My ears had begun to sprout sores, my clothes were tattered rags, my tree house was sopping wet from the fifty or sixty holes in the ceiling, I was sick and tired of tromping through mud and slush to get to my waterlogged home in the jungle, and I consequently slept wherever I could find a corner in town. Tarah and I had been crashing in Ellen's 'A' frame right across from the general store for two weeks,

165

and the comforts of a solid roof over my head were indescribable. A local woman had been raped (nothing new) in the woods by 'E' street recently, so we were all on the look-out for possible rapists. Mousaka guarded us from any approaching evil, though, so we weren't too afraid.

Tarah had found footprints around the house Sunday evening, and heard an Englishman's voice in the woods nearby. She naturally assumed it was the Cat come to take me home, full of my stories of impending rock star glory as she was.

"No, Cat is in England, and he's married with children," I argued, but Tarah was sure it was him. She twisted a strand of hair around her index finger.

"Gabby, I'm your friend and you can just trust my instinct," she whined. "I've got ESP and telepathy too. It's the Cat come to get you." She was absolutely positive, in her pubescent way. I didn't want to believe it, but since I had become such an avid watcher of the stars and three blue ones still followed me around, I couldn't quite allow myself to discount her theory altogether, either.

"You really heard an Englishman?" I asked, hoping she would say no, hoping she would say yes. Damn, just when I'm getting normal, I thought to myself.

"Yes, I swear he was talking to me," she said matter-of-factly. Tarah didn't think it one bit strange that a man would hide in the woods and talk to her. "He said he couldn't come out because too many people knew him," Tarah continued, "And it was Cat Steven's voice!"

"Did he actually admit he was Cat Stevens?" I asked, still not convinced. "It could have been some weirdo, waiting to jump you and rape your young bones." I was still full of reasons why it wasn't him.

"Look, Gabby, you can just ignore him if you want to, but he won't go away." Tarah pouted, and went to play with Mousaka. He had, by this time, grown into a hulking brute who weighed at least seventy-pounds, and he was only a pup! Ask me how I fed him (he fed himself chickens, that's how).

So.

Cat Stevens wanted me back, I thought to myself. I wonder what he did with his wife and kid... maybe he dumped them and came here to find me, realizing that I was what he had been searching for all along, wanting to find his equal, his soul-mate, his twin. That's it (the bullshit gets deeper), his wife is in England, filing for divorce, and he has decided to come back to California and play music again. He probably owns land around here, I heard that lots of unknown but famous people own land in this area, and come here to get away from the raging crowds and their hysterical fans. Hmmm...that's logical. I wonder if he's out back now, I think I'll just take a look.

Thus, I began looking around every corner, searching for Cat Stevens, or the ghost of Cat Stevens, the phantom of my mind's obsessive compulsion, the illusory dream that never came true, the man in the bushes.

Chapter 11

*I'm being followed by a moon shadow,
moon shadow, moon shadow.*

Cat Stevens

Honoring the Ancestors

Mythical creatures do tend to hide, just like unicorns, leprechauns, and rock stars. They lurk in the cavernous crevasses of one's subconscious mind, as Frankenstein must have hidden in the laudanum dreams of Mary Godwin, that fateful year of 1816 in Switzerland, as Shelley imploded in Lord Byron's villa, and she attempted to expunge her fears and escape her sadness.

Was Lord Byron mad?

Were they all mad?

Or did the literary giants, including Byron's biographer and lady love, (each vying for his attention) along with Godwin and Shelley, experience mass hallucinations, demons, or ghosts? Was it a group vision, or a haunting creature, created from their mutual fears, as Mary's diary intimates?

Would I, too, dream up a monster and write a story about its creation and destruction? Oh, probably never, I had no ambition other than to be discovered someday by Cat (doing what?), my self-created obsession.

Ah yes, the subconscious mind holds symbolic creatures and the unknown is only a key to our mind's door. I certainly wish I had found my key because as the rain continued to fall, my fungus-infested brain took on newer and wilder fantasies. These kept me from any gainful employment since I was waiting for Cat Stevens, thus I didn't find it necessary to do anything constructive with my life in California.

I was one of those 'Type A' personalities with no initiative to back up my personal charisma. After all, I had everything I needed except a roof over my head that didn't leak, a real family, a lover, money, possessions, ambition. In short, what I lacked was a life. Why didn't I try to get a job in Fort Bragg when it was offered to me? Shall I tell the truth, and will you scoff at my refusal to comb my hair? I wanted the beach wind to blow it and the sun to bleach it into blond, curly ringlets, 'au natural' beach girl style.

My roots never grew in Northern California, my seed was scattered onto rocky ground, my house was built on sand and sadness, my mind went the way of all those who follow their obsessions to the exclusion of reality. I was a wastrel, a scoundrel, a prodigal. Even so, I enjoyed keeping up with current events, especially if they were radical.

When I wasn't hanging out on my favorite cliff over the beach in Mendocino, playing guitar and watching the seagulls, or guarding one of numerous sinsemilla plots my friends farmed, or hitchhiking up the highway towards Oregon for some good times, I could usually be found in the Seagull restaurant with my cronies, eating bread crusts and drinking cup after cup of coffee (free refills and sympathetic waitresses).

A lady friend was telling us about her latest adventure in the Big Apple, where she had recently visited her mother. Right about this time, Ronald Wilson Reagan was elected president, and we all thought he was the Beast, Mr. 666 himself (Count the letters). Since he had displayed so little pity for welfare recipients in his latest policy changes to improve the budget for those in his income bracket, Arianne's story wasn't too awfully difficult to believe, it was just awful in general.

"I swear, they tattooed welfare people with I.D. tattoos before they could get their checks," said Arianne, a beautiful twenty-year old wastrel herself, who wore bright cotton dresses, local wildflowers, and sandals. She had ventured home to Mama to pick up some cash (something we all did, sooner or later), and became shocked at some type of bureaucratic foul-up that made poor people victims of their keepers, or so she said.

"Naw," Tarah countered, "You must have been dreamin', Lady, why would they tattoo anyone?" The thirteen-year-old Tarah continued to munch on her bread crusts, while I pondered the argument, and slurped my fourth cup.

"It's probably illegal to do that, Arianne," I said, although I didn't disbelieve her story.

"It might be, but they did it," she said, sullenly.

169

"How come people allowed themselves to be tattooed?" I wondered.

"Maybe they needed the money," growled Arianne. "Maybe they had to put up with it." She was in a terribly dark, black mood.

"Hey, isn't Ronnie supposed to be the Beast in Revelations?" Tarah asked, since she often read my *Thompson Chain Reference Bible* in the evenings and during rainy days.

"Well, we really can't interpret the Scriptures so completely," I said, knowing how confusing the Bible could be.

"I don't give a shit who the fuck Ronnie is!" screamed Arianne, upsetting some diners nearby. "I saw the tattoos, all right?" She slammed down her cup, which would never hold coffee again. She was adamant, she was unmovable, she was dead serious.

"What's the deal over here?" the hovering, red-headed waitress asked. She was more employed than I'd ever be, I thought. "You guys need to cool it, okay?" We innocently nodded our assent, and she smiled at us indulgently. We knew more bread would make its way to our table that day. She padded off to wait on someone else.

"Hey, let's be careful, huh?" I murmured. "The manager is right over there." We all stopped arguing for a moment to notice the fat, bald-headed, middle-aged Establishment Person watching us. We didn't want to get kicked out, we lived in this place.

"Yeah, okay," breathed Arianne.

"So," whispered Tarah, "What's the deal with the welfare tattoos?" She looked expectantly at Arianne, who supplied the answer.

"It was supposed to be a method of keeping pimps from getting their girl's checks," Arianne explained, tapping her poor, cracked cup lightly on the table, "But to me, it's discriminatory."

"So you're saying this is really happening in New York City right now?" Tarah asked, incredulous at the thought. She was beginning to be convinced, however, little adolescent left-wing cynic that she was.

"That's what I said," Arianne said, beginning to fume slightly. "In New York City, right now, they're doing it."

I was, for once, speechless.

"And did you know anyone who fought back, refusing to be marked?" asked Tarah. Arianne gave her a dirty look.

"Yeah, I know some people who didn't like it."

"You know, the Beast requires all who worship him to take his mark in their forehead or their palm," said Tarah. Smug and well-informed, she sat back, convinced Christian that she was. Tarah didn't fear anyone or anything except God, and she believed He was her true Father, who would protect her.

"Hey, Jesus Freak, my mother lives in Harlem" Arianne allowed a dramatic pause "and she fought back."

I had to say something, since I was eaten up with curiosity. "So what happened?" I blurted, waving down the waitress for another cup.

"Yeah," Tarah added, "What did they do to your Mom?" Tarah was used to anything and everything happening to Moms, even to the extent of abuse by boyfriends, which had recently happened to her Mom. However, Tarah's Mom had originally bitten her boyfriend in an undisclosed area of his anatomy, which any woman with an ounce of sense would never do while in bed with a man. Arianne's Mom had simply refused to be tattooed.

"And the worst part was, the New York Focus said it was all a mistake!" exclaimed Arianne, ignoring our questions for the moment. She grimaced at the severely cracked cup in her hand, its life now over.

"Really?" Tarah and I both blurted out at once.

"I mean," exclaimed Arianne, obviously confused at man's inhumanity to man, "What the fuck!" A tear trickled down her peach-fuzed, downy soft cheek. "How many people now have those nasty numbers on their wrists?" She looked royally pissed.

"Strange occurrences in Gotham City," breathed Tarah. "Sounds just like Nazi Germany!" What a mind on that girl.

"Luckily for Mom," continued Arianne, "She didn't go for that crap, and held out until they gave her her money."

"That's good," I said.

"Boy, your Mom must be smart," added Tarah. Arianne sighed heavily.

"But Mom got evicted while she was waiting, and now she lives on the street." Arianne began to snuffle softly, and tears rolled down her tawny face. We all stopped eating to pay our respects and comfort our friend whose Mom was in worse shape than she was.

Imagine, living on the streets in New York City. It must be rougher than here, we all agreed. At least we had the ocean and nice people around.

Life on the street was something we were too well acquainted with, but at least our parents lived in houses. This was a final blow for Arianne, and I wondered what would become of her, rootless and ungrounded as she was now, with no where to return to should she decide to go home. Arianne shook her long, curly, chocolate-brown-with-red-highlights hair, and gazed at us with her enormous, hypnotic, azure eyes.

I blinked.

"So, do you think Ronnie was behind this latest abnormal request?" I asked the group, ever the political mouth.

"Yeah, I'd say he's behind it," said Arianne.

"Should people fight the system if they think policy is fucked up?" I asked her. Arianne took a dainty little nibble of bread, considered my question, and chewed her two crumbs of bread. She didn't say anything at first.

"I say, fight the system anyway!" Tarah, the youngest Leftist-Marxist-Anarchist in our group, always said 'fight the system.'

"I don't know," commented Arianne, chewing with more ardor, "I haven't eaten in three days and I'm too starved to worry about it anymore." She looked around for the waitress, hoping for some more bread. "Who gives a shit about us or the system?" Meaning: If we don't care about ourselves, who else will?

She had a point.

I was reminded of the girl in the car with those drunken bikers who said much the same thing. I was reminded that our lifestyles bespoke of thoughtlessness, carelessness, and ignorance of tomorrow. I decided not to think about it anymore, something I did often.

"You always fast, how can you do it?" I asked the lithe and beautiful Arianne. Forget the propaganda, I wanted to know how she stayed so skinny. My weight had once again soared up to at least one hundred and sixty plus pounds, and on five feet eight inches, that wasn't a very pretty sight. I have small bones after all. The gut hung way over the jeans, the thighs were cottage cheese....I was attempting to become a bulimic, because my attempts at anorexia had failed, due to lack of restraint. I regarded all the svelte ladies around me, and wished I could be like them, especially Arianne, because she was gorgeous. Juniper once told me I ate too much at one time (while I was raiding his refrigerator one more time), because I didn't know where my next meal would come from, but he didn't realize that I ate that way during my stint at Burger Prince, where the burger was just too apparent.

I wanted to be a starving artist, but all I ended up as was a fat transient, running out of roofs to crash under. Swansong had two house guests, the folks on 'E' Street were tired of seeing my friendly face at dinner time and bed time, Redfern had already let me crash at his treehouse numerous times, and Juniper was even getting fed up with my frequent fridge raids.

River was a loner by nature, Betsy Albionacious had another child under her already crowded roof, and the woods were too damn wet to live in. I constantly sought shelter from freezing, driving, pouring rain that fell day after day, week after week, month after month. I was becoming run down and bummed out, I was losing all semblance of normality, I was entering into the last stage of the twilight zone, I was about to become gravely ill, and very much afraid for my life.

Mousaka, the brute animal who was my very closest friend, stayed faithful throughout my journey, even though I was a fat piggy and he had to fend for himself. Shows you something about my character. Oh, I fed him chunks of mozzarella cheese, loaves of sourdough bread, pieces of meat when I could find them, fillets of salmon when I could scrounge them off the fisherfolk, but a one hundred and thirty pound dog (by this time he was huge) needs dog food, not people food.

He caught plenty of little animals in the forests nearby, but later on he began to catch bigger animals, too big for him to drag home. Mousaka protected me well one eventful night soon after the meeting at the Seagull, as I was peacefully preparing for a pleasant evening at Ellen's 'A' frame. Tarah was out with one of her numerous fellows (she was naughty fourteen by this time), and I felt very fortunate to have a dry house to sleep in for one more night. All mellowed out, I relaxed and listened to my favorite group, 'It's a Beautiful Day,' momentarily stepping out to leak my

173

lizard (no bathrooms in Albion). Suddenly, an ominous rustling in the woods nearby interrupted the natural flow of things. I wondered if it was a person I knew, a dog, a wild animal, or a faithless marauder come to end my life and mutilate my body.

The ominous rustling emerged from the bushes in the form of Samson, a hellacious monster of a brute who hated me because I told Ellen he was a scumbag and a loser. Fancy me, saying that. He leapt at me, thrusting his ugly, overgrown bulk right into my face. I feinted with my fists, then zoomed into the house. Samson was right behind me, all six feet of gloriously lumbering blubber minus two centimeters of brain matter sloshing in his head.

Enter Mousaka!

Now, by this time, Mousaka should have been called Moose, or Bubba the Brick, or something to that effect because he was just huge, and bloodthirsty from all his hunting. He took his first chunk out of Samson's probably diseased calf, then went directly for the buttock, latching on while Samson screamed in agony, and tried to run away. Picture a two hundred and fifty pound hulk of a man trying to run with a one hundred and thirty pound dog hanging onto his gluteous maximus, and you get the picture. I was laughing hysterically as Samson finally got loose from Mousaka, and hightailed it to the road, with Mousaka loping easily alongside of him, snipping and snapping at bits of flesh every every few steps to keep Samson in line.

I was totally relieved, but something nagged at me. Was he the person who had left footprints around the house, and called to Tarah from the bushes? Nahhh...my mind never had enjoyed reason, so why start now? Different footprints from the Cat's. I was sure of it. But something else had begun to nag my usually numb subconscious. Even though I had relied on instinct and gut feelings to guide me in my hitchhiking escapades, the complacent lifestyle of a local bum almost did me in. There was something else out there besides my mystic Kitty Cat, something fearful like a psychic vampire (Albion was full of them, legend said).

Terror struck deep in my heart as I contemplated probable enemies I might have in the area, and I began to feel mortal. My protective armor that God reserves for insane people was wearing off. Maybe Mousaka wouldn't be around the next time I had a big problem. Maybe the next time evil came around, I would lose the battle and get nastied. Maybe my fateful saga was determined to end in the beautiful headlands and coast of the Pacific Northwest. I might never see Lawless again, or Mama (I really missed her, it had been two years since I'd seen her last), or Gerhart, or Renee. I trembled as I lay me down to sleep that night, frightened of the raw, naked beauty of this place, where people died fairly often, and women came and went with the tides. I fell asleep and dreamed of a white poney.

My white poney came to me, prancing lightly on his butterfly feet, teasing me, drifting with me off into the dreamland where the forests held no evil faces, and unicorns danced in the moonlight. We tarried awhile in this land of silver and jasmine, while amethyst walls and a crystal river beckoned me to cross. I lay down at this clear, smooth river that had only the slightest ripple of a current, and watched dappled trout lazily swim to and fro amidst the pebbles, clearly visible underwater, by the light of the moon. I dreamt I was crossing the river, and came upon Cat Stevens.

He wasn't who I thought he was, only a faded man in pastel robes, speaking a language I didn't understand. Yet, I wanted to go with him, but he said no. My prancing white poney waited patiently on the other side of the river, so I crossed again to the other side, where bent blades of grass still marked the spot where I had lain. My poney tossed his pink nose, flaring his nostrils and breathing horsey breath on me. I attempted to lead the white one back to Cat's side of the river, but he had other ideas.

We began a long journey that followed a cobblestone path towards the crystal city. I could just barely glimpse turrets and gables of purple, pink and crimson glass, with jewels inlaid that sparkled in the full moon's milky glow. I suddenly was overcome with an urge to go live in this crystal city, because the walls promised me joy and happiness, if only I could ever find my way inside them. The emerald glade where I had slept faded as we trudged our lonely way up the winding path, and shadowy Cyprus trees blocked my view of the city. My white poney and me were dreamin' again, black rocks ebony faire in Mendocino....

I awoke with a start as sun poured into Ellen's loft from the skylight. The last vestiges of my white poney left me as I grudgingly let go of his protective embrace, and met the new day alone, all alone again. Something was missing, where was Mousaka? Climbing down to the cold, hardwood floor, I walked outside and whistled. No Mousaka. Hmmm.

Wandering over to the grocery store to buy some sourdough bread for breakfast (I ate a whole loaf back then), I asked the folks loitering around if they had seen my pup.

"Yeah, I saw him yesterday," River said, "He was stalking the chickens at old Farmer John's place." River characteristically scratched the top of his balding pate as he thought about my dog dilemma.

"Oh shit," I said. "I hope he didn't eat one."

I figured he did.

"You really should teach that animal not to stalk chickens, Gabrielle." River kinda gave me a 'Well, what can you do?' look and strolled over to the post office. I asked Tarah, who was coming out of the general store with her Mom and some packages, if she had seen Mousaka today, not yesterday.

"Have you seen my pup?" I was really getting worried, because he never strayed from my side, especially at night after I was in bed.

"Gabrielle, I saw him last night over at the creek by some sheep," she answered, looking at her Mom for assistance.

"Which creek?" I asked. "Near Farmer John's place?"

"Yeah, that's the one," she said.

"Oh fuck," I said, starting to cry.

"You don't think anything happened to him, do you?" Tarah noted my strange expression, and immediately offered to help locate the elusive Mousaka. "See you later, Ma, I gotta go find the dog," she said, waving bye to her Mom, and coming to my rescue. A true friend.

We looked high, we looked low. We looked on the beach, behind restaurants, in back yards, over hill and dale, and beyond. No dog. Oy! I wanted my Mousaka!

That night, just as we were ready to have a bite to eat over at Ellen's place, one of the guys in town came over and paid us a visit. My first greeting was "Have you seen my dog, Moon?" He shrugged his shoulders as in 'no,' but gave me some moderately good news, judging from the condition I was in that no news was good news unless it was about Mousaka.

"Sorry about your dog, Gabrielle," he said. "I wanted to tell you about Samson."

Oh, Samson huh? Yeah, tell me something I don't already know. "Did you know he tried to kick my ass last night?" I fumed, frothing at the mouth.

"Uh huh," said Moon, "That's the reason I came over." His kindly grey eyes gazed down at me, and I felt his friendliness envelop me. He felt very safe, and I needed it right then. Moon wouldn't make idle threats, I thought to myself. I guess Samson found that out pretty quickly. I had no doubt about what had transpired between Moon and the awful Samson. I wondered if he (Moon) broke any bones (Samson's).

"That asshole is twice as big as me, but half the size of Mousaka." I sniffled back a few tears. "He's been gone all day, and I don't know where he went." Full-fledged tears erupted, as I mourned my lost pup. Something bad had happened to him, I just knew it.

"Yeah, he's gone all right, we ran him out of town," Moon commented, handing me a hankie for my snotty nose.

"You did what?" I inquired, thinking the unthinkable. "You ran my dog out of town?" Moon looked aghast, and I realized he wasn't talking about my dog. I'm so slow sometimes, I silently mused, that it's not even funny anymore. Completely forgot my earlier thoughts in order to think only of my lost puppy dog. Waves of fear washed over me as I briefly allowed Sara's voice in my mind, and heard her screams on the freeway in Miami. No, I can't think about her, I just can't. "Sorry, Moon," I apologized, "Now what about Samson?" Moon just stood there with an odd, faraway look on his old, weatherbeaten face. He and others looked out for me the same way I looked out for Tarah. That's how it was in Albion.

"Samson bragged around town about how he was gonna beat you up," snarled Moon, "And some of the guys got a little pissed off about it." Moon put his hand lightly on my arm, as if to say 'we like you,' and said, "He doesn't have that many friends in town, Gabrielle."

177

"So you guys should have run him out before he came after me," I growled back. "But I really appreciate the effort, and thank you," I said, softening at the hurt look on Moon's face.

"I know you miss Mousaka, Honey," said Moon, hugging me for a moment.

"Yeah," I sniffled. That's about all I could spit out, because the loss of Mousaka had turned me into an emotional wreck. What about that nice crystal city that beckoned in the dreamy moonlight, would I ever reach it alive? I thought not.

"You might still find him," he said, although we both knew Mousaka was in trouble. "Don't cry, Gabrielle." I sniffled some more, and tried to look normal.

"With my dog gone," I sighed, "I'm dead meat."

"Maybe you should think about returning home to Lawless, Gabrielle." He looked me in the eye, patting my shoulder. "We love you, but there isn't a future for you around here, you know that." Yeah, I did. My ears had become pits of pain, with scabs running down to my jaw bone. My health was hitting the pits, and my safety was no longer assured. Where the fuck was Mousaka?

"I need my dog, man, then everything will be cool," I said, turning to walk into the woods and call, one more time, "Mousaaaakkkkaaa...."

Later that evening, around ten o'clock, River came knocking at my door, and I let him in. "Gabrielle, I have some bad news for you." He looked ominously ashamed, and unhappy to be the one to bear bad tidings.

"What is it, is Mousaka hurt?" I leapt into action and hyperactivated, jumping around the room, bouncing off the walls. "Where is he, do you know what happened to him?" River looked really uncomfortable, and softly said,

"They have him at the general store. He was caught with another dog killing sheep. Farmer John shot the other dog in the leg, and ran him off the cliff. Mousaka was taken prisoner."

"What the fuck for?" I screamed. "Did he kill any sheep?"

"I don't know the details, but they plan to keep him overnight at the store. Don't ask me why." River couldn't handle my dismay, and turned to go. "He's had it, Gabrielle."

I didn't believe it, and ran three miles to the general store alone to get my dog. I banged on the windows, the doors, the wooden beams, the sign out front. I heard Mousaka snuffling inside, and moaning to come out to me. "Mousaka," I softly whispered, "It'll be all right, I'll get you out tomorrow. Don't you worry, puppy dog, I'll come and get you in the morning." I cried big tears, and slumped down at the door that imprisoned my dog. Stupid fucking weird people! Why did they have to keep my dog hostage? He snuffled and whined inside, thumping around trying to escape. I pressed my face against the glass window, and tried to see inside. His furry nose steamed the window, and we momentarily touched through the glass.

I went home.

Next morning, bright and early, with the sun streaming in and spring in the air, I got up to go get my dog. Stepping outside, I noticed wildflowers blooming everywhere. What a beautiful day to take Mousaka to the headlands in Mendocino, where we could watch the seagulls dive and crash into the water for fish. That's what we'd do, I decided, we'd enjoy the cloudless day, and be together. We might even move back to Lawless. An old, rattletrap pickup pulled up, spewing gravel from the makeshift driveway all over me, and I noticed something in the back. The driver was a woman who wore a tan uniform with a patch on either arm. Uh-oh.

"Are you Gabrielle?" she said.

"Yes, I am, who are you?" Not bothering to answer, she simply said, "Your dog is in the back of the truck."

"He is?" I asked, walking cautiously to the rear of the truck and peering in. I hadn't heard any barking.

There was a bloody, furry mess inside the bed of her truck. It was my Mousaka. He was dead.

I couldn't believe it, I couldn't handle it, I tried to pet him but I got blood all over my hands. It looked like they slaughtered him with a machine gun or something. "You owe Farmer John forty dollars for the sheep this dog killed," the bitch said.

"I what?" I screamed, ready to punch her lights out. She backed away from me, not wanting to get hit. I would have. "My dog is worth more than that, and I want to know who the fuck killed him!" Hysteria took over as I cried and cried and cried. She said nothing, and got into her truck to go throw away my Mousaka, my friend, my puppy dog. I swear, my hair turned blond that day. I felt it go grey at the roots. How could these people imprison my dog, then sacrifice him at dawn like bunch of creepy cultists? I really knew it was time to go away from this place, because I was next on the hit list. Those grocery people had supposedly been my friends, but who was my friend, anyway? My dog was dead. My white poney was only a dream. I was too alone.

Before you knew it, I was headed back to Lawless on a Greyhound bus, leaving my troubles behind (or so I thought). As I watched the lazy, hazy fog wrap its tendrils around trees, ferns and sand dunes, I watched my life go by too. I vowed to return to this place someday, this raw, dangerous place that took life so lightly. I hadn't even said good-bye to Tarah, I couldn't say good-bye. I loved her too much to ever say good-bye.

Little girls, don't cry, please don't cry.
I'll never forget you, for as long as I roam.
Please don't worry, I am fine,
I have found my dream, in your eyes, in your eyes.
I searched, I searched everywhere, even, even L.A.
Barefoot, barefoot and poor, I was alone, I thought I was alone.
But He was there beside me, every step,
every step I took was toward Him.
I found my dream, I found my dream, in His eyes....
Last Friday afternoon, headlands blue,
I did na' care for anything.
My dog and me, were dreamin' again,
Oh black-rock ebony faire, oh black rocks in Mendocino.
The sea, she was calm, thus spake the wind, gentle wind.
The trees, they call me by name, windy, windy names.
Oh black rock ebony faire, oh black rocks in Mendocino.
I see, I see Ya write crosses, across the sky,
east and west, east and west.
I'm outta here.

Chapter 12

*I won't quit to become
someone's old lady.*

Janice Joplin

The Ritual

I was twenty-one years old, and on my way back to Lawless, Oklahoma in the summer of 1981. I was already falling into a great, big, horrific depression. Gorgeous redwood trees and Pacific Blue, those were the organic things I was leaving behind, but the deeper issues involved people. Ragtag me with carefully cultivated dreadlocks hair and shaggy legs, dressed all psychedelic with tie-dyed tee-shirts, no bosom tighteners and old, cracked leather sandals. I wasn't ready to return to the land of dust bowl dreams and too much television, and Oklahoma wasn't ready either for this misplaced California flower girl to set her dirty feet on its repressive doorsteps.

Hurtling towards infinity on a silver race dog while it belched hot black air into the hotter red air surrounding humidified Oklahoma, I caught a glimpse of what it would be like to be back in the Buckle of the Bible Belt with my non-friends and no peer pressure to share. I caught a feeling of pure terror as I locked into that silver dog's mission to return me in one grimy piece to Lawless, home of the most Seven-Elevens per square mile in the continental United States. In my alienated opinion, the only culture to be found here was "I Love Lucy" reruns and the three-month old pile of *Village Voice* newspapers that a poor, worn-down Brooklyn restaurant owner still nostalgically saved on his check out counter.

My hometown loomed in the distance, and even though the porta-potty smell of the silver dog's greasy, slimy seats was making me gag, even though I had barely slept a wink in three days on this slow-dog bus, even though the bald preacher man in the next aisle had been trying to feel my leg up every time I dozed off just for a moment, I still wanted to turn around and hitchhike back to the

Pacific Blue and get my money's worth on a highway trip to never-never land. I was that unhappy to be returning to the dusty dust bowl, home of Mega MacDonald's and a place where vegetarianism meant cows that ate a lot of grass.

Yeah, I was home pretty soon and got off the bus in the middle of a hot day in June while the Mall loomed dangerously like a huge blood-sucking tick that was frequently serviced by Lawless inhabitants doing the Mall Walk. Downtown Lawless had once been faintly attractive in a run-down sort of way, with rattle-trap three story Victorians once gracing its sleazy little heart. Now, high tech had taken over, shoveling under those lusty bawds that once housed rats and cockroaches in their flophouse rooms, leaving only the giant tick to suck dry every citizen of Lawless who walked into its neon denizens, clutching their credit cards in a greasy grip. Bermuda shorts were the rule back then in Lawless, anything two inches above the knee being an affront to the Lord, thus spake the preacher man who ruled pentacostally in Charismania.

"I said kneel," he might scream as his writhing sheep kneeled in obedience and hoped for some miracle and their salvation from sin and boffing their secretaries on Wednesday (but what the Lord didn't know wouldn't hurt 'em, they figured).

The cast of characters who inhabited the bus station this busy day swarmed around me, sweating great big clods of fume, peddling their wares on the strip where Lawless met its seamier side. "Say, baby," the purple, double-breasted suited black man said, as he rolled up to me in his limousine that had seen way too many better days. I had just disembarked and was shaking the porta-potty smell out of my nostrils, inhaling instead the semen encrusted scent of Lawless' nighttime crowd at the bus station who had left their organic flavor on the grey-green vinyl seats after a night of mutual jerking off in the bowels of the bus station's dark cavern.

I was home.

"Honey, I got a big black dick just waiting for you to suck it," he cajoled, wheeling slowly past me with a gold-toothed leer and a tentacle hand grasping air in hopes of grabbing my tits or shoulder or something, I dunno.

I just said "fuck off and die," and made my way home to Mama's house. I hadn't gotten very far when he came back behind me and nearly ran me over, spitting something gruesome out the window of his rusty chrome and yellow ride which hit me on the thigh, but I didn't really care because I was home and that's where the heart was, I heard somewhere.

Not wanting to call Mama or anything, just so I could maybe change my mind and go somewhere besides Oklahoma, I walked past the Mall Tick and wandered down Fort Kill Avenue, near Old Town Lawless where every year, some of the richer, indignant citizens would petition the City Council of good ole' boys to cut down those "doll-ganged trees, those dad-blasted leafy plants," because the horizon was not available when you had to look through trees to see it, and that was the scenery that made Lawless Oklahoma.

Forget about the fact that Old Town, rough as it was, housed the only trees left in Lawless which created a very small air supply for the citizens who inhabited the rest of its boundaries, forget the fact that Old Town was the only place left with beautiful and seedy sleaze-bag Victorian houses. They were coming down too, yelled the good ole' boys. "We need another MacDonald conglomeration right in the middle of that run-down crime area full of bums and dope addict bikers."

Yes, I pondered, it was quite a trip to be back in Lawless, Oklahoma. As I trudged the three miles to Mama's house, I noticed two white boys trying to hang a black boy off the stairwell in the front of their elementary school, two attempted muggings in the only jogging park in Lawless, and one car wreck which leveled a pedestrian who was stupid enough to try crossing the street in the middle of the day in broad daylight with no traffic. The car then swerved to avoid hitting an oncoming refrigerated pork truck, and slam-banged into the sign that touted "Lawless High," my old alma mater, as the "Only School with Good-Lookin' Cheerleaders."

Made it to Mama's house but she wasn't home. Got the neighbor to open the door for me and petted the dog, Foxy, who had been living there ever since I rescued her from the pound five years before. Fixed myself a greasy egg sandwich with mayonnaise and pickles, which, in the middle of a hot day in June didn't sit too well, but I didn't care, because it fit my mood to feel sick.

Back in Lawless, USA, I quickly became bored with the local neighborhood rounds, especially when I first spoke to good old Dad, at Hoggies Hamburgers, where he worked as manager. I had just cruised in, hoping for a free handout to increase my overall cholesterol and depression, and I didn't expect him to be glad to see me, but after all he was once my Daddy-oh. Might as well eat myself into oblivion since I'm stuck here in this horrific town where the farmers still worship the Corn King every spring with a virgin and a free sex show in the pasture.

"Hey Dad," I chirped, "what's shakin' in the burger kingdom?" I was munching on a Pork T sandwich, and couldn't think of much else to say to the father I hadn't seen in over two years. Daddy-oh couldn't have been less thrilled to see his prodigal daughter on Hoggie's doorsteps eating hog and growing armpit hairs with no bra.

"You sure have put on some weight, Gabby," he commented observantly. He nervously looked around to see if any of his friends or customers noticed my hippie appearance and purple sunglasses. "This is the only Pork T I plan to buy you because I'm flat broke." He pulled out both his polyester pockets to prove the point. I gave him the once over and took another greasy, dripping bite of hog jowl sandwich.

"Yeah, well I missed you too, Dad," I said, beyond caring about appearances or conversation. "Especially since you never wrote me a single letter." I finished off the last bite of greasy, breaded and fried Pork T, then began sucking on my strawberry milkshake. Sure, I'd gained a couple of pounds, I noticed, feeling my gut expand, but so what?

"I hope you plan to get a job, soon," he said, staring at my huge fat-laden tits which were shakin' and doing a dance. "But you'll have to wear a bra in Lawless." The old fart jumped up to bitch at the counter girl for not filling the salt and pepper shakers properly, which surely encouraged business from the good ole' boys who ate at Hoggies, since they enjoyed seeing him set the servants straight.

"Go get 'em, Dad," I called, feeling my oats from the shot of grease that plummeted down towards my expanded stomach cavity.

184

Time for my three hour nap, I thought to myself, then I'll get some pizza for dinner. It was back to the cream cheese and ice cream for my depressed soul, because I had nothing to live for in this filthy town.

"You need to spill less salt, Shandra, unless you want it to come out of your paycheck, girl," he yelled at the poor, ignorant black girl who was fresh out of junior high from Alabama and married to an Army puke stationed at Fort Kill.

"Have a heart, Old Fart," I called out to Daddy-oh because the poor, young, terrified girl was trembling and crying trying to scoop up the three or four granules of salt which probably cost five cents per pound at the most, but Dad acted like they were granules of pure, spun, designer gold. This was her first job and since her husband was a private and she had three kids already by the time she was the tender age of nineteen to support, he would kick her black ass all over the crib if he caught her without that paycheck.

Daddy-oh continued to harass his help, supported by the increasing audience of impatient customers who were lining up for their daily dose of cholesterol, saturated fat and animal by-products. Dad wasn't coming back to my table, so I decided to follow him down to his little basement office, hoping to get a little fatherly attention. All I got was a resounding, 'Get out, I'm busy!' so I decided to go home. I just loved my old man. He left me looking for a male support figure for years to come.

Things bumbled along like this between me and dear old Dad for a week or so before I figured out that he didn't really care for my company. The realization hit home when my brother Gerrie told me the following news after dinner one night, while Mom was napping. We snuck into my bedroom for a conference, just like in the old days. Gerrie whispered, "Dad told me to keep you away from his and Dana's house." Poor Gerrie, he hated to be entrusted with such nasty news. I was shocked, but not surprised.

"You mean, he doesn't want me to come over, but you can?" I asked, incredulously indignant.

"That's the deal," said Gerrie.

"Is he ashamed of me, or something?" I was pissed to infinity, and would stay that way for the next year, until things changed between my father and me.

185

Gerrie said, "Yeah, he's so full of shit. I don't even want to go over to his house, anyway." Raising his voice to the level of background Muzak, Gerrie continued. "He's one fat, righteous dude when it comes to sinnin' daughters," meaning me, of course. "But have you checked out his financial hazard on wheels?"

"Yeah, I saw that new Continental car his girlfriend was drivin' the other day," I said.

"Piece of garbage on the street," he snidely laughed. "Pussymobile."

"Ain't it the dirty truth?" We choked and cackled at that one.

"What about this shit he says 'I'm broke!'" Gerrie asked. Looking at me for confirmation, he shook his head.

"We all know how much cash the old man carries around with him, but what about the new Frederick's of Hollywood wardrobe Dana gets every year, and how about those trips to 'Vegas last summer?" We grinned simultaneously at each other.

"He sure is one pussy-whipped kinda guy!" I laughed, hiding my dismay at Dad's unchanging parsimony towards his 'real' family.

"A real sucker-face," Gerrie added.

"Too bad he screwed Mom out of all their savings," I continued, "He's blowing it all on booze and gambling."

Dad used to be a straight and narrow family man, but that was before he got his pussy whipped overseas, and became a veteran of Korean love, not to mention American nastiness. But I didn't help matters any with my poor attitude, and Gerrie had given up on Dad a long time ago. Might have had something to do with the fact that Dad had tried the same number on him, promising him a place to live years before, and ignored him from the time Gerrie was a young boy with a learning disability. Dad couldn't stand imperfection.

I wandered the streets of Lawless, fat, funky, bra-less, and derelict. Shop owners shunned me, my old friends (I have any?) disowned me, restaurants wouldn't hire me, neighbors wanted to spy on me. Only Mother, old-fashioned Mother, public school cook Mother, would have anything to do with me.

"I'm so glad you're safe," she would say, wrapping me in her older, worn-out work reddened arms.

186

"Air, Mama...." I would squirm, but I craved the attention. At least someone believed in me, I thought, looking at my poor wardrobe and fat-laden body.

"I always told your Father," she continued, "That if you lived long enough you would make something out of your life."

"You told him that?" I asked, pleased and basking in her warm kitchen love.

"I sure did," she said. "And even when he told everyone that you and Gerrie weren't his real children I told everyone he was lying through his teeth, that son-of-a-bitch." Mom never let Dad slide when he lied about us kids to the neighbors.

She took me to the doctor and spent at least one thousand dollars to get my ears cleared up, which also took over a year and a half to medically happen. I was a wreck. Mentally, physically, and emotionally, I'd had it. My dreams consisted of me, wandering the streets of Anytown, USA, searching for a bed. It was weird. I would wake up in my old bedroom at Mama's house, safe, secure, and relieved to be at home (although I wished it wasn't in Lawless). But every evening before I went to bed, I would take the dog and walk the streets, looking for my three bright blue stars. I never saw them again. On and on.

Finally got a waitress job at the local fish dive, but one dollar an hour didn't quite cut it so I ate most of my wages in breaded calf fries, gizzards, and well, you guessed it, I blossomed into a full-fledged hoggie myself. As a once thin but now very fat hippie friend once astutely said, "Old vegetarians never die, they just go back to meat." I became increasingly bovine in appearance, sprouting new and bigger flab folds on my already hefty-but-finally-healthy body. Something had to change, something had to give, somewhere, someone had to help me. I was drowning my sorrows and my personality in food, floundering in an ocean of cholesterol. Finally, an old friend showed up and changed my life forever.

Renee was back! I had been in town for half a year, and managed to develop an alcohol tendency, so took to frequenting the cheapest bars I could find, sort of looking for love and all that. I was almost ready to find a boyfriend, since I wasn't hitchhiking anymore, and could afford to finally be a sexual being with out fear of being raped in the night by some hard dick who wanted some too. There I was, hanging out at the old Prancing Pony Bar, a decrepit biker's hangout where beer and dope flowed freely among the motley crowd, and a place where men treated me like a biker broad, which was just fine with my sensibilities. In waltzes Renee, my old partner in crime, with her entourage of black, afro-adorned friends. Seeing her crowd made me immediately comfortable, so I downed my beer with one big gulp, and rushed over to the bar to greet her.

"Renee!" I jowled exuberantly jiggling all over. "What are you doing in this dive?" Remembering my disheveled appearance, I ashamedly compared my bovine body to her athletic frame. Obviously, Renee had been tanning, too, but my tan was pretty dark, due to my olive complexion. Hopefully, she wouldn't notice the many layers of fat which hid my personality under them. Piles and piles of cellulite stood between me and my former best friend.

I just knew she would look down at me with disdain and drop me forever because I was so fat and funky, not to mention weird. I was wrong. She thought I was normal! "Gabrielle!" she exclaimed, "Where the fuck have you been for the last two years?" Renee was green-eyed, light brunette beautiful, balleted to perfection from years of the dance. She surreptitiously glanced at my protruding gut, and noted the hair on my legs. No comment forthcoming about either.

"So what's cookin' gorgeous?" I squawked loudly for all the men in the bar to hear that I had a friend in town.

"You're cookin', baby!" she squawked back and we clapped hands and hopped hips to say like hello in a black girl way. The afro-crowd danced a jig with us, keepin' the beat to our song themselves. They didn't say much, just watched the white girls act silly. We were real inside out Oreos.

"Where ya' been all my dreary life, hon?" I asked, wondering how I survived six months in Lawless without her fun-loving presence (Renee was an original California girl from Sacramento, so we always had spoken the right language).

"Baby I been doin' on the strip," she said, as we both erupted in laughter all over again. Doin' the strip meant watching the whores over by the Second Avenue bus station as they seduced their johnboys and slung a little pussy. We used to do that all the time, I mused. Back when we were young and alone.

"Girl, you don't never change," I exclaimed, and her cronies nodded in agreement. Probably all their Mommas were livin' the Life on Second Avenue so they got to watch for free. A somber note crept into Renee's jingle bell voice, and she gave me a weird one.

"I heard from Prentiss Tribbly you joined up with the Moonies, or somebody like that," she said. Prentiss was an old ex boyfriend from back in high school who used to string me along.

"Say what?" wondered the black boys aloud. "She don't look like no Moonie to us." They scratched their sweet young bodies in complete unself-consciousness. "What's a 'Moonie,' Renee?"

"That guy is such a pud," I snarled, glancing at her crowd to get some agreement. They nodded their somewhat nappy heads with me. "I don't look like no Moonie lover."

"That boy's never been very bright," said Renee, lightening up now that the truth was out. "What'd you ever see in him, anyway?" I snickered at this latest addition to my already soiled personal history. Renee snickered too, as did her fellow ladies and gentlemen.

"I liked his cucumber," I said, motioning with my hand in an obscene pumping gesture. Michael Jackson's twin before the nose surgery piped up suddenly, unable to restrain himself any longer at my latest display of physical delights.

"You named Gabrielle?" the boy asked. He looked to be about sixteen or seventeen years old, and wore a black vest with green hiphuggers. From the sixties, or what? I wondered if his daddy knew anyone named Belzebubba, or drove a low rider, because he looked like that guy in the canary yellow limo who had gave me a little spit down in front of the bus station.

"Yeah, that's my name, what's yours?"

"My nomenclature be 'Judd,' to you, lady." Evidently the leader of this particular little gang, Judd pulled out his pick, and began to pull his hair outward, towards the sun. He also clutched his booty every now and then when he thought we weren't looking, reminding me of his male brethren who occasionally had a habit of doing that very thing. Big deal. Some guys pick their noses in addition to scratching where the sun don't shine. Maybe, I thought to myself, guys in general are just nasty.

"Gabrielle, why don't you come over to my house so I can shave your legs?" Renee said, sucking down her Corona with a lime. Shave my legs? I thought she didn't care. Hmmm. Maybe it might not be a bad idea. Renee looked at me again, changing my initial impression that she had not noticed my slightly altered, Northern Californian, feminist-carpenter, neo-new age sixties look. Well, maybe I just imagined the feminist-carpenter look as I was much too fat for manual labor. "Shave your underarms too?" she asked, no longer pretending to be anything but shocked. I silently sucked down my beer, and ordered another round for the teenage crowd. They were old enough I thought.

Renee then suggested spaghetti at her house with Mischi, Heidi, Schuppie the oldest dogs, Skeeter and Yoda the Cats, then Peter and Bernie the birds, not to mention the fish, Sylvester the White Fish, and Muffin, that poor mongrel dog that Renee and Klaus ran over with the Datsun, and took to the vet. We traipsed en masse out of the bar to Renee's funky Datsun, standing around in the dusty parking lot, squinting our eyes at the evil Oklahoma sun.

"Let's go shave your legs," Renee said, Michael Jackson, or Judd, as he affectionately called himself, followed us to her car, where we said good-bye to him and the giggling boys and girls, and exited the scene. The Brothers Johnson and the Ohio Players were waiting in our subconscious minds, reminding us by their presence of that lost time, long ago in our earliest, teenage, dad-supported youth, when we had driven a brand new car, listening to "Songs in the Key of Life," by Stevie Wonder. It was once more time to cruise the strip and watch the prostitutes, only this time we were in our twenties and should have known much better.

I hung out with Renee for the next week, even though the zoo was huge and smelly. I liked her house, which I had once, long ago lived in. The menage overwhelmed me, but I felt back at home in the old, funky house in Lawless' once homey, now sleazy district of town. Renee's live-in boyfriend Klaus tolerated my presence, and played tennis all the time while Renee and I plotted what we would do for fun that night which usually involved a halfjack of Jack Daniels under the tree in the front yard. Klaus, brown-eyed, brown-haired, tawny tanned body terminally clad in white tennis shorts had a brother, luckily, which made things all the more comfortable. It was time for my lizard to be let loose, I decided, and what better time than at Renee's house where leering eyes couldn't find me and slimy minded guys couldn't pick me up because I wasn't a hitcher anymore, oh no, it was time to lay the bad dreams aside.

I wanted a boyfriend, and I planned to get him soon.

"Why should I have to shave my legs?" I asked her later on that night in the bathroom with the clogged toilet, rubbing my calf and feeling the dark, spiky, long hairs that adorned my legs. Renee gave me an exasperated look and whipped out her razor blade, clicking it into its stainless steel Daisy razor shaver, advancing menacingly toward my well-woolied legs.

"Because," she said, lathering me up all the way to mid-fatty thigh, "Guys around here like bare skin." Skitt skitt went the razor, sharp on my poor, unadorned legs, pulling up roots of those hairs that grew there so long they felt like family, but I let her do it anyway, even though I felt truly naked that night in the bathroom all lathered up.

"What's the deal on Klaus's brother," I asked, willing to let her shave me only if I was gonna get some soon, because I had been such a little virgin, except for a brief fling with Michael in Oxnard, and after all, I was a pretty hot woman, some said.

"He's comin' over tonight," she said, skitt skitt went the razor, and she wanted to shave under my arms too, but I wouldn't let her until I actually saw him, and knew it was true that I would finally get my hands on a real man.

"What's he like?" I asked, meaning is he really for me and will he do the job right, because that's all that really mattered. I was hot and this was Oklahoma and there wasn't much else to do in this forsaken town except maybe smoke crank and get drunk and watch the whores on Second Avenue.

"He knows how to take care of a woman," Renee said, finishing my legs and looking me over. "Have a hit for yer heart," she said, handing me our friend Jack.

"I hear a bike outside rumbling," I slurred a couple hours later as we sat on the living room couch watching the tv and getting

191

bored because it was night and we wanted to be prowling but we were waiting for Hans to show us the way, the truth and the light down here in humid Oklahoma where in a town of one hundred thousand you have so much crime that people don't bother to watch the news, they just buy Rottweilers.

"That's him," she slurred back, downing the last of Jack and handing me an empty bottle. Renee lurched to the door to open it and here he came, all six feet of him and I was immediately in love with my new man, Hans.

"Got a joint?" he asked us, looking me over real good and I knew he wanted me in that way because his stomach growled and that's always a sign. I was just absolutely bowled over by his stink which he brought in off the street. He might as well have brought in his hog too, because the gasoline fumes emanating off his leather-clad hide made me afraid to light the joint Renee handed him.

"This is Gabrielle," she said in a madam's voice as if to introduce the best of her working girls to her highest paying customer. "She's just back from California."

Hans, Klaus' brother, was a sight to behold. He was a biker...a real, low-down, greasy-haired, tattooed, cradle-robbing, bitch-slappin' biker. He lived with a gang in their clubhouse here in Lawless, USA, and had a German ancestry which stretched way back to his great great great grandpa's castle. My German fixation had arrived, and Cat Stevens was finished. Pretty soon Hans and I had discovered the joys of sharing our stink right there that night at Renee's House of Original Sin, and Hans became my man to beat all women with a stick.

"Oh, baby," I crooned as he jumped on the couch later that night after Klaus had come home from playing tennis and was porking Renee in the bedroom "Hit me again," I sighed. We had a real combat scene going in the red bedroom that was my old lair, and I was entrenched in his biker kingdom, wanting to be his sordid biker queen. Within a week of brutal love play, I was riding the back of his hog, and feeling the Lawless wind blowing through my hair as we terrorized Mall walkers with his hog's fiery blast.

Hans, in his black leather way with bright brown eyes and wispy hair demanded I quit the Kitty Cat, even though I was finally getting some attention from his fan club cronies, who were writing me letters. I let him bug me for a while, saving up the letters for an RSVP I guess, knowing it would have to end in order for me to enjoy my German fantasy in Biker Heaven with Hans.

"You either burn those or give me up," he demanded, along with other commands such as "Get on my hog, bitch!"

"Okay baby," I would croon, shining the chrome on his bike and frying him hamburgers with lots of onions and mustard on Renee's old ramshackle stove. "But they keep writing to me," I would half-complain just to titillate him some more before he blew his stack one morning when we were sleeping in the red room and he found my hidden love stash of mail from London.

"Bitch!" his top blew off, "What's this other man shit I see?"

"Uh oh," I squirmed, "Ya found 'em, huh?" Yes he had and I tried a lame excuse such as something like the lack of culture in Lawless drove me to it but he didn't believe me one bit and I had to throw all the perfumed pretenses away before the fan club nabbed me and made me send 'em money, I dunno and I didn't care, I was in love with my biker man and wore his motorcycle chain around my waist all the time now. I even shaved my legs for him, not that he needed it. He was one full-blown motherfucker, and really told me what to do a lot, especially when it came to getting on his motorcycle among other things.

"I said clean the hog better this time," he would bellow, and I scrubbed harder and harder, hoping he would slap me just a little to wake me up and make me feel alive in this boring Lawless town in the Bible Belt in Oklahoma which was not okay by any means.

We sped around in our own little worlds on his hog, a rebuilt, bored-out Harley Davidson, drilled to perfection, while the rest of humanity sped around us and my hair got even more full of tangles. Didn't look to me and Hans like anybody much gave a shit where we went or what happened to our asses, so we continued to speed faster and faster and get drunker and rowdier and more bruised up every day.

Since I had moved in with Renee, Klaus, Hans and the zoo, Mom and I had a much better relationship than when I first got home from California all weirded out from the silver dog trip and smelling like porta-potty. She probably figured if she didn't see what I was doing to myself, it wouldn't bother her so much, and besides, at least Hans had lured me into staying in Okieland, right when I had been seriously considering hitching my way back to the dangerous Pacific Blue. She liked my greasy biker, because he treated her better than he treated me, which she didn't see and figured couldn't have been hurting that much anyway. We went over to do laundry and visit all the time, and she was happy I wasn't a newspaper headline and instead, was living across town in Lawless close to her.

She had hung in there with us, cooking those little kiddie meals at school even though her old bones were tired and probably couldn't take much more working since she had hit seventy, cooking supper for us at home every night, and breakfast in the morning. Renee, Hans and I ate at Mom's house as much and as often as she would put up with us. New age Mom. "What does 'this sucks, that sucks' stuff mean, anyway?" Mom asked me one morning, "And why did you send me that leaf in the mail?" I felt a bit unsettled at her reminder of my previous life as a transient hitchhiker in Northern California, and tried to evade the questioning.

"I have to go, Mama." Feeling very uncomfortable, I wandered into my bedroom, where Stevie Nicks albums hung out with Journey. Still the same room. Mom hadn't changed anything since I'd moved in with Renee and the menagerie way back when. She wouldn't let me off that easily.

"Was that some kind of pot?" she asked. "I thought pot looked like that." No way, I couldn't let this happen today because I was jonesin' wanting something real bad.

"Mom, I told you I don't smoke pot. Now, why would I send you a pot leaf, anyway?" Got ya fooled, Ma. I needed a joint like the hog needed oil.

"Well, Gabby, you did mention it in your letter. You said, 'I'm enclosing a little herb to make you feel better. It's guaranteed to stop any kind of headaches, sleep problems, or glaucoma.'" The old lady looked at my shakin' self and smirked a bit to show me it was cool, so I relaxed and tried to get away to my herbal stash.

Hmmm. Got me covered, don't ya, Ma? "Well, you know I was out of my mind, Ma. Why do you have to bring that stuff up now?"

We talked some more about this and that, and my search for a job entered the conversation because I wanted to follow in Mom and Pop's footsteps to the culinary world of Lawless' biggest service industry, the restaurant business.

I was trying to get a job at the local cafeteria, a big monstrosity that served hundreds of people fabulous (maybe not exactly fabulous) food in a large atmosphere. My dream come true. Along with my German fixation, I had a job fixation. I was going to move up into restaurant management, and finally get my Dad's attention.

"Mom, just drop the weed talk," I complained. "Heard any job news lately?"

"Okay, you're right. I'll give you a break, this time." Mom quipped, finishing the dishes as she always did, right after dinner. "Would you believe I talked to the manager of Furltons Cafeteria?"

"You did? About what?" Wow. The restaurant of my dreams was looming on the horizon, and I was about to actually get my foot in the door at Furltons.

"So. Did he offer me a job, or was it merely a social visit, Mom?" I stood in the doorway, aimlessly picking at a wart that had suddenly sprung up on my chin, and waited for Mom to put the last dinner plate in its place. There.

"Sweetheart, I do believe Mr. Bobkins asked about you," she said slyly, allowing the tension to slowly build. Mom began stacking the coffee mugs above the sink, and I couldn't take this teasing anymore, so I blurted out,

"Moooommm! Will ya just please tell me what he said?" I dried off the last piece of silverware, for by this time, I was too agitated to sit and watch her work in the kitchen.

"Well, I do believe he said something about needing a bus girl to come work the afternoon and evening shift," Mom said finally, as she turned around, and began banging the pots and pans around. That woman had an overabundance of energy when it came to the kitchen. I'd make a great bus girl after living with Hans, I thought to myself. I could play the straight Bible Belt act at Furltons for all the blue-rinsed set, then go home to my leather honey and beat some meat.

"So, did you tell him I needed the job?" I was not to be restrained, and ran around the dining room table to rummage through my things for the appropriate restaurant manager interview type stuff. Digging among the torn blue jeans and tie-dyed dashikas, I found a semi-tweedy business suit Mom had bought me in the hopes that I would someday conform, much as she once bought me Barbie dolls which I traded for toy guns and marbles. I was about to become the fastest rising star in my family, a bus girl at Furltons. I went, I conformed, I applied myself, I got hired. Before long, I got a raise. I bought myself a designer biker bitch leather leotard. Renee and I were hanging out at her house quite a bit, and as I slid into progressively more responsibilities at the store (Furltons was the 'Store'), good old Dad began to sit up and take notice. He actually started to talk to me about the restaurant business, as he had when I was a kid, long ago, and we shared our experiences on a daily basis. His store was right up the street from mine, and since it was so close, I dropped into Hoggies quite often. Before I knew what was happening, I found myself comparing inventory deficits with my father and actually enjoying it.

"Hey, Gabby, good to see you," old Pa would say, as he busily rang up the hourly sales on the registers. "I'll be right out there, get yourself a cup of coffee on me." He would limp to the back of his restaurant (an old war wound left his back in bad shape), where he would remain for approximately fifteen minutes, then emerge into the dining room.

"We rang up seven thousand in sales last Saturday, and it was only five o'clock," I would say, drinking my coffee black, like his. Yech.

"My food cost is eating me up," he would complain. "The help are wasting too many french fries, and I don't know where the cheese is going." He would nervously glance at his watch, and I would say something to this effect:

"Our biggest problem is the head office," I would say, grimacing at my coffee which tasted like crude oil. "They send nasty letters any time we have a discrepancy in hours or payroll." My consternation at all the paperwork and numbers would be apparent, and sweat would bead my fevered brow.

"I know what you mean," he would comment. "I get them too. Chaffondra, get to work cleaning that grill!" Looking at first the girl, then me, Pa would say, "Be right back," then stomp over to berate the terrified Chaffondra.

"Ever since I got that second promotion," I would say as he returned to his seat after leaving the poor girl in tears, "All Bobkins does is give me more and more paperwork." I hurriedly glanced at my watch.

"You really should have thought twice about taking that job," Dad would commiserate, "You know what responsibility goes with it." He looked around at the paper strewn tables, in the wake of lunch hour rush. The dining room blinked on and off like orange and black neon, cloning MacDonald's in all except the clown himself. Hoggies had a pig, razor-back style-to advertise their colon inhibiting, lard-packed wares.

"Yeah, but look at you," I said, nervously computing various sums where appropriate in my paperwork which lay before me. I was an Establishment Girl, transformed into pallid hamburger after only one year in Lawless' fast food business grinder by day, and a low-down scum sucking biker queen by night. "Fifty-nine years old, and working sixty hours a week." I exchanged harried glances with Dad, who noticed the ketchup stains on his polyester blouse for the first time. He absently wiped at the offending, bloody blotches with a napkin, to no avail, of course.

"I know, I know," he griped. "It's a pain in the ass when the head office calls and bitches about labor, but when we're busy, we need help." Dad got up to go chase down an elusive counter girl, yelling at her to sweep the dining room. I swept up all my paperwork that I carried everywhere in a briefcase, in the event that I might find time to finish it at home, or on the run. It was my only way to escape Furltons, which was only too happy to pay me twenty hours a week overtime as it was.

"Gotta go, Dad," I called, waving at him as he harassed his grill man about overdone Deluxe Burgers.

"You really should come by the house this Friday night, Gabby," he said to me as I hit the super storm trooper vacuum front door, which opened only after a die-hard shove, in order to keep its expensive air-conditioned contents freezing cold. He limped up to the other side of the counter, facing me as I fought gallantly with the thick glass and chrome door. "We're having vegetarian lasagna for dinner."

Dad looked at me expectantly, but I stalled. "Sorry Dad," I breezed, "Hans and I have a date at his Mom's house for dinner that night." No way, Jose, I didn't want to go to Dad's house. I'd rather face the screaming bitch, Hans' mother, his lovely royal German mama who haunted all our goings on with the wide-eyed power of her checkbook. Dad looked slightly embarrassed. It had been quite some time since his initial disapproval of my bra-less state, but I still wouldn't come to his house.

"Well, maybe some other night," he murmured sadly, watching Chaffondra fuck up another order. "Chaffondra, I tol' ya to sweep, not cook!" he screamed as several good ole' boys nodded their fat pink jowls in agreement. Them young girls oughtn't be allowed to cook when there was plenny of older women to do it better, they all seemed to agree, slurping their coffee and slinking in with their black Havana cigars to stink up the restaurant's already fat-laden air.

"Yeah, sure Dad," I answered, ignoring his outburst. "Maybe some other night." I went back to my duties at Furltons as second assistant manager, which was no mean feat, since the first assistant had absconded with the money and took off two months earlier. I was filling in for him on top of my duties, in the sixty employee restaurant.

Wow.

Was I tired!

After visiting dear old Dad, it was time to go see my good friend and confidante, Renee. Maybe she would have a scotch for me after work. Freshly dry and off the hallucinogenics, I had begun to rely on booze to give me a buzz. I could quit anytime. Establishment Oklahomans who had big time job gigs couldn't afford to be caught buying pot and illegal substances, so I protected my new uptown status by not associating with hard-core types except on weekends with Hans, and I let him buy all the drugs he wanted with my money. I just didn't do 'em anymore.

I hanging out with a German biker and I was also almost running a large restaurant. My dark and kinked out honey bear would pick me up from work on his Harley Davidson, and we would go to the clubhouse where his gang stayed, and drink beer. Most of the guys were rough looking, but I thought they were kind of sexy, in a naughty sort of way. They were always after me to sneak off with them, but I was afraid of Hans and his attitude. One hot humid day I strolled into the clubhouse like I owned the place, looking for Hans, as usual, who was lounging by the bar. Couple of the guys made passes, perhaps because of my bare minimal leather attire, but nothing concrete occurred because Hans was watching.

"Yo woman," said Barley, a good-looking junkie in his middle fifties with jailhouse tattoos and a bitch in every town who claimed to be his bride. "You need some action, Honey?" His gristled appearance and randy stench did nothing to turn off my attraction, for I was a true biker bitch and wanted them to come harder all the time. Hans glared at me and said,

"You go near him I'll fuck you up." I flirted with disaster, carrying Barley a beer and opening it in his face, splurting foam, getting his attention even hotter than before.

"Don' you worry 'bout a thing, little lady," he slurred, already reeling from his morning of injected stuff and something called Peruvian mist. He liked to mix horse with coke in order to feel his body crackle with fire, and cool the jonesin' stemming from his beleaguered brain. Old fart couldn't do much for me anyway, I mused, so why risk it?

"I'm jus' bringin' ya a beer," I said nonchalantly, glancing at Hans who was glaring my way. I pranced back to his side of the biker barn, where the Slaves of Hell kept their loosely knit gang of thugs. Hans slapped me clear across the room, and told me to stay away from any of the dudes or else I'd be slinging pussy elsewhere. I was so devoted to his lusty self and his evil ways that my soul's fire stayed quenched, I stayed his bitch, and we happily traveled the trails of Lawless, treading on uneasy ground.

It was a Lawless lifestyle, but what the hell, we didn't care because we had no culture anymore, we had no Pacific Blue to soften our heated minds, we only had each other and the wind. I was a subservient biker bitch, and I liked it. Quite a change from 'Crazy Gabby' who roamed California, but, like I said earlier, flow with it.

Chapter 13

*If Christ were here there is one thing he
would not be—a Christian.*

Mark Twain's Notebook

The Feast

"Are ya down, Homegirl? "I called through the door after work that Wednesday, hoping to catch Renee at home and not out partying, like she usually was by seven p.m. on weeknights. I heard a gurgling coming from the bathroom, so I figured she was trying to flush the old, funky toilet. I cruised through the living room, dodging cats and dogs and sayin' hi to the birds that hung over Klaus' chair where he usually sat and chain-smoked Marlboros.

"In here," hollered Renee as a whole wad of toilet paper came gushing out the door into the hall, barely missing my feet since I jumped out of the way just in time. "Shit!" screamed Renee and I couldn't help but snicker.

"Looks like it to me." She glared at me with a real live go to hell look, and I figured it was time to sca-doodle outta there before she asked me to help her clean up the sad brown stinky muck that had flooded the hallway, scaring Heidi and Schuppee the dogs right outta of their gourds. They sniffed at the stuff timidly, then padded outside to sniff their own, which I'm sure they preferred to ours. "Well," she pouted, handing me a bucket, a towel, and a sandbox scoop which we kept on hand just for these type occasions, since the toilet couldn't handle toilet paper or even larger poops. "Ya gonna help, or what?" I figured I'd better, although I'd rather sca-doodle, since she was my friend and those were probably partly my turds that floated around in the hall.

"Yech," I exclaimed, holding my nose and scooping while the cats looked on imagining we were scooping our own kitty-litter box because it sure wasn't their turds we were pickin' up that evening when I'd rather have been drinking a scotch. Finally got

200

the stinky mess over with and I said to Renee, "It must have been a big one to make the toilet puke."

"It was," she admitted, "I ate too much of that damn Korean food last night."

"That explains the paranormal stink," I said, noticing that all the animals had left the room and the two poor birds were practically gagging in their cage in the living room. "Got any of that air freshener stuff?" I asked.

"Let's step outside," Renee answered with a shudder, and it was a good thing too because we were gonna need some oxygen tanks real soon otherwise. "Better bring the birds," she said, "they look kinda sick."

Renee finally got out the booze much later on that night, when I was about to shake to pieces from my strong desire and by this time the house smelled a little bit better but the cats still wouldn't come back inside. I had decided, after she shaved my legs back in ancient history, that we should not succumb to that insistent siren, the lure of drug abuse, and I was still trying to stay off the stuff, although I hadn't been successful all the time.

Temptation, you know.

"I've had enough," I preached that night after cleaning up all the poo-poo, "for LSD has fried my brain, just like an egg in a hot skillet, and I can't stand the flashbacks." Pompous and clean for a whole past two months, I was ready for the change of life.

"Not so fast, Gabby," Renee countered, "I've got some killer weed, the kind that kinks your hair." She pulled out her plastic baggie full of hopeful green buds, crystal dreams from California. I couldn't take it, I wanted no reminders of that beautiful place I left behind.

"Look, just don't offer me any, okay Renee?" Surely, she would understand. She did. Renee walked over to her cabinet in the dining room, and swung the door wide. The look in her twinkly ever-glade eye was mischievous as ever, and as I turned to gaze into the open cabinet abyss, I was falling into it already.

"How about a little drinkie-poo?" She teased me with a bottle of Chevas, then dug out the Crown. I couldn't stand myself, and half-searched for a little Jack to add to the quorum.

201

"Oh, baby, oh sweetheart," I said, meaning the booze, because that's what it was, my sweetheart. It married me. The worst thing was, I didn't realize that I had changed over so quickly from one dependence to another until it was too late, not too many seasons later, to go back to my former, non-alcoholic self. I was a scrambled egg in no time "Yeah, I'll take a little sip," I said, as we grabbed a couple bottles and headed for the tree, underneath which we'd sit 'till the moon turned over and the dawn's early rays burned our blood-shot eyes.

Life clung on to me, tenacious as it was, and my love affair with Hans blossomed into a full fledged megalove that lasted until several unfortuitous events caught up with me and slammed my head into a brick wall. I was just hanging out and minding my own beeswax one fine spring day, and noticed Hans' hog out front of the clubhouse. I saw Leather Lips sitting on the porch and drinking a beer with another biker bitch from Wichita Falls, Texas who I didn't know, and asked her if she'd seen my Baby. The other biker bitch turned to smile at me and I noticed her black eye and missing front teeth, but that wasn't unusual when you hung with these kinda guys.

"I seen him," the fifty-year-old German poodle groomer said, "But you bes' stay outta there yourself." Leather Lips was the oldest biker bitch in the club and had been around the longest, so if she was giving me a warning I should of taken it and scrammed but I was young and stupid in those days.

"But he's my honey pie," I told her, tromping up the broken-down wooden slats that served for porch steps, "He won't mind if I just peekie poo." Now, Leather Lips had seen better days and they weren't living with bikers, if you know what I mean. Her frizzed-out blond hair and leather G-string bikini showed off the faded, jail house tattoos she wore better than most of the guys. She also packed a shiv for if and when anybody fucked with her. Leather Lips was a ballsy biker bitch who didn't take too much shit off anyone except, of course, her old man.

"You go in there you'll be one sorry motherfucker," said Leather Lips, scratching her crotch. The other bitch who was just visiting shook her head and snickered a bit which got me suspicious because I had noticed several hogs parked out front with Texas plates and wondered if there was a party he didn't invite me to that day.

"We brought in a little crank," said the Texas bitch, and I figured out that that's maybe why they didn't want me in disrupting business and all that but I was hip and they all knew it so it should have been kasj, but it wasn't. "It makes 'em mean," she said.

"I'm gettin' sick of you-all tellin' me what I can't do in my clubhouse too," I snarled, causing the two ladies in leather to reach for their shivs, which I noticed, luckily, and apologized before I got my face all cut to pieces. Never mess with a biker bitch, that's my motto. I waltzed into the clubhouse like I owned the place, and saw several unbathed biker dudes lazing around drinking beer which made the super heated place stink up like a whorehouse in Texas, or a bayou swamp filled with garbage in the summer.

"Where's the old man?" I asked Chin Chin, who was the only Korean they let join the club, mainly coz he killed a guy once in full view of the gang, and they were so impressed they took him in and let him hide out from the law at the clubhouse. Chin Chin had beady little eyes and hooked fingers that constantly looked like they wanted to pluck something, like he plucked his victim's eye out during the fight, I figured. He was a dangerous dude and had so many tattoos he didn't need any clothes except maybe a jock strap although that part had a tattoo too.

"He not here," snickered Chin Chin, which was a lie and I told him so and went searching for my honey bear who I hadn't seen in over three days and I wanted some attention from right now. I strolled to the bedroom, stepping over several sleeping bikers sprawled in puke and entered the den of iniquity where the Slaves of Hell initiated their women into the club. And I saw this humping creature that turned out to be Hans on top of some little slut teeny-bopper bitch so I immediately became enraged and hit him in the face before he even knew I was there.

"Arrrgghh!" he screamed, jumping off the little brat and slamming me into the wall real quick before grabbing my hair and pulling me over the bikers' passed out bodies into the living room where he could punch me and pistol-whip me in front of everyone to show off his macho male attitude. I musta passed out because I woke up in the front yard, to the best of my recollection, and forgot who I was for a while, I think. I don't remember much about it. My beating by Hans went on for a long time, evidently, and somewhat addled my brain. I wandered around Lawless aimlessly after the concussion, and finally found my way back home to Renee's house two days later, she told me, where I promptly swore off bikers forever. Renee took me to the doctor to have him stitch up my bleeding face which today still holds the scars from Hans.

I decided to get the hell outta her place before the old man came and finished me off so I tried to find a cheap apartment and decided to go straight and even sold off my leather leotard, although I secretly hoped that someday I'd find another German biker with a heart. I moved into a cheap little place in Old Town, and had lots of time to ponder my situation. I figured I was better off without Hans' sweet love, but I missed him all the same and told Renee to tell him where I lived after I was gone for two weeks, but he never came by. Just as well, I thought, I need to clean up my act and try to be a straight Establishment Girl.

Luckily for me, I found another outlet for my obsessive self downstairs where some boy musicians had a recording studio that thump-thumped me all night long and even vibrated the walls like an Oklahoma thunder-boomer in spring. I liked to trade off one obsession for another, although I didn't notice it at the time, and my personality was wanting to be released so it could pursue the pursuit of happiness, staying busy and all that.

Furltons was becoming an increasing drag, and I wondered if my greying hairs would soon fall out, because the stressful job I was in demanded all my attention, and I had no time for myself. I considered quitting and returning to college. But could I actually survive Academia? I had dropped out twice, and I was truly frightened of my lack of ability to stick with anything, although I had stuck with Furltons for way too long. The sounds from the studio beckoned me too, and I wanted to drag out the acoustic-electric Alvarez Yairi that Hans had bought me in a fit of passion before our big fight, back when he was still enamored of my charms. I wanted to play guitar.

Events soon decided my life for me, because I was offered a third promotion and twenty-two thousand a year to move to Austin, Texas, as first assistant manager of a Furltons store there. I turned them down, and they gave me the boot. I got no unemployment. When Furltons says go, you go, or you go. Relieved, I applied for grants to the local community college, and as usual, I was successful. It was back to school for this party-girl and that called for a drinkie-poo!

Shakespeare interested me that year, as did Chaucer, Spenser, and Sappho, reawakening my literary soul. Adrienne Rich, Erica Jong, Alice Walker and Marge Piercy caught my eye in my spare time, and I made all kinds of time to read, since I was now a born-again feminist. I parked my little old shuddering Datsun which Klaus had given me when I moved out, probably hoping I wouldn't call the cops on his brother. I bicycled to work on my old worn-out Takara, worked part-time in the dormitory snack bar, and tutored students in Cotton College's English Department Writing Lab, Room 333. "I used to be a biker bitch," I'd tell anyone who'd listen, "But now I'm just a biker." Folds and flabs of fat disappeared before long, so I attracted a couple guys but nothing serious coz like megalove had done me wrong.

When there was a music jam downstairs, I conned the guys into letting me join in. I also found it easier to take classes in English than anything else, so I had an excuse to read full-time for the first time in my life, and my grades were actually quite decent. But I was a lonely girl, a ripe peach just waiting to be plucked, for Renee had moved to Germany with Klaus, and I had no one to turn to in Lawless except good old Mom. Dad decided I shouldn't waste my time getting an English degree, so all he ever said anymore was that same, slightly altered refrain, 'Don't ask me for money, I'm broke, see?' as he pulled out both pockets in his, by now, characteristic trait.

The boys in the studio became increasingly interested in my guitar work, but I wouldn't jam with them at their church, even though they assured me I wouldn't be labeled a backsliding Christian in the popular churchgoer, Bible-thumper lingo prevalent in our Oklahoma Bible Belt. "Look, dudes, I know you're cool," I'd say, hitting the deep and resonant 'E' on my box, "But no preacher man is gonna tell me not to say 'fuck,' get it?" The boys looked at me incredulously as I strummed in time to Neil Young's 'Cowgirl in the Sand,' trying to get the 'A-minor/D-minor' switch just right.

205

They weren't incredulous with my playing, which was at best beginning mediocre, no, they were simply shocked at my foul mouth, the sweet things.

Shifting his bass to the floor, Sid, the studio's owner-manager looked at me soulfully with his big, innocent, puppy-dog eyes, and said, "It's not like that, Gabby." He unplugged the bass from his Randall amplifier, and turned it off. "Why don't you try it," meaning Bible study, "Just for one Sunday at the Stable?" The Stable was a coffeehouse type place where boho Christians went to congregate and jam.

"Forget it, I refuse," I said with great vehemence in my voice which he ignored. Looking around the studio, Sid picked up a small, cheaply-printed songbook with a lion and a lamb smirking on the front cover.

"See this?" he asked, opening it up to page thirty-three, and showing me the song written there. "This song is written about you," Sid explained, and it was a nice song, but I still didn't want to subject myself to the preacher man's rule.

"I like the song," I explained patiently, "But I hate church, Sid." Banging on the drum set, my guitar still slung over my shoulder, I illustrated my point. "Forget church, dude. Let's jam!" The other guys, Charlie and Benjamin picked up their stuff to play along since they did whatever the group think warranted, which was what I would soon learn was the pentacostal way.

On and on. I just wasn't interested, but I finally relented (naturally) one day while we were jamming, because the pastor came by to play a song with us. Page thirty. He was kind of cute, and wore Levi's with a Grateful Dead tee-shirt. Norman worked as a carpenter and was involved with church, but he didn't spend a lot of time taking up donations. I finally agreed to play in his group on Sunday, because, as he said, I could dress any way I wanted and leave after we finished playing. Damn. A new obsession had sneaked in the back door when I wasn't looking.

Sunday morning arrived, sunny and hot, and I wanted to go rock climbing that day, because the prickly pears were blooming and the prairie dogs were singing and the buffaloes were humpin' and the creeks were running and it was so beautiful out there in the wild, rattlesnake-infested Wichitas that I couldn't sit still for a freaking sermon, uh uh. I called my old Explorer friend Wayne, who still hung around Lawless, to see if he wanted to be my belay-slave on Crazy Alice, a five-eight route that was a favorite for climbers who liked to curl their toenails on the Zoo Wall in the Narrows, and he said "C'mon" so we went.

All my former buddies from Police Explorers were cops now, except for my martial arts expert buddy Wayne who had lived in Alaska for two years with a wolf dog. He and I got back together as often as we could to climb, and we had recently bought new ropes, hexes, friends, and harnesses along with some new green and blue climbing shoes for me. I was beginning to learn the art of lead climbing, but it was precarious business.

Forget church. Got out my Merrells and had a blast that hot sunny day with Wayne since he was my belay-slave, didn't need to climb on a tight rope except on Dr. Coolhead on the Zoo Wall right next to Crazy Alice which was five-ten with a bullet and kicked my ass clear to Texas. Sid was cool when I returned that night to the studio, because he knew I wasn't really quite a normal girl to be traipsing off into the woods at the drop of a hat and that I had some problems like alcoholic ones that I didn't exactly want to deal with not to mention my hermit ways.

Sid, being a real friend and not a church geek offered to introduce me to a friend of his, a woman healer and artist named Sara, who had designed the cover of his latest album, Throbsong. I now realize that Sid saw my mental/spiritual problems, and was only trying to get me well although at the time I didn't realize that I was even sick. A few days later, I fell asleep, and had this dream, which freaked me out totally because I didn't think God really wanted much of anything to do with a sinner like me who wouldn't go near a church even if it bit me.

I was lying by a stream, surrounded with pink and purple wildflowers just like Pacific Blue in California and I was reading my Bible. The natural beauty just knocked me out but I knew I was supposed to read so I turn to Revelations 21:10, and read the following passage: "And he carried me away in the Spirit to a mountain great and high, and showed me the Holy City, Jerusalem, coming down out of Heaven from God. It shone with the glory of God, and its brilliance was like that of a very precious jewel, like that of a jasper, clear as crystal." Sounded like somewhere near Albion, California to me, I thought to myself, wondering if I had to go back to Lawless or if I could just stay there forever by the Pacific Blue.

I felt my spirit gently disengage from my body, and float into the eternal aura which surrounded every living person on Earth. There was no time or space in Heaven, or in the spirit world. I found myself standing before an amethyst crystal palace with pillars of pink-amethyst that reached farther than my eye could see. "This must be the New Jerusalem that Jesus Christ spoke of, the same Holy city that I have studied in Revelations, the Garden of Eden that He has prepared for us," I figured to myself, although if anyone else had been around I'd a asked their opinion.

"Oh God, why have You shown me Your City, do You intend to take me Home now, Father?" I wondered, standing and gazing in awe at the sparkling pillars of my future home, and I was filled to overflowing with such incredible joy that I woke with a start from my dream/vision, or so I thought.

"This is exciting," I mused, lying by that same old stream, that good old stream that looked suspiciously like the Russian River in Mendocino County and filled my heart with gladness, and harbored white poneys and rainbows. An emerald glade, my hideaway by the river-creek. Look, over there! A white poney dancing in the ferns, my white poney prancing in the green grass... he neighed at me then faded into the mist for a while and I tried to figure out just what to do next.

I opened up my Bible, which had fallen by my wayside as I fell into sleep to Psalm 84:1. I read: "How amiable are thy tabernacles, O Lord of hosts!" I couldn't stop with just that first one, so I read on, finishing the entire Psalm. I suddenly had this overwhelming feeling like I was entering a rainbow, and the crimson red color just barely touched the top of my head. Suddenly, I felt myself breathing in the color red, and breathing myself right up! With a poof! I plunged into orange orange, and tasted citrus on my lips and tongue. It traveled all the way into the back of my throat, and I smelled the spores and droplets of Sunkist oranges. Not knowing what else to do, I resumed reading: "My soul longeth, yea, even fainteth for the courts of the Lord: my heart and my flesh crieth out for the living God."

I was, by now, covered and filled with a dome, a rainbow dome, a sky of colors-yellow, green, blue, indigo, violet. My awareness had expanded as I moved up into yellow, and felt the velvet lemon cream in my mind. Tasting tart lemon/orange orange on my tongue, I erased all past unhappiness and confusion, filling my heart instead with gladness and joy at the sight of the Lord. Maybe I'd get to stay here and never go back to Oklahoma—maybe Oklahoma was nothing but a bad dream, and I'd wake up in Swansong's Moon Room. The Bible said: "Yea, the sparrow hath found an house, and the swallow a nest for herself, where she may lay her young, even thine altars, O Lord of hosts, my King, and my God." There went that white pony again into the trees over there by the stream under the cherry blossoms; I whistled but he just looked at me and pranced off.

"Maybe I'm dreaming," I said to myself, "But this stuff sure seems for real so maybe I'm not." I made a horrendous attempt to stay asleep but alas, I woke up and there it was, Lawless Oklahoma, sprawled beneath my California girl feet. "Aw shucks," I moaned to no one in particular, "I guess I'm stuck here after all."

A week later, Sid convinced me to go to Texas to meet his best friend, Sara. "She's too incredibly cool," he said, "ya gotta meet her to believe it."

"So, like what's so fascinating about some old lady who paints horses?" I asked sarcastically, not wanting to trust anyone except myself.

"Her personality is like, electric," Sid said. "C'mon, what else do you have going on today, anyway?" Well, it was true, I didn't have too much in the way of excitement that weekend except the usual five hours spent with Shakespeare, so I said,

"Yeah, all right, but she better not be boring." Sid snorted at my wise-ass ways, then we hopped into the truck and split. We traveled to Tipton, Texas, a few days after I woke up from that totally strange dream, and I met Sara. She painted primarily horses for a living, and lived with her daughter in a huge farmhouse, with nine cats, two dogs and two horses. Initially, Sara and I talked about life in general and what it was like to be a Christian in a

209

convoluted world with churches that were stranger than fiction and the people who indulged in orgiastic, spiritualizing get-togethers that characterized the Charismatic movement in my area of the United States. "Sara," I asked her, "What do you think of all these judgmental preachers who ask for your money and spend it on larger and larger plastic steeples?" She shook her grey-haired paint-splattered head, and dabbed lightly at the white horse she was currently commissioned to paint. Seven thousand dollars per horse. Kinda looked like my white pet Snoflake poney who I used to feed watermelon during the old childhood days back in long ago land.

"Gabrielle," she said conversationally, not knowing I used to have a white poney pet, "You should be riding this horse instead of worrying about what other people think." Dab, dab, dab. There, his flared-pink nostrils are finished, now it's time to start on the hooves.

"Ain't it the truth, though," I agreed, watching her paint. I was in total awe.

"If you spend enough time with animals," she philosophized, "people problems just fade away." Sara looked at me with her wise grey eyes, then went back to the nostrils. Dab dab.

"Sid here thinks I should regularly attend church," I griped, "And listen to what Norman has to say." I was slightly confused by this time, which was nothing unusual for me, and my identity was at stake. No self-respecting Christian organization would ever claim me, nor I them, so why bother? I wondered. But, on the other hand, that dream really bugged me. Maybe the Lord was talking to me and I wasn't listening.

"I think you should follow your heart," Sara answered, tapping her sable brush in a small jar of turpentine. Her slightly gnarled hand performed wonders with a light swish of the brush.

"Yeah, right," I moaned, remembering the trouble my heart had gotten me into with Hans my old honey bear. I still missed the Life, but had gotten used to being extremely bored and straight without any whips, leathergoods, or motorcycle chains to keep me excited. Sara stopped with the turpentine and gave me her full attention. What beautiful eyes she had. What good vibrations. I think I like this lady, and I can't figure out exactly why. Sara said,

"When the time comes for communion with others, you'll know."

"What others?" I wondered aloud.

"The crowd at the Stable," she answered. Sara resumed painting the black hooves on her white poney, and I felt some modicum of peace.

"Do I gotta?" I whined, not wanting to go near those plastic steepled monstrosities that dotted the landscape of my existence, making me want to puke at every sight of their loathesomeness.

"Ya gotta," she answered with the surety that only years of knowledge brings. "Ya don't gotta embrace the personal theologies," she explained further to my fevered consternation, "just step in and check 'em out.'

"Oh, I guess you're right," I moaned, like a little brat afraid to eat her liver and onions, "but they really make me want to puke."

"What you don't know can hurt you," she said, referring to the tide of charismania which swept Lawless with a large broom stick. "Ya gotta know 'em before ya fight 'em." I was beginning to understand her understatements and homilies—if I was to be informed, I had to visit the false prophets and see their wily ways for myself. The Bible did mention many false teachers who could even fool the Elect in the last days. Hmmm. It made sense to me.

"Well, at least there are a couple of normal Christians around," I said, remembering the crowd at Waterford who saw little men. "Two that I know of."

"You'll meet one or two more," she said, "and don't forget to read your Bible."

"Can we write to each other, Sara?" I asked her. "You're the most sensible Christian I've met yet, besides Sid." I wondered if I should tell her everything that had transpired between Sid and me. A black cat walked by, and strolled over to me so I could pet it. A calico cat followed, jealous of my attention to his friend. I petted both of them, and pretty soon, a Manx wandered in to join us. Fine, I'll pet all of you, and scratch your little kitty cat ears, too.

"Of course we can," she said sweetly. "I'm especially interested in a poem of yours that Sid sent me about a white poney." She stopped painting, and put down her brush. Taking off her glasses, Sara gazed at me full on, locking eye-beams. "Will you tell me about him, sometime? I'd really like to know more about you, Gabrielle." On the way out to the Bronco, Sara pointed out her two dancing poneys, Cinnamon and Clove, who were prancing in the pasture, eating wildflowers and alfalfa grass. I fell in love immediately, totally entranced.

"Go ahead and pet them Gabrielle," Sara enjoined, noticing my excitement. I let out a shrill whistle, and the two poneys rushed over to where Sara, Sid and I stood.

"Look," said Sid, "they came to Gabrielle's whistle."

"That's how I used to call my horse," I explained, basking in the horsey warmth of Cinnamon's nose, and Clove's soft neck. The horses and I nuzzled each other happily, while Sid and Sara watched with some amazement. I always did love the poneys. Sid and I drove home in silence that day. We had been doing a lot of private prayer warrior type stuff on the sly, and getting some awesome results. One of our friends, Scott, had fallen in love for the first time because we prayed him a girlfriend and she suddenly showed up. Another of our friend's sick grandmother was healed of cancer while unconscious on her deathbed in the hospital, which wasn't very hospitable as most of them aren't. We didn't talk about this stuff with just anybody, and apparently hadn't wanted to tell Sara our great news. Would she have understood? Sid had a knowing look in his eye when I'd bring up telling Sara about all the praying stuff, as though she might already know, but he never breathed a word to me about telling her, so I figured he didn't. It was powerful help from God as far as I was concerned, so why talk about it? It was just a pure secret, that's all. Who would believe us?

I relented about church after meeting Sara, who was normal after all, and began playing guitar in the music ministry, while Sid thumped his bass guitar, and the huge speakers that hung on both sides of the stage reverberated with our music. What a trip! I became engrossed in what Norman had to say about God and people in general. He was a true philosopher, and a gentle person. Norman supported his family with his carpentry around Lawless, while his wife attended Cotton College, majoring in news writing. I had to respect the guy. People in the church began to talk to me, and I to them. I received letters reporting the latest church news, and began wearing dresses (I have always hated dresses) to church.

In church, things were getting totally out of hand, as was the pentacostal way in Lawless that season of the Lord. Norman was reaching greater and greater heights, as churchgoer voices filled the air, and every once in a while a histrionic in a tight dress would swoon and cry out in a loud voice, voicing her opinion in some foreign tongue which was unrecognizable by anyone present. Religious education in the Bible Belt. No wonder their kids were on drugs, they'd do anything to escape their parents. I'd say to Sid, "Who's the histrionic in the tight dress?" To which he would reply,

"Oh, you know her, she's the lady who's kid is on drugs." Things like that. I was so good and pure, white as the driven snow (yeah, the snow in Chicago that is frequented by dogs, maybe). Church was so much fun, I was really getting into it. Until the Elders threw Norman out, that is. For supposedly having casual sex with the church secretary. Get outta here.

Lickety-split and before a person could quote the Scriptures, as they all did quite often, the church took a vote and decided to expel him, leaving the reins of the holy carriage in those dirty and deceitful hands of the Elders. Leaders of the pack, they extended their condolences to Norman and his family, graciously allowing the poor fallen sheep to remain in their flock and attend services, if they wished. And they wished.

So I felt like a real jerk sitting next to the fallen Norman, who I still to this day do not believe would have casual sex with anyone, since he was obviously devoted to his wife. Services took a turn for the worse, right about the time that Norman was relieved of the pulpit to that loud-mouth, big-bellied, pot roast of a man, the former district manager of McBurgers, Sam Houston. Yuck. He screamed so loud at the flock each and every Sunday, his purple varicose veins nearly popping out of his fat, ruddy face, that I had to ask him to cut it out. My ears just couldn't take it.

"Brother Sam," I said, "There's something I'd like to discuss with you," this being supposedly an open organization where even the fallen, guitarist-sheep could bleat if they had something to communicate. We nodded to passing little lambs who had just embarked from Sunday school and were probably on their way to wring some little black necks, since there weren't any blacks

213

allowed in this here church since Brother Sam took it over, no sirree Billy-Bob.

"I'm too busy now to talk," he said in an undertone, as he shook the hands of his men parishioners, and kissed the brow of a select few of their ladies, the younger ones in the tightest dresses with just a trace of bodice showing through.

"Come on Brother Sam, I need to tell ya somethin'," I pleaded.

"Give it up, girl," he snarled, kissing another sweetie on the well-rouged cheek as she passed by in a cloud of Charlie. Okay, so I gave it up that day, but tried to talk to him again the following Wednesday, after a particularly harrowing harangue that didn't make any sense. I wondered if he had been hitting the Chevas that morning, because he sure looked it.

"Got a minute, Brother?" I asked, as he wheezed his way past me, toward the relative safety and seclusion of his official quarters, Norman's former office. No minute for me.

"Nope!" He smiled sweetly, shoving his way down the corridor between sheep, eying each potential tight-dress for future reference. I finally gave up, and spoke to another Elder about it the following Sunday, when I had the good fortune to catch his slimy ass outside of the men's restroom, and cornered him.

"What's the matter with Sam?" I asked the Elder. Slightly miffed, I had relapsed the previous week, and was now drinking again, so had less patience and virtue.

"Why, Brother Sam's just full of love for his flock," explained the geek.

"How come he screams at us?" I bitched, not convinced that former burger managers could love anything but a french fry. "Are you deaf?" I asked his puzzled face. "I myself wasn't but I'm getting there."

"The Lord has blessed Brother Sam," said the Elder, a loathesome issue of his father's loins, "And gave him to share his news with all of us." The Elder smiled sweetly, and I saw the gleam of Sam Houston in his jaundiced eye.

"Well, I don't doubt that," I said, although I did indeed doubt it, "But it's the yellin' that puts me out." I rubbed my ears that still reverberated with Sam's latest symphony of noise.

"He has to scream," explained the Elder a little too patiently and with great condescension, "Because some of the flock won't listen otherwise." The Elder rubbed both of my shoulders a little too much, and stared at my tits, supposedly done with talking and wanting to get down to business the preacher man way. He began to insinuate his body into the pelvic region of mine before I finally got a grip on things, and wrenched my way free. No one was coming.

"You creep!" I hollered in my old hitcher way, and kicked him in the shin, mussing up the carefully pressed charcoal slacks he was wearing, then stomped heavily on his patent leather shoes. He was lucky I didn't kick him clear into the Hereafter.

"Owww," he yelled, "You little vixen, you..."

"Don't you ever come near me again," I hissed, "or I'll give you a vasectomy!" I wasn't even streetwise anymore, and look what I had to put up with. The jerk limped away, cursing me not quite under his breath. I was so outta there.

As soon as I cleared out of that church scene, I fell prey to other pentecostal movements in the area, and evangelists drew me to their circus rings, time and time again. I was addicted to the spiritual atmosphere of their followers, and wanted to play my guitar to accolades. I wanted an audience, and the approval of some pastor, so soon after ditching Sam's church, I wandered into a Little Yellow Fence type place, looking for some action. (They all had cutesie names in Lawless). The preacher was speaking in tongues to himself, so I had to wake him up and tell him I was in his office. He took a few minutes to give me his focused attention, but still interspersed his speech with little, foreign refrains.

"Hello?" I said to his mumbling form in the sharkskin suit. "Hiya?"

"Are you there?" he asked finally focusing his eyes enough to see me.

"Yeah, I'm Gabrielle," I said, impressed with his prayer power.

"I thought it might be the Lord, come to redeem us," he said in a whisper, still lost in his trance. Reminded me of Hare Krishna in the temple of the melon back in California. Only this time, I was under his spell, and believed what he said was true. I can't believe I believed all that junk, but I did, right up until I had been playing in his church with the others for three months, three times per week not counting rehearsals. I was one well-trained sheep about to be led to the slaughter if I didn't wake up soon. Time to take a break from the church scene, and go back to my old self. Not without a fight though, and that was what I was getting into there at the Little Yellow Fence.

Before I knew it, the guitar player in the tattered jeans had been replaced by me on Sundays, even though he played fine and had been a church member with his wife and two very well behaved kids for two years. Not only that, but the pastor was collecting money for a trip to South America in a pair of three hundred dollar boots that were displayed for all to contribute in on an altar in the center of the church. His wife danced around in a red dress, false eyelashes, and six-inch-high heels, red also. What a show! She fell into a swoon beside the altar that held the expensive boots, moaning as her husband relayed his by-now-quite familiar story about how his dear wife had bought the shiny leather boots for him. "I'm taking these boots to South America," he sang out as she swooned, and both looked fondly at the boots in question.

"Ohhh," went the sheep, bowing their prayerful little heads. "Ahhh."

"I don't expect a gift from you, my brothers and sisters," he went on, "But my trip to South America will be a long and dangerous one, fraught with the illnesses of third world nations, and I may not return alive." His wife wailed in punctuation, and the crowd oohh'd and aahh'd in unison, locked into his cold little spell. Something was fishy in paradise, I thought to myself, and I wanted to get to the bottom of it. In my very forward manner, I approached Brother Johnson and his dear wife, Emelia, to ask them the biblical precedent for their unusual behavior. Not much of a Bible scholar myself, I did peruse the pages of my Thompson Chain Reference: King James Version to cross check their actions (expelling a man from the music set because of poor clothing, praying for money, etc.), and surprisingly enough, the Lord would have them handle things in a slightly different way. But would they be receptive to intelligent, vocal intercourse?

"Dear Brother and Sister," I cajoled outside in the parking lot, lisping in the approved pentacostal lingo.

"Yes, Sister?" the pastor asked as his wife looked at me askance as if she were on valiums or some 'ludes. I took a deep breath because I knew this one had to be fast.

"Can you spare a moment to talk about why you expelled the rhythm guitarist from his musical duty, and why you think it's wise to pray for money?" I got it all out in a big rush, since I knew they were in a hurry to go to lunch. Sister Emelia squirmed around on her stiletto heels, while her husband, sharply clad in a pink silk blouse and polka dotted neck tie, murmured in an unknown tongue, presumably a prayer, but with him, you never could tell. His patent leather shoes were shiny, as was his slicked back, permed hairdo. Brother Johnson spoke first, after finishing his speech in tongues to himself.

"Gabrielle, where are you, where are you?" And he went back to murmuring, gazing skyward as if he were searching for divine answers. Where am I? I thought I was here.

"I thought I was here, Brother Johnson," I commented, beginning to get fed up already with these two and totally losing my cool. He finally, very briefly, glanced at my eyes and then avoided any further eye contact. Shifty motherfucker, and to think I once believed in him.

"You haven't been coming to rehearsal these last few weeks," he began, "And I want you to know, you are in danger of losing your soul." He posed primly, with his little snout far up into the clear, blue, cloudless sky (this was before chemtrails), as Emelia continued to squirm, and pulled on his sleeve to whisper,

"We have reservations, Darling," pout, pout, "can't you talk to that... ooh... woman later?" She completely ignored me and looked over at the parking lot, anxiously. Her piss-yellow with orange-orange trim gas-guzzling Cadillac was in plain sight, still parked where she left it one and a half hours previously.

Brother Johnson continued to murmur in prayer, but gave me a 'go to hell' look. "God spoke to me last night," he said.

"Uh huh, and what did He say?" I snidely asked.

"He said you ride your bike too much," said the pastor with an omniscient expression on his prissy, pimp-like face.

"Say what?" I almost screamed, "how come He didn't tell me?"

217

"Because you never show respect for this church," he complained, checking his lapels for soot (from hell?), as he comforted his ailing wife. "And you always skip Friday night rehearsals."

I was fed up to here and felt like maybe Sara meant visit the churches for a little while then get away before you go completely crazy because I was about to and told him, "Look, I go to college full-time, have two jobs, and come to rehearsal three nights per week already," I griped. Hey, nobody tells me not to ride my bike, forget it. Checking out his wife's anorexic frame, I added, "A little exercise might do you both good, but that's not what I wanted to discuss." I could feel the Wichitas calling me, while I wasted time with these two soul snatchers in a dusty parking lot. I wanted to go rock climbing, and I had recently purchased a good bottle of California red I wanted to drink. In communion with myself.

"We really must go," Emelia said to me, and she tugged her husband's expensive arm with a manicured hand and disappeared behind her mellow yellow Caddy. She unlocked his door and drove away, presumably to nibble on the most expensively arrayed carrot sticks she could find. I was disgusted, and wanted out. Here came the guitar player in the tattered jeans, maybe he'd prove more intelligent than they did.

"Yo! Man!" I hollered in a risque heathen voice. "How come they kicked you off the musician stage?" I suspected the answer, but wanted positive proof. He gave me more than that, and I was sorry I asked.

"Brother Johnson says that for the good of the church, I shouldn't be seen playing in tattered jeans," he explained (never could remember the guy's name, come to think of it), "But until I find a better job than the one I have at Long Jockey Silver's, I can't afford new clothes."

"You look all right to me," I said in consolation.

Stuffing his hands in his pockets, he continued, "After all, I got the kiddos to think about." I thought he was very humble, and his kids were the best behaved in the whole church.

"Yeah, well I think it stinks, and I'm quitting the music group!" I said, vehemently. He looked confused for a moment, then spoke as if an idea had just hit him. Uh-oh.

"Gabrielle, God just spoke to me and told me something about you," he said. He at least looked me directly in the eye, however brief the moment. I'd come to appreciate direct eye contact in a pentecostal, charismatic community where anything went, and women did things in church that they wouldn't dream of acting out in the local Lawless Mall Tick.

"You mean, He told you something about me, and didn't tell me?" I asked, incredulous that my luck could be so bad twice in one day in the same parking lot. That sounded like something Brother Johnson might come up with, and I was suspicious. It's true what they said, I rode my bike too much.

"You need to quit riding your bike all the time, God told me," he said, sanctimoniously. I looked at this skinny runt of a guy, who I was trying to avenge, and all I got was misplaced judgement? I decided it was time to get out of the AO.

"I have a funny feeling about this," I said to his skinny self. "I think you should reexamine your relationships with others, and pray hard, all the time." Calmed down and cooled off, I felt it my Christian duty to dish out as much advice as had been dished out to me. He looked at me skeptically, as a cat might to a mouse that told it to go chase some bacon. "And don't give up the guitar just because Brother Johnson is too expensive for you," I added. With that, we parted company, older, wiser, and more gullible? I wondered....

Back I went to scale the bald faces of my beloved Wichitas, while the Little Yellow Fence sang themselves right out of town. Some of the local citizens criticized the Fence for unorthodox preaching, and other sundry elements that had the Christian Community in an uproar, so they moved outside of the city limits to a newly-built, plastic-steepled church. It was right next to this other church where known Satanists conducted their ceremonies, which made me wonder why a pentacostal church couldn't legally stand within five hundred yards of a liquor-selling establishment, even if said establishment was the best Italian restaurant in Lawless that only wanted to serve a little wine with the calzones, yet those so-called Christians chose to exist next to a devil's den. Bible belt laws made absolutely no sense to me whatsoever, and it was truly a compelling question. But I didn't stick around to answer it.

One day, a good friend of mine who played fiddle, dobro, and mandolin in a bluegrass, newgrass band, came over to see how I was doing, since I had sworn off the church scene forever. He was worried about my salvation, being a recently recovered alcoholic himself, and wanted to ease me back into the Christian view of things. He also had a mouthful of gold fillings, which he displayed, and I thought they were quite new, since he used to have cavities. They didn't come from any ordinary dentist, I was soon to discover. Beware! The Evangelist From Hell had arrived....

"Yo, Butch!" I sang out, as he drove into my driveway and parked next to my long-since-deceased Datsun. Waving gaily at me, he leapt out of his rattle-trap, and yelled,

"Have I got something to show you!" Clad in faded-out, tattered and torn overalls, covered in dust and grease, his blond hair begrimed with gunk, Butch had obviously just come from his garage, where he rebuilt engines, and resold cars.

"You don't happen to have a beer, do you, or a couple of bucks for a six-pack?" I asked. Back to my old tricks, I was once more transformed into a beggar, but this time at least I was in school, and had my own roof. Shaking his shaggy blond head, Butch's deep green eyes caught mine, and I discerned a mad twinkle that certainly wasn't there last time I saw him, which was a week before.

"See my teeth?" he asked in a conspiring voice. Opening wide, he motioned me to come closer for an oral view. I saw a very gold and flashy mouth.

Hmmm. "What'd ya do, rob a bank?"

"No."

"Okay, your Mom paid for the dentist, right?"

"No."

"Are you gonna tell me, or do I hafta beat it out of you?" I snarled in a pseudo-menacing tone, just like in my biker bitch days when I hadda be tough, as they say. I snarled in a joking manner, of course. Butch was 6'6, two hundred and forty pounds.

"Gabrielle, you've got to come with me to see the evangelist who's at the Holy Mother of Church in Dunkin," he said, closing his gaping wound of a mouth in order to speak, after showing me his treasure trove of new fillings. I wasn't in the least bit interested, and had ignored the Little Yellow Fence's frequent calls to my Mom (I hadn't a phone), imploring me to return to their lair outside Lawless city limits. No possibility whatsoever, uh uh. Me no go. I was more than happy to be drinking myself silly each and every night that I used to rehearse, and hanging around the studio, not to mention riding my beat-up, blue Takara which I was rebuilding into a fine, racing machine. Forget church, that was my motto.

"Sorry, dude, you know I hate church," I answered to his dismayed frowning face, hoping for a free beer anyway. Not so easy to dissuade this guy, though, and before I knew it, I was on my way to Dunkin, Oklahoma and the Holy Mother Church where Brother Moses had cast his spell. "This is the last time I'm going near a church, you got me?" I told Butch, as I rolled down my window to let my long hair fly and tangle in the wind. We were doing eighty miles per hour, as Butch was anxious for me to get to church.

"I know, I know," he said, "But this guy is a miracle worker, Gabrielle!" He reached into his bag, and shoved some papers at me, while using his left knee to handle the car.

At eighty. Should have known. "What's this, newspaper clippings?" I asked, not wanting to shift through the pile of trash sitting on my lap, where Butch had risked our lives to put it. "A dentist in church?" I read aloud, questioning what I was reading. "You've got to be kidding, Butch!" I yelled, slamming the pile down into the back seat, where papers immediately began flying everywhere, including out the back window. He slammed on the brakes, and pulled over, screaming at me to pick up the pieces. His devotion was awesome to behold, and it should have warned me about what I was about to witness.

Weirdness, and lost sheep, being led to the slaughter by the evangelist dentist from hell, and Butch was one of the chosen few, according to Brother Moses himself. As we all bowed our heads in prayer, I looked around me at the farmers, and shopkeepers, and mothers and children, and teenagers, all bowed at the request of the strange looking California beachnik kind of guy who was parading around in white robes with his wife, a lady of animal and inhuman eyes. I held my breath.

"Oh God, almighty power that exists in the air," he intoned religiously as the crowd all held their breath. "Almighty energy that pervades our atmosphere, Almighty Mother who protects us all, I ask for a miracle now, and that You descend from Heaven and heal our guests tonight." The Moses looking character who looked surprisingly like most of the guys on Venice Beach, led his temporary congregation deeper and deeper into a group hypnosis, with his rising and falling vocal intonations, and subtle suggestions. In half an hour, I was one of the few people who were not sound asleep. I nudged Butch, but he was completely out of it. Then, the great evangelical-hypnotist began to sway to his own music, and people began waking up, and looking (oddly enough) into each other's mouths. Moses and his much younger wife went around checking each and every mouth with their sterile gauze and frequently sterilized mirrors, exclaiming in exaltation every time someone displayed a gold filling.

"See," he preached, "the Lord has done a mighty work tonight, and healed many teeth." I wasn't convinced, but how could anyone explain it? Even the media was writing about these first person testimonials that were frequently brought to the attention of the press during Moses' two week stay in Dunkin, Oklahoma. And that wasn't the worst of it. My friend, a very down to earth kind of guy, swore his gold teeth were from the ablutions of Brother Moses, and Butch never lied. So, I got on good old Moses' mailing list for future reference, hoping to discover what exactly he was all about. It couldn't be God. Those innocent Oklahoma churchgoers looked too hypnotized, and ignorant of lying, thieving, conniving evangelists, and I noticed how much money they gave him that night. Each and every one of them turned their pockets, purses and wallets inside out. One policeman, who I knew from the Little Yellow Fence, put his .357 Magnum in the coffer, not having any cash on him. Talk about group-think! I hightailed it out of there, just as fast as my little legs could carry me to Butch's rattle-trap, and he drove me just as fast as he could, especially after I told him what I thought of the 'Brother Moses' routine.

"Butch, that guy and his wife are evil," I told him as we plummeted down the only hill in Dunkin. "I could see it in their eyes."

Looking at me like I was the craziest thing since the Slinky, Butch intoned lugubriously, "Gabrielle, he's a miracle worker, and you call him evil?" Obviously miffed at my display of non-seduction, Butch had given up my soul and resigned himself to the fact that I was indeed doomed to the fires of Hell. "You've been hanging around that recording studio too much," he said, "and Brother Johnson spoke to me the other day about your other nefarious activities."

"Oh?" asked I, as I shuffled in my seat. "What are they, or does he just suspect evil doing, since he is so psychic when it comes to humans other than himself?" Okay, I was becoming sarcastic, but this was ridiculous!

"He told me that God spoke to him about you," Butch continued in a superior, elderly kind of manner. "Gabrielle, I'm trying to be a friend, because we all love you in Christ's body," spoketh Butch, my saviour.

"That's terribly sweet of ya'll," I ascertained, belching under my breath. Too many peanuts for breakfast, part of my new diet designed to melt off pounds of flesh in only a few months. He wasn't finished yet.

"God told Brother Johnson that you spend altogether too much time riding your bicycle," Butch told me, his snout poking far up into the ozone layer, his holiness apparent to all who weren't saved, his gold teeth flashing in the afternoon sun. This was too much for me to take.

"Why don't you let me off here?" I asked his priestliness, attempting to escape any more pedantic litanies before I threw up my peanuts all over the car seat. "I can catch the bus to Lawless." Please. Let me out, now!

"Of course I won't let you go ride a bus, Gabby," Butch said with pure menace. "You know I love you too much for that." Butch was gearing up for the grand finale. "Let's just take a little detour, shall we?" Oh no! It's the hitchhiker's nightmare all over again, he won't let me out of his car! But what does he want with me?

223

"You're full of shit, Butch," I said, never one to let an argument pass unmentioned. "Biblically speaking, so is Brother Johnson and Brother Moses." What do you have to say about that?

"How can you blaspheme?" he asked me, terrified of the fires of hell that would consume me at any minute if I didn't stop.

"And furthermore, if you don't take me home, which was the original plan, I'll make it a point to file a police complaint against you," I threatened, meaning every word of it.

"I was only going to stop at Brother Johnson's house on the way home, Gabby," Butch whimpered, obviously dogged by my fierce attitude. "We could have a little Bible study." He looked at me with big, tearful, completely blank green eyes, and I stared him down.

"Never!" I screamed heinously.

"But why not?" he whimpered again.

"Not on your life, Bud," I said with a stern voice. After thoughtfully looking out my window at the rushing trees and houses of Dunkin, I explained, "Maybe you should read your Bible, especially about what Jesus says about 'God the Father,' something Brother Moses missed, 'Turning a man out of the tabernacle because of his poor attire,' something Brother Johnson missed, and the bit about 'avarice being the root of all evil,' something they both missed."

"Read the Bible?" he asked in shock. "I only listen to sermons because Brother Johnson said he could interpret the Bible better than us." I was on a roll, so I finished him off, ignoring that last little outburst which sounded suspiciously like medieval Catholicism, a fairly goddessy religion in its own right, what with the Mother Mary and all supposedly being closer to God than Jesus. Who was Bud thinking would interpret for him, the pardner?

But poor Butch was engulfed in total charismania. "And think about this," I said. "Many false prophets and teachers will arise in the last days, doing miracles to fool even the elect, which is us, Butch."

"I don't remember reading any of that," argued Butch, regaining his strength, "but surely, Brother Moses and Brother Johnson would never do anything that wasn't in God's Word."

"They wouldn't, huh?" I asked.

"No," he said with a vengeance, the manic gleam in his eye all but paralyzing me, "and they would tell me if there were any false prophets anywhere around here!" Then, in my imagination, he bleated like a shorn sheep, on the way to the wolf's tummy, right before the salsa hit him.

"You got me there," I said with a sigh, weak from grappling with the great cobra, the lying snake, the pentacostal license to pluck a few souls. "They probably never read past Genesis, anyway." Finally, he was taking the road to Lawless, and I was taking the road to freedom from the pentecostal-charismatic movement's awful embrace. My love affair with the church scene, which had lasted a full year, was finally finished. My love affair with the Lord, Yeshua ben Josef could begin in earnest.

I began a very serious Bible study of my own, and wrote research papers for Cotton College's English Department using the Bible as a reference. That was no small feat in an agnostic, academic environment, but I always did love a challenge. Chaucer always did say in his round-about way that paying the pardner wasn't necessarily the only way to get to Heaven and I wondered in my heart of hearts if all those sheep in Pentecostal Charismania were hoping that 1984 was gonna be any different and if it was would paying the Pastor suffice?

Alas, alack! What would Geoffrey have had to say about all this fluff?

Chapter 14

Spirituality leaps where science cannot yet follow, because science must always test and measure, and much of reality and human experience is immeasurable.

Starhawk

The Dance

I pedaled harder and harder, studied laboriously, and continued to work at my two jobs—one in the Writing Lab at Cotton College, and one at the snack bar in the boy's dormitory. I cycled to work and to class, stopping only when it rained on my little world, lost as I was in thoughts of Shakespeare's Venus chasing her lovely beauty, Adonis, and the wild boar who would prove to be Adonis' death. My opinions at this time were highly theoretical, almost heretical, if you will, to the saints of Cotton's English Department. Shakespeare had his sights on a young boy, I would say, and since his characters often pretended to be women disguised as men, who were, in real life, male actors disguised as women, it was not inconceivable that in his own, warped, humorous way, William chased his quarry in a poem, or a short play.

So far was I steeped in my own, literary mythology, that I regarded all other opinions as merely helpers to my primary cause; that was, the exploitation and exposition of William Shakespeare at his finest hour, the hour in which he pursued that evil, elusive boy, Adonis, in the form of a lusty woman, Venus, and plucked him up off his poney on that forest floor with a mighty arm, and carried him away to breathe sweet breath into his ear, alone at last with beauty and lust.

My short exposé shocked the prim, newly doctorated schoolmarm who had recently transferred to Cotton College to begin her life as Ph.D., but all she could really say was, "You need to buy a typewriter if you are going to graduate school," and, in a lighter fit of jealousy, she added "you were a shoo-in at Big

University in Normal." Big was where I had been prematurely selected for a graduate assistantship.

"But Doctoress Prim," I said, "you must open your mind and air its musty closets," and Doctor Prim reminded me, sternly, of my borderline grade in her class if I didn't pursue more eclectic areas of research.

"There is no such thing as a Shakespearean scholar in undergraduate school, dear," she said with a smile, "so you really should stop wasting your time and mine with these frivolous pursuits."

"You don't understand," I used argued, "Shakespeare left all kinds of evidence to prove my theory that he was Venus."

"Tch, tch," she would cluck, shaking her tightly bunned hairdo, "you really are a lost cause."

I wouldn't give up, but said instead, "There's a copy of a receipt from his patron, Rizzly, for one thousand pounds! He got it for writing "The Rape of Lucrece."

She gave me a funny look—what receipt? her eyes seemed to ask.

"And then Rizzly dropped Shakespeare for Marlowe, so Shakespeare artistically killed him off in Venus and Adonis." Such an obvious connection, any open-minded lit crit could figure it out. "Don't you get it?" I pleaded. Clear as mud.

"I never saw any such thing," Doctor Prim huffed, then stalked down the hall on her sensible shoes, leaving me to smugly consider my status here at Cotton College.

"I might be just an undergraduate," I mused to the listening secretary, who was fairly dark and not treated with much respect around this neck of the woods. "But at least I do my research which is more than I can say for most of this tweedy set."

She agreed completely, after spending half her life as a Cotton English Department gofer and semi-slave. "Fo sho, honey, you just set 'em straight, I'm right with ya," she said. We snickered and I reminisced about my favorite professor, the ethereal Dr. Schollweise who had decided she'd had enough of Cow-Poke Academia and moved back to Greenwich Village to pursue her real love, The Arts. Not much of that around here, I noticed glumly, checking out the grim walls and linoleum floors that Cotton had recently installed with the thought that they would impress the Board of Regeants enough to get more money for less education for the less fortunate who went there.

Since I had studied Shakespeare for four solid years, and he was my very favorite author, the brief chit chat with Doctor Prim bothered me not one tiny mite, for I knew that my knowledge of Shakespeare came from many hours in many research libraries, and an open mind to help that knowledge grow.

It was a sign of my increasing ignorance of reality, lack of diplomacy, and total devotion to the art of literary irrelevance that led me to finish and publish my opinion of Shakespeare's fantasy life. Trouble was, Dr. Prim and Proper with the Bun couldn't see the humor in my message, and I received a 'D' for devotion to Shakespeare, not the 'A' I so richly deserved.

Imagine her shock and dismay when, two months later, my trite little piece was published in none other than Shakespeare's Yearly, an off-the-wall underground magazine of parody, pun, and limericks with meaning. Dr. Prim actually couldn't have cared less whether I lived or died, but as one overseer of my undergraduate work, she felt it incumbent upon her academic soul to advise me against future perils in graduate school. "Perhaps you should take up maintenance work," she had tittered, handing me back my soiled pages, stamped with the sideways smirk of a crimson red 'D' on page one.

"You'll see, Miss Prim," I replied, barely able to conceal my hatred of her tightly wound, yellow bun and today's sailor outfit in tweed which she wore with brown penny loafers. "I will someday publish this work."

"Certainly, certainly," said Miss Prim (an unmarried old maid), "but you'll have to change your whole presentation to do it." As if she could tell by my presentation. "Shakespeare was a serious playwright, and you seem to take his humor lightly," she added with a shade of disdain and her recently doctorated knowing manner.

"Don't you see?" I asked her frowning face. "He thought it was funny to be frivolous." Needless to say, I flunked her class on literary interpretation that semester, but I didn't care that much about it because I was lost in my wonderland of faerie tales and dreams. Dr. Prim would not allow me to leave her classroom without one further admonition on the last day of class, and since I already knew what was coming I tried to escape by bolting out the door. I heard her voice sing out as I ran out of the building,

"You should buy a typewriter," she sang, "or at least apply for janitorial work so you'll be able to support yourself after college."

Undeterred by her lack of enthusiasm, I was still toiling away at Cotton, sleeping the bleak nights away in my little one bedroom apartment in Old Town, Lawless, Oklahoma, because I didn't have too long to go until I reached the zenith of my endeavors, the great dream of all dreams, graduate school at Big University in Normal, Oklahoma. Only two semesters left to go, and I would be free of Lawless' awful embrace. Besides, the apartment was bright and I had a lot of beautiful green plants. Felt like a jungle. My jungle.

I had the strangest dreams living up there all alone. I had become such a hermit that my dreams somehow took over reality to the extent that I disdained the local media, listening only to my records, reading only my books and journals—radio and newspapers were out of the question. This lack of mental interaction with reality sometimes surprised me, because I would dream the news in living technicolor. Like for instance, the night we bombed Libya.

I was snoozing away after a long involved study period, my mind resting from its bombardment of Virginia Woolf and Spenser's Faerie Queen (I was taking Twentieth Century Lit. along with Sixteenth Century, and it sometimes got confusing.)

Suddenly, without warning, I plunged into North Africa, and found myself strolling with none other than Colonel Khadafy. Quite conversational and friendly with each other, we were examining his military arsenal. It should have been strange, since several U.S. Army fellows were trying to rescue me, but as the Colonel and I gazed at his howitzer collection, I noticed my white pony prancing by my side, and knew I was safe from harm.

"Better get lost, guys," I yelled at the gaping soldiers who must have felt my death was imminent. "You'll get killed if you try to rescue me." The Colonel and I exchanged smiles, and I could tell he agreed with my instructions to our brave boys overseas.

229

"C'mon, we can get you out," they yelled back with typical military bravado, and it wasn't that I didn't appreciate their efforts, I just didn't need any help.

"Don't you see my poney will protect me?" I asked them, never once disturbing the ongoing monologue of my companion in khaki, Colonel Khadafy. My white poney pranced along as we viewed the various and sundry of Libya's military might. Tanks, rocket launchers, AK-47s—only an expert could name them all. I was merely a passer-bye, and unworried about escaping Libya and the Colonel, unless he got fresh, of course. Then something woke me up.

Pounding at my door, a loud, obnoxious pounding. What time was it? Nine o'clock in the evening, I must have slept forever. Planes circling overhead. Helicopters. In Lawless? Sara breathlessly burst into my apartment, slinging herself onto my one and only couch.

"C'mon in," I offered, although she already had. "Have a seat."

"I was in town and thought I'd stop by," Sara said, in between breaths (were the stairs that rough?). "You heard the news?"

"What news?" I asked, still half asleep and confused by her visit. We hadn't seen each other in at least three months, and she usually gave me warning before she danced into my life. Not that I minded her coming over tonight, because I was through studying for the evening. What was she jabbering about, anyway?

"Oh, I forgot you never pay any attention to the real world," she said quite snidely, but I put up with it, because she had a few quirks herself, and I kinda liked the old broad. Never one to listen to the radio, I wasn't really interested in local or international events, especially in the middle of the night.

"You're right," I said. "I don't."

"You're such a studious girl," Sara said sweetly. "With your eyes shut tightly and your head in the sand like an ostrich." She smiled as if she never said that, and I ignored her as if I hadn't heard it either.

"Want some tea?" I asked, wandering into my kitchen cubicle to prepare some anyway. To think I had once been politically advised in California. Now, I was steeped in my literary realm, and could hardly step outside for a fresh breath of reality.

I hardly was aware of my switch from Obsession One to Obsession Two to Obsession Three....I was also still hitting the juice every evening as soon as the sun went down, signaling to me that the bar was open.

"Yeah, I'll take a cup."

"Chamomile or peppermint?"

"Chamomile. Notice the air traffic?" asked Sara, as she straightened her coat out to sit for a few. "Looks kind of unusual, don't you think?"

"Yeah, maybe there's a special tonight on helicopter rides over Lawless," I answered from the kitchen. "Lemon or honey?"

"Got any sugar?"

"No."

"I'll take mine black."

"It's extra strong chamomile," I warned her from the kitchen. "Sure ya don't need a nip to sweeten it?"

"I like my sugar," complained Sara. "So I'll just take my tea straight."

"You got it, Boss."

"It's nice to see you again, Gabrielle, but you seem rather complacent," commented Sara. "Involved with school?"

"Totally," I replied, carrying her tea into the living cubicle. "It takes real devotion to detail, and I don't have much time for outside interests these days." Having a seat on the floor at her feet, I took a sip of chamomile tea, which I drank to calm my terribly upset stomach. Didn't do much for my liver, though, which needed more than a chamomile flower could give.

"Gabrielle," she said with a weird, scared look in her eye, "I think I should tell you that we just bombed Libya an hour ago." Sara nervously began pacing the small living room, which I had made more homey with a Iranian tapestry during a Middle Eastern obsession, and my energy drained right out. "That's why the air traffic is so congested tonight." She took off her coat, trying to calm down. "I heard Fort Kill is on red alert."

"I really should listen to the news more," I said, not a little bit shocked, but trying not to show it. "Today's Army is so efficient that by tomorrow Libya will be gone entirely."

231

"I don't think they'll bomb the entire country," she said with more sense than I had at the moment. "But it's still a nasty thought, that we are killing innocent people over there." Sara seemed close to tears, and I felt pretty sorry myself.

"Sometimes I hate being white," I complained. "Don't you?"

"It's truly an embarrassment," she agreed.

"I mean, Americans are the most arrogant race on the planet."

"Not to mention the laziest," she said.

"Why do we have to enslave, take over and maim and kill?" I wondered, remembering my talk with the Colonel, which was relatively peaceful considering what we just did to his country.

"They bombed a heavily populated area," Sara said, waiting for my reaction. "They killed some people, maybe Khadafy himself."

"And I would have missed it if not for my white horse," I slipped, Freudian-like. "What parcel of land was fortunate enough to get the Big Heat?" I asked. "How'd they do it?"

"The Air Force used F-111 jets to drop a few little bombs on Khadafy's headquarters," explained Sara. "What white horse are you talking about?"

"I dreamed I was visiting Khadafy just when you showed up," I said, struggling for some composure. "We were having a little tete-a-tete." I was slightly weirded out. Was Khadafy dead? Did I just converse with a ghost? Not that I had that much respect for the man, but still, I hated violence, especially when it was American made.

"You said something about a white poney," pressed Sara, "Are you still lost in that mystical never-never land?" We had corresponded over the past year about various and sundry, and after hearing all about my white horse dreams for too many times, Sara suggested I see a shrink to rid myself of these fantasies.

And that, from a horse lover!

"Yeah," I mused, "He protected me from Khadafy's amorous advances." Seeming disconcerted, Sara pondered my predicament.

"You mean you dreamed about Libya just now?" she asked. Almost swooning, she breathed," it's a gift, Gabrielle." I didn't think so, but I didn't want to argue just then.

"Aren't you the one who disapproved of my 'mysticism' not long back?" I asked, sneaking a few barbs in edgewise to keep her alert. "And now it's a gift?" True to form, Sara had an answer for everything. She too went through obsessions on a regular basis.

"You were so wrapped up in the church scene I was worried about what latent mysticism would do to your mental health," she shrewdly countered. Yeah, right, I thought to myself, but changed the subject

"How long are you in Lawless?" I asked her.

"I just stopped by to see if you wanted to make a few bucks and write me a research paper for the book I'm working on," said my friend. Aha, I knew it, she was exhibiting yet another sign of compulsive behavior, because we both knew that Sara always started these projects, like writing books, then never found the time to finish them. "Since you're pressed for money, and I'm pressed for time, will you do it?" she asked.

"Sure," I said, never one to pass up a gift horse. "What on?"

"Sixteenth Century dramatic development. It's for a textbook I'm writing." She finished her tea and put her coat back on. Sara had a tendency to wear black and purple, and tonight was no exception. Black jeans, purple blouse, black coat, grey hair, black Reebok tennis shoes-she was a sprite in the night, and she whisked out my door as quickly as she had whisked in.

"Love to write a paper for you," I said, thrilled to death at this literary opportunity to prove myself.

"I'll pay you a hundred dollars," said the fleeing artist Sara, pausing on the stairs to give me a parting hug. "I need it in one month, tops."

"Are you sure you aren't just doing me a favor because I'm behind on my rent?" I asked, a sneaking suspicion darkening my horizon.

"Of course not," Sara said, toying with her satchel. "I don't have time to do the research, and you do." Pausing to collect her thoughts, she added, "You did mention how broke you have been in your last letter..."

"Well, thanks," I said sheepishly as she handed me two fifties. "I promise to deliver on time." Sara silently descended the stairs to her van, as another chopper circled Lawless. Red alert while you sleep, I thought to myself. And I dream of white poneys. "How are the horses doing?" I yelled as she entered her van.

233

"They miss you of course!" laughed Sara. I loved her two poneys, her babies with those tossing airs, and those light prancing hooves. "Want to come to the farm next month?" she asked, reading my mind and my heart.

"Can't," I answered sadly. "Have to make it some other time when school's not in session." Sara waved good-bye and reversed out of my gravel pit of a driveway. The old faithless Datsun stood at attention, both front tires flat, both bumpers dying a slow, rustful death. Me make it to Tipton, Texas, a full, four hours away? Not in that heap!

True to form, Sara never finished 'the book,' although I did turn in that paper to her on time. I got an 'A' in my Sixteenth Century class, too. Sara was the kind of friend who flitted in and out of my life for the next several years, just when I needed her the most. That hundred wasn't the only time she gave me assistance, just the only time she gave me financial assistance. Getting my poems published in an obscure literary anthology was one method Sara employed to project me on my way to non-stardom, along with asking my advise on literary endeavors of her own, which made me feel important.

Sara and her two horses, Cinnamon and Clove, were three of my best friends in the whole world back then, and they were ever faithful and true. I think Sara had extrasensory perception when it came to my spiritual motives and mental health, because her letters always arrived when I needed them the most, and filled me with hope, buoying me up with good news, enough so that I could resume my struggle for enlightenment at Cotton College in Lawless, Oklahoma for yet another day.

Sara had a habit of popping in and flitting out, light sarcasm dripping from her lips, proverbs of life's harsh realities readily on her tongue, new projects always on the horizon. I definitely wanted to see more of my middle-aged female friend—she was short, to the point, and always invited me home for dinner.

Chapter 15

*He who travels far will often see things far
removed from what he believed was Truth.
When he talks about it in the fields at
home, He is often accused of lying, For the
obdurate people will not believe What they
do not see and distinctly feel,
Inexperience, I believe, Will give little
credence to my song.*

Hermann Hesse

The Trance

One bright hot humid sunny day, much like most days in bright hot
humid sunny Lawless, Oklahoma, I was wheeling my bicycle to
the local Seven-Eleven to buy some nachos with cheese and
jalapeños. I had been such a studious little thing, not interested in
men because I was just so busy studying Chaucer's naughty stories,
until I looked up, and there he stood, the man of my dreams.

The man of my dreams had to have several particular points in
order to snag my attention and my heart—my guy must speak
German, (like the dear Hans I used to have), be big and tough, and
remind me of my biological heritage, since I had compulsively
decided after leaving Hans that I was really pure Kraut.

It wasn't a wonder that I couldn't fill all these requirements in
Lawless, but suddenly there he stood. Tall, muscular, blond, and
with a lovely little smirk on his broad, dusky face. I was
enthralled, especially when I heard him speak to the cashier.

"Can you take ziss back, bitte?" his overly saur-krauted accent
asked, handing her a broken pair of sunglasses. Watching his well-
muscled arm extend across the counter in a non-threatening
manner, I got a glimpse of the man's methodology. The
countergirl, a mere Southwestern wisp of a thing, batted her
eyelashes at him and his clipped, Germanic accent which I am
certain knocked her rocks off since she seemed to be from Lawless
herself. I crunched a chip, which was drenched in cheese, nuked to
perfection. I commenced to drooling over this blond hunk.

"What'sa matta with 'em?" the counter girl asked. Pausing only briefly to glance at the obviously sat on sunglasses, she adoringly asked the more pertinent question which was, "Where ya from?" Coquettishly gazing at him with her pimpled, adolescent face, she gently pawed the paw which held his sunglasses, touching his fingers lightly with a flirtatious gesture of her own, that little hussy.

"I sat on zimm," he whispered, "but we won't tell anyone, ja?" He gently grasped her flailing hand, covering it with his manliness and she just about wet her little Lawless panties. Oh, smarm alert, I thought to myself, I can't stand this sequence anymore and besides I need to pay for my nuked chips. Blurting out my presence, I interrupted their little scene.

"Hey," I hollered none too politely, because they were beginning to wind around each other right in the store with customers staring. "The nachos are one-oh-six, right?" Slamming my money on the counter, I scrammed. He was cute, I decided, but gross and a cradle snatcher. She couldn't be more than eighteen years old, and he looked to be about thirty one or two. That much of a man needed a real woman. I stood outside, and unlocked my yellow bumble bee Centurion Facet with the new racing rims. I munched another cheesy nacho. Couldn't get the guy out of my mind, which he must have picked up, because he quickly exited the store and tried to pick me up.

Opening line: "You're not from around here, are you?" he asked, gazing longingly at either my nachos or my tits, I couldn't tell right away, but I can tell you now, it was my tits. Jerk. But dammit all, that accent gave me kinky shivers all up and down my German spine.

"Obviously, you just heard that line a minute ago," I said. "I gotta go drive a bus, so see ya." So suave, I knew how to handle men like him.

"No," he said quickly, "don't leave just yet."

"Why not?" I asked, hopping on my yellow racer.

"I want to talk wiss you," he said softly. "You work driving a bus, ja?"

"Actually, I just do it for fun," I answered. "Where do you work?"

Not 'what is your name,' because his name was prominently displayed on his left breast pocket. Detlev. "Next door in zee automotive shop," said Detlev, that stupid grin still on his Kraut face. I was hooked. A real German. My dream come true.

"Oh yeah?" I asked, finishing the chips and taking off on my yellow steed to pedal the two miles home and acting hard to get hoping he would follow me (which he did, of course.)

That insistent siren called me to my death upon the rocky island, and I died happy.

Va-rrooom Va-rrooom! went his motorcycle, a twelve hundred cc V-Max. He totally outran me in like a New York minute not only that but I let him follow me home like a very forgetful hitcher and he followed me upstairs with a wolf on his face and I let him in then said, "Can you help me with my German Conversation 4113 class?"

I had been struggling in 4113 with because it was a senior level course and I needed it to graduate so's I could mosey off to Big in Normal, and besides if he couldn't write 'Hoch Deutsch' and say 'iccckkk' with a sharp 'k' then a breath instead of that easy blue-collar 'issshhh' nonsense which any moron trying to learn German could pronounce, he wasn't my type. He gave me a baby-blue look which licked me up and down and all around obviously hoping for more than a little German Conversation but then on the other hand more might come later so let's get the homework over with, ja?

"Ja Ja, but of course ich hilfe du mit deine Schule Arbeiten," he said sweetly, taking off his black leather jacket which had like totally wowed me and flexing his muscles just so I wouldn't get the idea that this relationship was going to be anything but physical and I thought sure, why not, I picked him up off the street so what can I expect it's been way too long since I had a schon Worst, anyway and besides he just said 'ich' with a 'k' sound then a breath so he must have some kind of class.

He didn't have that much class I figured out later on, but we learned a little German that night and did some other things I had better not mention or my reputation might be at stake. I wouldn't want anyone in Lawless to think I was a loose hussy who picked up men in those days or that all that hitchhiking left me needing a couple years to catch up with the rest of the women in Lawless.

I acted interested for a short time pretending we had something in common besides the obvious, which wasn't half bad, but before I knew it he had practically moved in with me, and before he knew it I had kicked him out. Why? Something about no references, and lots of hot air. He would say things like, "I used to own a Porsche," and "I haf five daughters in Germany," to which I would reply, after a time, "show me your transcripts," and "why is it you don't have a better job?" to which he would reply, "I'm moving up into management," and "they lost my transcripts in Germany," that sort of dialogue.

I spent all the money on us and everyone should know by this time how broke I was what with struggling through college and two jobs, etc., but he continued to drink all my expensively dark imported German beer, just the same. My brand new roomie at that time who had needed a cheap place to stay when I needed some company and was a nice wild girl like myself, threatened to move out if I didn't get rid of the creep, so I had to rethink the situation, which I did. Yeah, he was a German all right, but he had become something closer to a germ, or perhaps, even lowly as a worm, which probably would have had the sense not to pick him up in the first place just because of a lousy accent and some cheap muscles.

The grand finale arrived after one month of hot and heavy.

I had recently discovered through a drinking buddy of mine that Detlev wasn't anywhere near what he seemed. The V-Max, which we va-roomed on all over town, was in actuality his married girlfriend's, although he kept telling me different to which I had begun to say,"show me the title," and come to find out he was also one of Lawless' more famous bar sluts which could have had disastrous effects on my health if I didn't end it right away.

We were standing outside in the sunshine, soaking up the rays, and for the umpteenth time, I asked my favorite question. I asked him why he couldn't prove a single thing he kept describing to me, such as his Army escapades, which were geographically incorrect not to mention impossible, and his lack of visible diplomas, not to mention diplomacy. Detlev, true to his fashion, began to cry, but this time, I had had enough of his tears.

"I can't prove anyzing to you," he whimpered, "but I love you, it's true." I couldn't figure out what initially attracted me to him, and by this time, even his accent was suspect. I displayed my leadership qualities and dealt him a domineering Germanic blow.

"Get lost, Detlev," I snorted. No tears in my eyes. "You're full of shit, and you know it." He wailed some more, looking at me every few wails to see if my reaction had softened, but it was no go. He had to go. He was a cheap piece of ass, that's what he was. A slut.

"But what we haf' togezer izz so beautiful," he whined. "Could you gif' me jus' one chance more?" Sniffle, sniffle, he wiped his red, inflated nose. "I swear, I get zee transcripts!" he swore vehemently on his bleeding heart.

"Give it a break, Detlev, I don't give a fuck about your phony education," I screamed like a banshee, shoving him across the yard and in the direction of his hovel which was a mere three blocks away from mine, located in the slummiest section of Lawless imaginable. I had moved from my second story apartment to a sprawling, basement-like dungeon with no windows and mildewed walls in order to escape the criminal element lurking in Oldtown, and to have a backyard for a puppy dog to protect me against villains and rapists after the old lady on my corner in Old Town was raped and I figured I'd better sca-doodle or be next.

Detlev gave up and stumbled to his Vega to drive home to his immaculately kept lair, where he continued to seduce young maidens with his phony credentials and exciting Prussian accent, heartlessly robbing them of their maidenhead and their few paltry dollars.

I heard Detlev was a bar slut at the Old Mad Hound Club, the one where they have nude dancers and illegal sex shows (we got laws against that perverted stuff in Oklahoma), but I only saw him there once. In the three months since I'd thrown him out the door of my dungeon, he had gained at least twenty pounds and was sprouting a thick, altogether funky shit-brown beard. Detlev was no longer the hunk who had initially attracted me. He eyed me hornily and explained his latest grandiose plan to leave Lawless, but I couldn't see how that was possible since he had no job anymore. He said he got a lot of money for his Vega, and had a tidy sum saved up on top of that. Sure he did. You would think since I linked up with him because of his German accent, and not much more, that I would learn my lesson and seek more in a man than a date with my German fixation, but this was not true. I still wanted a German boyfriend because I was, I had decided, completely German, considering my biological entrance into the world from the loins of my unfamiliar Kraut parents.

So, in order to achieve my love-goal I began hanging around this German bar in Lawless which was called Gertrude and Helga's (in honor of the two dykes who owned it), instead of trying to find my right kind of guy on the street or in front of Seven-Eleven over nuked nachos and cheese. All the other German women felt sorry for my pitiful self and let me chatter away the evenings with them, even offering to set me up with men they knew from the Old Country, which they all pined after with great, sorrowful expressions. Pretty soon, I was yakkity-yakking away like an unhinged ratchet motor-mouth and saying 'Tschuss!' with the best of them, a result of my German minor at Cotton College, and lots of German Conversation, 4113.

Before you could say 'Der Wiener Schnitzel,' I was introduced to Peter from Berlin by one of my many smiling benefactors, who understood my search for all things Deutschland. He was tall, dark and handsome, muscled up and ready for action, although he didn't say too much. Peter came with glowing references from Helga and Gertrude who knew him from the Old Country, and I was surprised that I caught him so quickly since he was such a tall dark hunk that he could have any female in Lawless, German or otherwise. I conveniently ignored the fact that he spent most of his time in a bar. After a whirlwind romance that lasted two weeks, during which time my roommate finally quit threatening to move out and actually did, Peter and I made an earth-shattering decision. (I never was one to draw out a romance and see what occurred; I was for getting with it right away.) Thus, we developed plans for my immediate trip to Berlin that summer.

I was twenty-seven years old and nearing the completion of my Bachelor of Arts degree. I had been corresponding with the Free University of Berlin, to sort of justify my trip to that city, and planned to finish my degree in German (what a laugh—I couldn't count to twenty in German!). But, it sounded good to unsuspecting ears as I spread the news to my family and friends that I was going to Berlin, moving all my things to Berlin, giving away my dog and leaving America for good to be a German.

Ja.

Naturally, everyone had thought I was over my wanderlust since I had been back from California for quite some time, but I had had them all fooled. I was still crazy as a loon. Peter went back to Berlin, and his sister, who lived in Lawless and worked at Gertrude and Helga's, reassured me that I would never hear from her brother again. I was staunch in my defence of our true love, even if it was only two weeks in duration, and sure enough, he sent me nine hundred dollars, wired from his bank to mine, for a plane ticket. I sca-doodled to Berlin on a Big Bird just as fast as I could say "Bye-bye Lawless!"

Imagine Peter's dismay when he realized what I brought with me—two bicycles, three suitcases, a guitar and two backpacks. They would not fit into the little Volvo his friend let him borrow to pick me up from Tegel-Flughafen in Berlin, so we had to call a taxi to haul it all off to his mother's apartment, where he lived.

Oh shit, his mother's?

Maybe I misunderstood him when he said where we would be staying, I thought he said 'our own apartment,' or something to that effect. And the things his mother did to get rid of me would fill Hitler's heart with joy. At least I had my yellow bumble-bee Centurion Facet racing bike, not to mention the fancy white Cannondale with black anodized rims, pink BMX tires, and racing cog that should have belonged to a road bike but I was just such a macho dudewoman I had to get hard on myself. I had bought these two flying machines with left-over grant money which was one reason why I was still so poor and frequently had to live on beer and noodles.

I could afford to ship the bikes because I had a sympathetic friend at the airport in Lawless who handled shipping and gave me a nice price (free!). I could afford the bikes themselves because I had a real job by this time as a public school substitute bus driver on top of my job as Cotton Writing Lab tutor. As far as I was concerned, summer vacation was here and school was out. It was time for a little fun in Berlin. I got comfortable in the apartment while Peter's mother scoped me out. She had obviously never seen an American in her whole life, and tried to converse with me about how my job in Berlin would most certainly be in a beer house. Evidently, Mrs. Peter's Mother, the lady with the plastic shopping bag, would never figure out that I was here to finish my degree and marry Peter, or that we would soon have our own little love nest in the sky, somewhere in downtown Berlin near the Ku'damm, Berlin's very cool main drag. Kurfurstendamm that is.

I wanted to hang out with all the punkers who stayed strung out at the Zoo, or Zoologische Gartens as it was properly known, right at the corner square of Ku'damm. Everything could be resolved with a little bit of slang, and when my friendly professor from the Free University of Berlin called me, I figured Peter's Mother From Hell would finally get the message about my mission in sunny Berlin, and sit up and take notice that Gabrielle had arrived.

It stayed sunny for about two days. Then, the temperature dropped and so did my humane-up-until-that-time treatment by Peter's Motherfucking Mother. I had just kissed him good-bye as he left for work at six-thirty that morning, when suddenly, I found myself standing in the stinking hall, wearing nothing much to speak of, and she wouldn't let me in. I pounded on the door, I screamed. I whispered, I cried. Luckily, I had his keys....

Before you knew it, I had outsmarted the crazy, white-haired, obviously depraved little lady creature from the dark lagoon, and I was relaxing in the bathroom, after observing the unusual toilet. I must add my description to the already existing literature available, just to keep you up to date since the Germans have reunited and we might someday enjoy the master race's race for superiority once again in this hemisphere. Most people in most cultures treat human waste like any other waste—they discard it as soon as possible and don't dwell too long on what shape it is, or the color, or the texture, oder the odor, odor, odor. Sigmund Freud may have thought he had it all figured out, but think about this: Why did the man have such an interest in 'anal fixations' and 'anal retention' and 'anal' this and that? Perhaps it would behoove us, as inspectors, observers, and sometimes admirers of human behavior, to more closely examine the toilet training Sigmund might have had as a young tot in Vienna.

How could the young man grow to become a leading psychoanalyst unless he first closely examined his own, personal excretions? How could Germans build toilets with little platforms for their shit to fall on, leaving the water covered hole for the flusher to fill and swoop the offending poop, only after each and every individual had ample time to view his body's fabulous makeover of what was once strudel, sausage and beer? Odor notwithstanding, German toilets lead to a greater understanding of the culture as a whole if one but dares to look. On the platform of the German toilet, where all poop must rest indefinitely, lies the answer—it's in the sausage.

So, I finished admiring my lovely, smelly, vegetarian turds, and hopped into the bath to wash the feces off my butt. Ah, a nice hot bath in freezing, sleeting Berlin, what a pleasure. Imagine my dismay and surprise when my bubbles were so rudely interrupted by a shocking torrent of ice cold bathwater—the bitch had turned off the hot water from her water heater, and I was left with cold bubbles and a freezing butt! I screamed at her in broken English, and she screamed back in broken German. Something like 'Nicht verstate Americanish....'

"Sure you don't, you wench," I snarled, "I'll get you back, just wait until your son gets home from work." The war was on. Well, I thought later, it's five o'clock now, and I've been hiding behind some books for a very long time while whatsisface's mother shows me to her old lady girlfriends, pointing a long, gnarled finger at me, the finger of a witch who would shoot me for her stew if I wasn't careful. Where was that Peter, anyway? Seven o'clock arrived, and still no Peter. German tv sucked, and I was getting weirded out. The Lady of the House mumbled something about the Bier Garten again, intimating I get a job there. Suddenly the phone rang. "Peter?" I asked, since she allowed me to answer it. "Where are you? Your fucking mother is driving me crazy!" His drunken voice wavered uncertainly over the receiver, and I heard the loud shouts of drunken German banter in the background.

Oh fine. "Meine kleine schnacke," he slurred sweetly. "Sex-kitten."

"Look, you fool, whyn'cha get me outta here?" I bitched, having had enough of Hell-in-a-Day.

"Just another few minutes," he cajoled, "come join me." I would if I could, but can I get back into the apartment afterward? Peter whined a little more about how his friends wanted me to come meet them, the thought of which I didn't much care for any more than the drivel I was having to deal with here in Berlin with the Plastic Bag Lady. Surely this is temporary, I reasoned with myself. Next morning was faintly drizzly, faintly sunny, very cold for July. I wheeled my bicycle (the mountain bike) out of the basement where I had kept them both locked up, and headed for my favorite Irish Pub in the Europa Center to have a nice, hot Irish coffee. By noon I was blitzed, and by that evening it was all over. I tried my key in the lock, but that witch had sneakily changed locks so even poor Peter couldn't get into the apartment.

Wow.

Suddenly, the realization that I was shit-out-of-luck in the middle of an unfamiliar West German island in a hostile East German state in the middle of the night struck me as ludicrously insane, and I realized that those nasty pedestrians who yelled at me each and every day were nothing like the folks back home, who at least minded their own business. You mean, I'm not a German? I asked myself, not having anyone else around to talk to except the wild pigs in Peter's favorite nearby walking park where the polizei would arrest you in a Berlin minute for setting even an inch of mountain-bike tire onto its sacred pedestrian realm.

Wait a minute here, I told myself sternly, I thought I was a German! Where are my ancestors? But naturally, no one answered my call, so I pedaled off into the drizzly night to find my truest love, Peter the Seuffe. When I wasn't hunting down Peter, my other favorite ride was to wander downtown towards Charlottenburg to check out the bike shops, hop on Spandau to have a cup of milche kaffee, then wind around back to Seimensplatz, where we lived nearby. The Grunewald green passageway was my forest home, and continued to beckon me (at the risk of life and limb crossing several busy downtown Berlin streets), because it held the only path that cars were not allowed to drive on. Other cyclists crowded its tiny, winding roadway each day, leaving me with a slight feeling of camaraderie, which I lacked elsewhere in Berlin. I continued to search for friendly faces, forgetting that I knew no one in that rebuilt city except Peter and his friends. I even began applying for bar jobs until my gig at the University came through (now that's a laugh).

No one would hire me, however, except this one sleazy old corner bar, rank with the chemical and feral smell of men's bathrooms, whose owner took a fancy to my pink-flushed, healthy cheeks. I was a bar girl before I knew it, and tips were great. I would hop on my little Cannondale mountain bike and pedal madly down Siemens Stadt to Heilmannring 4, where I lived, change out of my black spandex tights, which were de rigeur in Berlin that year, pedal madly back to Spandau (hopping a U-Bahn if it rained, which it often did), and meet Peter at his favorite bar on Wilhelmstrasse. It was fun, I stayed drunk, and we all had a rollicking time.

But life with Peter left much to be desired. As much as I drank, I still couldn't hold the vast amounts of beer that other Germans managed to consume, especially Peter and his friends. That wasn't the problem. Die gross Probleme was the fact that Peter and his friends would often disappear until the next day, leaving me to fend for myself in jolly Berlin, even though he managed to get me new keys (much to the Mother From Hell's chagrin). I didn't appreciate her increasing hostility, nor his decreasing presence in my life. All the cycling in the world couldn't erase my dissatisfaction with Peter and his lifestyle, not to mention my own. I also expected his mother to plant a bomb in my bedroom any day now, or poison my food, or have me arrested by one of the numerous polizei who roamed the neighborhood.

As it happened, I lucked out as usual, and ran into an American GI who had helped me exchange dollars for marks on the Lufthanza flight from Frankfurt into Berlin. He walked into my bar one day as I was pouring beer for the local gentlemen after lunch time, before the evening rush. It wasn't too busy, but I was the only waitress there, so I constantly rushed around, filling mugs and pitchers, and emptying ashtrays.

"Yo! Gabby?" he called out to me, almost causing me to spill a pitcher of dark frothy on the bald, courtly old gentleman's head who I was serving. I turned, my apron jingling with change,

245

hurriedly marked several x's on my customer's coaster, and ran to greet my long lost American buddy.

"Homeboy!" I effused.

"Gabby!" he effused back.

"Man, this place is almost too German for me to handle," I finally said, after hugging Stan so tight for long minutes and holding his tightly wound body close mine. I was almost in tears at the sight of his Army uniform and the 'flat tortilla' (green beret) he wore on his head which connoted Special Forces.

I felt I was about to be rescued from the Gulag.

Stan, a deep rich, chocolate-brown thirty-year-old Army Captain stationed in Berlin, was the epitome of American manhood. His short afro was trimmed to tiny ringlets, his stance was tall and strong, his manners were impeccable, and he extended an arm to help me out of my predicament. "So, you got time for a drink tonight after work?" he asked me as I maneuvered around the multiple tables that crowded my tiny place of employment. I checked the cuckoo clock on the wall over the bar—three o'clock.

"I get off at five," I answered, pouring another pitcher for the portly gentlemen who had held up their empty ones. "Can you meet me then?" He very gently touched my hair, and looked me over. My spandex was a little too tight, but I needed the tips. I squirmed under his appraising gaze.

"Sure," he said, "where shall we go?" Stan thought for a moment, then answered his own question, possibly reading my mind. "How about the Irish Pub at the Europa Center on Ku'damm?" I almost squealed with glee! We were going to one of the few places in Berlin (that I knew of) which was frequented by Americans and American bands. What a relief.

"Oh, Stan, I'm so glad you came here today," I said, sniffing back a tear. "I'm so lonely in Berlin, I don't know what to do."

He acted a bit surprised, and said, "What about that guy, Peter whatsisname, who you told me about on the plane?" A hopeful gleam filled Stan's eye. "Didn't everything work out?" I recognized that look, that horny male look, but I didn't care anymore. Stan probably had tons of girlfriends since he had been stationed in Berlin for three years, and one more wouldn't make much difference. Besides, I needed a friend.

"Be right back, okay?" I said, rushing to fill another order for yet another portly, well-dressed German gentleman on his extended lunch hour. I could have had any one of many prospective sugar-daddies in Berlin, but I wasn't interested in that particular kind of relationship.

"Sho, Baby," he said, then sat down to have a dark brew and watch me work. Stan was the Man, and my odyssey had changed course just a little. Not much else was happening. After several weeks of lonely roaming, and several more weeks of attempting to negotiate with my previously-friendly liaison from the Free University of Berlin, I realized school was out of the question for me. It was my fault, really. I had arrived in Berlin exactly two days late to enroll, and even though I had a special permission slip, I didn't follow through and provide actual admissions requirements. So, school was not going to happen this semester, and neither was anything else.

Moving into an apartment of our own might have saved our relationship, but I doubt it. I tried to talk to Peter repeatedly, but all he wanted to discuss was our impending marriage. Yech, I thought, anything but that. "Peter," I would say, "how come we can't get our own place?"

To which he would answer, more often than not, "Soon, we get married soon," with a drunken leer on his face. Smiling, he would plop another five mark piece on the bar table, and motion for a friendly fraulein to bring us two more. Then, true to character, Peter would light up one of those horrible German non-filters, and lovingly feel up my arm.

"But Peter," I would complain, "it's terribly boring in Berlin."

"Gabrielle," he would reply, "it will all change when we get married, now drink your beer." He would suck down another bottle of lukewarm beer, and another, and another. Could it be possible that my Peter was avoiding the issue? Finally, I couldn't take the charade any longer. That was about the time I decided to hit the road with Stan. It had been four long weeks since I left Lawless with all my worldly possessions (minus my old, red, Datsun pickup which Mama had bought me and my worn-out furniture), and I was ready to change residences. Naturally, Peter acted upset, and ranted and raved about how much he loved me. His mother stood idly nearby, listening to our conversation.

"I love you Gabrielle," Peter wailed, tearfully wiping his eyes on a napkin. "You just can't go back to America!" But I was staunch.

"Look, you're never going to move away from your mother's house," I replied. "You spend all your money on beer!" I didn't wipe my eyes, that's for sure. The Mother From Hell listened intently, a tiny smirk playing on her lips. She got the drift, even if she 'Nicht verstate Americanish.' Poor Peter was beside himself, but I held my ground.

"I'm waiting for my mother to die," he whispered, glancing over at her frail, bent body, "and then we can keep the apartment." I stared at him incredulously, my eyes rolling to the ceiling.

"You what?" I yelled, the irony of it all finally getting to me. "I don't want this apartment, I want to go home! And furthermore... and furthermore, you can wait until hell freezes over, because your mother will never die!" I was warming up to a crescendo. "She's not human!" We both looked at his mother, who immediately said, "Mensch...." I got away soon after that. Stan and I had been visiting on the sly, hanging out at the Irish Pub when I wasn't working, and one night I just didn't come home to Peter's at all. His Mother From Hell noticed, naturally. Peter freaked. It was okay for him to stay out all night in the bars with his friends, but for me to not show up for one single night was a double standard and a half.

"So," he accused, "you don't love me?" Peter stood in my bar the next morning with his hands on his hips and a pouty Jim Morrison style look. Here's this arrogant, two-timing German male and he wants to know if I love him? I thought to myself.

"What exactly would you like me to love about you?" I countered. Not that I was that lovable, but I certainly couldn't get into marriage, uh uh, not this party animal. I had a barmaid job, good tips, a decent German accent, and lots of male companionship. Why did I still live at Peter's Mom's place?

I dunno.

I finally broke Peter's heart, and he let me go. I moved into Stan's place, and started to have a little fun in Berlin. We frequented such bars as Ascot's, which was rustic, gloomy, well-populated and friendly. I also began to hang with the local mime-skinhead types who went there for beer and talk. Things could have just partied on like this forever, but I fucked it all up one day on the U-Bahn, and scared myself right back onto a Big Bird to Lawless.

I was drunk, as usual, and farting around on my white Cannondale when it got dark, and I got too far from home to know where to turn. I did my usual thing, and hopped a train, hoping to emerge somewhere near Siemens Stadt. Oops! I emerged somewhere near Friedrichs Felde, and found myself entering increasingly hostile territory. Guards carrying ancient Soviet submachine guns and rusty automatic pistols patrolled the deserted stations, as we passed into East Berlin. I was so drunk I couldn't figure this out, and I actually got off the train and headed for a check point. I took out my passport and showed it to the guy standing at Alexanderplatz, expecting him to pass me through. He took one look at my passport, inhaled a toxic breath of my alcoholic state, and said, "Sind sie bloerd?" He rolled his eyes, and laughed. "Was wollen sie hier, oder wissen sie?"

"What?" I squeaked, terrified at the gun in my face. "Aren't we near Siemens Stadt?" Practically speechless with surprise and an almost supernatural fear, I swayed in place, holding my bicycle tightly in the gloomy tunnel, and stared at his khaki uniform buttons and his shiny black boots.

"Sie sind eine Amerikanerien, und versten mich gar nichts?" he snarled. Looking me over some more, obviously collecting his thoughts, he was caught unaware by my next, very undiplomatic move.

"Huh?" I blurted out, then promptly threw up all over his shiny black boots. He recoiled in disgust and released the safety on his submachine gun with a loud 'click.' Oh shit! I thought, feeling much better after the megabarf. Am I in the wrong place at the wrong time? Is this not Siemens Stadt exit? I ran back to the train, hopped back into my caboose, and took my little bicycle with me. Forget Berlin!

I was going back to Lawless, USA where the buffalo roamed freely on the prairie, and the Indians still lived in tipis on

249

weekends. It was time for a good old fashioned pow-wow, and I wanted to hang with the homies, singing and drumming round the fire in a moonlit, starry night

I called up my dear old Dad, since he had all the money in the family, and begged him to rescue me. Even though he had his bad points, they did not include leaving his daughter in Germany indefinitely, especially in hostile Eastern Europe, because the world had not yet been blessed with a reunified Deutschland, and the Berlin Wall was still patrolled with machine guns on the DDR side. Stan took me to Tegel Flughafen two days later, and I rushed up to greet the sky.

So much for my German fixation.

Chapter 16

All mankind's inner feelings eventually manifest themselves as an outer reality.

Stuart Wilde

Spirits Speak

The Big Bird was a slow ride, but it gave me lots of time to rethink my situation, particularly my situation back in good old Lawless, Oklahoma, back in the good old USA. Funny thing about Lawless, I thought to myself as I attempted to breathe the recycled air that the Big Bird offered as an alternative to the 'smoking section,' I never realized how friendly the people are back home. Yeah, I'd originally wanted no truck with Lawless inhabitants back in my biker bitch days, but now that I was almost a college graduate, things took on a slightly different shade and hue. How could I ever hate the Mall Tick? I asked myself, it's the only place in town that opens at six a.m. to allow the elderly a place to walk without fear of being mugged. Not only that, but Lawless has the only Comanche language institute in the state of Oklahoma. I gazed at the lady sitting next to me and wanted to ask her if she was from Oklahoma, but at the last minute reason prevailed, and I actually locked up my motor mouth.

We landed a solid fourteen hours later in New York City, where I whisked my two bicycle boxes through customs by pretending they had been examined because I didn't want 'em chopped open like I saw all the other boxes were, and I hauled ass to make my Dallas flight by the total skin of my teeth. We stayed on the ground for the next three hours because of lousy weather conditions, which was infinitely better than crashing to the ground because the plane was out of control. I didn't mind; I wanted to dream some more about Lawless, my home in Oklahoma.

"How long were you in Berlin?" the bald-headed middle-aged plastics salesman in the seat next to me inquired, noticing the Berlin tags on my carry-on. He wasn't exactly the thrill of my flight, but I hadn't spoken to anyone since getting on at Tegel

Flughafen, so I decided to chit-chat a little to pass the time to Dallas.

"Six weeks," I said, "and it was pretty exciting too, especially when I almost got arrested in East Berlin for public drunkenness." The salesman, who had been eying my bod (as most men have a habit of doing,) gave a horrified gasp as he sipped his third martini.

"How did you escape?" he asked in total awe. "Did you call the Embassy?"

"No, I just kissed total ass," I answered, remembering my frantic attempts to polish the vomit off that DDR guard's shiny black boots, which must have won his approval because he finally let me go back to West Berlin, frightened, sober, and ready to get the hell out of the AO.

"Ohhh," said the salesman, a horny gleam lighting his jaundiced eye. He obviously wanted to know how to get me to totally kiss his ass by the way he gave me the Big Eyeball, and he asked, "Do you do that often?"

I decided to change the subject and tried to ignore the jerk for the rest of the flight. "I have to study," I said studiously, dragging out my German Conversation textbook to illustrate my point, and I did need to finish those six hours of independent study which I had stupidly enrolled in, thinking it would be easy. It just wasn't fun to study German in Germany when all I wanted to do was search out American newspapers to read a little English for a change.

Finally landed in Lawless, and Wayne picked me up with a six-pack of Fosters Lager ready at the helm, which I drank in two hours flat and got drunker than an old coot. The booze on the plane hadn't fazed me one bit, although I tried with all my heart to get snockered. The heady, humid atmosphere of Lawless Oklahoma air at night was enough to turn me into one soggy sponge. I soaked it all in on Mama's front porch and said to Wayne, who soaked it all in with me, "Sure is good to be home."

"Yeah," he agreed. "When ya want to hit the rocks?"

"Soon," I said, "ya still got all your gear?"

"But of course," he answered, "ya still got yours?"

"Uh huh. Wore out my Merrells climbing Dr. Coolhead on the Zoo Wall, though."

"No sweat, I can resole them for you in a heartbeat."

252

"Climbed the one called Top Rope Route yet?"

"Where's that?"

"On the north side of Mount Scott," I answered. "It's a sustained five eleven face climb that will kick your ass all over Oklahoma. That's why most of us have to resort to a top rope."

"Let's do it!" Wayne said excitedly. "I got a new belay-slave last year, ya know."

"Really?" I asked. "Is it a girl?"

"Ya gotta be kidding, Gabby," Wayne laughed. "Most of the women around here are afraid to break their nails."

"Uh huh," I agreed, "and afraid to pick off ticks, too."

"They sure are missing out on some good times," Wayne said, hitting another can of Fosters. "Climbing will be the rage in a couple of years, just wait and see."

"And until then," I said, grabbing a can myself, "we'll dominate."

Mom and I had a fabulous reunion the next morning, because she had been asleep when I arrived deep in the darkest night at two a.m. Even though I didn't have anywhere to live except at her house I still had my life, I thought almost miserably, remembering my many exploits that could have ended in tragedy. Cycling in a large foreign city while shitfaced on 15.2 percent beer wasn't the safest pastime for a young female to indulge in. I didn't tell her about it though, she had enough to worry about.

"Mom," I said as we prepared coffee and I downed three Advils for my blinding headache, "you wouldn't believe all the museums I saw in Berlin." Mom was busy fixing breakfast for my brother, who had to be at work in thirty minutes, so she just barely managed to chit chat while at the same time sling some hash and eggs into a skillet.

"Well, you know your father and I always tried to instill an appreciation for culture in you and Gerrie," she said, referring to the many castles we visited in Germany in between my weekly raids on Deutsch farms with my thuglets.

"It worked," I slightly lied, "I spent a lot of time around Charlottenburg and the Zoologische Gartens." A lot of time drinking in the courtyards, maybe.

"Did you locate your biological parents?" she asked shyly, always worried that I missed out on not knowing them. I gave her a big hug as she stirred three eggs into some onions, green peppers, tomatoes, and jalapenos, our favorite breakfast since we were young tots. "I wondered if you'd come back to Lawless if you had found them."

"You don't need to worry about that," I explained, trying to convince her that I could care less about those mysterious foreigners whose squirt in the night produced an unknown child. "I just wonder if I'm maybe part black," I joked, trying to get a rise out of her Arkansas born-and-bred attitude. She cracked up, and ruffled my slightly frizzy hair with a work-reddened hand. Mom was getting older, and more tired, but she had caught on to my tricks.

"Oh," she said flipping the omelet mixture, "I'm certain of it."

Weird how you notice little things when your eyes are open wider than before. I was hungry for Italian food the following day while I was still waiting for my baggage to make it from Dallas, and I moseyed on over to my favorite place which was run by the guy from Brooklyn, Bono. "Say, Wild Girl," he called out as soon as I was seated in his totally art deco dining room. "You was outta town a long time, huh?"

"Too long," I sighed, picking up a worn and faded copy of the *Village Voice* to read while Bono prepared my vegetarian antipasto, noodles with cream sauce, and fresh-made Italian garlic bread.

"Sorry I can't serve ya wine," he said as he sat down for a quick New York minute. "Ya know those thumpers from the Yellow Fence stopped that when they got me busted."

"No shit," I said, sipping a Corona which was under alcoholic content so was allowed. "Are you gonna try for the license now that they're gone outta town?" I asked.

"Uh uh," he answered, shaking his sweaty head and wiping his face with a red cloth napkin. "Day's always more thumpers where dose came from, an I don' wanna fock wit 'em." We exchanged a couple wordless glances, then he hopped up to get my dinner, which his wife, Nina, was watching in the kitchen.

"Don't blame ya," I mumbled to his vanishing form, not wanting to think about the thumpers and the Bible scene.

I read something about crack cocaine in Harlem in the *Village Voice*, when Bono called out from the kitchen, "I'll bring ya the latest issue," he said, "I keep 'em in the kitchen until I've read every last word." I looked again at the date on my copy of the *Voice* thinking, Brooklyn can't be that great or he wouldn't live here. Maybe all my misconceptions and preconceived notions about Lawless were wrong, I forced myself to consider. Maybe I was a stuck-up jerk who didn't know which side my Italian bread was garlic-buttered on. Maybe Lawless was actually the best place for me to be. Fancy that, I mused, reading about the gang killings, the race riots and the gay bashings in New York City. Culture has its price.

Back home in Lawless, I rejoined the American (human) race pretty fast, and finished up my last two semesters of college at Cotton. I bounced around in an old yellow school bus, picking up and depositing kiddipoos, while juggling German and Algebra to finish my degree. It was a relief to once again drive my old pickup, and drink cold Coors Lite, listen to English, and see familiar faces. Never did Lawless look so good as now. I was a new person, and enlightened by traveling to another world on top of that. But then the grunge hit me, and I got involved with Prentiss Tribbly. Yech. He began sniffing around the house some, cruising by and honking his car horn, just kind of letting me know he was available, so to speak. You would imagine that since I was finally over my German fixation once and for all that I wouldn't immediately launch into yet another fixation with my past. Alas, alack! I did. "Say honey," he said one day as he was slow-ridin' by in his midnight blue Cadillac Seville, its feelers just barely touching the curb as he slunk slowly to a stop. "Why don't you and me get together?" I was busy combing my German Shepherd, Shiloh, who I had recently acquired as a college graduation present from my Mama, and great grey and white tufts of hair cascaded from my metal curry comb as I yanked and pulled on Shiloh's tortured fur.

"Huh?" I said to Prentiss, for it had been many long years since high school, and I didn't think of him except in fleeting memories of the way he made me feel like a special person with his wit and his charm back when I was a young filly and didn't know the wiles of men. He was kinda cute, I mused, In a modified-soul kind of way, for Prentiss was really black during high school, but the Army had taught him to speak white to get ahead. I wondered if he still listened to the Brothers Johnson like we used to do together. Uh oh, I was starting to feel those longings again.

His curly, kinky hair felt like it was already in my hands, and my fingers were already running up and down his arms—no, stop it! His eyes looked deeply, soulfully into mine, and I felt what it was like to once again kiss his soft, cherry lips. I felt his warm breath on my neck, on my back, on my...I couldn't stop, I didn't want to stop dreaming about the love affair we had so long ago. I was fair game, and weak from my trip to Never Never Land. Prentiss had a nose for weakness, I would soon discover.

He stepped out of his ride, all tall, skinny, skanky six feet four inches of him, his green eyes and dark brown face giving me the once over. Did he think I was that easy? "Honey, I heard you a rock climbing fool," he commented, his slight paunch already saying 'middle age,' although he was only thirty. My pointed little ears perked up—I always fell for compliments. Exuding the desire to have Prentiss love me again, I all of a sudden couldn't concentrate on anything else but having his rapier wit at night when I most needed it. So lost was I in desire that I combed Shiloh a little harder, and she whined to make me stop.

"Shut-up, Shiloh," I told her to quell my aching heart, which the man standing before me had broken into little pieces when I was a senior at Lawless High. Prentiss stood a little closer and I got a whiff of his cologne, and admired his extra taut, tiny calves, and knobby knees. He really was a well built guy, when you thought about it. "You did, huh?" I asked him. "From who?" Prentiss smiled, and rubbed the small of my back in that old, familiar gesture as we stood out in my front yard that fall. I knew I was doomed to repeat myself with him, just to get a taste of those cherry lips of his.

"I never reveal my sources," he whispered, his very white perfect teeth displayed in a wide, wide grin. "How's about we talk about old times?" I yanked Shiloh a good hard one and she practically screamed in agony.

Prentiss Tribbly and I began a hot and heavy courtship that lasted for a full seven months. He had joined the Army eight years earlier, and was now a Staff Sergeant stationed at Fort Kill, the Army base next to Lawless. Prentiss was half German and half black, a mix that truly attracted me, given my taste in music and men. Only trouble was, Prentiss didn't act black at all, he acted pure white. Pure superior German white, to be exact.

We fought constantly, just like in high school.

"Why can't we go rock-climbing," I asked him two months after he picked me up in my front yard. That was my continual nagging (he said) refrain.

"I'm too freaking busy!" he snarled again, looking up from his crossword puzzle to give me the evil eye. Weird, I thought to myself, seems like he used to go outside once in a while. It was a bit strange when I took him for a teensy weensy five mile hike in the Wichitas and he ended up turning back after half a mile because he suddenly remembered some urgent correspondence he had forgotten.

"Are you sure you don't have time to finish this hike?" I had implored, almost begging him to come with me because I was lonely and wanted to get some exercise with my man. Prent had smiled that charming smile of his, huffed on another cigarette, and promptly said "No." No more explanations, just "No." He's just too busy, I figured, he'll do more things with me once he catches up on his correspondence. I always had an excuse for Prentiss, because I didn't want to lose the only homeboy I'd ever really loved, even more than Hans, who I was finally over.

That didn't keep me from pitching a hissy fit one morning, though. "You son of a bitch! "I screamed, throwing his clothes out my door. "Don't bother calling me anymore." Prentiss had once again begged out of a planned evening with me, for the fiftieth or sixtieth time, turned on his answering machine just to screen my frequent calls, then showed up at my house the next morning, full of excuses and wanting some nookie.

"I won't call you bitch," he snarled as he gathered his things, and he didn't either. Oh, a week went by and I thought I'd ring him just for old times sake, because I still wanted him, you see, he reminded me of our high school fling which had lasted two whole years, the longest relationship I'd ever had with a man, and I was hung up on his cajones.

257

"Prent," I would tell his machine, "call me, I'm sorry." But he didn't and after two weeks I went over to his house only to find his old girlfriend's Malibu out front, and she was married, too! That bastard, I thought, I'll never ever fall in love with him again. That wasn't true, of course, but I tried not to.

Then our love affair ended, much like it had ended when I was in high school, and Prentiss dumped me, just like before. I was devastated. What was it about men who treated me like shit that turned me on so much? Did I respect them more, or what? That question remained unanswered, but I finally figured out that my search for personal identity was really a search for the security I lost when Mom and Pop broke up, and I was hoping to find it in a man from my past. Figured it out much later, of course. Security, security, how many of us have any real security? I picked up my pieces after Prentiss refused to see me or talk to me on the phone. I listened to Sting and Heart, crying my eyes out for the only man I ever truly loved, and finally got my Bachelor of Arts at Cotton College that spring. Then, in early summer I got that magnificent official letter from Big's English Department saying that it was time to begin graduate school at Big University in Normal, Oklahoma. I immediately began sobbing when I read the news, "If you wish to accept the offer of Teaching Assistant, please sign along the dotted line and return this to the English Department."

Mama was proud of me and Dad once again sat up and took notice. I was ready, willing, capable and able to be happy with my life. I met a black officer during a bicycle club cookout and mountain bike race that summer, and began a relationship with him. I didn't love him like he loved me, but he was a hunk, fun to be with, and a nice guy too. We began to travel to bike races together, and hiked in the Wichitas. Maurice helped me with my bills and helped me regain my self esteem. But, true to my nature, I couldn't stay with him for long, because he was too nice. We broke it off after only two months, and I was again alone with my thoughts and my dogs. Now I had dogs, plural: a German Shepherd and a Rottweiler pup, Shiloh and Sasha, my two best friends in the world.

August rolled around, and it was time for me to journey up to the big university in the sky, Big University in Normal, and begin my illustrious, although short-lived career in acadamia as an English teacher. I arranged for a house and dog sitter to watch the place so I could commute to Normal, a one hundred and sixty mile round trip. "It's worth it," I told my Mama right before I left for my first day of classes at Big. "I'd rather live in Lawless than just about anywhere I can think of." She smiled at me like I was crazy or something, then kissed me and said,

"Just drive carefully Honey. I worry about you sometimes." So off into the new world of graduate school I traveled, off to my own office in a very large, very beautiful university where anything was possible and a person could meet all sorts of interesting characters.

I was still lovelorn, and love-worn, but at least school gave me something to do with my life, and people looked up to me because, as I proudly told my Dad that fall, "I'm working on a Masters degree."

"Yeah," he grumbled, "but when you gonna get a real job?"

I guess I suddenly had a dowry or something in Lawless, because as soon as I was home from Big for the weekend, Prentiss Tribbly began sniffing around my house again! He called me up one Saturday and stated his business. "I want to spend my whole life with you, Gabby," Prentiss moaned, breathing heavily into the telephone. What did I ever see in that guy? Now that I was a Masters candidate, and half-assed serious about my studies, I was stauncher and stronger when it came to trifles like 'men.'

"But the last time we talked," I answered, holding my space carefully, "you said to get lost!" He sure sounded sad and contrite, but I wasn't quite ready to give up my freedom. Feeling sorry for him as his voice cracked with desire for me, I listened to his plea anyway.

"But you know I love you," Prentiss moaned some more. "Why can't we be together?" Did he really miss me? He sounded seriously sorry. Hmmm.

"I'm pretty busy these days," I said, "what with school and commuting and all."

"I don't want to take up your time," he assured me.

"Well, I dunno," I hedged.

"I fucked up, I know I did," he whined, "but you gotta remember the good times we had together."

"Well, Prent, it's like this," I said. "You dumped me, and I'm pissed." He sure was good in bed though, and I was crumbling fast. My resolve weakened quickly.

"I was really confused, Gabby, because I knew I was in love with you and it scared me, but now I'm ready for the real thing."

"Oh, you are, huh?" I asked, my ears perking up. "What do you mean, the 'real thing'?" I wondered if he meant marriage, which would be heaven, coz I always loved him, and if he married me, that would prove he loved me too.

"I want to be your man," he breathed, listening closely for my expected reply. "I want to be with you and spend my life with you forever." Funny that I didn't take my experience with the old man and my job in management and put it to good use in this particular instance, remembering that he didn't want me until I did something laudatory in his book. Anytime I rose up in society, the sharks came hunting for my blood. No, common sense didn't have anything to do with my feelings for Prentiss Tribbly. True to form, I said, "I'll be right over!" and jumped into my Datsun pickup to drive to his heretofore forbidden house. We were back together, the most unlikely pair Lawless had ever seen. He swore he loved me, was my love slave, hadn't been with any other women during the seven months we had been separated, and wanted me back for a 'serious relationship.' I sort of swallowed his story, among other things, but fear lurked in the chasms of my subconscious mind, reminding me of past love follies.

I wasn't too sure about this. Yeah, I still loved him, but he had hurt me so much when he dumped me twice that the proof should have been in the pudding. Ah, but what a fine love affair we were having in between my commutes to Big for school, when I should have been studying English instead of Prentiss Tribbly. Within three weeks he had a key to my house. Within three months, we were married. Love Birds At It Again in Lawless, a story-book romance about two lovers who fall in love three times, then marry and settle down forever to have a very successful life together. I conveniently forgot that he was the one who once made me infamous with the nomenclature 'Crazy Gabby,' back in '79. All I could remember was that in '76 we broke Renee's bed.

Basically, I drank constantly as soon as the honeymoon was over, which was three days after we got married when he clammed up and wouldn't talk to me or let me bring my puppy dogs into the house, or go anywhere with me or do anything with me either. I tried not to let things get on my nerves, and told myself that Prentiss was just going through a phase and would snap out of it soon and then we would be happy, all that type drivel. At least I had some friends who weren't smoking crank in Normal, because the old friends I had around Lawless were dopers and dealers galore, except for Wayne, who worked as a plumber and still went rock climbing with me, making Prentiss extremely jealous.

I would commute to Normal, where I was having a fine time teaching English to the eighteen year old kiddipoos. I was also making Leftist connections, learning about our government's dubious drug smuggling activities, reading political exposes printed by the Christic Institute in Washington D.C. (a non-profit law firm crusading for the underdog), and writing wilder and wilder literary theories than any English Department should have to deal with. My self esteem rose in Normal, then fell in Lawless, but after a couple of months of negative Prentiss Tribbly, it fell in Normal too, so I drank more to kill the pain. I had a friend, a youngish forty year old art teacher who let me crash at her house with her two teenagers, and we hung out together at all the hottest debates and lectures. Just as soon as I could get away from my classes, I would meet Sally Alice at the local boho establishment where we would drink cappuccino with Nicaraguans and Ethiopians. Belatedly, I would phone home with the request to come home, but Prentiss always encouraged me to stay in Normal (for some strange reason). I kept hoping he would miss me, but he seemed glad to have me gone. Uh-oh.... Trouble in Paradise.

My teaching was going splendidly, but my literary theories left much to be desired. I was so certain of my awesome powers that I never took anything seriously—alas, alack! This was unwise, for I was no Shakespeare or Chaucer. My grades suffered, and I gradually became disillusioned, although a couple of professors attempted to guide me in the right direction. It sure was fun while it lasted, though, and Sally Alice and I rode our mountain bikes all over Normal, visiting art galleries, drinking Fosters Lager, and having a rollicking old time. I just didn't bother to study.

I always had this thought in the back of my mind that I should be home in Lawless. I called Prentiss one evening, planning to travel home for the weekend, and he wouldn't have it. I was sitting in Sally Alice's kitchen, watching her cook some veggies in the wok. She was lean, lank, petite, lovely, and spoke French. She turned to meet my gaze, her grey eyes flashing with fun. "You know he doesn't want you at home, Gabby," she said. Slapping another slice of onion into the wok, she added paprika and curry. Wiping her hands on the dish towel, she reached for the soy sauce. "Dinner's almost ready," she yelled into her daughter's bedroom. I wrung my hands, and reached for the phone.

"You're right, but I have to try to make it work," I said, belatedly. "I'd really rather stay here with you and the kiddos." Sadly, I dialed the phone. We had been married for a mere three months, and he didn't even want me around at all. Perhaps it was due to the fact that he had flunked out of college, and was jealous of my attempts at acadamia. Perhaps it was because he was too busy with his night job at the local theater where he ran the light show. Or, maybe there was something else amiss in paradise. I shuddered to think what. I dialed.

"Hello?" a strange voice answered Prentiss' phone. "Who's calling, please?" I was somewhat surprised to hear the voice of some guy, since Prentiss was so particular about answering his own phone. He also hated my dogs, which should have warned me about his personality.

"Is Prent at home?" I asked, twisting the phone cord in nervousness. Sally Alice stood by the counter, listening and shaking her head. She had been through a couple of divorces herself, and knew the score.

"Sorry, he's busy," said the voice. "Who's calling?" This is bad, I thought to myself.

"It's his wife, "I said, "now will you get him on the phone?" Then I added, "Who are you, anyway?"

"I'm Bernie," the voice lisped, only slightly more polite than before. "You must be Gabby." Did I detect a tone of ridicule and scorn? Who was Bernie? Wait a minute, I thought I met him one night at the Prancing Pony bar, where Prentiss just had to take me because of some band that played there. They were probably out wenching while I slaved away at Big. "Sorry Hon," Bernie said, "Prent's not home right now." I heard a muffled voice in the background, I couldn't tell whose.

"Fine," I replied wearily, "just tell him I called." I looked at Sally Alice as I hung up the phone, and suddenly burst into tears. Why didn't he love me? She patted me on the shoulder.

"Don't let it get you down," she said. "We'll just go to that lecture on Central America tonight." She finished stirring the veggies, adding mushrooms at the last minute. "Did you know the C.I.A. is recruiting at Big U tomorrow?" I shook my head, sniffling a little, still daydreaming about when Prentiss and I broke the bed. That was such a long time ago, and he seemed so different these days, but I knew he was still the same Prentiss I had loved in high school—bright, articulate, and funny—that's why I married him.

"So, what are we going to do about it?" I asked, rallying to the cause. Sally Alice appreciated my change of tone, and offered me a Fosters from the fridge.

"That's the way, Kid," Sally Alice said, grinning her mischievous grin. She rummaged through her desk and brought out a thick pile of fliers. "Don't worry, we've got plans for those devious suckers."

Next morning, I was passing out "Ban the C.I.A. From Recruiting On College Campuses" pamphlets, and this smug-looking, cocky, trench-coated white guy wearing Ray-Ban sunglasses saunters up to me and smarts off about my activities, saying, "So, what have we got here?" Smirking, he reread my pamphlet, and I got a faint whiff of his cologne. I noted the Vasque hiking boots he had on, but felt an immediate dislike for his arrogant attitude.

"You can read, obviously," I retorted, taking him for a right wing conservative antagonizer. "Go away."

"But don't you think the C.I.A. should recruit guys and ladies here?" he asked me, taking off his Ray Bans to give me a glimpse of his big green eyes. Kinda cute, in a smart-assed way, but I'm married, I told myself with a cautionary tone. "No I don't," I answered, but he continued to pursue his line of reasoning.

Shaking his black-and-grey curly hair, he added, quite reasonably, "Where should they go to recruit, prisons?" Looking me full in the eye, he presented his theories on C.I.A., government policy, and covert activities for the next hour, until I had to go back to my office to get ready for class. I cast my eyes down to his bulging cucumber, that trouser trout he kept barely hidden inside his tight, faded Levi's and invited him to walk with me to my office, so I could show off my book collection. As we entered the room, he sat himself down at my desk like he owned the place. "What a cocky bastard he is!" I thought. He thumbed through my books by Noam Chomsky and looked at my posters of South Africa while I worked on a couple of freshman papers I was trying to grade fairly.

"I would invite you out to dinner," he said, eying my wedding band meaningfully, "but I can see someone's already taken care of that."

"You're right," I told him, thinking he was just like every other man I knew, out to get what he could from women.

"You're allowed to have coffee now and then?" he asked.

"Oh, I have total and complete freedom," I said, furiously trying to finish grading the endless mound of research papers I kept assigning to my students, my fans.

"One of those relationships, huh?" Dave asked with a nasty gleam in his eye.

"No, and I'm really busy so you have to leave now," I said, flustered at his presence which was making me feel strange and uncomfortable. Dave gave me a funny look and said, "Don't get nervous Gabrielle. I'm just joking with you." He still made me nervous. Perhaps it was his long, lean, well-muscled body and piercing aqua eyes that turned green when he was happy and blue when he was mad, maybe it was the way he looked at me appraisingly, and seemed to see my deepest soul. He's a jerk, I told myself after promising to meet him the following Tuesday for cappuccino at the boho coffee shop. He only wants one thing and that is your little tush.

I couldn't have been more wrong. Turned out his full name was David Mark Hanlon, he was twenty-nine years old, a published novelist, a screenplay writer, an Airborne Ranger Green Beret, and a hell of a nice guy. He soon took me under his intellectual wing, and gave me someone to talk to over coffee. His aqua eyes remained green in my presence, and I sensed a caring soul underneath his macho right wing political propaganda. He just needed to read what the other side had to say about things, and I was just the person to persuade him to do so. Naturally, it took me a while to figure out his real motives, which were innocent since I was indeed a married lady, but we began to meet for cappuccino at the local establishment because I really was lonely for male companionship, where we argued our different theories twice a week. I began to look forward to these meetings and he became a good friend. He was one of the most attractive, intelligent men I had ever met in my life, yet I denied any attraction to him on my part, simply because I was monogamously married to someone named Prentiss who didn't love me at all.

On weekends, when I would go home, Prentiss always seemed busy and preoccupied. He wouldn't have anything to do with me in bed, so I was slightly frustrated in that respect, but more than that, I was losing all semblance of self esteem because of my relationship with him. He would often disappear for days at a time, taking his clothes with him. I always assumed it was because of something I did, since he constantly told me how unsuited we were for each other, and how he wanted me to move out so we could be friends. I didn't want him to leave, and had already considered dropping out of school because it made him uncomfortable to have an overly educated wife. It wasn't obvious to me how brainwashed I had become. "But why did you want to marry me?" I asked him one morning as he was packing to go stay with 'friends.'

He stuffed the last shoe into his suitcase and snarled, "You wanted to marry ME!" I guess he forgot he had originally come to my house asking for my attention, but since I fell for it, it was probably my fault after all.

"But Prent, can't we try to salvage this marriage?" I begged, trying to get him to remember his once powerful love for me. Once phony is a better word for it. Maybe he married me because he needed a cover for his covert activities, which I finally suspected after several months of marriage on the rocks.

"Why don't you move out?" he yelled. "It's my house, you know."

265

"But I want to live with you," I pleaded. "I know, let's get some marriage counseling, okay?"

"No!" he screamed as he picked up his suitcase and slammed out the front door.

Speaking of rocks, I believe I mentioned earlier that Prentiss claimed to be a rock climber. Chouinard hexes, Wild-Country friends and other lead-climbing paraphernalia hung all over his bedroom wall, but as far as actually climbing anything, Prentiss couldn't even climb stairs. He liked to talk good equipment, and pretended to know all about lead-climbing. It used to attract me, but as I stood looking at the equipment and the house still vibrated with his angry exit, I realized it was all a facade designed to impress his friends. Come to think of it, Prentiss looked pretty pitiful compared to Dave Hanlon, I told myself later that night as I sat in the living room watching tv with my puppy dogs, who were thrilled and surprised to be in the house for a change. They were used to sleeping next to my bed at the old house, and confused when I moved to Prentiss' house where they couldn't anymore.

No, I decided, Prentiss was gangly, knobby, and funky. Not to mention anti-sexual. He just wasn't hunky at all or in any way shape or form, yet I would never ask him to divorce me, because for some weird reason, I was obsessed with this teenage image I had of him. "He sure is intelligent," I told myself, as he had told me so many times before. "He flunked out of college because he wasn't interested."

Prentiss was my husband, and represented security, and that's what I had been lacking for the past thirteen years, since my parents broke up and left me unsettled. I wasn't about to divorce the only man I had ever really loved, I'd kill myself first, I'd drop out of school, I'd do anything to keep Prentiss. The past life I had with him, to me, was my last ditch effort for a sense of safety. I had tried California, I had tried school, I had tried Berlin, I had tried drugs and alcohol, but nothing could save me from the fear I had developed over the years. Nothing, not even Prentiss Tribbly. I began to harbor suicidal thoughts on my way to and from Normal after he came home three days later in a hateful mood and wouldn't talk to me any more at all. I would dream about running my truck off the road at ninety-five plus miles per hour, thoughts I had never before entertained. I would drink beer after beer, scotch after scotch, always seeking to obliterate any feelings in my heart, any thoughts in my head. I began to have blackouts. Then, I dreamt of my white poney.

It is night time in the city, what city I cannot tell. My white poney and I are wandering the streets, and I leave him for a moment to go visit a friend. I enter the door of an old apartment house, and climb upstairs on rickety stairwells in a dank, smelly hall. My friend isn't home, so I hurry back downstairs, endlessly long stairwells, with a frightening sense of impending doom. I finally emerge into the dark, foggy night, but my poney has disappeared. I call him, searching everywhere, crying out his name, but he is gone. As I wander the streets alone, lurking shadows frighten me, but I am more afraid of losing my friend, my white poney who loved me so.

I meet with some old friends of mine from Lawless High School, who tell me they have seen my white poney, and offer to lead me to him. I feel afraid of something, but I hurry to find my friendly horse, wanting to stroke his forehead and kiss his neck once again. They lead me to a courtyard, then laughing, they dance away. I find him lying on his side in a pool of blood. He has a knife stuck in his throat. He is dying, his crimson blood streaming warmly down my arms as I hold his head, crooning softly that I love him. His brown eyes begin to flicker and fade as he lies dying on the cold, hard ground. I sob, wanting his life to last forever, wanting his friendship to never end.

My friends laugh, dancing back into the courtyard. They ask me if I'd like them to take my poney to the vet, but it is they who have stabbed him, and left him lifeless in my arms. They laugh and laugh, as my poney breathes his last breath into my face, the last horsey snort I will ever share with my white poney, my white friend, my white love.

And Snoflake dies.

Chapter 17

The Group Heals

To say that I had reached a low point in my life at this time would be an understatement. I was one unhappy cookie, and things were about to speed up and get worse. I didn't worry about my karma too much, since I stayed nice to other people, and tried to help as many friends out as possible. Lying, stealing, murdering and adultery were not my style, nor was the fine art of backstabbing (although I did tend to gossip too much). Yet I had a sick ache in the pit of my stomach that had never been there before. I had a very bad feeling about all this.

Moseying along the highway to Normal one bright day in October, right when the leaves had begun their auburn changes, I listened to my favorite group, Shadowfax, as they played the Shadow Dance and Brown Rice. All was seemingly okay on the surface in my New Age revery, but lurking just below boho land was a hazy, grey underground—and like a cold, black, scaly snake, the subconscious desire to off myself slithered there.

Swigging from a bottle of Jack at nine o'clock in the morning was one way to achieve that particular goal, albeit subconsciously, and as I swayed to and fro in my bucket seat, my pick-up swayed to and fro on the highway. I swayed a little too much to the fro, and found myself looking out at the world from the vantage point of my sunroof, smashed into the trunk of an elm tree that stood in a field of marigolds and alfalfa. A big old milk cow said, "Mooo....," and went back to chewing her cud, thoughtfully it seemed.

Oh, to be a cow and not in this mess. I didn't want to be reincarnated as a cow, which was against what little religion I had left, just to become a cow for the moment would be sufficient for me. At least I wasn't too beat up. I wore a seat belt at all times due to my fear of smashing face first through a windshield and surviving as the masked woman. My old Datsun had had it though. Old Faithful was wrapped around a tree, leaning crazily on its crushed right fender. A huge, black, nasty, Oklahoma vulture like the kind that always followed us climbers around in the Wichitas swooped close to the truck, hoping for a bite to eat, I presumed. They'd eat anything, as long as it was dead.

I wasn't dead yet, but all that time I wasted wondering how fast I could swig down Jack had temporarily distracted me from the task at hand, which was driving my truck to school and my job at Big University. How would I explain to my boss that I survived a wreck but couldn't see straight enough to call in sick? What's more, how would I explain my terribly alcoholic breath to the two Smoky Bears who had just pulled up to investigate my little wreck? Big and Burly squeezed out of his patrol car, and sauntered up to where I was sitting on the ground, viewing my poor pick-up. He cleared his throat, took out his pad, and began assessing my situation. They cleared their throats, reached for their guns, and mowed me down like a field of grass. I must have been hallucinating that bright sunny October morning, because I could have sworn the two Smokies were about to shoot me. Had shot me. How many of them were there?

"You all right, ma'am?" he asked. Then, sniffing the air around me, and surely noticing my blurry vision (I thought I saw two patrol cars), he blinked and said, "May I see your license, please?" Oh shit. I tried to stand up, but fell over on the grass. I don't think he assumed I was injured—I think he correctly ascertained I was drunk. The bottle of Jack in my cab confirmed his suspicions, and he pulled it out as I fumbled for my license. Where was it, anyway?

"Officer, I canth explain everything," I mumbled, stumbling around the misshapen carcass of what was once my freedom on the road.

He began to look pissed, and in a matter of fact voice, pronounced, "Drinking and driving is illegal." He pulled out his handcuffs, and added "So why don't we just skip the walk and breathalyzer, and take a little ride down to the station, hmmm?" Clasping my hands in front of me, I obediently followed his orders, and stiffly walked with great difficulty the thirty paces to his car.

"What about my truck?" I asked him, trembling in terror and what was soon to be D.T.s. My poor old funky Datsun looked just terrible wrapped around that tree over there, and the cow still stood there in the flowers and alfalfa chewing her cud. Even the

269

bobwhites still called 'bob-white, bob-white,' and I heard the hoot of an mouser owl nearby. Yes, everything and everybody was just super-normal except for me, and that was about the way things would stay, too.

"Don't worry," the two officers said in unison, after reading Miranda to me. "You are allowed one phone call." They sure did look alike, but with my bad vision, you never could be certain. My poor little pick-em-up stood crazily against that elm tree, undrivable, unusable, and soon to be for sale, for I was on my way to jail, and someone had to raise the bail money. Good-bye mythology, hello reality. I became the proud recipient of a free stay in jail, and a suspended license for 'Driving under the influence of alcohol.'

Prentiss, sweetmeat that he was, managed to sell my mangled truck for parts and scrap metal in a week, and got me out of jail. "Why the rush," I asked him, "you could have just left me in for six months and kept the truck."

Prent, who had surely enjoyed his week without me, said, "I would have, but I got a good deal on the truck." He looked at me appraisingly. "Hope you don't mind, but I spent the cash on some things I needed around the house." I was too tired and too weak to care. But something had been worrying me while I shivered and shaked my way through seven days of delirious tremens.

"Did you call Big for me, Prent?" I asked him. He smiled in his characteristic manner, that sort of lopsided 'I know something you don't know' smirk.

"Yeah. You're not fired," he said a little too cheerfully. Hmmm. Why the smirk then?

"Boy," I sighed, "that's a big relief." He was quick to point out that that wasn't necessarily the case, because he never had been one to support my literary endeavors in the past, and he certainly didn't plan to start now just because of a little quirk in my routine.

"Don't expect me to drive you to work," my husband said, "because that's your problem, and I'm going to the field for three weeks, anyway." Sauntering over to his Volkswagon, he unlocked my door. How chivalrous of him, and how unusual. I had the sneaking suspicion he was just showing off his license to drive. Forget him! I would drive anyway. I had to get to work, didn't I?

I cleaned out my meager savings account, the one Prent didn't know about, and bought a used Chevy Love with almost 100,000 miles on the odometer. With no insurance and a suspended license, I set out for Big University exactly eight days after my wreck, and reached my destination with no ill effects to speak of. Even though I stayed sober for the drive, I was craving a drink so badly that I bought a six-pack of warm Fosters at the liquor store on my way to campus. After downing a couple in the parking lot, I felt a bit better. That was before I found out about my grades in Error Analysis, a graduate class in rhetoric taught by one of the stuffy professors who scorned me.

Sliding into my seat a mere five minutes after class had began, I couldn't understand the hateful glare I got from old Doctor Roth and his graduate student admirers. Surely they had been late once or twice in their academic careers. Dr. Roth extolled us on the virtues of philosophical analysis in his anal retentive manner, little tufts of greasy grey hair shimmering inside his floppy ears as he spoke. "Even as we speak, research in error analysis continues," he murmured, as forty pairs of young puppy dog ears strained to hear his every monosyllable, and forty pens wrote furiously, copying every single utterance in its entirety.

One bright young pup piped up with a comment. "It is such a great project that pioneers have begun inroads in such various fields of literary analysis as deconstruction, right Dr. Roth?" The favored student wearing Phi Kappa Phi stood up, preening as Dr. Roth patted him on the head.

"That is correct, Sean," the hairy professor replied, "I can tell you have been paying attention in class." Consulting his pile of crumpled notes on the podium, Dr. Roth asked the class, "Does anyone remember the date of my lecture on last decade deconstruction and its effects on modern day literary theory?" At least thirty grubby little hands leapt up, and sounds of 'Oh, me please,' and 'No, me, Dr. Roth,' filled the dusty sunlit air. Typical English class, typical professorial bullshit. I never listened, never took notes, maybe once in a great while read the text, and finally got what I deserved for my efforts.

At the end of class, after all the studenten had dragged out their JanSport backpacks, bought at the local 'Big Sport' bookstore, Dr.

Roth deigned to pass out our exams. Mine arrived with a scowl, and I got up to leave the classroom before looking at it. Surely, I nonchalantly told myself, I've got a 'B' at least, that test was a piece of cake. Maybe I even got an 'A.' I carelessly hiked two buildings over to my English Comp class, where I reigned superior as New Age English teacher. My students loved me, but my professors did not. "Hey Tom," I yelled to one of my long-haired freshman, sticking my paper in my backpack, "ya better haul ass to class, Dude."

"I'll be there, Gabrielle," he called back to me, finishing up a conversation with several of his hippy buddies in the courtyard. I loved my students, and they loved me. I decided to wait until after class to look at that paper, somehow intuiting its grade and not wanting to get depressed right just yet.

"Hello, people," I said as I took the podium and faced my forty semi-attentive students, a motley crew of hippy kids, skinheads, straight Greek geeks, and one black man from Ethiopia. "I have in my pocket a possible failing grade, and I really need some cheering up."

Sounds of "No sweat, Gabby," "That's rad, man," "It'll turn out all right," and "Don't let it get ya down," filled the classroom as they perked up and sat at attention. I then made my next announcement.

"We're gonna have a little testie-poo today, a pop quiz." The shit hit the fan and chaos reigned as my heretofore friendly students became a pack of wild dogs, and I feared for my life. "Zip lips, people," I said. "You're giving me a real pain in the head." They continued to grumble and mumble and slunk way down low in their seats, glaring at me with pure seething hatred. I had frequently assigned light reading, perhaps a short story or a few choice words on pronoun usage, and my students rarely had time for such trivia, since they always had other more important matters to attend to. The pop quiz was my method of choice which I employed in order to wake up my sleeping beauties and make them come alive, telling them that they were becoming more motivated by taking my tests. I always gave them a quiz over relatively obscure exercises, which they flunked, of course, then I allowed them to retake the exam one week later, by which time they diligently devoured whatever they had considered trivial drivel the week before. I always gave them the best grade out of two, but they got the message anyway, and actually studied once in a while, which was more than most freshman English teachers could ever hope for.

One of the other things we did was have debates. Today, after everyone flunked the pop quiz, they got out their notebooks and research to debate the topics, "Do black people talk that way because they are ignorant?" which was a highly inflammatory topic, to say the least, and it provided me with no small amount of mirth as I sat in the back of the room to observe Student Court. Each student had a textbook-anthology that I had prepared for the class that was chock full of research. It was up to the student to decide what to use. For example, in the class debate today, students had material from slave journals, linguistic texts, anthropological studies, sociological studies, racial violence, apartheid articles from several publications, and last but not least, Ku Klux Klan treatises. I did the research for them, to encourage them to think.

"I think black people talk funny coz they ignorant," said one white boy from Alabama. "It sez here in this book that the Grand Dragon himself knows blacks have smaller brains than whites." The young man from Ethiopia smirked, silently enjoying the debate. A hippy-chick who worked at the boho coffee shop and sold dope on the side to put herself through college took issue with the Alabama boy.

"Did you not bother to read the treatise entitled 'Linguistic Development from Africa to America'?" she asked, getting slightly red in the face from the effort of confronting ignorance.

"No, I don't need to read none of that stuff," he answered. "The teacher sez we only have to read what we want to debate." I had to interject.

"Billy-Bob?"

"Yas ma'am, Mizz Gabby?"

"I said it would be wisest to read everything in the packet."

"But you said we didn't get no grade for this debate, Mizz Gabby," he whined.

"I said you did get a grade for the persuasive paper after the debate."

I spoke sternly, hoping he wouldn't start bawling like he did when he got too excited. "Oh," he mumbled, "I misunderstood the instructions." I sat back down and shut up for the remainder of the debate, preferring to let the students handle everything.

"Well, Billy-Bob, it doesn't help your argument to ignore the fact that blacks in the eighteenth century wrote books and sold them, now does it?" my hippy child student Beverly said. She was a sharp one, even if her daddy was in jail for dealing tons of grass in the seventies.

Billy-Bob from Alabama looked uncomfortable and scratched his crotch. "Well, they probably didn't really write them," he mumbled.

"What?" said Beverly, "speak up, will ya?"

"I said they got some white folks to write for them," he yelled, losing his temper and the debate.

"But can you document that comment with research?" Beverly shot back at her opponent. Billy-Bob scratched his crotch again, and seemed deep thought for a moment.

"Can you repeat the question?" he asked.

The audience groaned, and the student judge said, "Next panel, please."

"You lose, sucker," said Beverly with a triumphant smirk. Student Court was definitely in session, and things got hot for the next forty-five minutes. My pop quizzes were only five minutes long, because I didn't like to waste valuable class time on little exams. I finally wrapped things up as the bell rang, and reminded my students to study hard next week for their next Pop Quiz, and they were still arguing about black linguistic development as they filed out into the hallway. Even Billy-Bob was talking to Niki from Ethiopia, asking him if his tribe swung through trees and ate insects. Bright bunch of kids, I thought to myself as I swung through the giant glass doors that led to Gittinger Hall's courtyard, pulling out my treatise on Error Analysis. I glanced at my paper. A flat, solid 'F' stood out in bold red ink. I screamed "Oh crap!" at the passersby, but no one even noticed.

Students flunked out of Big all the time, it was no big deal. What could I do? What could I say? Where could I go from here?

"You all right, Mizz Gabby?" asked Billy-Bob, who had heard my scream and came running.

I shook my head, handing him the paper to see for himself. I was always honest with my students about my failures, figuring it would make things easier for them when they had to face their own. Billy-Bob let out a long, low whistle, and said, "You in a heap of trouble, huh Mizz Gabby?" I looked at him with tears in my eyes, knowing that I was indeed.

"It's time for a little liquid persuasion," I told Billy-Bob

"I'm with you," he said, so we trudged to the nearest bar and he bought me a couple of double scotches and I listened to his stories of what Mama had done to him back behind the pig barn when he lived on a farm just outside of Mobile. Terrible story. Three hours later found me wandering all over Normal alone and on foot, my other classes and responsibilities forgotten in favor of Fosters, scotch, and vodka martinis. Somewhere or other I had gotten myself totally blitzed (was it Lennie's Bar and Grill, or was it Butterfly Gardens?). All I could remember was stumbling off campus into the nearest drinking establishment at two-thirty in the afternoon with some young pup who told me a sad tale about incest. I had awful breath and no money left. I had lost my wallet, torn my Indian blouse, lost my keys, and skipped all of the other three Composition classes I was expected to teach that Tuesday. Oh shit. How did I get in this mess? I wondered. It was getting dark, and I couldn't remember where I parked my truck. Something was nagging at the back of my mind, something about a meeting I should have attended for the English Department. Wait a minute, there seemed to be a problem with one of my professors, let me think—I remembered then what the stew was about, and why I went on such a rampage of a drunk in Normal that day. My grades. I was flunking out of graduate school, and was certain to lose my assistantship.

Suddenly hit with the most crashing sense of doom and total depression I had ever experienced, I began to heave big, heavy sobs, catching my breath in gasps, nearly doubled over with the pain of my changed existence. I walked into the Expresso Shop and bummed a quarter off one of the students who was studying there, and called Sally Alice. She wasn't home. I then attempted to

275

contact Dave Hanlon, but when his answering machine came on, I remembered he had a writing lecture to give in Arkansas that week, and wouldn't return until Friday evening. Shit. Where is that pickup parked, anyway? Pulling one last warm Fosters out of my backpack, I slurped it down in an astonishing gulp, and looked around me with wet, blurry eyes. Big University in Normal, Oklahoma, the land where those who are reared in Lawless go to succeed in life after the Bachelors degree. I was soon to be on my way out, hell, I was on my way out, and graduate school was to be no more for this girl. Might as well drive the ninety miles back to Lawless and Prentiss Tribbly, my dear, uninterested husband of six months.

Where did I park that truck? I couldn't escape the fact that alcohol had not improved my already strange personality, but I craved release from the pressures of my life as always, and stroked the bottle to find my way home to a numb reality. Might as well finish this beer, I decided, but it was already empty. After walking around campus for two hours, according to my watch, I spotted the old, worn, rusted out Chevy, and hopped into it to cruise home. It was getting late, and a long drive lay ahead of me, so I stopped at the liquor store for a litre of Scotch with a hotter than hot check. I was thirsty, I reasoned, and a couple of nips along the way might make me feel better about breaking the news to Prent about quitting school at Big. He was my only hope for empathy, and I knew I could count on him if I was really depressed and needed a friend. Surely he would come through with loving arms, accept me as I was, and give me some sound advice for the future.

With these promising thoughts in mind, I set out for Lawless, a litre in my lap, no license in my wallet, my brains cells bursting with a 1.5 alcohol content. I don't remember anything about the trip. All I can recall is what happened when I arrived at home in Lawless that Tuesday night in October. Dimming my lights so as not to wake Prent, I rolled silently into the driveway and lumbered out of my pick-up, the bottle in my fist. After taking one last swig to make me more alert and able to communicate my sad feelings to Prent, I unlocked the front door, intending to slide into bed and awaken him with a soft, loving kiss.

I heard slapping noises in the bedroom. Sasha and Shiloh began scratching on the back door to be let in, but I knew Prent wouldn't like it if I let them in the house with his two cats there, so I ignored the scratching. Slap! What was that weird noise? I saw candle light flickering, and figured Prent might be awake and slapping himself? No, however strange he was, he didn't self-flagellate as far as I could tell, even though his frequent bouts of temper suggested otherwise. What could that be? I wondered, should I call out and let him know I was home, because he didn't expect me until Thursday evening, and it was only Tuesday. The cats purred, and I smelled fried food in the kitchen. He must have made something fattening for dinner, since I wasn't home to see it, I thought.

Slap! Tired of skulking around the house, walking on eggshells like I didn't actually live there or have a right to come home unexpectedly, I strolled into the bedroom to see what was going on. Not one to be suspicious, since I was usually so drunk I couldn't tell much about anything anyway, I was shocked at the display in the bedroom, in my bedroom, on top of Prent's and my wedding present from his parents, the waterbed.

Lying spread-eagled, Prent was face down with his naked butt still red from his lover's latest slap. Bernie, the mysterious voice who often answered the phone when I called from Normal, asked Prent if he would like another one before they went any further. Neither noticed my presence, as I was quiet as a cat. "Well, pussy, you want it some more, or shall I drill you now?" crooned Bernie, his fingers sliding in and out of Prent's slimy butt. Gross!

Prent, obviously in pain, cried out, "You're hurting me," and then whined "why don't you like me?" As Bernie's delicate little wrist pulled and tightened the twine he held at the small of Prent's back even more, causing Prent's hands to turn crimson and purple from no circulation, he slapped Prent again, only this time with a leather belt. Prent seemed to love it, and let out a loud moan (I think he spurted). Now, I don't have anything against S & M sex, even between consenting males, but I didn't think I should have to watch my husband get violently, digitally, butt-you-know-whated by his buddy.

"Ahem," I cleared my throat to announce my presence and allow the boys to regain their composure. "Would you two care to tell me how long this has been going on?" I asked, watching their surprised faces as Bernie quickly dropped his belt, and Prent squirmed, tied with his hands behind his back, face forward on the pillow. I was certain the mattress would be a mess, and I didn't plan to sleep on it after this little episode. The smell of feces and petroleum jelly assaulted my nostrils. I was actually too drunk to feel sick.

Avoiding my eyes, Bernie hurried into his jeans, and faded into the living room. I heard the front door slam, and Sasha let out a loud, rumbling growl. Shiloh began her howl, while Bernie slipped into the night from which he came. "You have no right to show up here in the middle of the night," Prent complained, still tied up and stark naked on the waterbed. I enjoyed his discomfort, even though my heart was completely broken.

So stupid, I was so stupid up until now, I told myself as I eyed the belt which Bernie had dropped on our bedroom floor. Scrawny little homewrecker, I thought, remembering Bernie's voice on the phone. How come I never guessed anything was wrong with our marriage? I guess I had wanted to badly to I believe in Prent that I looked the other way and denied his weird behavior. Smelled like a toilet in that room. "Untie me!" Prent commanded, "this damn twine is too tight!" Squirming some more, he turned around and lay upon his backside, that thin, shriveled cucumber having spent its load with another man. Yech.

"Ha!" I laughed ghoulishly, "just let me get my camera out and take a little pickie-poo!" My personality disorder notwithstanding, I was in danger of becoming lunatic, and Prent was in even greater danger of becoming my victim.

"No!" he squealed, trying to get up. He fell back onto the bed because one of his feet was tied to the corner post. I hadn't noticed that, but decided that this was the time to enjoy what was left of our relationship.

"So," I said in a more pleasant tone, "you like to be spanked?" I looked him over, noting his fat belly roll, which looked out of place on his otherwise skinny frame, and wondered what his commanding officer on Fort Kill would have to say about his

278

behavior. Too bad I'm not a gay-basher, I thought to myself, but maybe a little spankie-poo would do him good, maybe even give him another hard-on. Tears of anger began to drip out of Prent's beady brown eyes as I gathered the belt into a coil around my wrist.

"Leave me alone, you bitch!" he screamed as I swatted him a good one right on his spindly thigh, and watched his earthworm creep up into an asparagus stalk.

"How sweet," I said to my victim, "you've got a hard-on."

Obviously, Prent and I didn't last long after that particular night. I wound up finishing my litre of cheap Scotch, then hustled over to Renee's house (lucky for me she was back in town from Germany), and left Prent tied up on his bed. "If you hurt my dogs, I'll kill you, you son-of-a-bitch!" I threatened him before leaving, as he lay all trussed up in twine. "Touch them, poison them, hurt them in any way, and you die, you bastard." He lay speechless after his beating, and probably would have asked for more if I had been Bernie, but I had other things to do with my life besides spank my gay husband.

"What will you do?" he whined, cajoling and wheedling in fear of reprisals from me, I'm sure. The Army didn't like gay boys, and he didn't know for sure if I would turn him in to his commanding officer. I would never do that, because I believed in everyone's inalienable right to sexual privacy, but I let him stew, anyway.

"I'll divorce you," I answered, flinging some clothes inside my Chouinard pack for a long stay at Renee's house. "So bug off!" Depressed, suicidal and upset about my future, I depended on Renee as my last hope, my last grasp at life before I killed myself. I got on the phone to call her, but naturally, she didn't answer. What did I expect? It was one of those nights, hell, it was one of those months! So, off I went into the Lawless night, stars glittering overhead.

Hmmm, I thought, what kind of life will I have with no job, no marriage, and no hope for graduate work at Big? Might as well off myself, and get it over with. Can't face people anymore. Am a failure. Got to do something to forget everything, got to get drunk.

Eight days later I woke up in a parking lot in Amarillo, Texas, wondering what in the world had happened to me. I was filthy, my clothes were covered with unknown crap and funk, my hair was unmentionable, my mascara was running, my truck was out of gas, and I was out of hot checks. I got really scared and went to a pay phone that cold, foggy morning, still groggy from my alcoholic stupor, and scared to death of what crimes of passion I might have committed. Did I return and shoot Prent with the .357 Magnum he kept in his bedroom closet, wrapped in an old, oiled piece of leather chamois? Did I sleep with strange men? Had I acquired a disease? Finally, I got through to Renee with a collect call. Her response was not unusual.

"Gabby, where are you?" she yelled into the phone, burning my ear in accusation (or so I interpreted). "We've been worried sick about you!"

"Yeah, that's nice Renee," I answered bitchily. "I need some help." Too much booze caused my words to slur hideously, my brain cells tired out from too much partying.

"What's the deal, Gabby?" Her voice softened. She was a shrink by this time, and I could hear the therapist taking over, taking control of my life. I needed it desperately.

"I can't remember where I am, or how I got here!" I sobbed.

"Ask someone," Renee said quite reasonably, "then come back to the phone, okay?" Mellow voice. "I'll wait right here." I trembled and shook, and looked at the phone book.

"It's Amarillo, Texas," I told her, "can you believe it? Renee acted cool, as was her style since acquiring the Masters in clinical psychology.

"Find out what your address is, then wait right there," she soothed, "and I'll come get you, okay? As I sobbed into the phone, Renee kept silent. "Okay?" she prodded. "I need to call your mother and let her know you're all right."

"I'll stay here," I said, "Renee, just please help me!" After checking street signs and giving her a general address, I went back to my pick-up and fell asleep for the rest of the day. Nightfall came and went, I slept some more. By morning, she pulled up in her Nissan 300 ZX, and gassed up my truck, after which we drove back to Lawless, and I was sober for the first time in months. It was strange pulling into Lawless behind Renee's car, but she let me stay at her house, and I called my Mom to tell her I was okay.

"Gabby," Renee said to me over a hot, steaming cup of coffee. "You've got to get a grip on yourself." I sat there morosely involved in my self-pity trip, and she tried to reason with me about my substance abuse. I wouldn't listen.

"I don't drink that much," I said defensively, "I can quit anytime I want to." Scared shitless, I couldn't accept the fact that I had lost eight days of my life. Renee wasn't convinced, but tried another tack.

"Look at this book." She opened a psych textbook from Big to page 114. "It says right here that you have a borderline personality disorder, like I do." I didn't want to look, but I glanced at the list proffered anyway, my curiosity killing me. Hmmm. I'd never seen a book describe me so well before. Unstable relationships, substance abuse, binge eating, yes, that sounded like me. What was this? Severe mood swings? Frequent and inappropriate displays of anger? Suicidal behavior? That was me all right. Lack of clear sense of identity, hey, who wrote this book, anyway? Chronic feelings of emptiness, frantic attempts to avoid real or imagined abandonment... and it said you only had to have five of these characteristics to be diagnosed with borderline personality disorder, and I had all of them? Oh, shit!

I didn't think it would ever be possible to change my life and straighten up, especially since I was actually a diagnosable deviant. Fuck it, I decided, I'll just kill myself somehow. Maybe the razor blade thing would work. I went into Renee's bathroom, excusing myself momentarily from our conversation, and reached into the medicine cabinet for a Daisy razor blade. Slice, slice, ouch! I winced as a trickle of blood smeared into my shirt sleeve. This hurts! How many people don't commit suicide, I wondered, because it hurts? Renee didn't suspect me, so I managed to escape undetected into my suicide fantasies, but actually doing the job required more than a quick side trip to the bathroom. No, I pondered the situation long and hard before I came upon my next possible weapon against myself. A bottle of bleach. I took it out of the pantry closet, opened the white plastic bottle and sniffed. Didn't seem to stink that bad, a little acidic, maybe, but I took a slight taste to find out. Yeaachhh!

I rushed to the sink, swooshing water around in my burning mouth, trying frantically to cool my burnt tongue, almost screaming in agony at the taste, the smell, the feeling of bleach sliding down my poor, unsuspecting throat. Renee kept reading in the dining room as I frantically washed my mouth out. This is not going to be easy, I decided, I've got to come up with something a bit more clever. Pills? What kind? Drowning? Nahh. Jumping off a tall building? What if I didn't die? Nahh. I sat in the kitchen, my rear end firmly planted on the cold, linoleum floor of my best friend's house and planned my suicide.

It's got to be successful, I figured, because if it's not I'll never forgive myself.

Chapter 18

All unhappy families resemble one another; every unhappy family is unhappy in its own fashion.

Leo Tolstoi

So mote it be, blessed be

I stewed around Renee's apartment for a few more weeks, then summoned up the courage to find a lawyer and file for divorce, since I hadn't heard a peep out of Prent since that fateful night. Come to find out, a lawyer wasn't all I needed. He had already filed, on the basis of abandonment and mental cruelty. Fine. I had sneaked over to Prent's house to get my things while he was at work, and to check on my dogs who seemed none the worse for my absence. Apparently, Prent had taken my threat to kill him if he touched them seriously, and hadn't fed them any poison, or anything as toxic as the chemicals I had been considering for my impending suicide. Tuinal? Seconal? Zanax? What could I ingest to off myself that would be painless, easy, mindless, and one last happy trip before I went to the big sky? I didn't stop to wonder who would take care of my puppy-dogs.

Renee, sensing my ideas and suicidal motives, called Sara in Tipton, unbeknownst to me. I was living day to day, week by week, and scrambling for employment. I finally landed a job at Lawless' only all-black dance club, the Local Scene, and began my career (I told myself it would be short lived) as a cocktail waitress. "Doin' the butt, yeaw! Sexy, sexy, all night long!" Since I only saw things in black and white, a typical borderline personality disorder syndrome, my world was split into villains and heroes. Sara and Renee were my protectors, while Prent and the professors at Big were out to get me. I had hoped to find solace in love, music, drugs, alcohol, school, athletic competition, food, but whatever I attempted in life somehow didn't work out in the long run. It never occurred to me that perhaps I was the problem, perhaps only I could make my life work. Instead, I ran after fantasies, and finally found no fantasies to believe in anymore. Unable to escape the real world, I retreated further back into my shell, my microcosmic existence, than ever before. Black men at the club tipped me graciously and treated me very well, for it is so often than those who have been oppressed by society are still able to reach out and help another human being. In my case, it was obvious that I was one confused woman, unhappy in love, and relentless in my desire to self-destruct.

"Oooh, my mama," the lonely black soldiers would crow as I waltzed into the club each night at ten o'clock sharp. "You wanna be my honey bun?"

"Sure honey, "I always answered, "just let me take a load off first."

"Baby, I want to make it wid you," another man would say.

"I gotta get to those guys first," I bantered back, teasing and never touching, but then, they didn't expect me to. I would smile a sunny smile, and get great tips from these men, who were far away from home, and treated me with much more respect at the club than white guys in Lawless treated cocktail waitresses in other clubs. The black crowd in Lawless cherished their club, and they dressed up to enjoy the evening when they went there.

I was the evening to some.

I drank more than I sold, but no one told and everyone liked my service. Black ladies tipped me big, even though I recognized some of them as employees of Hoggies, Furltons, McBurgers, and Burger Prince, and knew they couldn't really afford one night a week at the local scene, where Margie G. reigned supreme, and everyone acted polite. In fact, if not for the gentle bar patrons and my kindly boss Margie G., I would have faded out sooner than I did. But, the day arrived when my blackouts were running together into one big blank, and Renee finally relinquished her psychological hold on me. That day was November 7, 1988. We were having dinner.

"Gabby," she told me, her fork pronging slices of stir-fried eggplant dipped in wheat germ and oat bran. "You've got to go into therapy and detox." Unconcerned, I downed a quick shot of Jack and ignored my plate of steaming veggies. Usually my favorite meal, tonight's entree of spinach noodles wrapped around asparagus and cheddar cheese along with crusty-fried eggplant just didn't appeal. I blinked at her double image, feeling threatened and put upon.

"If you want me to leave, just say so," I snarled nastily. "I know you look down on me and don't want me around, Renee." Shoving my plate away, I jerked out of my chair and stumbled to the kitchen cabinet for that other litre of whiskey. "Where are you, Jack?" I drunkenly wondered, wandering amongst the kitchen things, looking for my old buddy, Jack the Ripper, to rip my liver out of my body and my soul out of my heart. It had to stop.

"No, Gabby, it's not that at all," Renee said, dropping her fork onto her plate. "I care about you and want you to get well." Suddenly, her face fell, and a look of total defeat crossed Renee's green eyes. I could feel the sadness rolling off her in waves, but no, I couldn't let myself fall into her trap. I didn't want to feel anything anymore, especially pity from my so called friends. Shit, what friends?

"Bullshit!" I screamed, jumping off the cabinet counter. "You hate me and you know it!" Stomping out of the house, I got into my Chevy to cruise the bars in Lawless. "Just another starry night," I reasoned, "and I've only got myself to worry about." They just want to control my life and make me into someone else. No way I was playing that game. No possibility. Sure, she was a shrink, but what shrink can watch her best friend fall apart and do nothing about it? I began to feel worried that Renee or Mama might have me committed, but after that night, she quit telling me to change, quit bugging me about a few little drinks here and there, and generally left me alone to simmer in my alcoholic stupor. Poor Mama just waited in her house, her arthritis killing her, and hoped I'd come around once in a while to visit.

As far as Mama was concerned, I tried to be polite and reasonable, saying things like, "You worry too much," while she silently stirred me some vegetable stew on the stove. "I'm not too hungry, Ma," I'd say, then slink out into the night for another round at the bars, never stopping to feed my stomach or my soul, just getting gassed every evening to forget all about life and friends and family. As far as Renee was concerned, politeness was out of the question, because I was sick of her meddling in my affairs, and told her so. One participant was plenty at my pity party as far as I

285

was concerned, and she could just butt the fuck out! Of course, I reasoned, I welcomed the opportunity to live rent-free anyway, since she owed me a place because of our friendship.

Finally, I found the perfect answer to my suicidal question...I would do the carbon monoxide thing. My poor Chevy Love leaked so much exhaust anyway that a little extra from a vacuum cleaner hose attached to the rear exhaust pipe just might do the trick. And, I wouldn't feel any pain, because I intended to take a few Seconals (stolen from Renee's medicine cabinet) to relax me. Now all I had to do was decide when and where, write a literary and moving suicide note so my epitaph would be guaranteed eloquent, and go to sleep. All those who had oppressed me in my life would cry and mourn after my death. I would bequeath my poetry to Mom, who would cherish it (I did regret leaving Mom, but I had to do it), leave my puppy dogs to Renee, leave my bicycles to Gerrie, and leave my truck to Dad (just to remind him of how much he mistreated me and how much I loved him nonetheless). Yes, it would be a grand suicide, and everyone in Lawless would come to my funeral.

I began to envision myself floating in the sky above, watching all the black-clad mourners weeping and gnashing their teeth over the injustice of my death. Prent would confess that he was unfaithful to me with Bernie and get kicked out of the Army for it, the professors at Big would leave my poetry tacked to bulletin boards to remind students of a once great author who died at her highest point of literary achievement, a mass would be held in my honor at the Episcopal church in Lawless...wait a minute, what about my relationship with the Heavenly Father? Did I think He had forgotten me? No, I reasoned, He had simply allowed His vigilance in my life to lapse, taking care of more important duties than the upkeep of Cat Stevens' almost former wife. He would forgive me for my suicide, wouldn't He?

Where would be the best place to pull my plug, I wondered, or was there such a place (I was tempted to procrastinate further) in Lawless? Maybe I'd call in sick at work tonight...maybe I'd write my suicide note later on, like tomorrow. Maybe I'd do the dirty deed now, and get it over with.

Finally, the decision was made for me. My truck had just enough gas to last for about two hours, and the transmission was going out. It was either now, or never, at least where the Chevy was concerned. I spotted the Great Prairie Coliseum on Shardon Road, and noticed the marquis advertising an Arabian horse show that coming evening, Saturday night. What better place to commit my final act, the supreme act of self-mutilation than at a horse show? I loved horses with a passion, especially white ponies. There were sure to be a few in the Arabian herd that was on display that night, so at least I would die among friends.

Scribbling a long, drawn out last will and testament at Renee's house, I left it on her dresser drawer where she would be sure to find it upon returning from work at the Torpid Clinic. I grabbed the hose off her old, beat up vacuum cleaner. It had a couple of holes which I had periodically 'fixed' with tape and pieces of inner tube, so I didn't feel too bad about taking it. Renee would be glad to see it go, and probably go buy a new one right away. I stole some tape from the garage and some twine for my makeshift funnel for carbon monoxide poisoning. Piling all this into my little Love truck, I added a bottle of Jack I had been sipping on and "borrowed" a few Seconals from Renee's stash in her bathroom. Time to do the deed, time to run away again, only this time, I wasn't coming back.

Parking in the east end of Prairie Coliseum, I noted the increasing amount of traffic for the horse show. Too bad I couldn't take just a little peek, but the entry was ten bucks, and I had spent it on Jack, as usual. As I taped the hose to my exhaust pipe, as I settled in for the long haul, as I inhaled deeply of the toxic fumes, toxic alcohol, and toxic downers, I felt a gentle tug in my solar plexus, where the scar I carried since infancy lay hidden beneath my shirt. "It hurts," I hazily thought as I inhaled some gas fumes. "It hurts."

It's getting colder and colder, I can't breathe too well, my lungs are burning...it stinks in here, I'll bet my hair really smells like a garage. I can't see anymore, what's that at my door? Why doesn't anyone love me? My stomach hurts. Why did my parents have to give me up? Why couldn't they keep me instead of putting me in that orphanage in Germany and leaving me there to fend for myself...a just born baby girl with a hideous scar, left to fend for herself in a dirty, destitute and poor orphanage...where is that German bio mother, why did she let him burn me with that cigarette on my stomach, and hurt me so? I want to find her and kill her! I want to kill all of them for leaving me so alone, so abandoned...my stomach hurts. I'm sleepy now, it's time to go to bed, Gabby, you need your rest, you're just a little girl right now, but you're going to grow up to be big and strong, and do something with your life someday...oh Mother, Mother, you aren't German, you are American. You're my real Mother, you always have been, but where are you now? Why can't I let you help me? Who was that German woman? Mother, are you out there? Do you hear me calling you? I love you, Mother. My stomach hurts, Mommy, can you stop him from burning me, please, oh Mommy, please make him stop...don't leave me here, Mommy, please don't go, I don't care if he burns me, I want to stay with you, please don't go, oh Mommy, I think I'm dying....

Something is at the door. Who is it? Leave me alone, I'm dying! Who is it? I can't see you, I can't hear you, who are you, what do you want? Something yanked me by the arm and pulled me out of my truck. I lay in a stupor on the cold pavement, and felt sick to my stomach. Coughing, coughing, coughing up blood, I rolled over on my back, and vomited up Jack. I felt a gentle stroking on my head and a soothing female voice gently called my name. "Gabrielle, it's all right baby, I'm taking you home now." I couldn't see yet, and I vomited up more blood and Jack, but somehow the starry night began to revive me and the voice became more familiar. She wiped my mouth with a piece of cloth, and helped me to sit up. "Have a sip of water, baby, you're going to be all right," the voice said. I began to realize where I was, and how I came to be there.

"Why?" I mumbled, "why did they have to burn me?" I was incoherent to anyone but Sara, who knew about my scar, and saved me from myself. Her gray eyes shone with unusual light, as her short grey-brown hair shook with the Lawless breeze. Sara, all five feet four inches of her, had pulled me manually out of the car, and out of Death's clutches. "Don't worry," she soothed, "we're going home now, Gabrielle." And, after a while on the parking lot, I was able to stumble to her rusty old van, and move some paintings over so I could fit into the front seat.

"How did you find me?" I asked my older friend. She started up the van, then turned to look at me, a very few fine freckles punctuating her face from too much sunshine. Sara ahem'd a bit, then answered me.

"Renee called and told me about your problems."

"Strange that you're here," I slurred, slumped over with stomach cramps from the gas and the booze, worn out with the suicidal effort. Sara rolled the van out of the parking lot, and we headed somewhere south, probably Texas, I thought at the time.

"I was in town to photograph Arabian horses, anyway," she added. So, it was a twist of luck, once again, in my favor. Maybe there was a reason for me to live after all. I began to realize God might have plans for my life that I couldn't immediately see. But I felt like the sickest dog who ever lived, and turned to throw up out the window. Yuck.

"Shit makes me sick," I said as I retched again. "Where you headed?" She wasn't going anywhere in Lawless, that was for sure.

"How about we go to the farm in Tipton, and plant some trees, Gabrielle?" She knew another reason I would want to go there besides the trees.

"Will the poneys be there too?" I asked. Sobbing and wiping my nose with the by now soiled cloth, I wept unashamedly. "Can I please see the poneys?" Sara turned onto the highway headed south toward Texas. Did I discern a slight sniffle? Clearing her throat, with a voice gone slightly hoarse, she said,

"Of course. That's why we are going there." After handing me an apple to eat (I hadn't eaten all day, too busy drinking), she added, "Maybe we should talk about some of your problems, too." I didn't understand what she meant, was she another shrink out to commit me?

"What problems?" I blurted angrily.

"You know. Those painful memories you have about things," she answered gently. Very vague, but I was beginning to get her drift, because Sara was the only person who I had confided in about my scar. Only she and Mama knew the truth, although I was certain Dad had an idea about my stomach problems.

289

"Oh, you mean that," I said, not really wanting to discuss anything right that minute, so soon after an almost suicide which was infinitely more horrible than I'd ever imagined. It felt truly awful to be so near death, and I didn't enjoy it one bit. I didn't even want to kill myself anymore, because death was so gone, so out there, so not here where the life dwelt on Earth. "Forget suicide," I decided. "There's got to be a better way." Sara kind of looked at me funny, like she could read my mind, and she probably could, too.

"Have you ever heard of healing of memories?" she asked me. "It's the latest thing, and I've been traveling round, helping people deal with their past." She gave me a friendly look, and I felt encompassed by her intense energy, the same energy that propelled her to paint horses, the same energy that saved her from emotional destruction after being sexually abused herself as a child.

"Okay," I answered, "maybe you are right after all." Someone had to have the answer, and I was just too tired to deal with it anymore.

"Every injury and every hurt has a healing," Sara said wisely. "Jesus healed everyone who came to Him." I did agree that that was true, and the New Testament was a book I used to be well-acquainted with. Terry and I used to pray for people, I thought to myself. What happened to that special me who could reach beyond my own problems and pray for those sicker and sadder than I could ever be?

"What's my problem, anyway?" I asked Sara. Could she answer this one? Sara gave me a sharp look, because she remembered when I was strong, but she felt like I'd be strong again. So does Mama," I mused inwardly, so does that old lady who would give you the bread out of her mouth if she was starving.

"It's on the way out," she answered. "You have to believe God is true, and He will heal you." I did believe once, for other people, so why couldn't I believe for me?

"I'm supposed to be a Christian," I complained, admitting I wasn't very together. "All day long I self-destruct. It makes me sick." She said nothing, and with that in mind, we rambled on into the night, the stars twinkling overhead. I just wanted to go to sleep.

Next morning, after a long and sleepless night spent tossing and turning, I hiked out to one of the pastures before the dawn's first rays of sunlight cast their orange-pink glow onto the horizon. I was off to see the poneys, my lovely poneys. There they were, tossing their dappled grey and palomino manes, throwing their heads against the wind, galloping with each other into the day's first light. I whistled my old whistle, the one I once called Snoflake with, the one I used on my old pet poney back when I was a child. They saw me, and trotted up to the fence. Breathing their horsey breath fully, I felt some peace in my soul. Lovely poneys, I missed you this last year, I should have come sooner to see you. It was a warm morning, with thunderheads dancing above in blue-green bruises. Perhaps a storm would wash away my tears. The wildflowers bloomed all throughout Sara's three-hundred acre farm, while in cultivated fields, wheat and barley tossed their tasseled heads. A thunderboomer shook the earth while lightning flashed in frightening white fire. The rain misted at first, then fell lightly to the earth.

Warm drizzle quickly filled my hair, and I held my tongue out to taste fresh rain water. Hail began to pound the pastures, little round white marbles bouncing off the ground. I thought I could stay in this lovely storm forever, but just as the sun began to struggle out of the clouds, just as a faint purple, red and orange rainbow could be discerned in the distance, more rain fell. Sara crunched some gravel as she walked toward me, and stood petting the poneys while I lay my head against Clove's neck, smelling the rich, salty, pure horse scent, warm and full of life in my nostrils. The horses and I stood sopping wet in a rain storm, not minding it one bit. Sara stood silently for a moment, patting her favorite mare, Cinnamon, on the nose.

"C'mon, Gabby," she enjoined, "I've got some great coffee beans ground, and a huge pot of coffee to make for us." Her gray eyes danced with light and gazed deeply into mine. Glancing up at the sky just in time to see faint rays of sunshine through two ominous black clouds, I obediently relinquished my hold on the poney's neck, and followed Sara back to her Victorian farmhouse, where cats purred on the windowsills, and pink and yellow wildflowers bloomed in the front meadow.

291

We sat at the kitchen table, drinking strong black coffee with frothy, steamed whole milk and sharing small talk. What rich aroma her coffee beans created, what a nice morning to enjoy together. But when will I be able to be happy? I wondered. "So what did you do about that horse show in Lawless?" I asked. Sara might have missed a big commission because of me. She looked at me calmly over her coffee mug.

"I took some photos," she answered, "And made a few connections, then headed out to the parking lot." I studied Sara's slight figure, clad in black drawstring geisha pants and an oil-streaked cambric blouse. Tracing the lines of a horse's prancing body with her fingertips on the table top, Sara was ever the artist, even in the morning. "Then I saw your Chevy," she added, not without an ominous tone to her voice.

"But when did Renee call you?" I asked, confused as usual.

"A week ago," said Sara, crunching her toast with relish and gusto. "Why?"

"Oh," I said, "It just seems strange that you found me, that's all." I dipped my spoon into the honeypot, then drizzled it over my stone-ground wheat toast. Mmmmm. Sweet taste of honey.

"Yeah, well, life is strange," said Sara. "Could be you just can't escape life on this funky planet without thoroughly experiencing it, Gabrielle." We laughed about our unusual planet, our optimal paths, and our strange coincidences.

"So," I began, haltingly, "what can we do to get me normal?"

"You?" giggled Sara. "Normal? Isn't that a town in Oklahoma?" A languid morning passed in Sara's kitchen, while pink and yellow flowers accompanied our table. The flowers outside her French doors swayed in the thunderstorm, their fragrant heads dipping and thrusting in time to our conversation, it seemed. The early morning flower scent, commingled with the thunderstorm's wet intensity gave me deja-vu, and reminded me of some lost primeval garden where we must have once roamed in a far away time. I felt like I was in Northern California again, by the Pacific Blue watching whales spurt in the ocean's distance, and seeing seaweed wave directly underneath my feet. I relaxed in Sara's presence, her horses, plants, and herb garden, wishing I were out here all the time, feeling at home and one with the environment. An abundance of dancing negative ions pervaded my senses, assaulting my mind and body with an unearthly energy. I began to daydream as sunlight streamed into the kitchen's crimson and green stained glass window, the octagonal shape filtering colors in and out, in and out. Sara broke my revery gently that morning.

"Are you ready to begin?" she murmured.

"Begin what?" I asked drowsily, unsure of what she had in mind, but trusting her to somehow help me. I swayed uncertainly between fear of my past, and terror of what the future might bring.

"To invoke your past and begin again," she answered. Seated across from each other in old, carved oak chairs, and antique oak table between us, Sara and I held hands and said a simple prayer. That was easy enough. I began to truly experience peaceful feelings in my otherwise chaotic soul. After silently meditating for a few minutes, I felt ready to begin my ordeal which Sara had warned me would not be an easy one. Feeling that I was finally ready, she gave me some mental suggestions. "Remember what it was like to be a young child in Germany?" Sara softly asked. "How did it feel to be left all alone?"

"On the playground?" I asked.

"Earlier," she said softly. "Think back to an earlier time." Really, I only half-paid attention to her whispers, when suddenly, without warning, I was catapulted into my childhood, then infancy. I began to sob uncontrollably, lost in another world, a world of pain with no understanding. White, everything was white, there was no color, no shape, no picture on the screen where once I saw Sara's kitchen. I smelled nothing, tasted nothing, felt nothing but raw emotion.

I was lost.

Labyrinths of sorrow enveloped me, I felt so helpless and alone, I couldn't see anything but clouds, fog, and tendrils, threads that hung from above and below me, linking me to what? A voice said, "You must ask Jesus Christ to sever the bonds that you have with your biological mother." No! I wanted to cry out, but my voice was gone, and words wouldn't form on my lips. My heart cried out, No! But the voice urged me on, and then I saw a vague, shimmering figure, someone who loved me more than I could understand. Somehow, I knew this to be God, and I began to feel more powerful, more capable of movement. The voice said, "You were lost, and now you are found, Gabrielle." I touched the many tendrils that hung on me, locked as I was into that place where time and space didn't exist, the tendrils were all over me, linking me to what? The figure moved closer, and closer, then finally, I realized that this must happen before I could let go of my pain.

The voice said, "Relinquish your spirit to Jesus Christ. He is your mother and your father now, He is your savior and your life." I didn't want to say no anymore, and began to unhook the many tendrils and vines that hung on me, connecting me to events and people in my life. I handed them over to the figure in white, who stood by me now, closer than ever before. I unhooked the last tendril, the hardest to release, the one that connected me with my biological mother who I never knew, who allowed me to be hurt, then abandoned me in an orphanage. I let her go, and took the hand of Jesus, allowing Him to be my Savior.

The voice said, "You must ask for forgiveness from God, for hating your mother and the one who burned you on the stomach." It became easier and easier to do as the voice asked, for every time I let another painful memory go, my tendrils loosened up, and before long, I was standing alone, with nothing hanging over or under me at all. I felt immense peace, and a feeling of wholeness enveloped my spirit. All shadow spirits were gone. The voice said, "Gabrielle, you are like the Edelweiss that grows on a mountainside in Germany." And then I woke up.

"Feel better?" The voice asked, with a gleam in her eye. Brilliant light shone into the kitchen, the dawn arisen, the storm passed away. I was blinded by the light, but awake in a new world, a world in which I would have to take hold of my life, and live again. Sara handed me a piece of homemade bread with wild plum jelly. I slathered creamy butter all over a second slice of crusty white bread.

"I don't even crave a drink at the moment," I said, and we both grinned. Sara finished her third cup, stood up to straighten her jeans and put on her gardening gloves. I heard Cinnamon and Clove whiney to each other in the distance.

She looked at me expectantly and said, "Glad you feel better. Now how about helping me plant a few trees?" The poneys whinneyed to each other again in the green pasture, their voices sailing soft and pure upon the newly soaked air, and I wondered if they were whinneying at us too.

"Can I just for a second pet Cinnamon again?" I asked.

Chapter 19

Hope is not an option.

Mark D. Harrell

Closing the circle

To say things changed after that would be an understatement. Let's fast forward now to true romance. I am writing a letter to my man who is in Panama writing special ops instructions for the military. It went something like this:

Greetings Wild Man.

How's Panama these days? Enough about you, let's talk about me. I'm having a rocky life here in Lawless as usual, what with the mosquitoes, ticks and my friends. Finally killed all the ticks in the backyard, just in time too, because they had a plan, drawn up by their Master Tick, to storm the house in three days, but I neatly foiled their attempt with a hundred pounds of powdered sulphur in a barrier around the house. Bloodsucking little beasts.

I miss your face. I've been doing a bit of rock climbing lately, and I just returned from a monstrously hot day in the humid, tick and GI infested jungle, ravenous for cold water and a baked potato with salad at Old Plantation, and tumescent with the victory celebration of Renee's first, very assisted climb (or shall we say 'crawl'?) up Tiny Bubbles. And not a minute too soon, cos it was freaking hot out there and we were almost out of water. Especially bad was the fact that we started late and I took Renee on a wild goose chase over Canyon One and Canyon Two to Canyon Three and the path to real enlightenment, the path to Tiny Bubbles, only a few short minutes from the parking lot, but if you go my way, it's a few short hours.

Sound familiar? We barely stumbled out of the jungle at 2:30 and 95 degrees if you are not on the rocks. Renee mentioned that we should have brought breakfast and just fried up our eggs in leftover human sweat, and thrown in some wild onions and garlic for measure. She's totally disgusting in her eating habits, if you ask me.

This weird buffalo kind of groan-yelled at me just as we were making our escape in the RX-7, out of the underbrush and into the light. Ranger Ken says it's rutting season for the buffalo, and I believe it. This bull stuck out his tongue, took up the whole road and started pawing the ground, heading straight towards me! He was making these really strange noises, groaning and snuffling, and kicking up quite a fuss in the dusty prairie afternoon.

Renee thought the sounds I was hearing were from the radio, but I knew it was the Buffalo Bull from Hell out to gore himself an RX-7, so I made a quick detour to Prairie Dog Town, thinking we'd be safer there while the snorting, pawing bull snorted more snot and swaggered up to this unsuspecting van which had tourists sticking their heads out the windows.

We narrowly escaped heinous insurance rates. Your car was saved by me at the risk of my life. I thought about interposing my body between the car and that crazed animal, but such sacrifice proved unnecessary, as the lady in the van had it covered. I would have done it for the car. But, danger notwithstanding, the wild buffalo calls will lure me into the woods. With the blink of and eye and the flicker of the fullest moon, I'll be gone again, searching for the source of that ethereal stink, he of the Buffalo Groan-Yell.

Yes, it's true, I finally found myself a man, and we lived, laughed, biked and climbed together. But first I had a few things to sort out, namely my dance with alcohol. I finally realized what had caused me to fly like a comet out of Lawless into the dream of Cat Stevens. I was a borderline personality, just like millions of other American women with nothing better to do than get depressed and go crazy. It was easier for me to admit that I had a wild wire loose in my brain than to admit that I was an alcoholic, but AA set me straight in a New York minute once they got me in the door.

"You've got to try them Gabrielle," Renee told me one morning soon after I came home to Mama's house from Sara's farm in Tipton. "Going to an AA meeting might be the trigger to set you straight." Renee was once again fixing one of my favorite vegetarian meals, black bean and rice burritos with salsa and Swiss cheese, and I was once again sitting at her dining room table. Mama sat there with us drinking coffee and shooting the breeze, and I was jonsin' something fierce just waiting to get my hands on some Jack, but the doctor had told Mama that my liver couldn't last much longer, so she was watching my every move with a vengeance.

"I don't wanna go," I whined like a little baby. "Why can't you guys just give it up already, huh?"

Mama got really righteously pissed, slammed her old arthritic fist down on the table, saying, "I put up with your drugs, I put up with your wanderin', I didn't say nothin' when you married that gook Prentiss Tribbly although I coulda told you he wasn't normal," she paused for air. "But I'll be goll-danged if you think I'll let you drink yourself to death!" she yelled, bursting into great big wracking sobs that shook me up so much I began to sob too, losing my appetite entirely.

My heart couldn't take it. That just about put the lid on my bottle of Jack, I'll tell you. Old Mama was getting up in years and she was the only one who had remained ever faithful to me my whole life, telling me I'd make it through Cotton's meat grinder, helping me over my California hot tub ear problems, sitting up with me nights when I cried about Dad. I couldn't let her down after all she'd done for me, I just couldn't. I might be able to let myself plunge into this black hole, I thought, but I can't take Mama anywhere near it. "Okay," I mumbled, "I guess I'll go." Renee came over and hugged me tight, and Mama came over and hugged the both of us. I thought they were going to squeeze me right to death that Monday afternoon in August, right around 1989. I even got hungry again, and forgot about my trembles and shakes for a few minutes.

Soon after that, I called up the AA lady in Lawless and she invited me over to her house to visit and quell the feelings of impending doom I was harboring at the time. Her name was Zero and she had all kinds of drunks scattered around her ramshackle Victorian home right in the heartless heart of Oldtown. Stepping gingerly over a ratty looking guy sprawled out on the living room floor, who was stinking up the whole house since he couldn't have bathed in at least a week by the looks of him, I went into the kitchen to drink the AA staple, black coffee. "Hope you don't mind the mess," said Zero, handing me a cracked cup of very black coffee. "Some of these folks just don't have anywhere else to go while they are detoxing, you know?"

"I sure do," I told her, shakin' quite a bit these days myself from stayin off the juice for a whole week, which was truly a test of my love for Mama. But, I was determined not to break her old heart which had slaved in the school kitchens for all those hard years just so I'd have a decent life.

"I gotta tell you up front," Zero said, "I'm an addict, an ex-prostitute, and an alcoholic," which I could believe judging by the tracks on her arms and her prematurely wrinkled face. I tried not to be uncool, because the stink was getting to me from all the passed out dudes in the living room, and my stomach was gettin queasy from the black coffee, but I had to say something to her sparkling bright blue eyes.

"I'm, uh," I faltered, almost saying it, almost getting it out into the open for the first time but not quite.

"C'mon, you can say it," she prodded, and the biker-bitch me met the ex-whore Zero right then and there and we connected enough in friendship and mutual understanding that before you could say "Lawless is okay," I was standing up before a whole bunch of bedraggled people and saying,

"Hello. My name is Gabrielle and I am an alcoholic."

Oh and there's more of course.

I got clean and stayed clean, eventually traveled back to Northern California to spend four years working with abused street kids. Life went on, I finally had enough of the Left Coast and moved to the East Coast for a change of pace, got my M.S. degree and settled down to a very full life of country living and service to others. Along the way, people kept telling me, "Oh you look Czech," "Oh you look Romany Gypsy," "Oh you look Cherokee, Italian, Lebanese, Spanish...." I still didn't have a flying clue what in the heck I was and it became time to deal with the German thing. Oh boy, the German thing was back with a vengeance.

By then fully internet savvy, I posted online at a message board for adopted people looking for bio relatives, pretty much forgot about it and just kind of went on with my life. About a year later, a beautiful soul living in Germany finally contacted me one day. She is my dear Searchangel. Through her, I found out my fairly sordid

German/Czech bio history, and another door swung wide open. It's not pretty, but my life is definitely a page turner. Here are excerpts from our letters. [Note: These letters are the real thing, unedited, exactly as written. They are straight from the heart and I am thrilled to know my Searchangel and Angelika]

Hi Jules,

I was digging very hard—Metal Detector—and have great news for you....Just now I talked to your aunt Anna on the phone!!!! Yesterday I was thinking so much, how I can get more information. Again I searched on the website of [German City] to find somebody I can contact. Again I wrote to the Lutherian Church of Buerstadt and asked for help. This morning the Minister of this church sent me an email and wrote that your birthfather died in 2002 and that there is a woman in [German City] with name Anna Lukmann nee Groepl (born 1940, has 7 children by her own, one died), who is the sister of your birthfather. I searched the white pages for her phone number and called her. She was on the phone and I told her the reason why I am calling.

She told me, that your birthparents were divorced a long time ago but your birthmother remarried (last name unknown to her, but it was a man from [German City] again). Your birthfather never told much about all this and your siblings.... you read it right.... siblings!!!! Until the death of your birthfather she had sometimes contact to Angelika. She told me, Angelika never married but had a son and gave him away, too. She and your birthmother are living in [German City] at the time of his death. But you had some more siblings: Angelika was the first child, then second Siegfried (but died very young at around the age of 20 perhaps of cancer). There have been also sister Petra and sister Cornelia, which were given away (adopted or not, she didn't know). As far as she knew, only Angelika and her mother have contact together.

I then searched the white pages for Angelika in [German City], but there is no entry (if you don't want it, you are not registered there - like me, too). Which means, I have to write to the Registry Office of [German City] and ask for her recent address.

Hi Jules, are you back again?

Jules, I only want to tell you, don't expect to much from your new found family. Sometimes you will not get what you want, and I guess, this will be your family or a part of it (maybe I am wrong, then "sorry"). Anyhow, please take care of your emotional feelings. I am sorry that my English is not good enough to explain this in the right way, because words in another language can have another meaning.

Yesterday evening I got a call from a woman who told me this:

This woman got my message from the man in this house and sent a SMS to Angelika. Then Angelika was begging her to call me and to hear what is going on. Angelika is living with her or in her apartment since 26 years. She is a handicapped woman (I don't know what is her disease). Angelika was visiting friends and will be back tomorrow evening. At the moment Angelika is without a job and searching for a new one. She normally works in homes for old people (I don't know the name in English). The woman told me, that as far as she knows the father of Angelika was an alcoholic. The other 2 sisters grew up in children homes and or foster care. Siegfried died of cancer of the bones...and your birthmother never visited him when he was ill to death in hospital. Also—I don't know how long—your birthmother don't want any contact to Angelika.

This woman said, Angelika always searched for a family or sister, but also the sisters doesn't want contact or made a break. This woman spoke in a really very warm way about Angelika, so maybe Angelika is a nice person. The woman said, Angelika will be very happy about finding you (or you her... smile). As fast as I understood, also your birthmother has no contact to the other children. And sorry, Angelika cannot speak or write English, but the woman said, for this problem they will find a solution. My feeling was, that this woman take care of your sister very much.

I asked this woman if Angelika has black hair, but she said, all the children have blond hair. So I guess, you may have another father and that's why you were given up for adoption? I can call Angelika tomorrow evening, but I am not sure I will be at home because an uncle of mine from Australia will come to Hamburg tomorrow and wants to see me. If this will be the case, I will call her after tomorrow. Maybe then I will have more information for you... if, I will write it immediately to you.

Your Searchangel

Jules,

Yes, you wrote about this burning mark (but I just forgot it). Maybe I will ask Angelika about it (if she can remember). Yesterday I just thought it would be interesting to know what is written in your adoption records. Before I found Angelika I just wrote an email to the City Youth Office of Kreis Bergstrasse in [German City], because I got a call from Mrs. Heil that they have no records. And when I read the paperwork you sent to me, I found this about Kreis Bergstrasse. When I found Angelika I again wrote them, that the search is over and that their help is not anymore necessary. But by German law you have the right to see your adoption records or (as far as I know) to get copies of it. Maybe also in these records the name of your birthfather will be written down. What do you think about it?

Your Searchangel

Jules, I will contact the City Youth Welfare Office of Kreis Bergstrasse again to see if I can get the information. Your birthfather could be an American Army Buddy because in this area have been a lot of Army Bases until know. My stepdaughter was married to an American Army Buddy, too (now divorced). Once I lived for about 6 month in Mannheim, then near Heidelberg for about 8 years and also my son is born there, which is not far away from Buerstadt, Bensheim, Dossenheim. But if your birthmother was in the business of restaurants, it could be also any other foreigner.

In the years of helping adoptees I have heard many stories. Sometimes the birthmothers denied to have any contact. But mostly the reason was because their whole live they kept it as a secret and became afraid that when this secret will not be anymore a secret, it will disturb their new built family. But also sometimes after a while some of these birthmothers changed their mind and told it to the family. But I have never heard from a woman, who gave all her children to others and doesn't want any contact to

302

them. This is unbelievable to me. This woman also told me, that your birthmother with her husband now live in a financial secure (or very good) situation, whatever this means.

I will do my very best to get all the information you want and can get. Here in Hamburg I know a woman who is working for the City Youth Office of [German City], and she helped me in several searches. I only don't know she is in holidays just now or not. But I can call her and ask her about the law getting information of your adoption files.

I only hope you had warm hearted adoptive parents.

Your Searchangel

Jules, I just came home and must eat something now. After this I have to write a long email to you. But one thing I can tell you in advance:

Thank God every day that you were adopted!!!!!!!

Your Searchangel

Jules,

Yes, it's going to be such a bad story I have never heard before by my own (only in the news or in tv). But I should write from the beginning.

Yesterday I came home at about 9.45 pm because I met my ex-uncle Australia the whole day from (it's an uncle of my ex-husband, whom I found 4 1/2 ago after 48 years of separation in Australia, but he and my ex-mother in law had trouble one year later and have no contact anymore, too). Only to me he still is in contact by email or letters. There was a call on my answer machine from Mrs. Wagner (the woman Angelika live with) that Angelika will be at home at 9 pm and is very excited to hear from me/you.

Then I called Angelika. She has a very soft and warm language and my imagine is, she is a very much hurt person, but still after all what happened very warm hearted, very very kind and friendly.... and very very happy about your search for her. We talked together for about more than 1 1/2 hours!!!!!! And if I didn't make a break because I was so much tired, we would have talked some hours more. I like her!!!! I hope I can write everything in a chronological order as she told me so much, I tried to write down something when we talked, but it was to much. Angelika didn't know that you exist until 1984 when she found the family book by accident. This kind of book you get on your wedding with the marriage license inside from the registry office. After birth of a child every child birth certification will be included in this book. There she read your name. Then she started asking around in the family about all these years because she knew less about the past and her siblings.

Angelika told me this:

Your mother was very beautiful when she was a young woman. Her husband originally originates from Tchechien. He was a strong alcoholic, very aggressive and very violent. He has beaten his whole family including the children as much as he could. Angelika until today has physically and psychologically problems from his beating. Angelika said, her brother was mentally handicapped from the beating of his father (she said: my father has stupidly struck him). Angelika cannot say even which year her sisters Petra and Cornelia (called "Conny") were born, but she said, Conny is the youngest. Conny was born at home not in a hospital.

When Conny was some weeks old, her father throw her against the wall several times. Everybody was crying very loud, so a female neighbor couldn't bear it anymore and called the police. The police and the ambulance came, Conny was brought to hospital and the City Youth Welfare Office was involved then and took all the children away from their parents. It was written about it in the newspaper there. Angelika was 7 years old at that time, and all her siblings came in different children homes. Angelika remained in children homes up to reach the majority. After this it was not allowed for the parents to visit the children for a long time.

As far as I remember the parents lived separated since that time, but had the divorce years later. The new husband of your mother originates from Tchechien, too, and was a friend of her first husband. The rumor say, that this man is your birthfather. Her first husband knew that you are not his child and said, I will never have this child in my home or I will kill it (or all of you or kill mother and child, I cannot remember). So you have never been in their home. From hospital directly you came into the orphanage in Worms for some month until your adoptive parents took you out.

So I cannot tell you where did you get this burning mark on your stomach. Angelika told me, your mother never hit any of her children.

Jules, this I will send to you as a first part, otherwise your have to wait to long. But I will write the next part just after it.

Your Searchangel

Jules,

Your mother visited the children sometimes in the children homes. Petra came out and as far as I understood lived for a while with your mother. There were people who wanted to have Petra for a while, but your mother said to them, only for a weekend sometimes. After such a weekend they didn't bring Petra back to her and this case came to the court. The judge said, this kidnapping is not right, but it will be the best for Petra to live with there people. So Petra lived with them. Petra doesn't want any contact to Angelika.

Conny lived in children homes/orphanages and with different foster parents, was beaten there terrible, too. Conny had 3 children by her own (one died during pregnancy). Conny has a guardianship. Angelika said, something is wrong with her but couldn't explain ist exactly. So I think from this throwing against the wall and all other things happened in her live, maybe she has mental and psychological problems. Conny sometimes wants contact to Angelika, then she doesn't want. But Angelika hasn't seen her since she was a baby.

Siegfried had brain-harm from the beating of his father. When the children were small he wanted to kill all of them. The father was very ill, too with heart asthma. When he had to go some steps his face became blue, and this was the reason of his death, too. Angelika, too, has asthma.

In all these years Angelika tried to contact the parents from time to time in get in contact again. 4 1/2 years ago she visited her grandmother (the mother of her father). Her father came around and they had some trouble and he tried to beat her again. He said to Angelika, I have forgotten to kill you. During some other meetings before, he said to Angelika "I am so sorry for everything" and he

305

cried. But after the last meeting and these terrible words, Angelika decided never to see him again.

Part 3 will follow (when internet connection will allow it.....)

Your birthmother later married this other man (probably your father). This man also has a dark skin. She decided herself for this man not for the children. So Angelika said, she has thrown away all her children. He hates all her children and don't want to see them. He calls them all "hare" as a kind of showing that they are no persons, only animals. When Siegfried died, he said on the opened coffin: one hare less! Angelika was so much shocked about this, she became psychological problems for a long time.

Your mother and this man had an affair during her marriage. Also in this time another women got a daughter from him called Gabriele!!!!! But he decided to stay with Wilma. These Gabriele is a very intelligent woman who studied law. About 18 years ago she came to her father and wanted answers for all her questions. They had trouble during their discussion and never met again—as far as I understood.

Angelika said, in all these years she always tried to get in contact to her mother who is living very close to her. They took her as a housemaid!!!! for a while and treated her like a child. Angelika is not able to call her mother "mum" or something like that, she said always "Boss" to her mother (which speaks for itself).

Angelika also told me, that the father of Wilma tried to rape her when she was twelve years old, also his brother and her husband later (he always tried to touch her and so on, and she has heard that he sometimes travels to Thailand to have sex with children). When she this happened she had the possibility to reach a pistol. She called somebody and cried for help to take her out there or she would kill herself in between 2 hours. They took her out in this time.

Angelika said, only her longing for a family forced her all the time to try again a contact to her family. Angelika said, only twice in her life she got respect of somebody: from Mrs. Wagner (where she is living for 26 years now) and her female lover (Angelika is a lesbian) for now 3 years. Her female lover is a woman who had her coming out with 50 years, has 4 children from her marriage, to which she gives all her love. This is the first time in the life of Angelika, that she feels there is a loving family and that means everything to her. Her mother and or this man would force her to "throw away these cripple"! Angelika said, how can I do this, this woman every was there for me, took care of me, helped me for so many years, is very much physically handicapped, how can I leave her alone???

I could understand Angelika in many ways, because my father was a violent alcoholic, too (since 30 years now he is a "dry alcoholic"). He has beaten my mother minimum twice a week but never me when he was drunken (I am the only child). I also had a horrible life and can never forget, and I told her about it. She wants to write to me about her life because - I guess - felt my empathy. Angelika has someone who can translate English letters for her. Also she will ask the children of her female lover for an email addi, because they have a computer and perhaps internet excess.

Angelika now really is so much happy about finding you, you cannot believe it. She said, you are a part of herself.

Jules, believe me, after hearing all these horrible stories I couldn't sleep and had to take a sleeping pill. In my head there were cruising around all the things I have heard and how I can translate it to you. I hope you could understand everything—I gave my very best.

Your Searchangel

Dear Jules,

Angelika told me, that he has a sister with name Ella, and that this woman always was very kind to her (as I wrote before). Ella also told her, that Gottfried travels to Thailand (Siam) to have sex with children—and Wilma knows it!!!!

She told me, when her father visited you in hospital after birth he was drunken, and when he was drunken he was incalculable (because I told her that normally in a hospital it is forbitten to smoke), so it could be possible to burn you with a cigarette. Angelika told me, that her father has beaten her with a chain for dogs when she was a child!!!!

In 1984 Angelika visited her father and by the way he showed her this family book. There she read the first time your name and

307

asked him "who is this child". He said, that is not my child, it's the child of Gottfried. Later Angelika asked Ella about it, and Ella told her that you were adopted by Americans and brought to the States.

These are the news I have. I sent nearly all your pics to Michelle and also your "Resume", the rest are to large, and I will send them later. But Angelika will visit her female lover in about one week, so she will not see it before.

I hope, you had a nice weekend with your daughter und friends.

Your Searchangel

Hi Jules,

I just now I talked to Ella Spyris on the phone. She is your aunt because she is the sister of Gottfried [Name withheld] but has no contact to Wilma. She knew everything about you from Angelika. She was very nice and helpful.

She told me that Gabriele is raised up by her mother and stepfather by the name Gabriele [Name withheld] in [German City]. When she was young she was married to a man by the last name Schober but later divorced. She then married a second time and has 2 sons. Her second husband has a company (unknown which kind or name of it). She is born [Date hidden].

I can send a request to the residence registry of [German City] (German City is only a part of larger city like Harlem in NY) but have to pay the fees of about 8 €.

Your Searchangel

Dear Jules,

I will try to translate from Angelika:

Hello Julschen, the whole day I have been out to do something but haven't forgotten you. Have headache because of the weather, am very sensitive. Yesterday and today my mood hasn't been the best. These kind of days are not good for me but there is no sunshine every day. Will go to bed early where I like to watch tv. I like it very much comfortably. Soon I will have enough money for the flight to you next year. I am very exited and happy about it and to see you and your family. I will bring a translator with me, can understand a little bit if you can talk slowly. I also like to watch the body language. Here we talk English, too. I do it often. My little dog can understand English.

Once I had a relationship with a female American but only for sex, could understand nearly everything. She was in a fictitious marriage because she had to do with drugs. Without marriage she had to leave the country. She hasn't had a good language, only bad words. For me it is important to have a good body language and good words are coming out of your mouth. Yes, my new woman is a very dear, we fit each other. She has her apartment, I have mine, so it is wonderful to spend weekends together. Everybody need free space but this will work only if you trust each other. We are in love like big children. We can laugh about everything, if you could see it you would shake your head, or?

Have you ever been so much in love? Then you are feeling butterflies in your stomach, then the airplanes. Yes, that is life, I like to feel merrily. The grey of every day I don't like. Much more I like sun feelings, heart feelings. Julie, you are a real hetro, only one question, do you like to answer me? Do you smoke? I asked once. What are you doing during the day? What time you go to sleep? Are you not in such a good mood at mornings? I can get up mornings and tell you a whole novel so fit am I. So dear Julie, till later.

Heart greetings to you,
Angelika.

Dear Julschen,

It can be that I thought about it that perhaps our contact wouldn't be as before. But I never would like to stay between you and her. But I have no phone number nor email address of her. I really even don't know her last name. And Gabriele never wanted contact when I visited Wilma and Gottfried. I only now her from talking, not personal. But you can call the sister of Gottfried, Ellas phone number...Ellas can talk very well English because her husband is American. To the whole family Doerrich I have no contact. Sometimes I talk to Ella on the phone or meet her when visiting Wilma. Ella is the only one who has been always kind to me, and I like her very much.

I wish you and your family a good time.

Best regards,
your Angelika
From Angelika:
Hallo julchen,du machst sehr,viele sachen,auch mit, deinem Sport. Ich fahre viel Fahrrad. Laufe, viel, bin mit der natur sehr, verbunden. Geht es deiner mama gut? Wünsche mir das,es nächstes jahr geht, das ich zu dir fliegen, kann. Freue mich jetzt schon, darauf. Frau wagner kann nicht mehr, da sie krank ist, was mir sehr, leid,tut, da sie eine liebe ist. Aber julie was soll, man machen, gegen krankheiten, sind wir menschen, machtlos.Wir werden das, schon schaffen. Bei mir sind meine atemwege, nicht so gut, bei dir auch, glaubeich. Körperlich,bin ich total fitt. Bisschen rückenschmerzen, das haben viele menchen. Meiner kleiner dog ist so süss, er wird 12 jahre möchte, nicht daran denken, wenn er nicht mehr ist, Da ich tiere sehr liebe. Meine lieblings blume, ist die rose, vergleiche die rose mit dem leben. Rosen ohne dornen gibt, es nicht. Liebe Julie bin später wieder da.
Herzlich Anngelika, Frau wagner.
Ps deine mama, viele liebe grüsse, an alle in deiner familie.

The End.

Isn't that sweet? I found my half/sister in Germany, and we occasionally talk about our pets mostly via Babelfish email translation. Our families are wishing each other well and everything is all great. Okay, this is not the end, this is the beginning.
Sugary sweet with sugar on top.

Chapter 20

At some point I had to stop and smell
the beautiful, luscious roses.
I didn't realize they were being eaten alive
by revengeful, well-fed,
Starship Trooperish,
plant-killing bugs.

What happens between the worlds changes all the worlds

My editor tells me that what you are about to read is actually another book. Indeed, stories about our outdoor adventures are earmarked to become another book entitled *Living Green Cheap*. I am in the process of compiling a rough draft manuscript and it is next on my list of publications for Owl. For the moment, I will share with you some excerpts so that you can join in on our fun playing outside, working on the farm, and trying to live green cheap.

Life goes on here at our ever growing homestead farm. I hang with my beautiful daughter and her wonderful friends. We have teenage tipi parties that go on for days and days. I teach women about biking and permaculture, take local kids on bike rides, fix everyone's bikes, snowboards, and skateboards. These days the garden is so freaking huge that it scares me to look at it. I've enclosed a few articles to give you a better idea of what it's all about these days. Enjoy.

The Garden's online debut.

Hi Everyone. Welcome to spring at Cherry Plain Sanctuary Farm. Soon, I will be posting new photos of our upgraded farm, including pics of the new beds, expanded strawberry beds, blueberry bushes, and asparagus.

Let's start this season talking about strawberries. I'm a fan of letting them run wild. Isn't that what we all really want to do anyway? Why not plants too? I let them run wild in the summer, our family enjoys luscious strawberries from early, mid and late blooming flowers, then in the winter, the happy plants naturally die off and/or go to sleep. Springtime rolls around, many of them come back to life, the old ones just continue to compost, and I have a whole new crop of strawberries everywhere. That's just the beginning...I take this new crop, one plant at a time, and shovel carefully under it, then transplant each plant to a new home. Right now, we have four happy strawberry beds that also include a few garlics and perennial flowers.

We started with much less last year. I bought a total of maybe 20 plants at the Honest Weight Food Coop. Since then, we have probably 300 plants growing and I have given away probably two hundred plants to friends. How does this magical abundance work? Back to my original plan, you let your strawberries run wild! Then transplant them in the spring. Simple solution to an age old question which is, What do strawberries really want? They want LLAMA POOP! Oh, didn't I tell you? That's our secret...

Torturing bugs is not Buddha-like.

My wonderful friend, Dennis Phayre, former owner of the best vegetarian restaurant in the Capital Region, Shades of Green and fellow vegetarian, recently emailed me in response to my site and said, "So you like torturing hungry little bugs?"

In response to his response, I wanted to share my feelings about garden eating bugs with all of you spiritual seekers out there who believe that bugs should live long fat happy lives. I too am a vegetarian and I too love the Earth and all its wonders. Here's the saga of me and the slugs, which started out oh so Perelandra:

For the record, I don't like torturing them. It grosses me out. I kindly asked them to leave on multiple occasions. Then I picked them off carefully one by one into the hundreds. I have photos of kitty litter boxes full of slugs to prove it. Then finally one day I decided that it would be best for their spiritual evolution for them to fast, so I applied Slugaway, which is completely non toxic to humans and pets. The slugs fasted, they evolved, and they have reincarnated as butterflies, last I heard.

Weeks later.

For those of you who remember my slug issues last season, well, I have good news. The slugs are gone. I quit giving them bowls of beer after a few cases because all they did was get drunk, procreate, drown happy and leave many little slugs to take up their alcoholic pastime. I tried other remedies too. After using white vinegar and water to squirt the little buggers as they ate, rather than picking them up (eugh!), sprinkling diatomaceous earth around the plants on top of the soil as to not disturb the earthworms below, I took stronger action and ordered my first (not last) expensive organic solution.

I applied a healthy application of Escar Go, from Gardens Alive dot com, and finally, after a complete demulching of the whole garden (since it's so wet here we don't really need it), I checked on the lovely gardens today because it's rained for the past 12 hours.

No slugs, not even one.

All I can say is YAHHOOO!

I'm going back out there just to sit and stare in awe at the beauty of no more slugs in my gardens. [of course they came back].

Japanese Beetles Galore.

Those freakin Japanese beetles...for those of you who have asked how I deal with them...I put out traps fairly far from the garden, and I walk around with Dawn dishwashing detergent diluted in a spray bottle, and spray them while they eat. Between the traps and Dawn, I will hopefully salvage 98% of the garden. Also, plant mullein plants near your garden if you don't have them already. The beetles love mullein and it will willingly sacrifice itself to save your corn, tomatoes, etc. While they swarm the mullein, spray them with Dawn.

July 13th RED ALERT!!!

Either Dawn is totally poisonous or I just made the mixture too strong, because it totally hurt my plants. Yikes! Don't use Dawn. It's BAD for Plants. Sorry plants!

So, onto better things. Yech. Those bugs are annoying. Anyway, it's time I shared a few pics of our Farm this year. These pics are from June, I'm about to go shoot some more for July. At the moment, the tomato plants are about five feet tall, squash leaves are two feet across, we are picking zukes, peas, greens of course and literally gallons of strawberries from a small patch. I guess mixing three different types of strawberries together, adding perennial herbs and garlic, then lots of llama poop did the trick.

313

Let's hear it for mountain people east.

I'm waxing philosophical. It's easy to be green if you love the outdoors. Besides belonging to three food coops, harvesting our own wood for building and burning, growing most of our food, bartering, freecycling, recycling and buying everything locally, our year-round, outdoor family fun costs next to nothing because we have our own adventure equipment. I do 99% of the animal doctoring, haul all our dirt for the gardens, build the beds and keep our stable of bikes, skis, snowboards all tuned up. For wintertime entertainment round the woodstove, we read books and watch the llamas fight over their food. There are plans to train the llamas for packing, but right now, they are too busy playing outside in the snow to even consider letting me put a pack on their backs. My heartwork is in animal rescue, and all of our pets are "recycled." Let me tell you a little more about Mountain People here in New England, of which I am one.

We live on the MA/VT/NY border, on 18 acres of forest, high up a steep driveway, deeply into the snowbelt. The temperature drops 15-20 degrees when you drive from Albany, NY heading east to the MA border, which is only 23 miles as the crow flies. There's still no cell service here on Misery Mountain, which is in the Taconic Range of the Berkshires, and if you get lost up here on the ridge you could die and stink for quite some time till someone finds you, probably a four wheeler if you are lucky. We have moose, bear, wolves, bobcats, foxes and coyotes who share this space with us. Sometimes they surprise us out on the trail, where we take our llamas for hikes along with the dogs.

You can drink water out of the springs here, directly from this mountain. I have been doing it for almost 14 years. One of many mountain bike rides from my house is up the old trail (older than the telephone) to the top of the ridge, which winds up and down till you get to Massachusetts. Don't wreck, break down or otherwise hurt yourself cos it is still wild up there. Read above.

We trad climb in New Hampshire, where you can get 10 pitches of 5.8 and still get off the mountain in time for a swim in the river, The Gunks, The Dacks and even in Great Barrington, MA, where there's some of the best bouldering to be had this side of the Mississippi and a sick 5.10b called Endeavor to Persevere.

In the winter time we strap on our tele skis and snowboards, then hike up the closest mountain to earn our turns. Last year one of our most epic days was spent on Mt Greylock, small at only a few thousand feet, but the site of a 1930s battle between the Nazis and local ski bums for the Olympic medal. That's right, the Olympics were held on a little mountain in Massachusetts, with a top speed of 4 minutes to ski down that steep slope. The day me and my buds went there we took two hours to get down it, dodging trees and laughing the whole way down. Took a lot of beer to kill that cold pain. (Luckily at the top was a community cabin with a fire burning, so we are able to warm up before freezing on the way down.) A few years back, I won a new $1000 boat from American Whitewater at the local kayak festival on the Deerfield. I paddled my new boat on the West River in Jamaica Vermont. On the way there, I found six free new windows, which I strapped into my truck with the boats and took with me. We have free signs everywhere here in the East, which means you can really score good on garbage day.

The locals here take care of you. My goat recently died and I gave a call to my friendly farmer, who came over with his pickup and took her to his land to bury her since I don't have a tractor yet. I gave his brother in law (the divorced guy) a box of veggies and zucchini bread for their efforts.

Our driveway washed out, and the farmer's brother with the (undisclosed location) gravel pit brought a couple of tractor loads of gravel over and filled in the holes, no charge thank you.

The local bar in our tiny town of 200 (circa 1800s) is owned by a Salvadoran immigrant who caters to the biker crowd. They recently had another free pig roast complete with huge vats of Spanish rice. One big ugly biker guy came up to the Puerto Rican cook and asked if he was the one who made the dinner. When he said yes, the biker guy gave him a bear hug and said, Thank you! I thought he was gonna cry for a moment there. This year I gave him some strawberry plants for his very own garden at the restaurant.

We built 25 raised plus more beds in the past two years because my neighborly farmers give me unlimited free loads of topsoil, even loading it up onto my 210,000 miles on it still runs kinda rusty Toyota T100 pickup. Their grandchildren are eating produce from my gardens. Now we have a new greenhouse built out of cattle panels to continue our food production without giving up snowboarding this winter. My friend who owns a CSA told me we can grow kiwis too, and our little kiwis are quite edible.

I used to be a writer but these Eastern mountains got to me and now all I think about is being outside with the rest of the animals. Here's to a green life in the sweetest of the East.

Building a greenhouse.

To support our newfound fresh homegrown veggie addiction, I built a greenhouse out of... guess what? Cattle panels of course. We first used them to enclose the poopers, then for garden trellises and finally for a shed, but I have all kinds of ideas about correct use of restraints...so now they are a greenhouse.

Back to the cattle panel greenhouse. To avoid confusion, I built it *before* reviewing what everyone else has happening out there in the world of small scale cattle panel enthusiasts.

Here's our item breakdown:
3 cattle panels
2 2X12X10 rough cut planks
2 2X12X8 rough cut planks
6 X 6 foot metal stakes
4 2X4s
20 foam pipe insulators
greenhouse plastic roll
greenhouse plastic stripping
greenhouse plastic repair tape
12 X .99 cent clamps
hay bailing twine
1/2 inch staples
long screws for base
Tools:
good staple gun
electric drill
sharp box cutters for plastic
small hand saw
stake pounder

Here's the details:

First, I took apart our old cattle panel shed which was housing the lawn mower, hay bales for the poopers, and a few chairs. That took an entire day but provided me with much needed posts and three full size cattle panels.

Then, I drove down to the local rough cut lumber yard and bought two 2X12X10s and two 2X8 very thick heavy rough cut pine planks to use as a base for the greenhouse.

After screwing these together with the Makita, I then attached four 2X4s (resized to fit) to the top of the base to ensure a solid backing for the strips and plastic.

Then, the fun part. I hauled all three cattle panels over to their new restraining pen, much to their dismay, and proceeded to maul and woman-handle the unwieldy and obviously possessed cattle panels into a shape that would work for the hoop house. I tied them off with left over hay bale twine, and a few pieces of rope at the top, overlapping the panels to add strength, then somehow managed to get them into the frame of pine planks. Whew, that was a challenge! Took a whole day.

You should know that I have a love/hate relationship with cattle panels, and they are still angry at me for the extreme makeover. However they are by far the cheapest strongest option for the really low budget greenhouse/shed/fence builder and I still love them at the moment.

After getting those suckers into shape, I pounded four metal stakes inside the shed, as opposed to outside like my garden trestles, and began to pad them up. We had a stack of unused insulators in the basement, so I brought them up and padded up all places on the posts and panels using copious amounts of duct tape and insulating until I was out of foam. What people may not realize, as I don't see anyone else doing this online, is that cattle panels have little burrs that can catch and tear greenhouse plastic, so insulating them is the safest way to ensure the long life of your greenhouse. That took a whole day.

Now that the greenhouse frame was ready for some plastic, I emailed my buddy and mentor Daniel Dog, founder of Laughing Dog Farm in Gill, MA, and asked him where to get the good greenhouse plastic. Please note, home gardeners, using good plastic is the *only* way to build a solid greenhouse. He said a good product could be had from Griffins, and lucky for me they have a warehouse in Latham, NY. Yahoo! No shipping, although finding the place was a true challenge.

I bought a roll of plastic, enough for four greenhouses and the best price by far I'd seen anywhere, along with the plastic stripping (you have to staple the plastic onto it) and some repair tape, also useful for building the greenhouse. It really sticks.

Back to the greenhouse. In an almost anti-climactic moment I unrolled a little plastic, threw it over the top of the greenhouse and nailed the plastic onto the 2X4 base. Done deal. Added a strip to the front and back for "walls," using those great .99 cent clamps you can buy at Home Depot and taping a board to the bottom of each for weight, and presto framo, we have a very hot greenhouse. Whew!

Keeping on, Om Shanti
Jules

There's more of course.

What's the real price of a free lift ticket? she asks. "Ride for Free, Fact or Fiction" was first published in *The Mountain Gazette,* February 2000.

If you are a dumpster-diving dirtbag like me, the Northeast is the place to be this year. I know, complaining about lift ticket prices is the de rigeur thing to do, especially at the snowboard shop when you are trying to replace those broken Burton Mission bindings on the cheap…gotta pay to play they say. And then you also have a chance to talk about all that great backcountry stuff you did last weekend in the Dacks that took 18 hours round trip including hip-deep powder and a 3,000 feet elevation gain. There's always that story along with your rock-torn, sand-blasted tree-stomped aging body to prove it. Hey, I'm 49 years old, I can complain about pain if I want to. There's either free turns, earn your turns, or work for your turns, take your choice. If its liftserve you are looking for, the money exchange can be challenging, even on e-coupon days. Do you buy gas or do you spend your last $20 on a lift ticket? And what about food, cos those granola bars are getting way old. Me, I like my stuff free or greatly reduced, always have. I used to work in bike shops so I could use the tools I couldn't afford. Finally, after slowly building up my basement shop by buying used tools from retiring mechanics, I continued working in bike shops to acquire the bikes I couldn't afford. Then I got addicted to snowboarding after working in a bike shop that sold snowboards. My climbing rack is comprised of free swag found at the cliff, old cast-off cams from friends, and deals from swap meets. Just so you know, before any comments, I do use new ropes. Well, maybe not perfectly new... My whitewater kayaks are those that the shop couldn't sell cos they had five years of dust on them and were too big to fit anyone under 250 pounds. Who weighs 250 pounds and whitewater kayaks, anyway? The foam inserts came from a factory dumpster ... they almost float. Because of my fabulous volunteering skills, I finally won a new kayak at the Deerfield kayak festival one year in between beers. Stuff just comes my way.

Ya gotta eat right to live they say. I like organic veggies including fancy tomatoes and strawberries, so I grow them myself. Since good fertilizer costs a lot I also grow llamas and scoop their poop. I'm so lazy I fenced the garden next to their favorite poop pile so travel from one to the other is minimal. There's a really great food coop nearby so I work there and shop with coupons for sale items each week. Not cheap but still, our eggs and cheese come from the next little town, and the apples are local too. Trips to town don't cost much as our youngest car, a very beat-up purple Honda Civic hatchback with 171k miles uses minimal gas. Staying limber at my age means teaching beginner yoga once a week at the local library so that I can get a free yoga class and some pocket change. Think I'm kidding? You can stretch or die in my world.

It's probably understandable by now that when it comes to winter, there's just no way I'm gonna buy a ticket to a liftserve, and true to my lazy nature, I can't do backcountry every weekend. Besides, I work Saturdays and Sundays, a time when most people play, and I don't work at an office. Yes, it's true, I have forsaken all corporate trappings and work at area ski resorts as a Mountain Slave. I am a ski patroller at one mountain and a snowboard instructor at another. Both these titles translate into: Cheap local labor. The military precision of our incredible ski patrol team at very strict and jam-packed with guests Jiminy Peak in Massachusetts is rivaled by the unlimited tree riding/cliff hucking opportunities at wildly unregulated Magic Mountain in Vermont, where you can even hike up for free and earn your turns with your dog if he's leashed. I looked at all the resorts in our area (there are many in here on the NY/VT/MA border) and picked the coolest, non-commercial, telly ho mountain I could find to teach at this year. Magic Mountain in Londonderry, Vermont is the sweetest, I love that mountain. I teach a little and play a lot. Last year, I taught full time, Monday through Friday AND holidays at Jiminy so this year my new motto is, don't make your snowboard your corporate ball and chain.

Getting national ski patrol OEC training was easy, I just signed up and went to classes. Back in September, I thought it was so cozy and warm, sitting in class, practicing splints on other instructors. Drinking coffee. Once you pass the medical exams, ongoing mountain training lasts for a total of nine months. You begin to realize that you are also now officially a Mountain Slave and figure out how much work there is ahead. You start to feel the crunch of what happens when you screw up. Yes, that was my fault and it was a mistake. That was a major screw up and I understand the consequences to our guests on the mountain and to the future of skiing and riding here. Yes, I will attend training to make sure I never do it again. The payoff is great, however, if you are a dirtbag like me. I can visit other mountains by way of my ski patrol number, some without even so much as a letter of introduction. Mountains want ski patrollers on their trails, anyone can google ski patrol certification and you'll get gobs of free offers. Just this fall we could have stayed at Lake Tahoe for free and taken ski patrol training. Think about it, wouldn't you like to ride for free too?

There is a downside to my story. I've had to improve my technique enough to hang on ice off double black diamonds pulling a freaking 150 plus pound sled with a 200 pound guy in it. Hey, I'm 130 lbs and I am riding a snowboard. It's below zero windchill, at night, and the breeze has become a tornado. I'm tired, I'm cold, my teeth are chattering and my hands are ice cubes. Still, the patient needs first aid including ABCs and O_2, C-collar, extrication from the trees, backboarding, loading onto the sled, then sliding, successfully I might add, down the mountain to Hq. Doesn't that sound like fun to you? Oh, and did I mention that falling or losing the sled is obviously not an option. It's happened.

Have you ever tried snowboarding at night with a really big, two-foot long drill? How about carrying eight, six-foot long poles? Maybe you've tried refencing a closed trail while riding your snowboard switch. Then, there's always the student who run over your board repeatedly till the top separates from the bottom and you have to buy Tips and Tails off ebay to save your gear. The best news of all is, if you get injured on the mountain you get pee-tested! How's that for fair trade? As for teaching snowboarding here in the Great North Iced, at Magic the rope tow is no piece of cake so we end up walking up and down the bunny slope while chattering our teeth and freezing our butts off. Ten or 15 laps on the bunny are all the cardio I need for the day, but wait, there's more! Take the cold kids in after two hours of lessons, buy him/her overpriced hot chocolates and cookies, give them your warmies out of your gloves cos their hands are so cold, go back outside and do it again for another two to three hours, then hand the kids off to mommy and daddy. Explain how great the kids did, blah blah blah, oh that's okay, don't mention the hot chocolates and cookies, the kids were hungry, and what do you get? Certainly not a tip.

Then there's the other mountain where I taught full time last year. Picture this: Me with 11 little four year old kids, snowboards that they have never seen before, missing gloves, runny noses, peed in pants, sometimes even poop, vomit, crying, mom and dad disappeared for the ENTIRE DAY and I am trapped till at least 3:30 p.m. with this mob. It's six degrees outside, and our bunny slope with the Magic Carpet looks like an ice skating rink. We have to eat hot dogs and mac and cheese together as these are my charges for the day, including potty, snacks, naps and lunch. Shall I say more? It's not a pretty picture.

When it gets ugly, you just keep breathing, and tell yourself you are getting a free lift ticket this year. What defines free anyway? Free means you can come and go to the mountain as you please, oh yes, let me tell you about the good parts to my story. Free means we have this fabulous Hq at Ski Patrol where I leave my snowboard and gear and can suit up in style. Free means I have private bathrooms at both mountains (well, I admit one of the bathrooms doesn't lock and the little kids don't knock). There's the intructor's lounge at Magic where we can toss our crap, and the wonder of hitting the slopes at eight a.m. before anyone is on the mountain. Closing down trails at Jiminy with Ski Patrol after 10 p.m. can be really fascinating, especially after it snows then rains. The entire mountain is covered in unseen moguls that you must hop over while searching the trees for a wayward skier/rider who may have fallen off the face of the Earth.

Winter is getting older these days. I get up in the morning at six a.m. and I feel like shit. My rusted up, purple Honda is covered with ice and snow, the llamas are screaming at something that looks suspiciously like a coyote in the woods, the dogs and cats are hungry (again!) and I have to be on the lift at eight a.m. or else. Weather forecast for today is "wintry mix" and we all know that means freezing rain followed by sleet and snow. We'll get soaked to the bone on the lift, then become shellacked Ski Patrollers with sticks for fingers. There could very well be multiple accidents on the mountain today, with very limited employee parking as over 5,000 people are expected. Speaking of the mountain, it is half an hour away to where I park then I gotta walk and I'm still lying here in bed. The old man is snoring. Will someone please bring me some hot tea? Will someone go reboot the woodstove, start my car, scrape the snow off, feed the animals, drive me to the mountain, put my boots, knee pads, helmet and radio on, suit me up in my fancy red with a white cross Ski Patrol jacket, haul my sorry ass up the lift and carry those poles that drill those sleds down the mountain for me? I just really want to go back to sleep cos I was on my snowboard last night till 10:30 p.m. then finally went to bed, rode hard and put up wet.

Ride for free, is it fact or fiction?

The End Really. I hope by now, dear reader, you have had enough of me and my stories. For all of you out there who have stuck with this book to the bitter/sweet end (bitter start, sweet ending) please remember, my heart goes out to you and your loved ones who have had tough times.

Believe in yourself and those people you worry about while they are out there trashing themselves. Like my dear old Mom always said about me, "If she lives long enough she'll make something of herself." So will you, so hang in there. Here's someone to take with you on your journey:

aye dreme a' white poney

aye saw a white one in ma'dreme
where'er aye went, went he
protected me, 'e did, O yes
he luv'd me
jus' he an' me

ever tyme aye see a white one
ever tyme aye dreme a' he
somethin' skye, er Heaven comes
somethin' kind
an' good fer me

God is jus' fer lonely folk
an' hopes an' dreme er true
aye 'ave a white one fer m' own
white poney
jus' fer me

aye'll save ma' dreme, ma' hope secure
aye'll hold him close ta' me
ma' white horse cometh
soon ya' see
he cometh jus' fer me

what tha' white horse signifies
what he brings, ya see
he bringeth goodness, luv an' joy
ma' white one brings true luv
ta' me

A Note from the Author

Shouldn't we do more to help our world? Think about it.

It's simple to pierce the veil, but first we must pierce it with our hearts. What if each one of us were to stop shopping at places we don't like? Think about it. Could we pierce the veil and gain enlightenment? What if you and I and everyone else lived in community and got along? We could share gardens! We could learn to speak without talking. We could hear our friends voices in our ears before they called us on the phone. The veil is so thin, it's falling away with every sweet word we speak. We are happy and we live in peace. Say it sister.

Service is easy.

I really think the best way to free oneself from troubles is to help other beings. If humans aren't your thing, you can help animals, even plants. Help something or someone who is in your path, needing you. That's the first step towards freeing yourself from the chains that bind you. What can you do today to make someone's life easier? That someone can be a dog, a cat, a llama, a person. Rescue is real. Try it to ease your depression. I'll provide links on a resource page, but for now, just give it some thought.

If you have room, you can rescue a llama and its llama friend. Or if you have a truck, you can help your friend move. With tools you can fix someone's bike. With nothing you can be nice to an old lady. If you have something, maybe you can even take your llamas to visit nursing homes on Sundays in your minivan. You get the idea. Forget what people may tell you, it's okay to always be nice.

There's more.

You can make it a rule to always stop for pedestrians. Smile at someone who flips you off. Help a little old lady across the street. Sweep someone's steps for them. Find an elderly shut in and go visit her on a regular basis. Take a child to the park, read a book to someone who is lonely, buy tickets to a ballgame for a boy and his father who might not otherwise be able to afford them. Weed your neighbor's garden. Feed your neighbor's goats. Give your neighbors your best produce from your garden. You get the idea.

Here's another really big one. I know you probably are about to guess what I'm about to say so here it is. Forgive everyone and everything that ever pissed you off. Even if you don't feel it in your heart, just start telling them (you can do this mentally) that you forgive them. You can train your mind to release all that anger and thoughts of revenge, and your mind will eventually trickle down to your heart. and you will be completely free of what was ailing you. How does this happen? It's not about the people you need to forgive forgiving you back. Uh uh. It's about you forgiving them, thus releasing your attachment to that dark ugly blob thing attached to your psyche and body that has been tormenting you.

Speaking of Spirit Releasement Therapy, there's a lot to be said on that topic. First and foremost, you have to want to release those voices, that "friend," the blob on your head, the blinding shade over your eyes, the icky gunk in your ears that says it's your friend. It's time for light workers on the planet to let all that yucky stuff go. The dark ugly gelatinous blob thing you see in your mind's eye is not of this world and in fact, is not human. You let go of your anger then it has no choice but to detach because like any good parasite, it will feed upon its host until pulled off. You become an inhospitable host when you no longer draw negativity to you by thinking angry, unforgiving thoughts.

Just let it go. Need a prayer? Here is a simple one.

First invoke a circle of protective Angels to cover us. Then say the following words. "In the name of Jesus Christ, I cover you in the Blood of the Lamb. I bind the spirits that have attached to your being, and I send them up to God and the Angels for reprograming and reprocessing." See the mystical sparkling purple magical substance cover us, then watch the dark blobs begin to disengage. Have pity on these black tarry beings in their dark plight, and forgive them for they know not what they do. See them enter the tunnel of Light and travel up to God and the Angels, away from this plane of existence.

Oh believe me, I have to work on this myself. I speak from experience and it's a daily task not to get into road rage, little family stuff, big tiffs, snits, etc. All that stuff we like to wallow in attracts bigger nastier junk that eventually gets us into trouble. It's best to be aware of it, work on it, and let it go. I'm sorry I love you

325

works wonders. My daughter and I say it just about every day to each other because we know, deep in our hearts, that we love beyond measure. I'm trying to learn to say these words to everyone else. Do you think because maybe you've been bad that the Angels and protectors and God and all the rest won't help you? Forget it! You are beloved. Go ahead and say this prayer. Say it now.

People here in the West seem to get so depressed about their lives, but what about the many starving children in India who self-mutilate so that someone will give them food? There are three-year-old children in Bangladesh right now who work six to seven days per week using hammers to chop up D-cell batteries for the carbon rods that can be reused. Think about it, would you chop up a battery for the carbon rod? That's nasty work. At three years old?

There are people right now who have lost children and don't even know where they are, if they are safe, if they are hurting, if they are well...you know. There are people right now, many people who have lost loved ones. What I say to a lot of people is, if you are feeling sorry for yourself, get on your hands and knees right now, and starting doing it every morning, thanking the Creator for what you have. If you have your family, your health, food, a roof, a job, a car, when will it be enough for you to be thankful?

Being thankful is the best way to get happy. Even if you don't feel it, just go ahead and start saying thank you for all the wealth and happiness that's sitting in front of you. Get out there and do something good for someone else. Pretty soon you'll be doing it all the time. You know what I say when folks remind me that I'm super busy and ask me how in the heck I can manage everything? I say "I live a life of service to others. The more I serve, the more time I have." You can do this too. Find yourself a niche and start serving others. If you really want to get happy, find yourself several niches and start living a life of service... I call it tithing to the Universe. Give unto others, as you would have them give unto you.

And with that, I will say, it's been real, my friends.

Guten Tag.

About Jules

Julie, known as Jules, is mother to a wonderful daughter Reesa, and is happily married to Jerome Tracy, who has three sons. She wrote *Tripping with Gabrielle* in 1989, then moved from Oklahoma to Marin County, California where she started working bike shops. Jules eventually gravitated back East, then published her second book, *A Woman's Guide to Bikes and Biking*, in 1999. Her third book, *A Woman's Bike Book*, published in April 2010, is a titillating tale with color photos of women and even a few guys having fun on their bikes. Highly recommended.

Today, Jules is a member of the National Ski Patrol, and works for both Magic Mountain and Jiminy Peak. She also builds trails and rides backcountry with a local DEC ranger, and hopes to someday train with local search and rescue teams. She actively lectures local teenage girls and boys on the dangers of the road and how to provide self defense for yourself and your friends at all times. Jules has a long-term dream of becoming an acupuncturist, but that would necessitate passing Anatomy and Physiology, which so far hasn't happened. She hopes to provide community based acupuncture to inner city citizens who have never before been able to afford this type of healing medicine. Jules, also known as Rain in her reclaiming circle, is a chilled out, yogic mom, wife and farmer over 50 who is committed to living green and living clean. She has personally experienced traveling down the homeless hitchhiker road and doesn't recommend it. *Tripping With Gabrielle* is Jules' manifesto to the homeless, the runaways, the disenchanted, the addicted, the helpless and the poor of the world.

She salutes you.

The Wichitas, near Lawton, Oklahoma.

Beautiful wild creatures in Oklahoma.

About Owl Publications

I always recommend shopping at your local bookstore first to find copies of your favorite books. What would we do without them? Local bookstores and libraries are still the lifeblood of the hardcore, title searching, discerning reader. If they have some used books and a ratty old couch for me to sit on, I'm there!

If you would like to stock this book in your bookstore, rape crises center, homeless shelter, local library, or other place of business, you can order books at a discount directly from Owl Publications. If you are a reader looking for another copy of this book and your bookstore doesn't have it, please share our contact info with them. Owl Publications is all about publishing books to uplift the human spirit. Right now, in addition to *Living Green Cheap*, I am working on a new book entitled *Return of the Blue Star*, a tale of what happens when a community dials into an alternative universe, then brings this energy back home with them.

The Owl on her day off.

I was first inspired to write *Return of the Blue Star* while mountain biking with true shaman cyclists in Marin County, California. Several years later, while living in Hawai'i, I was exposed to a beautiful blue star looking thing in the sky that everyone on the mainland called "Haley Bopp." The Hawai'ians knew that it was no ordinary comet, and we stood outside our doors at night, together with them, gazing into the sky and communing with what seemed to be an intelligent, bright, brilliant blue angelic being cluster. The so called comet inspired me to write a new book, dedicated to what our lives can become, should we choose to co-create a new, more peaceful, cooperative reality together. Throw in a few shamans, a lot of permaculture, an intentional community, reclaiming witches, radical faeries, and you have *Return of the Blue Star*. She comes back, we learn more about how to live, and there's some extra special effects too, for the stargazer.

Contact us at: weathershaman@gmail.com

Best friends forever.